P9-ELH-198

PREPARING ART AND CAMERA COPY FOR PRINTING

PREPARING ART AND CAMERA COPY FOR PRINTING

Contemporary Procedures and Techniques for Mechanicals and Related Copy

Henry C. Latimer

McGRAW-HILL BOOK COMPANY

NEW YORK ST. LOUIS SAN FRANCISCO AUCKLAND BOGOTÁ DÜSSELDORF
JOHANNESBURG LONDON MADRID MEXICO MONTREAL NEW DELHI PANAMA
PARIS SÃO PAULO SINGAPORE SYDNEY TOKYO TORONTO

Library of Congress Cataloging in Publication Data

Latimer, Henry C
Preparing art and camera copy for printing.

Includes index.
1. Advertising layout and typography. I. Title.
HF5825.L33 659.13'24 76-6937
ISBN 0-07-036620-9

4567890 HDHD 8543210

The editors for this book were W. Hodson Mogan and Beatrice E. Eckes, the designer was Richard A. Roth, and the production supervisor was Teresa F. Leaden. It was set in Caledonia by University Graphics.

Printed and bound by Halliday Lithograph Corporation.

Contents

Preface		vii
Chapter 1	The New Preparatory Procedures and Techniques	1
Chapter 2	Paper and Composition Methods	16
Chapter 3	Camera Copy in Paste-up Form	49
Chapter 4	Camera Copy for Simple Multicolor Printing	80
Chapter 5	Applications of the Copy Overlay	102
Chapter 6	Artwork for Letterpress Printing	119
Chapter 7	Process Color Copy: Its Preparation	139
Chapter 8	Camera Copy for Rotogravure	168
Chapter 9	Posters	177
Chapter 10	Placing the Order	182
	Checklists of Printing Specifications	184
	Index	188

Preface

As a profession or an industry changes because of new technology—new processes, equipment, procedures, techniques, and capabilities—new informative literature is needed. The purpose of this book is to update production knowledge for designers and planners of printing of all kinds so that they may take advantage of new methods and capabilities.

The need for faster methods and the demand for lower costs resulted in much research and development after World War II. The findings of this search could best be applied to the photomechanical printing processes, particularly to offset lithography, which became the dominant commercial printing process. All the printing processes, however, have benefited to some degree because all use photographic techniques in engraving or platemaking.

The unusual feature of this change in the use of printing processes requires the printing user to transfer much of production planning to the creative planning stage in order to take advantage of the extra capabilities of the photomechanical processes. Time and cost factors are now controlled in the creative planning stage. In addition, the user or the user's advertising agency or art studio prepares camera-ready art and copy in the form of paste-up mechanicals. This procedure assigns the equivalent of the high-cost platemaking and typesetting operations of the engraver and printer to the user's art department to save both time and costs.

These procedures, which have been made possible by new technology, are permissible under *time* plate estimating, a system used by all printing processes except letterpress. Anything the user does to reduce the printer's time is to the user's advantage. The intermediate steps between the original artwork and that prepared for the camera are termed "art production." They include composition for the mechanical, which is equivalent to page makeup on the drawing board. Any form of composition can be used: phototype as well as galley repros of metal or typed composition.

As early as 1968, the Technical Association of the Pulp and Paper Industry (TAPPI) learned from a survey of 2,400 art directors that two-thirds of their departments were specifying or ordering process plates or separations and even printing.

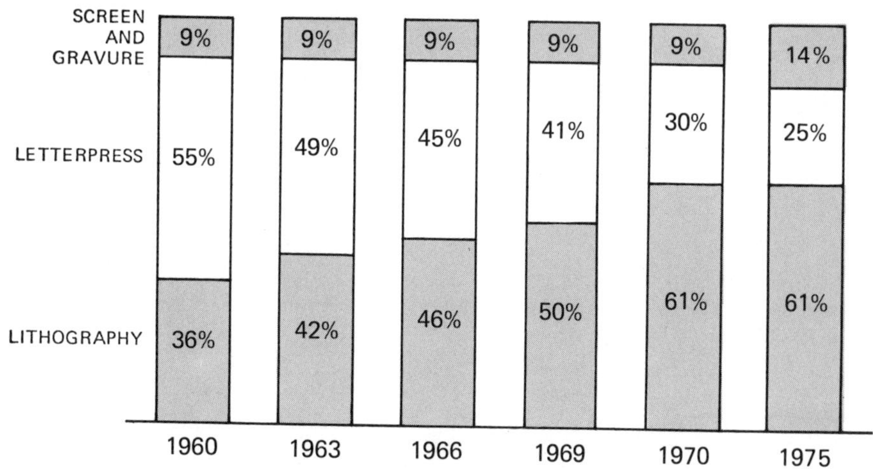

Use of printing processes for commercial printing. [*Source: U.S. Bureau of the Census*]

Art departments were handling much display composition with desk-top photolettering machines. Now, with the cost of a simple tabletop text phototypesetting unit (operated by a typist) as low as $4,000, art departments have started to do all the composition for the mechanicals and the negatives destined for publications printed by offset or by gravure. These replace the electros required for letterpress publications.

For several years electronic scanning machines have been used for process color separation negatives for all printing processes. Recent technology has added a laser beam that produces *screened* negatives or positives for any printing process in hours instead of days. Special camera copy, usually prepared by a color photo laboratory, is required.

With diversified printing methods and the predominance of photomechanical processes, it is important that planners and buyers of printing know the advantages and capabilities of these methods and processes. This book offers a how-to guide to the new procedures and techniques and the skills needed to handle them.

H. C. LATIMER

PREPARING ART AND CAMERA COPY FOR PRINTING

CHAPTER ONE

The New Preparatory Procedures and Techniques

FROM THE VIEWPOINT of the user printing production in the past consisted in planning and preparing material for the printer within the limitations of the kind of letterpress printing being used—commercial, magazine, or newspaper. A study of printing costs made in 1938 for the Association of National Advertisers dealt only with the press operation (efficient press size for the particular job); apparently engraving and composition costs were not a problem.

Advertising agencies were concerned only with the preparation and placing of magazine and newspaper advertising. Direct mail, dealer window displays and sales aids, and posters were considered competitive media to be planned and sold by lithographers and printers. Early in the 1930s, however, advertising and marketing research found that for national publication advertising to pay off to its fullest extent collateral printed materials were necessary. Both national advertisers and their agencies became concerned with the planning and preparation of printed materials.

After World War II printing and allied costs almost doubled. Both the printing user and the producer expanded their research, directing much of it toward the development of faster methods and lower costs. Initially platemaking and typesetting were the major objectives. As a result photographic masking methods replaced most of the manual methods used in color correction. Next came electronic scanning machines, which in hours can produce color separations for any of the major printing processes. Photographic typesetting methods progressed from the Intertype keyboard to optical character recognition (OCR), permitting a manuscript to be read by a computerized typesetting machine.

USE OF PRINTING PROCESSES TODAY

Data given in the U.S. Department of Commerce's *Census Report on Commercial Printing* (1972) reveal that offset produced 61 percent, letterpress 30 percent, and gravure 9 percent of all commercial printing in 1972. In addition, offset produced 75 percent of all advertising and book printing. Offset and letterpress are the two all-purpose printing processes, suitable for both short- and long-run printing, either single-color or multicolor. Rotogravure is particularly well suited to long press runs of publications with process color. According to a press manufacturer, a thirty-two-page booklet with 50 percent process color is produced most efficiently by offset for up to 750,000 impressions, by letterpress for 750,000 to 1 million impressions, and by gravure for more than 1 million impressions.

Newspapers

The American Newspaper Publishers Association (ANPA) reported in March 1969 that 405 daily newspapers in the United States were being printed by offset. It predicted that by 1979 fewer than 200 dailies would be printed on letterpress equipment and that more than 1,300 would be using offset presses. Quite a few of the larger daily newspapers, including *The New York Times*, are now using plastic relief press plates made from photographic composition. The *Times* has ordered $36 million worth of offset presses and equipment; *The Wall Street Journal* is already offset.

Business Publications

A check by the Standard Rate & Data Service for production specifications of business and farm publications with circulations under 50,000 reveals that more of them are now printed by offset than by letterpress. This development is due to the efficiency of web- (roll-) fed multicolor offset presses, which permit such publications to offer process color instead of two-color work at a low production cost.

Magazines

In national consumer magazines all three major processes are used for the full-circulation or regional editions. In June 1969 *Printing Production* magazine published a chart, based on U.S. Department of Commerce data, showing that 48 percent of all magazine printing was being handled by the photomechanical processes. In 1972 a spokesman for Du Pont was reported in the trade press as stating that, of the publications Du Pont advertised in, 87 percent used offset, 12 percent letterpress, and 1 percent gravure.

Folding Cartons and Packaging

The printing of much packaging material, such as folding cartons, has shifted to offset and gravure because of the high quality of process printing on boxboard achieved with the large high-speed presses. Such printing is technically the most exacting type of large-volume production (there may be as many as 20 million pieces in one printing) because of registering to 1/1000 inch and adjusting printed colors to appear as wanted under the various kinds of lighting in chain stores. The absence of the usual expense of curved electros, lockup, and makeready of a large four-color rotary relief press is an important cost factor in the use of photomechanical processes. Large five- and six-color sheet-fed offset presses can be made ready to run in hours instead of days.

SWITCH TO PHOTOMECHANICAL METHODS

Additional information on the extent of the change in printing production comes from knowledgeable persons. In mid-1973, for example, an Eastman Kodak executive stated that 10,000 phototypesetting machines were in use and that about half of the volume of composition in the United States was handled by such equipment.

With the switch from letterpress to offset and other photomechanical printing processes, all of which require camera copy (the copy to be reproduced) in paste-up form, the printing user's production changed radically. New capabilities in printing became available. So did a different method of estimating plate or engraving costs: the *time* required for engraving work by the form of camera copy supplied rather than by the engraving size, as in letterpress printing. This time method of estimating plate costs is used by all processes except letterpress.

HOW PRINTING PRODUCTION HAS CHANGED

It used to be said facetiously that all a production man needed to know was a good printer and a good engraver. There was some truth in this quip: the other fellows did the work. The function of the art department was to turn over to production the rough layout, finished art, and the copywriter's manuscript to be set in type. Except for newspaper production art was to be reproduced on coated paper.

All this has changed. Today, for a national consumer publication advertising campaign all three major printing processes will be used, and negatives of the advertisements will be shipped about as often as electro plates. Advertising research discovered that for magazine ads to pay off to the fullest extent (six full-color ads cost about $250,000) collateral materials must be used: the various forms of dealer aids, merchandising programs and special deals, posters, direct mail, and local newspaper ads, as well as informative literature for the interested prospec-

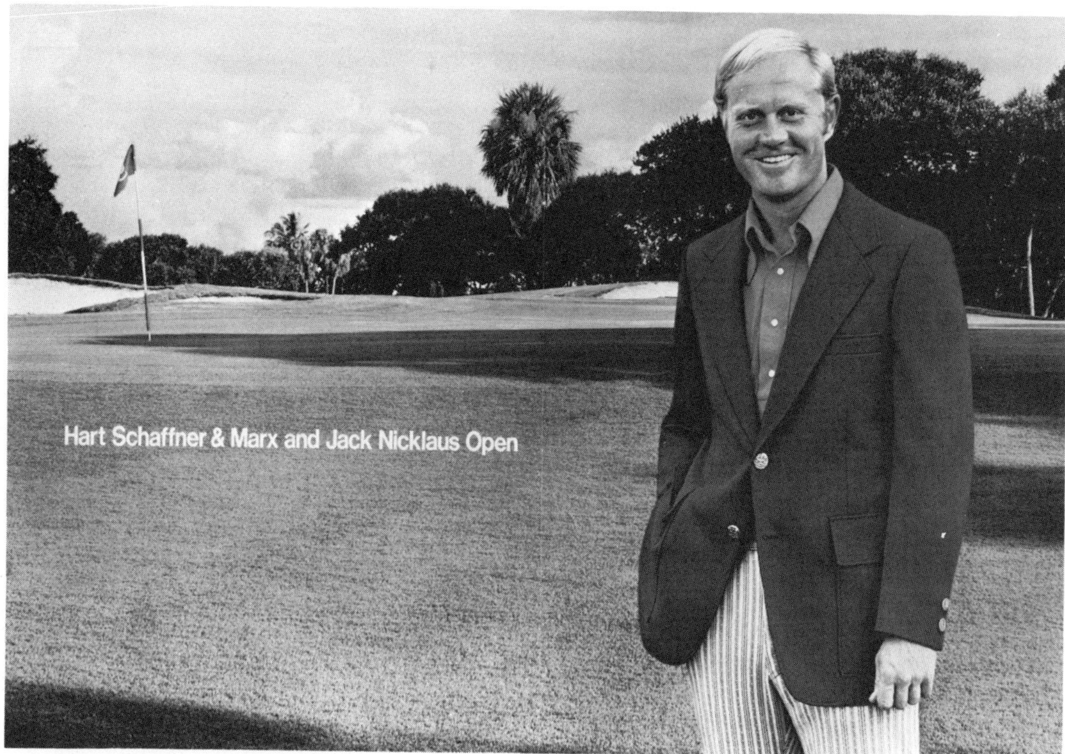

Fig. 1-1 Jack wasn't there when the picture was taken. In advertising, a full-color illustration is often made up of components that are combined or inserted. With color transparencies this job formerly was handled by the photoengraver; the process was costly and time-consuming. Today art production takes charge of such preparatory work and turns over to the producer camera-ready art, even for electronic color separations, for all processes.

tive buyer. All this printed material must be integrated and coordinated with the advertising idea or theme and with publication schedules.

The advertising agency naturally took over the planning, and usually the production, of the collateral materials and included them in the overall program and budget. Every conceivable kind of printing production is required; all types of printing papers are used, often in huge volume; and the quality planned for each type of material varies with the end use.

This planning, along with that of the publication schedules, is handled in the creative advertising stage. For national advertising the planning will be a team operation, with the art director a key member of the team; for an industrial account it is apt to be carried out by the agency account executive and the client's advertising manager; and for the local department store it is likely to be the responsibility of the advertising manager working with the merchandising managers. All will make some use of collateral materials. It is this kind of printing production that is responsible for the fact that 75 percent of all advertising printing is done by offset.

DEVELOPMENT OF ART PRODUCTION

The transition of advertising production from the production department to the art department was gradual. As late as 1961 approved rough layouts first went to production for recommendations on paper, the art medium and its preparation, the printing process, and so on, so that they might be kept within the limitations of time and budget. Since art had always handled photography and prepared the paste-up mechanicals and other camera copy for offset and rotogravure, it was not long before art learned production and time and cost factors and began using the new procedures made possible by the new technology to scale, position, and color-adjust process copy for "prepared" camera-ready copy. This development in turn transferred important operations from the engraver or platemaker to the copy preparation stage in the user's art department. The extra capabilities of offset permitted the making of all the different plate (process) sizes needed for the collateral printed materials from one set of color separations or the conversion of magazine color plates to obtain separations for about 25 cents on the dollar.

Meanwhile, the art director had become a key member of the creative planning group in advertising with greater authority, and his or her department began absorbing production for both platemaking and composition. For the latter, nonmetal composition as well as metal type could be used.

Work of Art Department Shown in TAPPI Survey

Fortunately a 1968 survey of 2,400 art directors by the Technical Association of the Pulp and Paper Industry (TAPPI; see Bibliography) revealed the changed character and scope of the work of their departments because of the switch to photomechanical printing methods. It was found that 76 percent of the art directors work directly with graphic arts suppliers instead of through the production department, as in the past. More than 80 percent specify or buy typography and paper, and two-thirds specify or buy plates and separations and even printing. Many art departments have absorbed selected production personnel to handle the time and cost factors of print advertising. The art director's authority now equals his or her responsibility; the director is the one to be satisfied.

USE OF REPRODUCTION COLOR PHOTOPRINTS

In the late 1940s reproduction-quality dye-transfer color prints came into use in preparing camera copy; later, Type C prints also were employed. These replaced carbro prints because duplicates of the color-adjusted originals could be made inexpensively. (Usually, multiple copies of artwork are required for different producers. One international account is reported to need thirty-two copies of all artwork.) These new color prints had a major effect on the development of art production, that is, the intermediate steps between original artwork and that prepared for the camera. Among the consequences were the following:

- Mixed art media could be reduced to a single medium, all in tonal balance and properly scaled or proportioned.
- Process color elements could be scaled, color-adjusted to suit, and positioned for an assembly of two or more such elements.
- Process elements could be proportioned for same-focus economies, using group color separation under time estimating.
- Offset and gravure could produce multiple plate sizes for different layouts from one set of color separations.
- A full-color illustration is often made up of two or more components. Dye transfer prints are used to position and blend the components and make any desired changes in hours. Such work formerly was done by the engraver or platemaker in a time-consuming and expensive procedure.

Several years later, developments in color transparencies facilitated their use for the same purposes. For an assembly, transparencies are emulsion-floated onto film, scaled, and positioned. This form of camera-ready copy is also used by electronic scanning machines to make continuous-tone or screened color separation negatives for all three major processes. Moreover, a 35-millimeter color transparency can be enlarged for a magazine page in one hour.

EXTRA CAPABILITIES

The extra capabilities of offset are used constantly by the designer, who employs the finest halftone screens (up to 300-line;

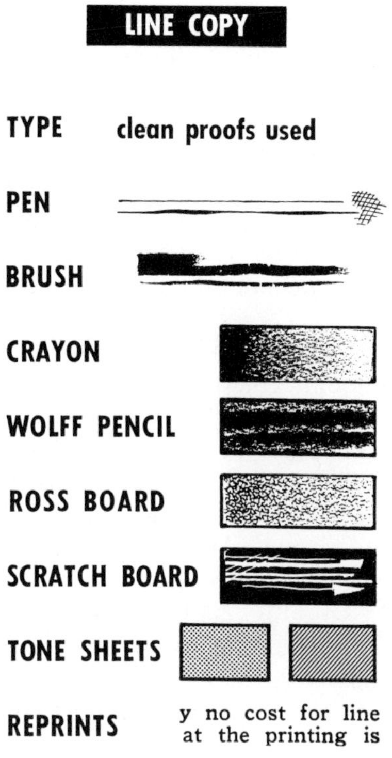

LINE COPY

TYPE clean proofs used

PEN

BRUSH

CRAYON

WOLFF PENCIL

ROSS BOARD

SCRATCH BOARD

TONE SHEETS

REPRINTS y no cost for line at the printing is

Fig. 1-2 Any copy that can be reproduced without the halftone screen.

TONE COPY

Fig. 1-3 Any copy requiring the halftone screen or another method to reproduce shades of gray or a color.

175-line is standard for good process color) on rough-textured papers such as antiques and text papers. With offset there are no restrictions on the choice of paper surfaces. Modern typefaces with their fine serifs and hairlines can be used on such papers because the ink is applied from a resilient rubber-surfaced offset cylinder.

In the creative planning of a tight-budget advertising campaign full-color (relief) magazine plates can be converted for the offset production of collateral materials; they can be enlarged or reduced within reasonable limits for the various layouts. The cost is about 25 cents on the dollar; color print proofs cost only about 10 cents on the dollar as compared with ink proofs. Since color correction for both offset and rotogravure is carried out on the separation positives instead of on the plate metal, this procedure is practical.

A unique capability of offset is large-size work in process color: window displays and posters that exceed the practical capabilities of photoengraving in one piece (about 15 by 17 inches). The use of a large color form for printing is also practical for offset because of the absence of makeready expense except for press adjustments, amounting to 8 percent of the usual makeready cost.

Offset has been stressed because it is the all-purpose process using photomechanical methods and is now the predominant commercial printing process. It is practical for both short and long press runs and is capable of both excellent and commercial-grade printing.

TWO KINDS OF CAMERA COPY

Just two kinds of camera copy are involved in making engravings or plates for the three major printing processes:

1. Line copy, or copy to be reproduced in 100 percent black or color, including type, reverses, rules, and art media illustrated in Fig. 1-2.

2. Tone copy, or photographs and other

artwork that involve reproducing shades of gray or color (see Fig. 1-3). In the camera back is a halftone screen that reproduces shades of tones in halftone dots of varying sizes.

Both letterpress and offset use the halftone method; rotogravure uses a grid of ink "wells" of varying depth to get light or dark tones.

Fig. 1-4

TIME ESTIMATING OF PLATE COSTS

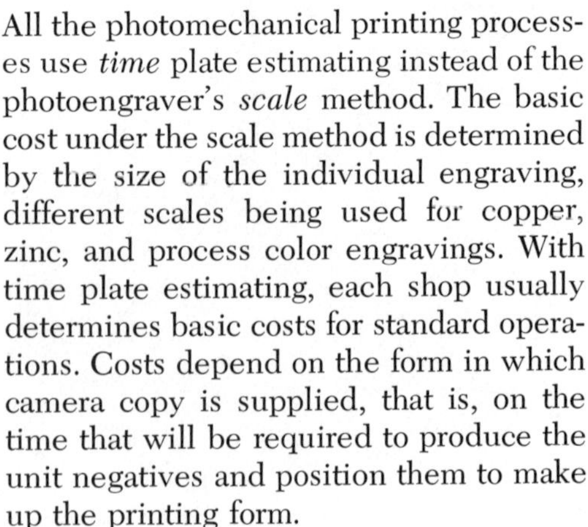

All the photomechanical printing processes use *time* plate estimating instead of the photoengraver's *scale* method. The basic cost under the scale method is determined by the size of the individual engraving, different scales being used for copper, zinc, and process color engravings. With time plate estimating, each shop usually determines basic costs for standard operations. Costs depend on the form in which camera copy is supplied, that is, on the time that will be required to produce the unit negatives and position them to make up the printing form.

For example, with offset the standard practice is for each shop to have a base plate cost for each press size. This cost includes the number of 8½- by 11-inch line negatives that will go on the press plate, the stripping of the negatives on the flat or form, and the making of the press plate. Thus if all line copy, illustrations as well as text and heads, is scaled and positioned on the mechanical paste-up, the base plate charge includes everything, and there is no extra cost for the equivalent of line engravings. If the shop must scale and position the line illustrations, it charges for the time. Only the halftones involve an extra cost.

If a job (even a booklet) has several tone elements, these can either be scaled and positioned on the mechanical or be proportioned as separate elements to be reduced as a group halftone. When the elements are positioned on the mechanical, one focus handles all of them, and individual stripping time is avoided. The line and halftone negatives will be combined. Proportioned separate tone elements are photographed as a group to obtain better detail and same-focus economies. The large negative is then cut apart, and the individual halftones are stripped into position.

When we take up the preparation of mechanicals in Chapter 3, you will understand why line copy is always scaled and positioned. You will learn how line copy is scaled in the art department and how tone elements are scaled or proportioned.

COMPOSITION METHODS USED TODAY

The photomechanical processes do not require metal type. When type is used, all that is needed is a clean black proof (repro). This proof is pasted in position on the mechanical as indicated by the designer's rough layout. The type proof can be of a made-up page, of a semi-made-up page (see Fig. 2-12 in Chapter 2), or of galleys of type as it comes from the machines.

In addition to metal composition, various "cold-type" methods are used on small print orders for which metal type would be too expensive. The text can be composed on special reproduction typewriters with book faces and margin alignment. Paper transfer letters, mechanical lettering aids, or desk-top photolettering machines may be used for display type. Much of this work is done in the user's advertising or art department.

PHOTOTYPESETTING

The major development in composition methods has been the use of various types of photocomposition on film or on paper for the paste-up mechanical. The objective of research in printing technology was to reduce or eliminate manual methods such as the operation of a Linotype machine. By the use of electronic and computerized equipment various types of phototypesetting machines were developed to fill differing printing requirements. These machines now range from the equivalent of a typewriter that sets phototype in sizes from 6 to 36 points and sells for as little as $4,000, through OCR systems that are activated by a coded typed manuscript, to very expensive computerized systems with memory banks that can retrieve selected old composition

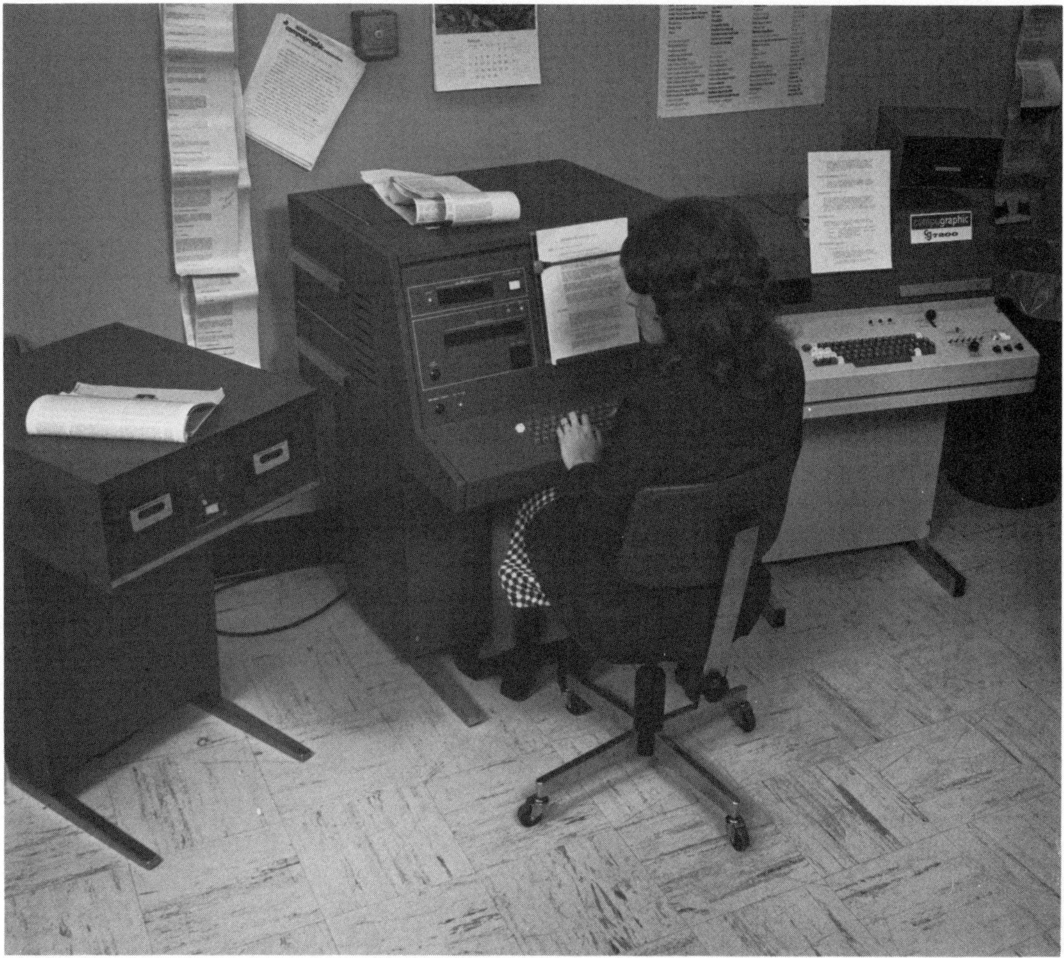

Fig. 1-5 Modern composing room for a weekly newspaper. The typist is operating a direct-entry CompuWriter phototypesetter unit of Compugraphic. ("Direct-entry" means that no preliminary perforated tape is necessary.) This unit, which has a total on-line system capacity of ninety-six fonts, is suited to applications requiring the frequent mixing of type styles and sizes.

and combine it with new composition. Such systems, it is claimed, can revise a metropolitan telephone directory in forty-eight hours.

Since most readers of this book will have a general knowledge of the principles of commercial printing processes, we shall not describe them in detail. It is timely, however, to explain the differences in the printing plates used by each process that are produced from the negative of the camera copy. We should also call your attention to the fact that all processes except letterpress use the principle of the one-piece printing plate, cylinder, or the like to avoid the expense of press lockup. Most of the equivalent of letterpress makeready is also avoided with offset and gravure.

PHOTOMECHANICAL PLATEMAKING

All three major printing processes use high-contrast photographic film for line copy. This film reproduces black and dark tones as 100 percent black; the light tones of a photograph or wash drawing drop out completely. Both offset and letterpress use the halftone method to reproduce tone copy; shades of gray are obtained in the reproduction by the varying sizes of the halftone dots, which are very small for light tones and are so large for dark tones

Jack's Slacks have the trim line and snap-back neatness only double-knits can deliver. Available in stripes, patterns and solids, in a full gallery of colors.

Jack's Blazer Suit combines the casual ease of a blazer with the always-right-everywhere good looks of a suit. Available in eight colors.

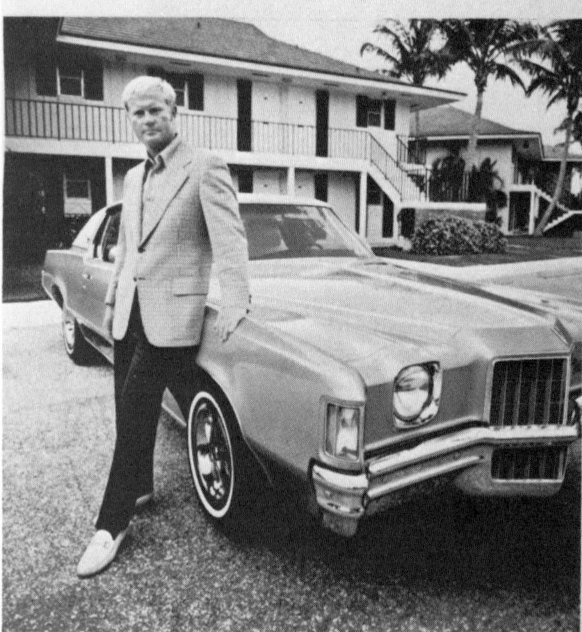

Jack's Tri-Color Sport Coat sets off slim solid-color slacks and his Pontiac Grand Prix.

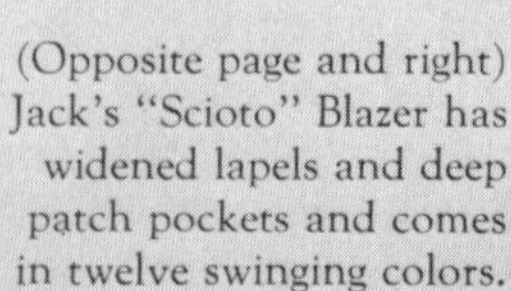

(Opposite page and right) Jack's "Scioto" Blazer has widened lapels and deep patch pockets and comes in twelve swinging colors.

Hart Schaffner & Marx tailors this Jack Nicklaus Wardrobe in Scioto Cloth™ of Celanese® Fortrel® polyester. It's the double-knit of the future, styled for today's leisurely living.

There is nothing like Scioto Cloth. It moves when you move. Gives with every action. Takes a lot of punishment. Scioto Cloth packs perfectly and travels terrifically. It never rumples or crumples or bags or sags.

Jack Nicklaus first got into double-knits for golf. Knit slacks gave him freedom of movement plus unwilting good looks. Now, that same free-moving thinking has sparked a whole collection of comfortable, casual, coordinated clothing that's as much at home in the office as at the country club.

Fortrel® is a trademark of Fiber Industries, Inc.

Suiting the American Man since 1887 • HART SCHAFFNER & MARX

36 SOUTH FRANKLIN STREET, CHICAGO, ILLINOIS 60606

Fig. 1-6 (opposite) No longer must the engraver separate, color-adjust, scale, and position each process color element. Art production now handles all such details in preparing camera-ready copy either for the engraver or for the electronic scanning machine to produce the color separations of the whole page.

that they sometimes touch, producing a tone that is 80 or 90 percent black. The film used is the same as for line copy, thus permitting the production of a combination line-and-tone engraving. The halftone method requires the use of a halftone screen in the camera back, either a glass halftone screen placed just in front of the unexposed film or a contact halftone screen in close contact with the film.

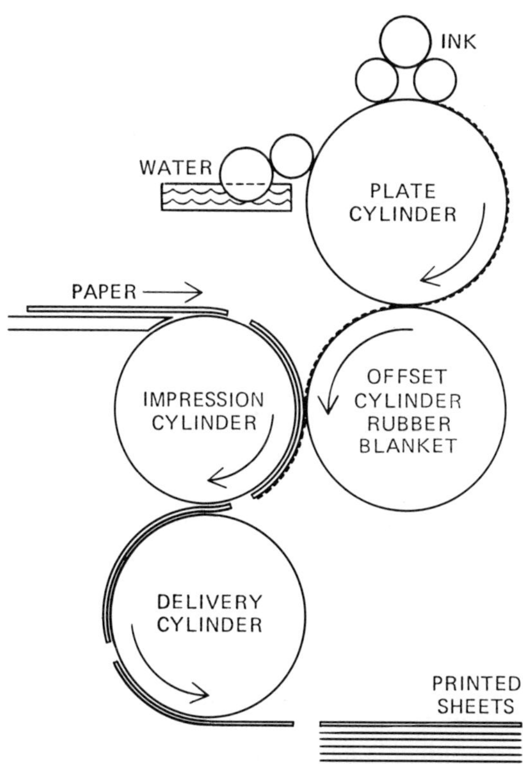

Fig. 1-7 The principles of the offset press.

To reproduce tone copy, rotogravure requires continuous-tone film (as snapshots do) to control the amount of light for the depth of the ink wells. The use of two kinds of film adds to engraving time.

ACTION OF LIGHT ON PLATE COATINGS

All photomechanical platemakers first make a negative of the mechanical and of any separate elements. With offset the completed unit negatives are assembled in binder's imposition on special goldenrod paper, from which the press plate is made by contact-printing in a vacuum frame. In photoengraving the individual negatives are positioned on a piece of glass. This "flat" of negatives is contact-printed on light-sensitive coated metal to make the engravings. Later the metal is cut apart to obtain the individual engravings. Rotogravure photocomposes the unit positive (continuous-tone) film from the line and continuous-tone negatives. Positioned in strips the length of the printing cylinder, the unit positives are contact-printed on a "carbon tissue" (a plate coating on a paper backing). The exposed plate coating is then transferred to the copper printing cylinder. When the printing form has been completed on the cylinder, it is prepared and etched to produce the ink wells.

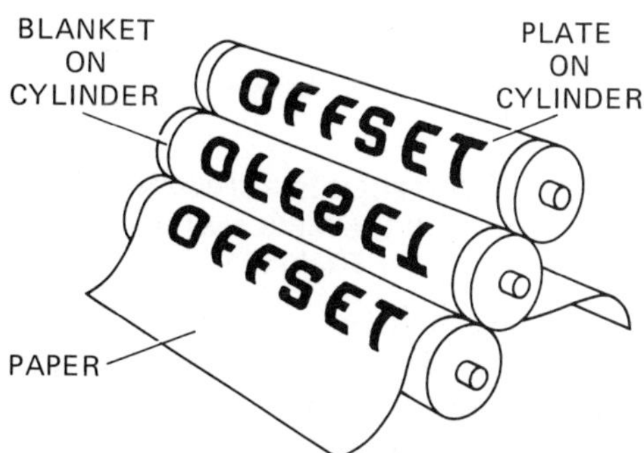

Fig. 1-8 Using the principle that grease and water do not mix in order to ink the printing image, the revolving plate cylinder first touches the dampening rollers and then the ink rollers. The ink adheres only to the greasy image, which is transferred to the offset cylinder and from there to the paper.

THE ACTION OF LIGHT ON PLATE COATINGS

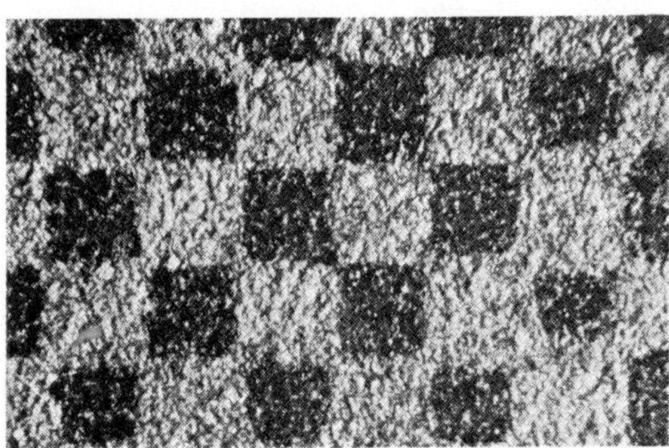

Fig. 1-9 *Offset:* The formation of a printing image that is developed to make it ink-receptive and to make the nonprinting areas ink-repellent. This is the planographic type of press plate, which resembles a black print on a large sheet of gray metal.

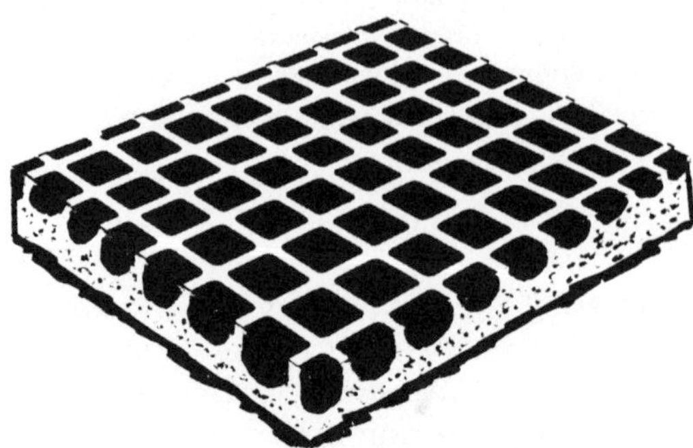

Fig. 1-10 *Gravure:* A resist image of varying degrees that governs the depth of the etching operation in ink wells. This is a form of intaglio plate, with the printing image below the surface. A scraper blade removes the ink that is not in the wells from the cylinder.

Fig. 1-11 *Photoengraving:* The formation of the printing image in an acid-resist coating that permits the subsequent etching operations to eat away the nonprinting areas of the metal, leaving the image in relief.

Commercial Screen Printing: A light-sensitive coating is spread on a fine wire mesh screen. Exposed to an assembly of photographic positives, the light hardens the nonimage areas. The coating under the black of the positive film image is not affected by light and is washed off to produce the stencil.

DIFFERENCE BETWEEN PHOTOENGRAVER'S AND OFFSET NEGATIVES

In making halftone negatives, the photoengraver purposely does not expose the plate for the final tones. The engraver allows a margin because there is a lateral reduction of halftone dots in the acid etching of the copper. The final halftone dot structure is obtained by etching to reduce dot size and burnishing to enlarge dots.

In contrast, the final tonal qualities of both offset and rotogravure are on the films to be contact-printed on the plate coatings. This means that from an original set of four-color separation negatives any number of different plate sizes can be made for the different forms of collateral material. It is also practical to make a "blowup" of a smaller process color piece to produce a larger size. The various sizes of wall calendars are produced by this method.

Fig. 1-12 A letterpress form of type and plates in a chase. It is used for shorter press runs on a flatbed press.

Fig. 1-13 An offset flat, or printing form, made with photographic negatives. The press plate is made photographically from the flat by contact printing.

Fig. 1-14 A large book form of type and cuts positioned on the bed of the press.

Fig. 1-15 An offset press plate being clamped around the press cylinder. This is equivalent to a letterpress form locked up and made ready.

EQUIPMENT USED FOR MULTIPLE IMAGES

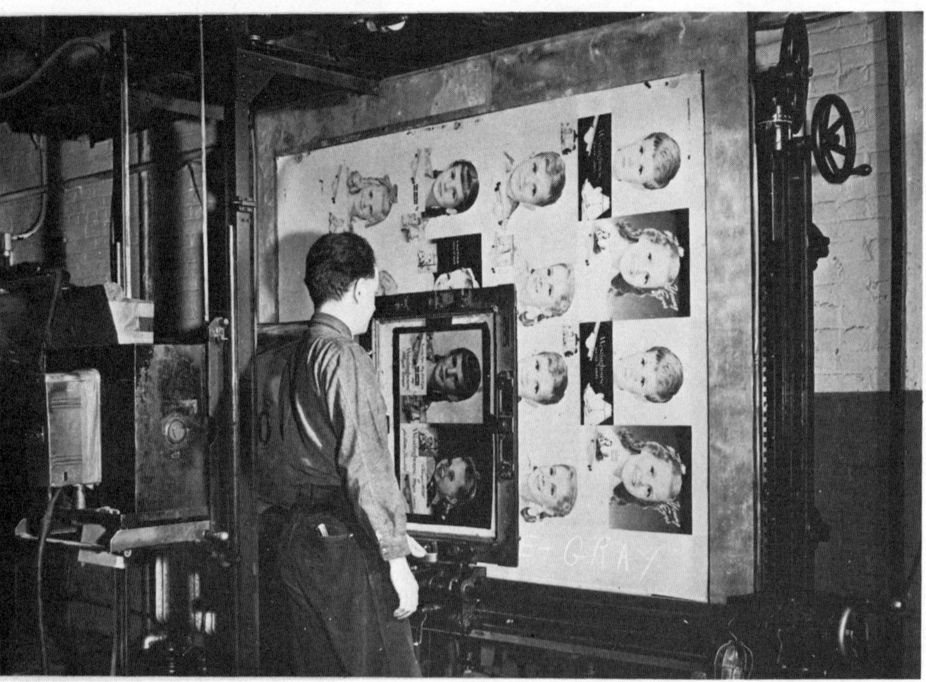

Fig. 1-16*A* This Rutherford step-and-repeat machine gives an idea of the equipment used for large press plates. Unit positives or negatives in a chase are exposed and repositioned the necessary number of times. Register is to $\frac{1}{1000}$ inch by paper tape.

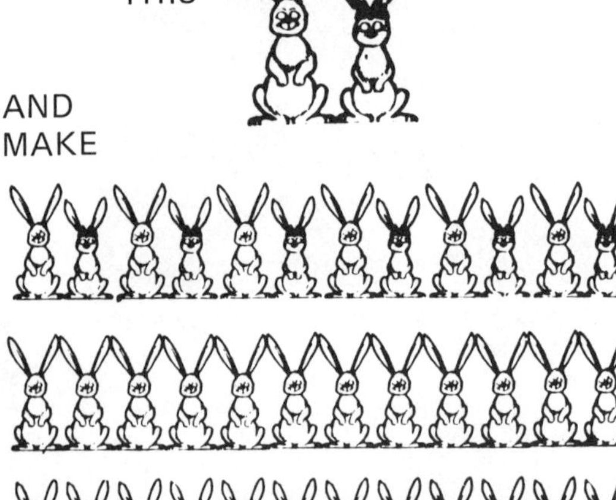

Fig. 1-16*B* This drawing shows the principle of step-and-repeat work with photomechanical equipment, which is widely used for process color work.

MULTIPLE IMAGES

Because the negatives or positives of offset and rotogravure have their final tonal qualities in the films, in both processes a step-and-repeat machine can be used to make multiples of full-color subjects (the equivalent of electro duplicates). Such multiples might include ninety-six labels on the press plate or thirty-two magazine color inserts. Under time plate estimating, the cost of even this quantity of images is nominal.

MULTIPLE IMPOSITION

When a printing order involves a large quantity, it is usually printed in multiples—two up, four up, and so on—on the press. The printing form of the job can be repositioned on the press plate by hand, or the job can be handled mechanically with a machine that is not so complicated as the step-and-repeat machine. Under time estimating, this procedure is much less expensive than the use of electros or relief plates.

LARGE PROCESS PLATES

Plans for an advertising campaign usually include the printing of large-size pieces such as posters, window displays, wall charts, and maps. Generally process color work is required. The lithographic (offset) specialists who produce this type of work have color cameras with a circular halftone screen as large as 60 inches, and they use projections for even larger work.

Here again the technique of having the final tones, including color correction, in the films, is to the advantage of the printing user, for this kind of collateral material (consisting of artwork in whole or in part) is frequently integrated with consumer publication schedules. Either the original color separations can be used, or the magazine color plates can be converted for offset lithography in the large sizes.

The use of a broadside, such as a 25- by 38-inch folded sheet, is extensive in advertising. Production can be planned to handle the job with a mechanical and reproduction color prints of artwork. Everything is in scale and positioned on the press plates, for with a color camera with a circular screen measuring up to 60 inches all the elements are handled on the four process plates. It is not necessary to strip each color subject into position on the four press plates.

CONVERSION OF COLOR PLATES

The process engravings or separations of any of the major processes can be converted for production with either of the other two printing processes. Full-color magazine plates and rotogravure separations are regularly converted for the production of collateral material by offset. Conversions cost about 25 cents on the dollar in comparison with the original plates or separations. If the conversions are to be used by a shop other than the one making separations, prior arrangements should be made by the user or customer.

PAPER AS A COST FACTOR

Most uncoated advertising papers are now surface-sized for use in offset printing. Very important to production is the fact such offset paper is generally considered equal in strength, bulk, and stiffness to a letterpress coated stock 10 pounds heavier. Surface-sizing imparts stiffness and strength, and the extra bulk is a characteristic of uncalendered paper.

On the average, paper stock accounts for 23 percent of the cost of commercial printing. With long runs of printed matter the cost of the paper is given special attention, and the printing process may offer the answer to questions of cost. On a weight basis 14 percent is saved when a 60-pound offset paper is used instead of a 70-pound letterpress coated paper. The uncoated paper costs about 12 to 18 percent less than the coated stock, depending on whether the expensive or cheaper grades of the two types of paper are compared.

Rotogravure uses either coated or uncoated paper in rolls, but the uncoated type must be calendered to give it the required smoothness even with newsprint. Screen printing uses 80-pound offset paper because of this paper's surface-sizing.

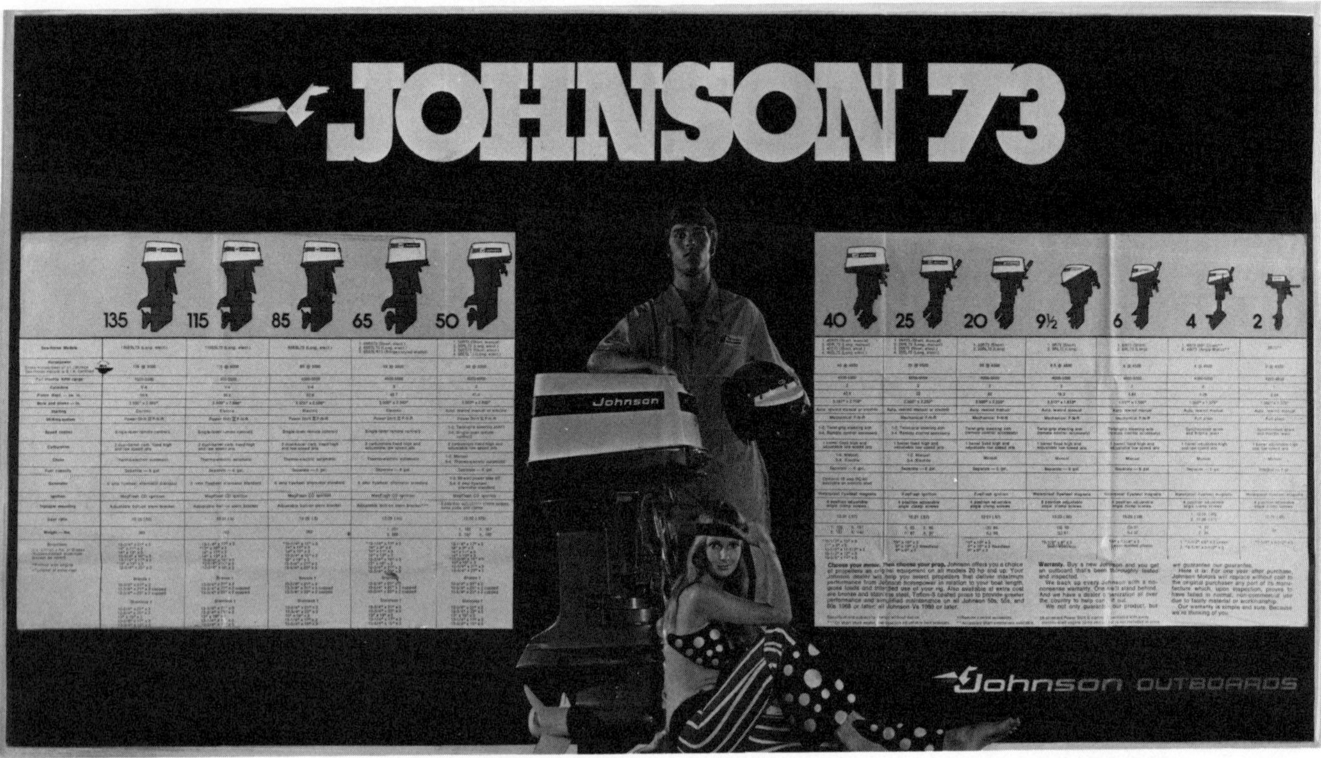

Fig. 1-17 Dealer poster, 3 by 5½ feet.

Fig. 1-18 Booklet, 9 by 12 inches.

Key Artwork in Two Sizes from One Set of Color Separations

Here are a dealer showroom poster and a dealer booklet for prospective buyers, with the key illustration in 6-inch and 26-inch sizes with the background design. Both sizes were made in a 175-line halftone screen from the original color separations by offset.

ADVANTAGES OF THE ONE-PIECE PRINTING FORM

The printing user should know something about the handling of pages or other copy units in making up the printing form that goes on the printing press, for this procedure has involved high-cost manual labor, particularly for multicolor printing. We have seen how pages are made up on the drawing board for the photomechanical processes by the preparation of the mechanical, and Fig. 1-13 shows how the photographic negatives of the mechanicals are positioned on a large piece of goldenrod paper (carbon tissue for rotogravure) to make up the printing form. After contact exposure of this form to the offset press plate or gravure cylinder, the printer has the equivalent of a letterpress form locked up and made ready without holding the press while the work is being done. The usual makeready for the halftone press areas is eliminated because both offset and rotogravure presses use rubber-surfaced cylinders to compensate for the necessary pressure on tone work. The high cost of letterpress lockup and makeready is the major reason for the shift of printing from letterpress to offset.

ART NOW CONTROLS PRODUCTION

In summary, it is apparent that time and cost factors for both art and printing production are now controlled in the user's creative planning stage. The wider scope of extra capabilities and new techniques necessitates a knowledge of contemporary procedures and techniques in the art department.

In advertising and other fields, ideas are boiled down to rough layouts; decisions on colors, paper, printing process, art media and their preparation, and usually composition have been made. The approved roughs go to the art department with any instructions and artwork for the mechanicals.

By using a mechanical you can make up a page on the drawing board with any form of composition. A knowledge of art production transfers the equivalent of some engraving and typesetting operations to the copy preparation stage to save time and costs (scaling and positioning, reducing mixed art media to a single medium, and the use of metal galley repro proofs cut composition costs in half) and controls the planning for the desired quality. You can also take advantage of same-focus economies, the use of conversions of electros or separations on hand, change plate sizes, and employ process color separations in a range of costs.

ORDERING RELATED COLOR PRINTING FROM ONE PRODUCER

Since offset can make all the different-size process halftones from one set of continuous-tone color separation negatives for the various forms of collateral material, such jobs usually go to the producer making the color separations. For specialized production such as posters or displays, which the principal producer may not wish to handle, the order to this producer should specify that a set of color separation negatives be supplied to the other producers. This avoids duplicating most of the color separation cost.

Bibliography Charles E. McHugh, *Dictionary of Advertising and Graphic Arts Terms,* Western Publishing Company, P.O. Box 1276, Poughkeepsie, N.Y. 12602; *Pocket Pal,* an illustrated booklet on the printing and engraving process, International Paper Company, 220 East 42d Street, New York, N.Y. 10017, annually; *TAPPI Survey,* CA Report 16, Technical Association of the Pulp and Paper Industry, One Dunwoody Park, Chamblee, Ga. 30338.

CHAPTER TWO
Paper and Composition Methods

MOST BOOKS ON printing or advertising production have dealt essentially only with the letterpress process. It should be understood that any references to the fineness of halftone screens suitable for various kinds of paper apply only to letterpress. For this process 120-line or finer screens require coated paper, 100- or 110-line screens can be used with supercalendered and English-finish paper, and newspaper stock is limited to 75-line or coarser halftones. The various antique-finish and text papers, together with the bonds, were best suited to line art.

TONE ON UNCOATED PAPERS

There are no such restrictions on tone copy in the other major printing processes. The 150-line contact halftone screen is standard for single-color commercial work with offset, and the 175-line screen is in wide use for process color work. With offset the paper surface has little connection

Fig. 2-1 These award winners in exhibits of commercial printing indicate the extent of illustrative treatment in tone and color. The majority of the examples are printed on uncoated paper by suitable processes.

with the fineness of halftone screens; in fact, even 300-line screens are used commercially.

Coated paper is used in offset when desired, principally for fine detail, extra brilliance, and spirit varnishing. Many advertising papers today are surface-sized and are used for both letterpress and offset.

Rotogravure requires a smooth calendered paper to lift the ink from the printing cylinder wells. Special rotogravure papers are made in both coated and uncoated grades including rotonews, which is used for newspaper color supplements. Because rotogravure involves long press runs and paper in rolls, the producer and the customer usually settle details on a carload basis.

Designers now have an unlimited choice of paper regardless of the art techniques to be reproduced. Their preference for the various antique finishes is shown by the winning entries in exhibits of commercial printing, such as those of the American Institute of Graphic Arts. As a prominent paper manufacturer puts it, "Paper is part of the picture." To quote a New York Type Directors study, "Papers of special character and impressiveness are considered one of the six major graphic design trends. . . ." Developments in advertising and book papers with their new finishes, textures, brightness, and colors offer a new dimension to the graphic arts designer.

Since the art director is now concerned with the budget and with reproduction quality as well as with the design of printed material, paper is an important part of art production. The cost of paper averages 23 percent of the total printing cost. Obviously paper is an important cost factor but one subject to considerable control for both advertising and publishing.

Form for Processing Inquiries, Orders

Paper in Sheets

Salesman .... Date ....
Customer .... Purchasing Agent
Address ....
Ship to .... Purchase # ....
Address .... Deliver ....
GRADE ....
QUANTITY .... (Sheets) .... (Pounds)
SIZE & WEIGHT .... M; .... basis weight
COLOR .... FINISH .... DESIGN ....
CALIPER THICKNESS .... 1-sheet .... 4-sheets .... pages-to-inch
☐ WATERMARKED ☐ UNWATERMARKED
GRAIN DIRECTION ☐ long ☐ short ☐ optional (one dimension)
DESIGN OR PATTERN NUMBER ☐ long ☐ short ☐ optional (one dimension)
TRIMMING ☐ machine ☐ trimmed-2-sides
TO ONE SIZE ☐ trimmed-2-ends
☐ trimmed-4-sides
PRESS SHEET ☐ Sheetwise ☐ Work-and-Turn ☐ Work-and-Tumble
REPRODUCTION METHOD (indicate which)
☐ Letterpress ☐ 1-color ☐ 2-colors ☐ 3-colors ☐ 4-colors
☐ wet ☐ dry
☐ Lithography ☐ 1-color ☐ 2-colors ☐ 3-colors ☐ 4-colors
☐ wet ☐ dry
☐ Gravure
☐ Photogelatine
☐ High-gloss inks ☐ metallic inks
☐ Finishing ☐ varnishing ☐ lacquering
☐ acetate laminating ☐ liquid laminating
☐ polyethylene laminating
☐ embossing
PLANT HUMIDITY REQUIREMENTS ....
PURPOSE FOR WHICH THIS PAPER IS INTENDED ....
PACKING ☐ Ream-marked in cartons ☐ Ream-marked in bundles
☐ Ream-sealed in cartons
☐ Ream-marked on single-tier skids
☐ Ream-marked on double-tier skids
☐ Ream-marked on 4-tier skids
☐ Felt-side-UP ☐ Felt-side-DOWN
SKID SPECIFICATIONS ☐ 4-way-entry ☐ 2-way-entry
runners ☐ short-way ☐ long-way
minimum distance between runners .... inches
maximum height .... inches
maximum weight .... pounds
Note — MARK SKID NUMBER AND ORDER NUMBER ON RUNNERS
SHIPPING siding on .... RR
plant can accommodate trailers up to .... feet long
☐ sidewalk delivery by winch-truck
Most satisfactory delivery hours
.... AM to .... AM
.... PM to .... PM
Receiving platform closed .... to ....
SPECIAL MARKINGS ON SKID-WRAPPERS ....
SPECIAL INSTRUCTIONS NOT IDENTIFIED ABOVE ....
SAMPLE FOR MATCHING ACCOMPANYING
NOTE: Be sure to send out-turned samples in advance of shipment

Fig. 2-2 This paper merchant's form gives an idea of the details that may have to be considered in ordering paper.

CONTROL OF PAPER COSTS

In designing the size of the unfolded printed piece, always make sure that it will cut efficiently from standard paper sizes, which are listed in Fig. 2-3. It is not unusual for a user to switch to a different kind of suitable paper to obtain the required standard size. Never make calculations to the edge of the sheet, for trim and gripper margins are required and bleed designs may need additional space. The trend today is to a page measuring 8½ by 11 inches rather than 9 by 12 inches.

Uncoated offset paper is surface-sized to make the lint stick to the paper. This characteristic gives the paper extra strength and stiffness, and since the paper is uncalendered, it has extra bulk. Therefore offset paper is generally considered equal in strength, bulk, and stiffness to a letterpress coated stock 10 pounds heavier. For long runs of color work this weight differential presents a chance to save more than 25 percent of the cost of

STANDARD PAPER SIZES: KINDS, STANDARD SIZES, REAM WEIGHTS, EQUIVALENT WEIGHTS

Standard Weights
BOOK PAPER (Weights per 1000 sheets)
Basis 25 × 38

Basis	30	35	40	45	50	60	70	80	90	100	120	150
17½ × 22½	25	29	33	37	41	50	58	66	75	83	99	124
19 × 25	30	35	40	45	50	60	70	80	90	100	120	150
23 × 29	42	49	56	63	70	84	98	112	126	140	169	
23 × 35	51	59	68	76	85	102	119	136	152	170	204	
22½ × 35	50	58	66	75	83	99	116	133	149	166	199	249
24 × 36	54	64	72	82	90	110	128	146	164	182	218	272
25 × 38	60	70	80	90	100	120	140	160	180	200	240	300
26 × 40	66	76	88	98	110	132	154	176	198	218	262	328
28 × 42	74	86	100	112	124	148	174	198	222	248	298	372
28 × 44	78	90	104	116	130	156	182	208	234	260	312	390
30½ × 41	78	92	106	118	132	158	184	210	236	264	316	396
32 × 44	88	104	118	134	148	178	208	238	266	296	356	444
33 × 44	92	106	122	138	152	184	214	244	276	306	366	460
35 × 45	100	116	132	150	166	198	232	266	298	332	398	498
36 × 48	108	128	144	164	180	220	254	292	328	364	436	544
38 × 50	120	140	160	180	200	240	280	320	360	400	480	600
41 × 54	140	164	186	210	234	280	326	372	420	466	560	700
44 × 64	178	208	238	266	296	356	414	474	534	592	712	888
35 × 46	102	118	136	152	170	204	238	272	306	338	406	
38 × 52	124	146	166	188	208	250	292	332	374	416	500	
41 × 61	156	184	212	236	264	316	368	420	472	528	632	
42 × 58	154	180	206	230	256	308	358	410	462	512	615	
44 × 66	178	208	238	266	296	356	414	474	534	592	712	
46 × 69	201	234	267	301	334	400	468	534	602	668	802	
52 × 76	250	292	332	374	416	500	582	666	748	832	998	

The weight differential in paper is important to the advertiser because of the following factors:

(1) The more weight, the more body to the finished advertisement

(2) The more weight, the less danger of gray areas resulting from show-through of material printed on the reverse side of any one sheet

(3) The more weight, the greater the cost of the paper

(4) The more weight, the greater the postal cost for material sent through the mail

(5) The more weight, the greater the thickness of individual sheets, as a rule, and the bulk of a completed booklet or folder.

The accompanying charts show regular sizes, regular weights for standard reams and equivalent weights per 1,000 sheets for different types of paper. The measure of weight in paper is expressed in so many pounds per ream. You may desire to use a 50 lb. printing paper (50 lbs. per ream) — or you may want a heavier type of sheet, weighing say 70 lbs. at slightly more cost. By checking the tables you can determine: (1) whether the weight you want is standard in the different paper types, (2) what the regular sheet sizes are, (3) how much poundage you will require in 1,000 sheets of any size.

Standard Weights
COVER PAPER (Weights per 1000 sheets)
Basis 20 × 26

Basis	50	60	65	80	90	100	130
20 × 26	100	120	130	160	180	200	260
22½ × 28½	123	148	160	197	222	246	320
23 × 29	128	154	167	205	231	256	334
23 × 35	155	186	201	248	279	310	402
26 × 40	200	240	260	320	360	400	520
35 × 46	310	372	402	496	558	620	804

Standard Weights
PRINTING BRISTOL (Weights per 1000 sheets)
Basis 22½ × 28½

Basis	80	90	100	120	140	160	180	200	220
22½ × 28½	160	180	200	240	260	320	360	400	440
22½ × 35			250	300	350	400			
26 × 40			330	396					

Standard Weights
INDEX BRISTOL (Weights per 1000 sheets)
Basis 20½ × 24¾

Basis	90	110	140	170	220
20½ × 24¾	117	144	182	222	286
22½ × 28½	148	182	230	280	362
22½ × 35	182	223	284	344	444
25½ × 30½	180	220	280	340	440
28½ × 45	296	364	460	560	724

NOTE: To convert from inches to millimeters, multiply by 25.4.

Standard Weights
BONDS, LEDGERS, SAFETY, WRITING PAPERS
Translucent, Xerographic, Micr Bond
(Weights per 1000 sheets)

	Substance								
Size	13	16	20	24	28	32	36	40	44
16 × 21	23½	29	36	43	50½	57½	65	72	79
16 × 42	47	58	72	86	101	115	130	144	158
17 × 22	26	32	40	48	56	64	72	80	88
17½ × 22½	27	34	42	51	59	67	76	84	93
17 × 26	31	38	47	57	66	76	85	95	104
17 × 28	33	41	51	61	71½	81½	92	102	112
18 × 23	29	35½	44½	53	62	71	80	89	97½
18 × 46	58	71	89	106	124	142	160	178	195
19 × 24	32	39	49	58½	68½	78	88	98	107
20 × 28	39	48	60	72	84	96	108	120	132
21 × 32	47	58	72	86	101	115	130	144	158
22 × 25½	39	48	60	62	84	96	108	120	132
22 × 34	52	64	80	96	112	128	144	160	176
22½ × 22½	35	43	54	65	76	87	97	108	119
22½ × 34½	54	66	83	99	116	133	149	166	183
22½ × 35	56	67	84	101	118	134	152	168	186
23 × 36	58	71	89	106	124	142	160	178	195
24 × 38	64	78	98	117	137	156	176	196	214
24½ × 24½	42	51½	64	77	90	103	116	128½	141
24½ × 28½	49	60	75	90	105	119½	134½	149½	164½
24½ × 29	49½	61	76	91	106½	122	137	152	167
24½ × 38½	66	81	101	121	141½	161½	182	202	222
24½ × 39	66	82	102	122	144	164	184	204	225
25½ × 44	78	96	120	144	168	192	216	240	264
26 × 34	62	76	94	114	132	152	170	189	208
28 × 34	66	82	102	122	143	163	184	204	224
34 × 44	104	128	160	192	224	256	288	320	352
35 × 45	109	135	168	202	236	270	303	337	371

Fig. 2-3 Paper data courtesy of Walden's Paper Catalog, 1976. For more comprehensive data on paper use, binding, folds, computation of ream weights of special sizes, and price, the *Estimator's Book,* published by the S. D. Warren Company, is recommended. It is usually available to paper buyers through Warren distributors.

paper. On a weight basis 14 percent is saved when a 60-pound offset paper is used instead of a 70-pound letterpress coated paper. On the basis of cost per pound the saving ranges upward from about 12 percent, depending on whether expensive or cheaper grades of the two types of paper are compared.

There is also a bulk-to-weight advantage in using uncoated papers, which include both the uncoated offset papers and the sulfate bristols, index bristols, and tag stocks, all of which take fine halftones by offset. An uncoated offset can be bulked to a thickness of .0085 caliper to substitute for cover paper. The quality and cost of bristols now make it possible to substitute them for heavy, more costly papers. In selecting a stock for return postcards, for example, it was found that an extra-bulking stock would save 19 percent in weight over a comparable heavy stock.

It should be understood that not all mill brands of paper have the same qualities. Some bulk more than others, and some are stiffer than others. In fact, particular brands are often referred to as "hard" or "soft" papers. Folding qualities also differ with grades and brands.

Selecting an uncoated paper also offers an opacity-to-weight advantage. The introduction of titanium pigment has permitted the use of a lighter-weight paper without loss of opacity. For example, halftones may be used on both sides of a sheet of lightweight opaque bond for statement enclosures and the like. Other papers also are opaqued, and it is not unusual for a more expensive paper to be selected without a material increase in cost. The use of a thinner sheet often makes a larger folded signature practical, or it can bring a mailing within the limitations of an automatic mail-inserting machine.

SELECTION OF THE MILL BRAND BY THE PRINTER

With small print orders paper costs are not important, and any brand can be used. With long runs of color work the choice of paper depends on printability, grain direction, and the sheet size to be used. The buyers select the kind of paper they want to use, but to handle problems of paper, ink, and press, offset printers select the mill brand on which their quotation is based. Large color printers tend to standardize their selection on several brands. Since paper prices per pound depend on the quantity purchased, by buying in carload lots printers can offer a lower price on these brands.

PAPER SPOILAGE

There is spoilage in all printing, both in the pressroom and in the bindery. For less than 5,000 sheets spoilage may run as high as 10 percent if bindery operations are required; for 25,000 sheets or more spoilage will be about 5 percent. Each passage of the job through the press, each color, and each bindery operation take their toll. Printers therefore take spoilage into consideration when they estimate paper requirements for a job. Because of spoilage and high press speeds it is impractical to print the exact number of printed pieces ordered, and by trade custom 10 percent over or under the specified amount constitutes delivery unless there is a written understanding to the contrary.

SPECIFYING INK COLORS

For flat (nonprocess) color work the best method is to attach to the copy a small ink swatch from an ink catalog. Sample colors are printed on both coated and uncoated stock, ink being identified by number. Widely accepted now is the PMS system[1] of matching ink swatch books for customer and printer. Each color or shade is identified by number with a detachable swatch for camera copy. All ink manufacturers have numbered formulas. A printer's estimate may quote prices on black and one PMS color, thus avoiding the expense of matching a colored sample.

A number of paper companies, among them Weyerhaeuser, have issued sample books of their colored papers printed with various PMS ink colors to show the result of combining the two colors. Art supply

[1]Pantone, Inc., 55 Knickerbocker Road, Moonachie, N.J. 07074.

Fig. 2-4 Art Directors and Designers Often Use Uncoated or Colored Advertising Papers

1. Envelopes have a display as well as a utility value. Illustrative treatment is unlimited.
2. Return coupons and postcards should be able to take pen and ink; postcards must meet postal regulations for thickness.
3. Package enclosures, shelf talkers, and the like are printed in such quantities that the cost of paper is an important factor. The thin opaque papers take tone work on both sides and reduce tonnage.
4. Softness is an important ingredient of literature for the infant market, and it is also desirable in cosmetic advertising. Paper is an important part of this characteristic of printing.
5. Cookbooks and recipe booklets should be printed on uncoated paper because of the chance of wet hands' making pages stick. There are no restrictions on art media with the offset process.
6. A contrast of cover and text is frequently desirable, and it affords a change of pace with magazine inserts. A heavier antique stock is often used for process color.
7. With higher postal rates, the thin opaque bonds keep the weight of printed matter down. They can be printed on both sides.
8. Special events telegram blanks require both process printing and the ability to take pen or pencil. An inexpensive stock for both requirements is handled by offset.
9. The various forms of merchandising coupons usually require tone reproduction and stiffness. Uncoated stock is frequently the choice.
10. Even uncoated blotting paper takes halftones by offset.

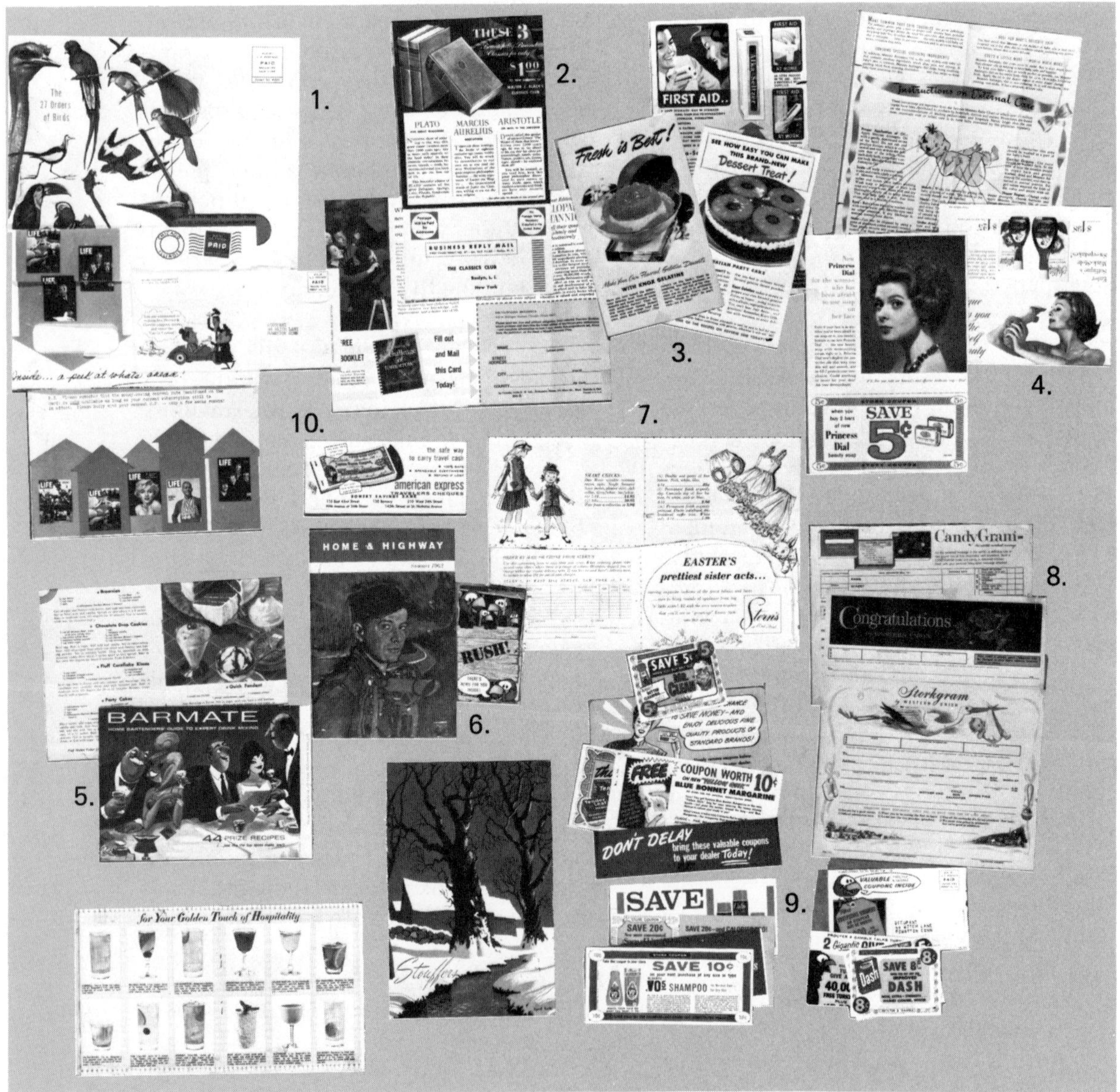

stores handle PMS art papers, geared to the standard ink colors, for layouts.

If a satisfactory color cannot be found from these sources, an artist's watercolor swatch can be supplied. Such a swatch should appear on the stock to be used. You should never submit a color on coated paper when uncoated paper is to be used; the same ink will look different on the two papers.

Ink Color Specifier

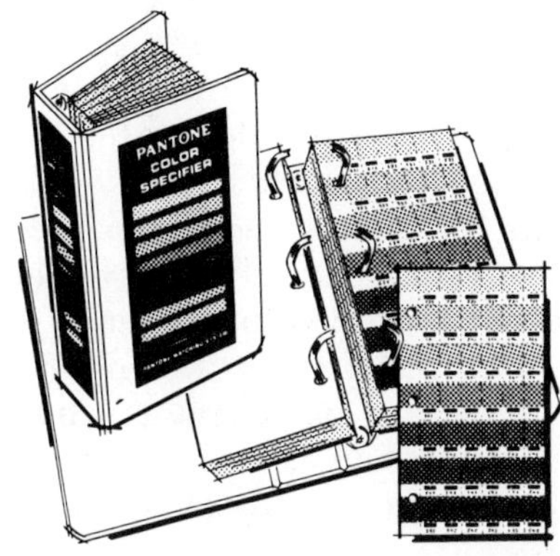

Fig. 2-5 Pantone® swatch book of ink colors for art directors. It has 6,000 tear-out chips of all the Pantone® colors on both coated and uncoated stocks.

MAXIMUM WORK AREA OF SHEET

With all printing processes, in selecting a job size that may be cut efficiently from a standard paper size, you must allow for the usual printing margins and for trims in the bindery. An extra inch for both sheet length and sheet width is usually sufficient, but inside fold trims (¼ inch) and bleed trims must also be considered. For booklets, magazines, and books you should obtain from the printer the bindery imposition: a blank sheet folded with pages numbered. The choice of imposition depends on the binder's equipment and color register needs, and you should not assume that the same imposition is always used for the same type of job. Folds should be made with the paper grain, usually the longer side of the sheet, but paper can be ordered "grain short."

PRINTING IN MULTIPLES

Except in the case of small jobs, printing is done in multiples—two up, four up, and so on—depending on quantity wanted. Since offset eliminates the high cost of the lockup and makeready of letterpress, it can take advantage of the economies of a large printing form. Two-sided printing is done by "work and turn" to save a plate and a makeready, and a booklet may use an imposition which will yield six copies in a long folded strip that needs only to be cut apart. Possible bindery economies should be considered in selecting the efficient press size for a job.

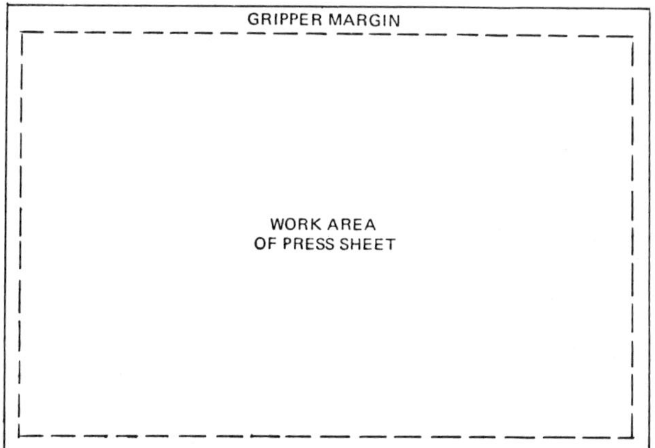

Fig. 2-6 The dotted lines indicate the maximum work area on the press sheet. At least a ½-inch gripper margin on one long side and an ⅛-inch trim on the other sides are required.

TYPE AND OTHER FORMS OF COMPOSITION

Since the graphic arts are being adjusted to the photomechanical printing processes, which can use any form of composition that can be photographed, even typewriter copy, we shall emphasize the nonmetal methods, particularly phototypesetting. However, a general knowledge of typefaces, type sizes, measure (length of line), spacing between lines of type, and the like is pertinent to all methods of preparing composition for camera copy.

The forms of composition used for camera copy can be grouped in three categories:

1. Metal, either hand-set or machine-set. Only good proofs are needed.
2. Photographic, ranging from desk-top lettering appliances to commercial phototypesetting machines operated by phototypesetters and by typographic services that also provide metal composition.
3. Cold-type, with methods ranging from transfer paper letters for large type and mechanical lettering aids to special electric typewriters with book typefaces. Such composition is used for small orders that cannot bear the cost of metal type or photocomposition.

Regardless of the kind of composition, the typefaces are essentially the same. The diagram of the metal letter *M* in Fig. 2-7 shows the details of a piece of foundry, or hand-set, type used for the larger sizes. Note that the point size (lines per inch) includes a shoulder to provide space for descenders (*j*'s, *p*'s, *y*'s, and so on); the type body allows space for capitals and ascenders (*b*'s, *d*'s, *f*'s, and so on).

In composition a letter or a punctuation mark is termed a "character"; the number of characters determines the space required for the particular typeface and type size. The height of a typeface is specified in *points* (there are approximately 72 points to 1 inch); thus, 36-point type would occupy ½ inch. Letter width varies, but the width of a line of type, termed a "measure," is specified in *picas* (there are 6 picas to 1 inch): a 3-inch column width is specified as 18 picas. Indention of the beginning of a paragraph and horizontal spacing instructions are indicated in *ems* (an em is the square of the type body used).

The Anatomy of Type

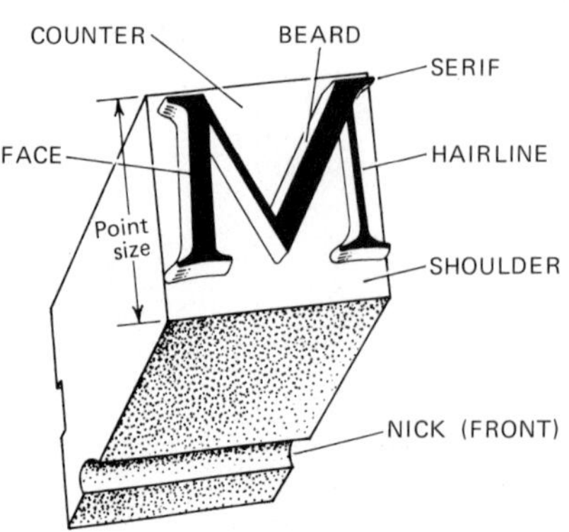

Fig. 2-7 A piece of foundry, or hand-set, type.

TERMINOLOGY

The design of a style of type, called the "face," is identified by name: Cheltenham, Bodoni, Futura. Machine-set text type, such as 8-point and 10-point type, is usually available in two styles of the same face, such as roman and bold or roman and italic, from the same Linotype magazine.

Type larger than 14 points, used for headlines, is apt to be individual foundry type for hand setting, but it may be machine-set; it comes in normal, condensed, or extended form and frequently in italic or boldface. Some styles are available in light or medium weights as well as in boldface.

The International Typographic Composition Association (ITCA) classifies typefaces as Old Style, modern, square serif, sans serif, and special, or miscellaneous (see Fig. 2-17). Since faces can fall into two groups, classification is not rigid.

The term "leading" refers to extra space between lines of type. The longer the line, the more space is desirable for readability. With hand-set type, leading is provided by thin strips of type metal. With machine-set type the mold for the type slug can be made thicker for leading, for example, 10-point typeface on a 12-point slug, like this line of type.

MACHINE-SET METAL TYPE

Practically all body or text type is set by machine: Linotype, Intertype, or Monotype. An operator at a keyboard assembles automatically little brass matrices of the characters to form the desired line of type. A lever is then pressed to let the molten type metal flow into the mold to form the type slug of the line.

The typefaces come in several forms: *roman,* the commonly used form with vertical stems; *italic,* which is slanted; ***bold,*** which is a heavier version of the roman; and ***bold italic,*** a heavier version of italic. Some faces are also available in small capitals.

The matrices are carried in a magazine; most type machines are equipped to handle two magazines. A magazine for body type usually carries roman and one other form, either italic or bold but rarely both. The Intertype catalog listings are shown in Fig. 2-9.

In general, machine-set body type is available in sizes from 6 to 14 points, but there are a few faces with smaller sizes. Display type sizes range from 18 to 42 points, with a few faces available in 48 and 60 points. Since machine-set type is cheaper than hand-set type, it is best to check and see if the face and size you want for display type are available in machine-set type.

MONOTYPE

Monotype machines cast individual type characters instead of line slugs. Many faces come in sizes as small as 6 points, but some come only in sizes of 14 points or larger. All tend to run as large as 36 or even 48 points, with some ranging to 72 points. Their selection avoids the use of hand-set type for some display faces. When machine-set type is no longer needed, it is remelted, as are any electros of hand-set type, which generally is not released.

Type founders publish catalogs of their faces and sizes, and typographic services that set type but do no printing publish lists of their faces and sizes. Printers supply customers with type sheets of what they have on hand.

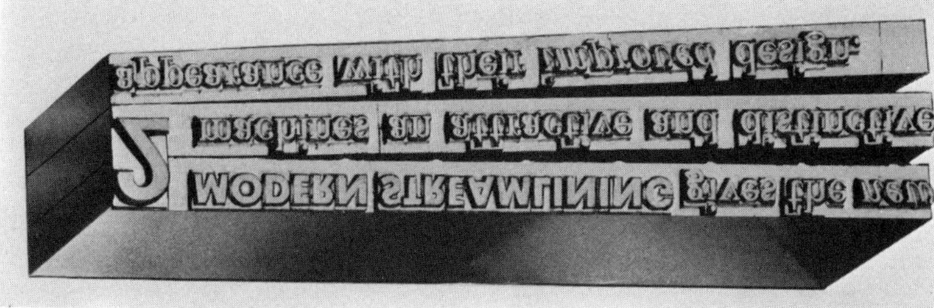

Fig. 2-8 Machine-set type slug.

11 Pt. Baskerville with Italic and Small Caps. Font 854 — Code WIOYJ

INTERTYPE matrices excel in type 123123

INTERTYPE matrices excel in type VBCVBC

Alphabet 130 pts. Figures .076. Characters to 1 pica 2.63
Special characters available. See alphabet section

11 Pt. Baskerville with Bold. Font 857 — Code WJEUP

INTERTYPE matrices excel in type 123123

INTERTYPE matrices excel in type 123123

Alphabet 133 pts. Figures .0761. Characters to 1 pica 2.58

Fig. 2-9 Machine-set body type: two magazines.

HAND-SET TYPE

Today hand-set type is used principally for display headlines. It generally comes in sizes from 18 to 48 points, but there are both larger and smaller sizes. New typefaces initially are hand-set; later, if the demand warrants, they are put on the machines.

Hand-set type is foundry type, purchased by the printer from a type founder. A typographic service also buys this type but does not release it when supplying metal composition to a printer. Instead, an electro of any hand-set type is supplied and positioned with machine type for a locked-up page. The original type is used for a repro proof and electros, but in either case hand-set type is returned to the typecases for reuse.

LUDLOW TYPE

A variation of hand-set type is Ludlow type. An assembly of Ludlow matrices of characters is positioned manually and locked in a special type stick, which serves as a mold for molten type metal to form a type slug of a headline. The matrices are put back in a typecase, and the slug is eventually remelted. The advantage to the printer is that his inventory of regularly used faces is reduced and he need not redistribute foundry type into the typecases. Newspaper headlines are usually set by this method.

6 pt. Spartan
8 pt. Spartan
10 pt. Spartan
12 pt. Spartan
14 pt. Spartan
18 pt. Spartan
24 pt. Spartan
30 pt. Spartan
36 pt. Spartan

Fig. 2-10 A type series.

Futura Medium
Futura Medium Italic
Futura Medium Condensed
Futura Bold
Futura Bold Italic

Fig. 2-11 A family of type.

The average printer carries only a limited selection of typefaces and sizes. The printer or the customer goes to a typographic service for a larger selection. Advertising typographers have the largest and most nearly current selections. With their local association they publish a directory of typefaces and sizes and the names of the firms that have them.

REPRO TYPE PROOFS

The most expensive form of composition is a repro proof of a made-up page of type. A semi-made-up page proof may position only the columns of text, perhaps with subheads, and display composition, widely scattered blocks of type, and running headings with folios, proofed without regard to position. A third form of repro proof consists of the galley proofs of the type as it comes from the machines: text, subheads, and display type, all in separate galleys. With these proofs the page can be made up on the drawing board by the production artist, and the cost of composition is cut in half. Today this form of composition is widely used even for letterpress when type matter is to be part of the engraving.

When repro proofs are delivered, they should be carefully checked for imperfections. The galley proofs should be of equal weight so that when they are pasted up, one column or page will not be darker than the next one. You should also make certain that columns of type are not "cocked"; otherwise, they cannot be aligned. Hairline rules should not be used because of the danger of portions of the lines dropping out; hairline rules should always be inserted on a mechanical with a ruling pen.

With the use of a mechanical only a proof of foundry type is needed, and the cost of composition has been reduced. Foundry display faces are the newer hand-set faces not yet on typesetting machines. The typographer does not release this type as metal but supplies an electro, while retaining the original type. Since only repro proofs of the type are needed for the mechanical, the cost of electros is avoided.

Photostats are used for reversing type or any element on the paste-up and also for enlarging or reducing type to get an exact fit of a headline.

COMPOSITION IN THE ART DEPARTMENT

With the offset printing process dominant in commercial printing and in use for 75 percent of all advertising and book printing, much of printing production is now handled in the art department, where the mechanical is prepared. It was the shift to the photomechanical processes and the use of phototype that caused this change. A survey of art directors by the Technical Association of the Pulp and Paper Industry (TAPPI) revealed that 83 percent of the directors now deal directly with typographers on a regular basis instead of working through the production department, as they formerly did. The reason is that art now is a key element in the creative planning stage and controls both time

Lithography's Place In Printing Production

By H. C. LATIMER

Educational Director, LITHOGRAPHERS NATIONAL ASSOCIATION

(The term lithography includes offset lithography, offset printing, photo-offset, photo-lithography, planography, etc. — the basic process is the same.)

IT IS GENERALLY ACKNOWLEDGED that each printing process has its own field. The purpose of this leaflet is to define lithography's field, and to group in concise form the basic reasons why lithography is selected as the process to be used in producing various types of commercial printing. This will help to show the newcomer in advertising and the non-professional printing buyer the applications and advantages of the process as well as its frequent economies. In some cases the choice of the paper to be used or the size of the printed piece may indicate lithography as the process to be used; in other cases, cost of the job including engravings will be the determining factor, the buyer getting a price by lithography as well as a price by one of the other processes when he thinks it advisable.

From the standpoint of cost, the lithographic process may be at a relative disadvantage in the production of certain types of jobs, chiefly those involving individual short runs. If these short-run jobs are made up entirely of straight type matter which can be printed directly from the type by letterpress or if the job is one where the higher costs of letterpress make-ready and engravings are not too important as cost factors, the economies in lithographic make-ready and higher lithographic press speeds may not be sufficient to offset the initial cost of making the lithographic press plate. However, as the length of the run increases (particularly when it is sufficiently long to warrant running the job in multiple units) or as the costs of letterpress make-ready and engravings increase in importance as cost factors, lithography soon makes up this disadvantage and becomes more economical. Lower costs are obtained for short-run jobs by lithography, by means of "gang running" several such jobs in one press run. In this way the plate and press costs are divided between the several jobs which make up the single press run.

The quality of work produced by any of the printing processes and the price for which a job can be purchased are dependent upon many factors. All of the processes are capable of producing good, bad and indifferent work, and lithography is no exception. With this process, as with the others, wide variation in quality is possible and considerable variation in price will be found. Quality of management, sales policies, appropriateness of equipment, experience and skill of the working force, etc. as well as price, are all basic factors in the selection of the lithographer or printer with whom to entrust the production of one's work.

The reasons for using the lithographic process usually come under one or more of six basic groups.

The Six Basic Reasons for the Use of the Lithographic Process

1 PAPER STOCK USED

When the choice of paper stock calls for fine halftones (120-line screen or better) on a rough surface stock such as: Fancy Finish, Wove, Antique or Laid Finish, Bond, uncoated Cover Stock, etc. This is possible because the ink is applied from the rubber-covered offset cylinder. Applies to such work as:

a. Folders, broadsides, booklets, etc. with fine halftones on an expensive rough surface or fancy finish stock for effect.

b. Process color work on uncoated stock. On long runs the use of an inexpensive uncoated stock, such as sulphite bond or halftone news, in place of coated stock required for letterpress, can make a considerable saving in cost of paper.

(Offset *coated* stock is used when desired—particularly for work to be varnished or for sharper detail or greater brilliancy of colors).

c. Letterheads with illustrative treatment calling for fine halftones on bond stock; also the advertising, 4-page sales, and dramatized letterheads, using halftones with sales copy.

d. The new lightweight opaque bonds printed both sides and carrying halftone illustrations. Much used for statement enclosures by department stores and specialty shops that want the "tone" of a bond paper.

e. Envelopes to match letterhead treatment, or to carry thru the art treatment or theme of a booklet or catalog. Also the "panoramic" (all-over decoration) envelope.

f. For letter campaigns where halftone illustrations are desirable, lithography reproduces the illustrations, the letter and the letterhead in one run; for many long-run form letters lithography has replaced the processing of the letterheads, doing the whole job in one run.

g. Direct mail literature, particularly broadsides, with large dramatic halftones and colors on the various fancy finish papers—handmade finish, homespun, etc., as well as on wove finish.

h. Children's picture books and many primary grade text books illustrated with attractive process colors and halftones on the text pages of soft uncoated stock lessening eye strain, and on which the lithographic process can put fine halftones.

i. Advertisers' recipe books with process illustration on an uncoated stock by lithography. Wet fingers do not cause pages to stick together.

j. Parts Books and Instruction Manuals using halftone illustrations on bond paper for its strength.

k. The new trend in stockholders' reports is to illustrated booklet form on wove or other rough surface stock. The same trend holds true in town and city yearly financial reports. Halftone illustration on such stock calls for lithography.

l. Lithography permits fine halftone and process illustration on uncoated cover stock for magazines, catalogs and house organs, stockholders' reports, etc. The cover of Fortune magazine is an example; Coronet's is another example.

m. Liquor and other expensive bottle labels on uncoated stock with halftones.

There are of course many other such applications calling for the use of lithography (magazine inserts, greeting cards, menus, etc., etc.). Lithography's ability to put fine halftones (frequently 175 or 250 screen) on the various uncoated paper stocks, *and not cost*, is the determining factor for the use of the process in the above types of prin*ing.

2 COST OF PLATES

With illustrations and color being used extensively in many types of printing, the buyer today is concerned with the cost of printing plates — halftone and line engravings, electros for multiple images in longer runs, wax plates for fine ruled form work, reverse plates for many types of multi-color work, and process-color plates — or their equivalent in printing processes other than letterpress. With the exception of electros, these costs are usually in addition to the printer's quotation when letterpress is used, but included in the quotation when lithography or gravure are used.

Because of economies peculiar to the process and of ways of preparing copy for economical reproduction, lithography frequently offers the printing buyer an opportunity to eliminate or greatly reduce, the cost for ...

... each of the four color plates are pulled on cellophane-like material and the lithographer has the equivalent of camera film screened positives of each of the color separations. Negatives, enlarged or reduced slightly, can be made from these. If the advertisement was printed by gravure, the advertiser secures from the magazine continuous-tone color separation positives on glass. In both cases the expense of remaking color separations is avoided and the cost for each set of color plates is usually less than it would be if working from the original art work. From art work in magazine ads it is possible to derive much in the line of dealer display material. Whole ads may be "blown up" to a window poster featuring a special offer, or just a part of the art work may be used in making up counter displays or window strips or booklet cover illustration, etc.

Photo-Mechanical Equipment Assures Accurate Register and Economy

For small size work such as labels, seals, or stamps requiring accurate register for colors, a negative of a unit containing many duplicate images is made with a "step and repeat" camera. A few "steps" of this unit on the litho press plate may give several hundred individual images on the litho press plate. All this work is done photo-mechanically to 1/1000 of an inch. Photo-mechanical equipment is used for close register work, regardless of size.

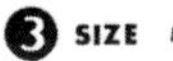

3 SIZE *Posters, Window Displays, Maps, Etc.*

Lithography's Place In Printing Production

By H. C. LATIMER

Educational Director, LITHOGRAPHERS NATIONAL ASSOCIATION INC.

(The term lithography includes offset lithography, offset printing, photo-offset, photo-lithography, planography, etc. — the basic process is the same.)

IT IS GENERALLY ACKNOWLEDGED that each printing process has its own field. The purpose of this leaflet is to define lithography's field, and to group in concise form the basic reasons why lithography is selected as the process to be used in producing various types of commercial printing. This will help to show the newcomer in advertising and the non-professional printing buyer the applications and advantages of the process as well as its frequent economies. In some cases the choice of the paper to be used or the size of the printed piece may indicate lithography as the process to be used; in other cases, cost of the job including engravings will be the determining factor, the buyer getting a price by lithography as well as a price by one of the other processes when he thinks it advisable.

From the standpoint of cost, the lithographic process may be at a relative disadvantage in the production of certain types of jobs, chiefly those involving individual short runs. If these short-run jobs are made up entirely of straight type matter which can be printed directly from the type by letterpress or if the job is one where the higher costs of letterpress make-ready and engravings are not too important as cost factors, the economies in lithographic make-ready and higher lithographic press speeds may not be sufficient to offset the initial cost of making the lithographic press plate. However, as the length of the run increases (particularly when it is sufficiently long to warrant running the job in multiple units) or as the costs of letterpress make-ready and engravings increase in importance as cost factors, lithography soon makes up this disadvantage and becomes more economical. Lower costs are obtained for short-run jobs by lithography, by means of "gang running" several such jobs in one press run. In this way the plate and press costs are divided between the several jobs which make up the single press run.

The quality of work produced by any of the printing processes and the price for which a job can be purchased are dependent upon many factors. All of the processes are capable of producing good, bad and indifferent work, and lithography is no exception. With this process, as with the others, wide variation in quality is possible and considerable variation in price will be found. Quality of management, sales policies, appropriateness of equipment, experience and skill of the working force, etc. as well as price, are all basic factors in the selection of the lithographer or printer with whom to entrust the production of one's work.

The reasons for using the lithographic process usually come under one or more of six basic groups.

The Six Basic Reasons for the Use of the Lithographic Process

1 PAPER STOCK USED

When the choice of paper stock calls for fine halftones (120-line screen or better) on a rough surface stock such as: Fancy Finish, Wove, Antique or Laid Finish, Bond, uncoated Cover Stock, etc. This is possible because the ink is applied from the rubber-covered offset cylinder. Applies to such work as:

a. Folders, broadsides, booklets, etc. with fine halftones on an expensive rough surface or fancy finish stock for effect.

b. Process color work on uncoated stock. On long runs the use of an inexpensive uncoated stock, such as sulphite bond or halftone news, in place of coated stock required for letterpress, can make a considerable saving in cost of paper.

(Offset coated stock is used when desired—particularly for work to be varnished or for sharper detail or greater brilliancy of colors).

c. Letterheads with illustrative treatment calling for fine halftones on bond stock; also the advertising, 4-page sales, and dramatized letterheads, using halftones with sales copy.

d. The new lightweight opaque bonds printed both sides and carrying halftone illustrations. Much used for statement enclosures by department stores and specialty shops that want the "tone" of a bond paper.

e. Envelopes to match letterhead treatment, or to carry thru the art treatment or theme of a booklet or catalog. Also the "panoramic" (all-over decoration) envelope.

f. For letter campaigns where halftone illustrations are desirable, lithography reproduces the illustrations, the letter and the letterhead in one run; for many long-run form letters lithography has replaced the processing of the letterheads, doing the whole job in one run.

g. Direct mail literature, particularly broadsides, with large dramatic halftones and colors on the various fancy finish papers—handmade finish, homespun, etc., as well as on wove finish.

h. Children's picture books and many primary grade text books illustrated with attractive process colors and halftones on the text pages of soft uncoated stock lessening eye strain, and on which the lithographic process can put fine halftones.

i. Advertisers' recipe books with process illustration on an uncoated stock by lithography. Wet fingers do not cause pages to stick together.

j. Parts Books and Instruction Manuals using halftone illustrations on bond paper for its strength.

k. The new trend in stockholders' reports is to illustrated booklet form on wove or other rough surface stock. The same trend holds true in town and city yearly financial reports. Halftone illustration on such stock calls for lithography.

Fig. 2-12 With semi-made-up page type proofs, pages of a folder made up on the drawing board.

8/9 × 12 picas
A suitable column width (measure) for readability depends on the type size and the spacing between the lines

8/10 × 20 picas
A suitable column width (measure) for readability depends on the type size and the spacing between the lines (leading). A widely accepted rule is that the line be 1½ to 2 times the length of the

8/11 × 23 picas
A suitable column width (measure) for readability depends on the type size and the spacing between the lines (leading). A widely accepted rule is that the line be 1½ to 2 times the length of the lowercase alphabet of the selected

Fig. 2-13 The longer the line of type, the more space between lines.

and cost factors related to production. In many cases the advertiser and the agency art department have absorbed production personnel.

POINTS ON TYPE COSTS

The basic cost for body, or text, composition is calculated for "straight matter," material set in a single typeface and size flush left and right. Lines with roman and italic or roman and bold type usually entail extra costs with metal type. Lines can be set flush left with an uneven, or ragged, right (no hyphenization), flush right with an uneven left, or centered. A narrow measure is frequently set flush left to avoid the unattractive letter spacing that would result from setting it flush left and right. Centered lines entail a premium charge. With metal type there is generally a premium charge for straight matter wider than 30 picas (5 inches).

Always remember that machine-set type is less costly than hand-set type. Check a type catalog for a suitable machine-set face and size.

SPACING OF TYPE

Measure and Spacing for Body Type

A suitable column width (measure) for readability depends on the type size and the spacing between the lines (leading). A widely accepted rule is that the line be 1½ to 2 times the length of the lowercase alphabet of the selected type size. This measurement is given in type catalogs. Another theory is that the measure should not exceed the width of fifty characters of the type used.

To illustrate, the above paragraph is shown in three different measures, each with different leadings, in Fig. 2-13.

Spacing Capital Letters in Headlines

A common problem in typography with metal capital letters involves spacing certain adjacent letters for appearance, particularly capitals 30 points or larger. For example, a word containing *A* followed by *V* or *A* and *T* next to each other may require adjustment (see Fig. 2-14). Your judgment will determine whether such letters should be brought closer together or whether other letters in the word should be spaced farther apart. Such spacing is usually adjusted on the drawing board, but a Photo-Typositor photolettering machine may be used. With the machine you can see the position of the letter before it is exposed. The smaller the bold caps are in a headline, the greater the space between the lines must be to command attention.

Display sizes of many of the popular commercial typefaces are available in the form of transparent self-adhesive transfer sheet letters. Greeking sheets (simulated composition) in 8- and 10-point sizes are sold for the text of comprehensive layouts.

With the photomechanical processes chapter initials are usually handled by means of transfer letters, which are inserted on the mechanical with the repro proofs of text. The proper alignment of raised and sunken initials is as follows:

RAISED initial aligns.

THE sunken initial should align at both top and bottom for best appearance.

TAVERN — AS SET – NO LETTERSPACING

T A V E R N — LETTERSPACED TO EXTEND "ERN"

TAVERN — LETTERSPACED TO CONDENSE "TAV"

Fig. 2-14

CENTER BALANCE

Balance falls under two forms –

Center Balance
(bisymmetric)
which is static
and all lines
not making a full line
are centered
under the line above

OFF-CENTER BALANCE

Off-center
balance
(asymmetric)
is dynamic and
has the quality of
motion (where cen-
tered lines should
not appear)

This style is considered the contemporary form.

SPACING

SPACING BETWEEN GROUPS OF TYPE

Related groups should
be closely spaced
to each other with at
least twice the amount
of spacing separating
it from an unrelated
group of type.

Use white space rather than separating rules.

PROPORTION

Proportion

Type face, size,
measure and
line space,
should conform
to the general
proportions
of the page.

UNITY

UNITY

RHYTHM

Fig. 2-15 Thumbnail illustrations of working with type courtesy of the International Typographic Composition Association, *Guide for Buyers of Typography,* Washington, D.C., 1966.

HARMONY

HARMONY

This is obtained
through the agree-
able relationship of
the various parts of
a design. Study the
border with the type
face to be used.

Shape • Size • Tone

Cooper

Fig. 2-16 Borders should reflect the typeface.

The end use of a printed job usually determines the choice of typeface, size, measure, and spacing. For books readability is very important, but for commercial printing, particularly advertising, the amount of space available for text or for blocks of type may outweigh considerations of readability.

CLASSIFICATION OF TYPEFACES

Typefaces were developed from the hand script of monks copying manuscripts in the Middle Ages, which produced a type style similar to that which we call Old English, used for decorative purposes at Christmastime. German script printing was an offshoot of this style. Finally, the less cluttered Italian lettering on Roman temples was adopted, resulting in the roman style of today's typefaces.

Typographers today generally group typefaces in five classifications: Old Style, modern, square serif, sans serif, and special, or miscellaneous. However, some typographers consider that certain typefaces fall within two classifications.

H

Old Style: Such faces as Garamond Old Style, Caslon 540, and Baskerville have moderately heavy and thin designer's strokes, with the inside curve of the serif originating from the curved pen or chisel stroke. They are popular book faces well suited to soft uncoated book papers. In advertising they are best suited to formal or dignified layouts.

H

Modern: These faces represent a transition from Old Style, with greater contrast between the thick and thin strokes of the letters and a slight difference in the serifs of many letters, which are more mechanical in design. The development of these faces with finer serifs and hairlines was due to the invention of smooth coated paper. Bodoni, Caledonia, and Craw Modern are examples of modern faces. For letterpress, these faces are not suited to the soft uncoated printing papers such as antique and text papers.

H

Square Serif: Typefaces in this classification tend to be heavier than those of the first two groups. They were developed to obtain bolder headlines for commercial printing, particularly texts in large sizes. Such faces include Craw Clarendon, Cairo Extra Bold, and Beton Extra Bold.

H

San Serif: This style of face without serifs came into use with the development of modern art and layout, in which details are eliminated. Examples are the Gothics; Futura, which is very popular in all weights; Univers; and Lydian.

Fig. 2-17

HSMA hsmanoetrguykjw

ABCDEFGHIJKL ABCDEFGH

HSM hsmanoetrguykj

AN hsmanoetr ANO anoet

Miscellaneous: This is a catchall classification of typefaces not included in the first four groups. They are used by designers for moods or special effects. Special faces are often employed by fashionable retail shops to capture a distinctive appeal.[2]

ABCDEFGHIJKLMN
abcdefghijklmnopqrst

Baskerville

HSMANOETRGUYKJW
hsmanoetrguykjwbfpcv

Craw Modern

HSMANOETRGUYKJW
hsmanoetrguykjwbfpcv

Craw Clarendon

ABCDEFGHIJKLMN
abcdefghijklmnop

News Gothic Bold

[2]Baskerville, Craw Modern, Craw Clarendon, News Gothic Bold, and many other typefaces are available in ATF Spectype transfer letters at art supply stores.

Selecting the Typeface

Selecting a suitable typeface and type size calls for judgment under specific conditions. Usually some compromise is necessary because of limitations of space on the layout, local resources, and, with small print orders, frequently cost.

For the beginner it is usually best to know type styles rather than specific faces. In advertising both display and text faces are closely related to the product or service being advertised. Industrial equipment, for example, is apt to call for bold or extra-bold square-serif or sans-serif headlines and for a modern face for the text because of their extra weight. A woman's specialty shop is likely to use typefaces of a more delicate nature, such as one of the miscellaneous display faces for small ads or a light sans-serif display face for large ads. The text is apt to be set in an Old Style face because it is lighter than modern typefaces.

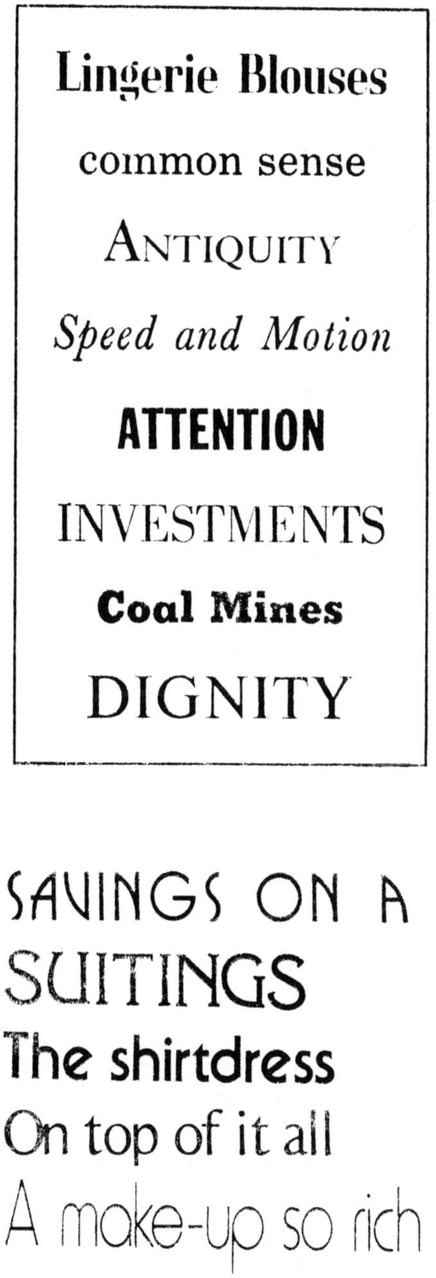

Type can suggest masculinity or femininity, dignity or the lack of it, exclusiveness, cheapness, modernity, or antiquity. Selection is a matter of judgment and taste, and rarely are one face and one size the best. The way type is handled in a layout does more for appearance than the face selected.

Lingerie Blouses

common sense

ANTIQUITY

Speed and Motion

ATTENTION

INVESTMENTS

Coal Mines

DIGNITY

SAVINGS ON A

SUITINGS

The shirtdress

On top of it all

A make-up so rich

Fig. 2-18 Two panels of typefaces, traditional and contemporary.

COST OF METAL COMPOSITION

As mentioned above, the basic cost of text composition is for straight matter, which is quoted either by the line or by 1,000 ems. Display type, whether hand- or machine-set, usually involves time charges for positioning in the page form. For an advertising layout this positioning and lockup can amount to half of the cost of the job. There are standard premium charges for mixing italic or boldface with roman text and for lines set in roman and small caps or in caps and small caps. In addition, there are charges for varying indention, tabular matter, centered lines, and straight matter more than 30 picas wide.

These premium charges for some forms of metal composition apparently are not an official trade custom in phototypesetting but are followed there to some extent. Cold-type composition is priced on a time basis.

MARKING COPY TO BE SET IN TYPE

Typewritten copy to be set in type should be on 8½- by 11-inch paper, with each page numbered and the last page marked "end." Your instructions for face, size, measure, and leading should be placed in the right-hand margin. The left-hand margin, which should measure 1½ inches, is

MARKUP OF COPY TO BE SET IN TYPE

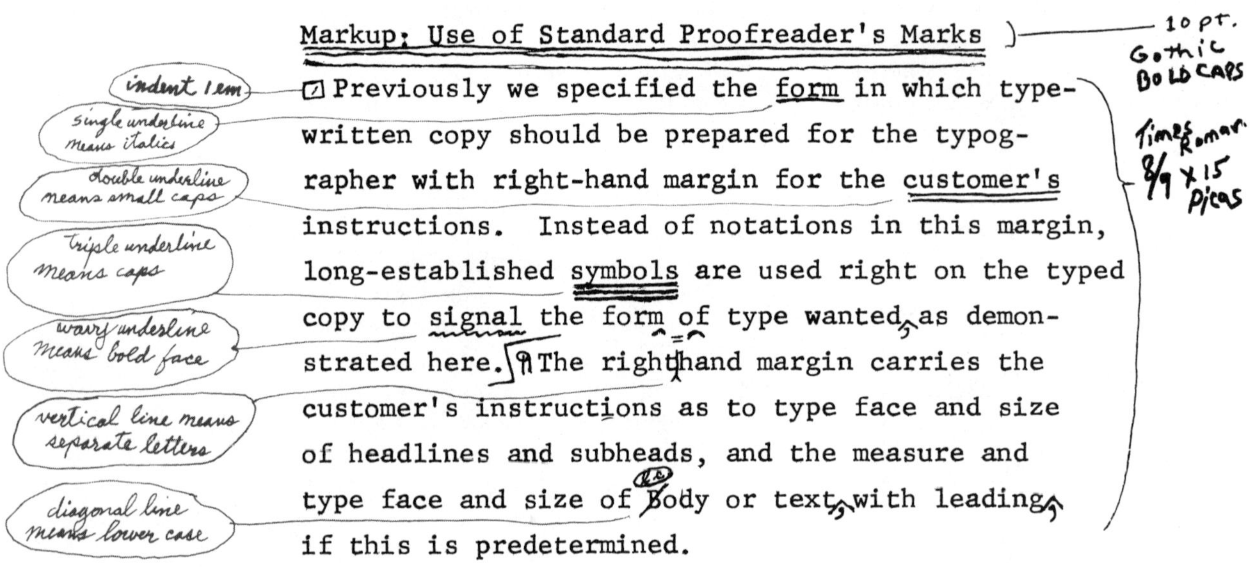

Markup: Use of Standard Proofreader's Marks

10 pt. Gothic BOLD CAPS

indent 1 em

single underline means italics

double underline means small caps

triple underline means caps

wavy underline means bold face

vertical line means separate letters

diagonal line means lower case

Previously we specified the form in which type-written copy should be prepared for the typographer with right-hand margin for the customer's instructions. Instead of notations in this margin, long-established symbols are used right on the typed copy to signal the form of type wanted as demonstrated here. The righthand margin carries the customer's instructions as to type face and size of headlines and subheads, and the measure and type face and size of Body or text with leading if this is predetermined.

Times Roman 8/9 x 15 Picas

LEFT 1½" MARGIN IS FOR TYPOGRAPHER'S MARKUP. CUSTOMER'S TYPE SPECIFICATIONS SHOULD GO ON TYPED COPY, NOT ON LAYOUT.

THE ABOVE COPY WITH MARKUP WOULD RESULT IN THIS TYPE SET:

Previously we specified the *form* in which type-written copy should be prepared for the typographer with right-hand margin for the CUSTOMER's instructions. Instead of notations in this margin, long-established SYMBOLS are used right on the typed copy to **signal** the form of type wanted, as demonstrated here.

The right-hand margin carries the customer's instructions as to type face and size of headlines and subheads, and the measure and type face and size of body or text, with leading, if this is predetermined.

Fig. 2-19 The marked copy above would result in the typeset lines to the right.

for the printer's instructions to the composing room: which copy is to be hand-set and machine-set, which machine is to be used, and so on. If there is considerable body type, as for a book, you should send two copies so that two typesetters can work on the job. Refer to the example in Fig. 2-19 for your form of markup.

If a made-up advertising page is wanted, a layout should accompany the typed copy and any separate blocks of type should be keyed (*A*, *B*, *C* or 1, 2, 3) for position. The makeup operator will position the metal. Markup instructions should not go on the layout but on the typed manuscript copy.

Words in the body type that should be set in boldface, italics, small caps, and so on are indicated by proper proofreader's marks, as shown in Fig. 2-19, and not by notation in the right-hand margin. Symbols and underlining are the typographer's language and should be used.

The standard proofreader's marks (Fig. 2-20) should always be used on the reader's type proof to indicate corrections. Their use avoids confusion as to what is wanted.

When ordering type, specify the printing process to be used and, if offset or gravure, the kind of repro proof wanted. The repro proof can consist of the made-up page, as for letterpress; the partially made-up page, to be completed on the

Punctuation	
⊙	Period
^,	Comma
(:)	Colon
^;	Semicolon
ʼ∨	Apostrophe
“∨	Open quotes
”∨	Close quotes
=/	Hyphen
1/N 1/M 2/M	Dash (show length)
( )	Parentheses

Delete and insert	
∂	Delete
∂ (close up)	Delete and close up
out see copy	Insert omitted matter
stet	Let it stand

Paragraphing	
¶	Paragraph
fl ¶	Flush paragraph
□ [2]	Indent (show no. of ems)
run in	Run in

Spacing	
#	Insert space
eq #	Equalize space
⁀‿	Close up

Style of type	
wf	Wrong font
lc	Lower case
cap	Capitalize
ic lc	Initial cap, then lower case
sc	Small capitals
c sc	Initial cap, then small caps
rom	Set in roman
ital	Set in italics
lf	Set in light face
bf	Set in bold face
3∨	Superior character
^3	Inferior character

Position	
] [	Move right or left
⊓ ⊔	Raise, lower
ctr	Center
fl L fl R	Flush left, right
=	Align horizontally
‖	Align vertically
tr	Transpose
tr #	Transpose space

Miscellaneous	
X	Broken type
⟲	Invert
⊥	Push down
(sp)	Spell out
/	Shilling mark (slash)
(…)	Ellipsis
see L/O	See layout
?query	Query

STANDARD PROOFREADER'S MARKS

Fig. 2-20 When ordering composition, provide the printer with marked-up typed copy and layout if for a made-up page. Blocks of type on the layout should be keyed by letter or number to typed copy for positioning.

Multiple-line heads should be marked to be set flush left or right or centered.

Narrow-measure text (to pass an illustration) should be set flush right or left with one side left ragged to avoid awkward spacing or hyphens.

When clippings of printed matter are supplied as text, paste them on 8½- by 11-inch paper.

When proofreading typeset matter for corrections, always use standard proofreader's marks.

To reverse type (show white on black) use a Photostat negative on the paste-up.

To enlarge type beyond the available sizes, use a Photostat positive or the newer proof-positive print.

Repro proofs of metal or strike-on type are usually sprayed with fixative to prevent smearing, but check to be sure that this has been done. Do not approve repros until you are sure that there are no broken or gray-spot characters, cocked text lines, or smears and that all corrections have been made.

CHARACTER COUNT TO LINE INCH

Count the number of characters (letters), punctuation marks, and spaces between words in an average line. These are *Copy Units*. Then count *Lines of Copy* and multiply by the number of *Copy Units* in the average line. This indicates the *total number of Copy Units.*

```
Education-To prepare us for
complete living is the function
which education has to discharge.
H. Spencer. Education is properly
to draw forth, and implies not so
much the communication of
knowledge as the discipline of
the intellect, the establishment
of the principles and the regu-
lation of the heart. Webster.
```

10 lines of copy

copy units in average line

10 × 30 = 300 or total number of copy units

☆ CASLON No. 540 Foundry

6[27] 8[20] 10[17.5] 12[13] 14[11] 18 24 30 36 42 48 60 72 84

ABCDEFGHIJKLMNOPQRSTUVWXYZ&

abcdefghijklmnopqrstuvwxyz

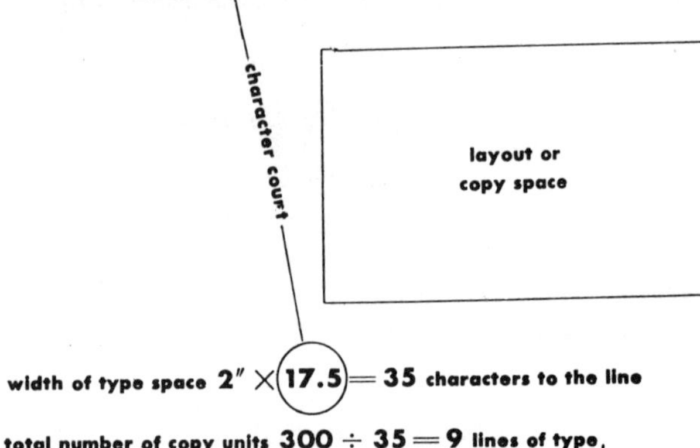

width of type space 2″ × 17.5 = 35 characters to the line

total number of copy units 300 ÷ 35 = 9 lines of type

Education-To prepare us for complete living is the function which education has to discharge. H. Spencer. Education is properly to draw forth, and implies not so much the communication of knowledge as the discipline of the intellect, the establishment of the principles and the regulation of the heart. Webster.

Typewritten copy is easy to figure since the number of CHARACTERS in a line can be measured with a ruler. Elite typewriter runs 12 CHARACTERS to the inch and Pica typewriter runs 10 CHARACTERS to the inch.

Fig. 2-21 [*Courtesy Monsen Typographers, Inc., Chicago*]

drawing board by the paste-up artist; or galley repro proofs, to be used on the paste-up mechanical with photolettering for display type or with mechanical lettering aids or transfer letters.

Check all final or repro proofs carefully for broken letters, cocked lines, and so on before accepting them.

For rotogravure publication ads on which copy has been sent direct, follow the publication's production specifications. These are quite special, usually including a transparent type proof.

COPY FITTING

Estimating Required Space

Since the art department now specifies and usually buys typography and the designer handles such details for magazines and books, commercial art instruction does not only include specifying typography. For a layout the artist must also be able to estimate the space required for the copywriter's typed text when set in suitable type.

Rough layouts are the result of planning. The copywriter receives his instructions: the size of the space or job, what is to be emphasized, and the components to be included. Before he writes the copy, he usually makes a preliminary rough to determine the space available for his copy. In a professional department he is rarely handed a layout and told to fill the indicated space with copy. Thus commercial art is concerned with copy fitting: how much space in a layout or dummy will be required for copy already written? Too often the layout artist does not know how to fit copy or specify type. Both are now the responsibility of the art department instead of production, as in the past.

Typed Manuscript Copy

Copy for text matter should be typewritten to provide word or character count, double-spaced, on 8½- by 11-inch paper, with a left-hand margin of 1½ inches, a right-hand margin of 1 inch, and a space of 1½ inches at the top and 1 inch at the bottom. The margins provide space for marking copy for type sizes, and with a pica typewriter (six lines to 1 inch) the page has room for 250 words, with a 60-character count, or about 10 words, to the line.

Approximating Needed Space

Space or type size can be approximated by ruling off several square inches of a specimen of printing that you feel would be suitable for the job and counting the words to obtain a count per square inch. From your typed copy you can estimate the total number of words and approximate the number of square inches of space needed for the type you like. If your calculations are close, send the typographer your type specimen and mark the copy and layout "Set to fill."

From a type catalog or local type service or printer you can get the number of characters per pica or per inch (6 picas) and compile a table of words per square inch:

Words per square inch	Point size 6	7	8	9	10	11	12
Set solid	45	37	30	26	20	16	13
Leaded 2 points	33	26	22	20	15	13	11

When you specify extra space between type lines (leading), you reduce the number of lines per inch. With 10-point type leaded 2 points, for example, you get six lines per inch instead of seven plus.

Character Count, the Most Accurate Method

Character count is a more accurate copyfitting method, to be used after author's alterations and changes have been made. Figure 2-9 shows two Intertype magazine face listings, each of which gives the number of characters per pica. Phototype catalogs and type sheets also usually show characters per pica. The Linotype catalog, however, uses the character count per line inch (6 picas). The Monsen explanation (Fig. 2-21) shows how to figure the number of characters in typed copy.

PHOTOTYPESETTING

The initial phototypesetter for text type was Intertype's Fotosetter, which was converted from one of the company's metal composing machines. Figure 2-27 shows how light passing through a stencil put the letters on film; an operator familiar with the machine's keyboard was required. Since this was a manual method, little time was saved, but the impression of the letters was sharper than with metal type because there was no squeeze spread of the ink.

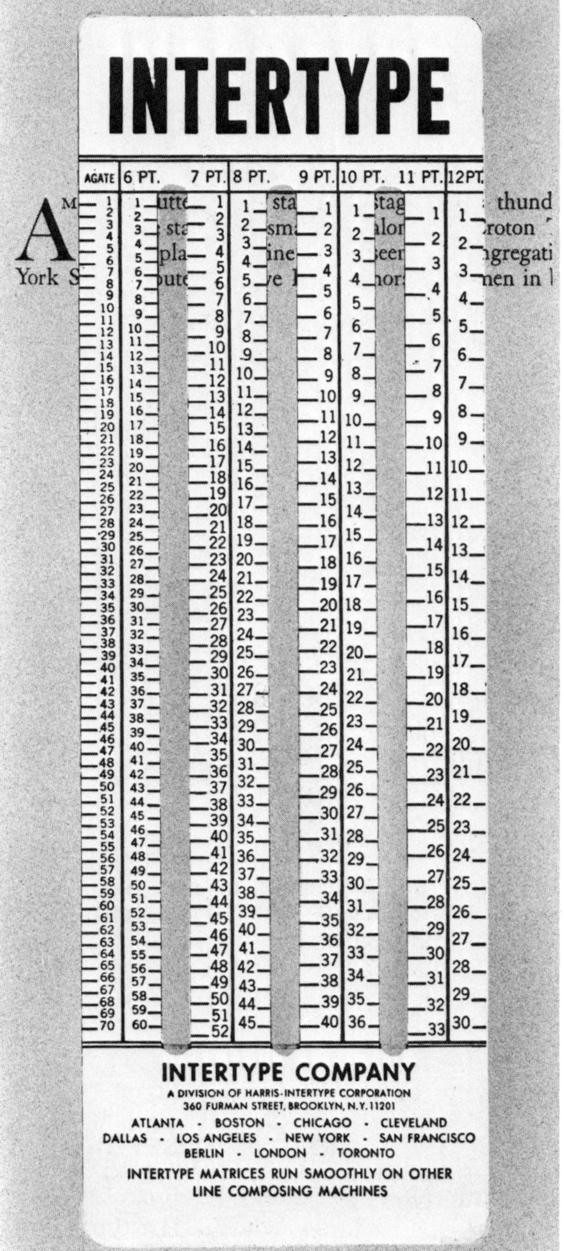

Fig. 2-22 Type gauge.

Curving a Headline

Fig. 2-23 The old method of cutting a type proof is now outdated.

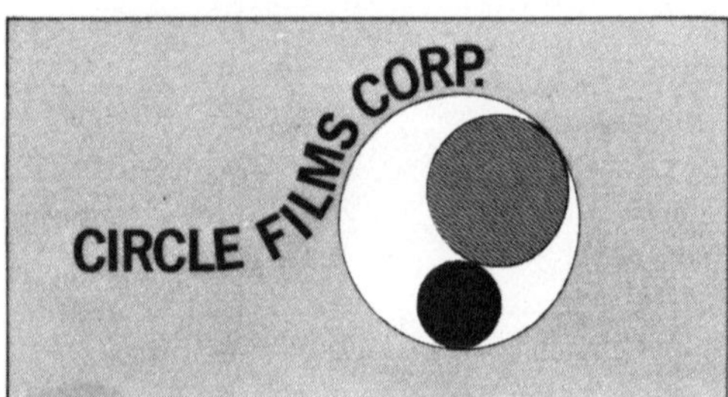

Fig. 2-24 The simplest method is to draw the curve in blue and then use transfer letters (sold by art supply stores) on transport film.

A. A rough layout for type such as this is not suitable for the typographer.

B. A more comprehensive layout such as this, with the copy fitting and sizes of type worked out, is needed. If the budget permits, the typographer can handle these details.

The Graphic Arts Monthly

C. With a comprehensive layout the finished make-up will be obtained with minimum delay and resetting.

Fig. 2-25

PHOTOTYPESETTING SYSTEMS FOR THE PRINTING USER

Intertype's Fotosetter, the first of the phototype machines, was the last typesetting machine to use the Linotype keyboard. The practical aspects of automation and use of a typist called for a faster speed, which could be obtained with a special typewriter keyboard that produced a perforated paper tape or a magnetic tape. At first, a "raw tape" was produced which disregarded type specifications (face, size, measure, etc.), which was fed to a computerized unit prepared for such detail, and which produced a second tape that activated the typesetting unit to produce the composition in galley form on paper or film.

The initial objective in the early phototypesetting research was speed, capabilities, and volume. Some of the equipment cost millions of dollars and could do such things as setting a page of type in seconds and, with computer memory banks, store information for retrieval and use or discard it. It was claimed that a fat telephone directory could be revised in 48 hours—the dead listings were discarded and the new listings inserted in their proper place.

Fig. 2-00 Input for phototype by means of keyboard with video screen. Typist can see result of keystrokes and correct errors on tapes or diskettes. *(Courtesy of Dymo-Graphic Systems.)*

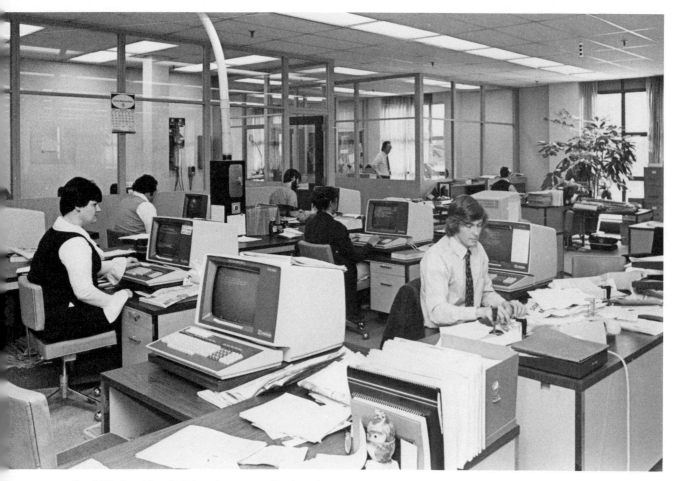

COST OF PHOTOTYPESETTING EQUIPMENT PLUNGES

With the developments in word processing and the advent of simple, unsophisticated, direct-entry phototypesetters which a typist could operate, selling for as low as $4,000, this equipment began to be installed in printing users' art and advertising departments as well as in editorial offices.

Viewing panels showing the result of the keystrokes were added to the keyboards producing the tapes or other forms of input such as the computerized magnetic diskette or a magnetic cassette tape, to permit correction before tapes were made. Some of the more sophisticated commercial typesetters can handle the tapes of 20 or 30 typists.

Some of the more recent phototype systems, such as the Linoterm and Comp/Set 4510, with video screens, not only show the composition from the keystrokes, but by pushing a command key can do some composition positioning—such as double column, and "flush left" or "flush right" or center.

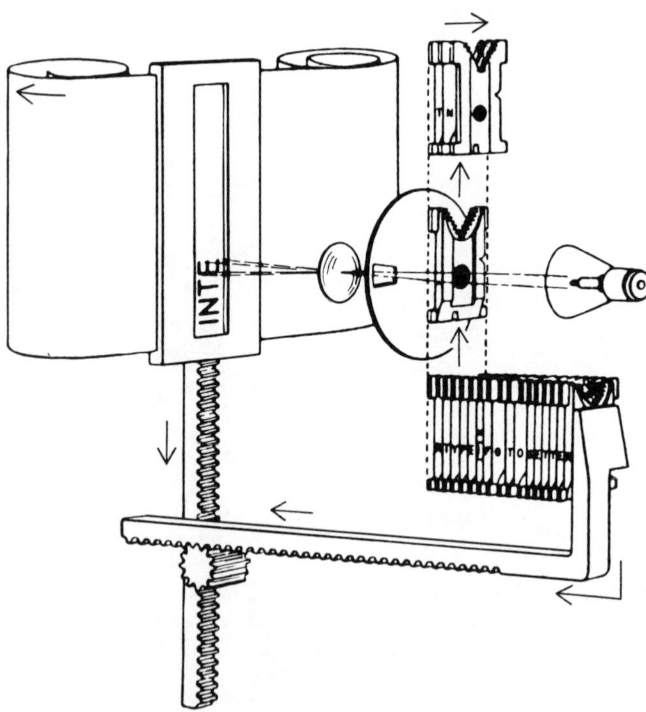

Fig. 2-27 Intertype's Fotosetter (1947), the first phototypesetter, used the brass matrix of the Intertype metal typesetter as a stencil. A beam of light projected the stencil image onto film to compose the line. A manual operation, this has been designated as the first generation of phototypesetting methods.

Fig. 2-28 This keyboard of Dymo Graphic Systems is representative of the newer phototypesetting models with viewing screens for a few lines of the typist's work. These come in justifying and nonjustifying models and may be augmented with optional equipment and accessories.

We previously mentioned OCR devices which can read typed manuscript and produce forms of magnetic media to serve as input for most commercial phototype systems and thus avoid the keyboarding operation. Practically all makers of phototype systems sell the Computext OCR page reader for the direct-entry typesetters, and there are other more expensive OCR units.

More suitable for the in-plant shops is the Dymo bar-code page reader, which reads a bar code under each character instead of the typed character. The typing is done with an IBM Selectric typewriter by using a special spherical one-piece type font, i.e. :

This page reader also produces the magnetic input media and, if wanted, a perforated paper tape.

THREE GENERATIONS OF PHOTOTYPESETTING

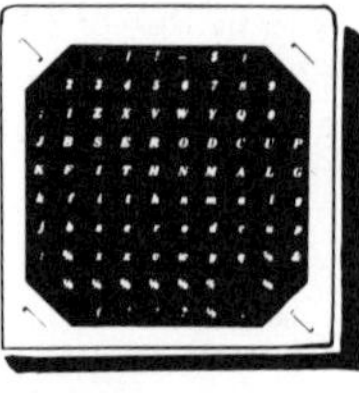

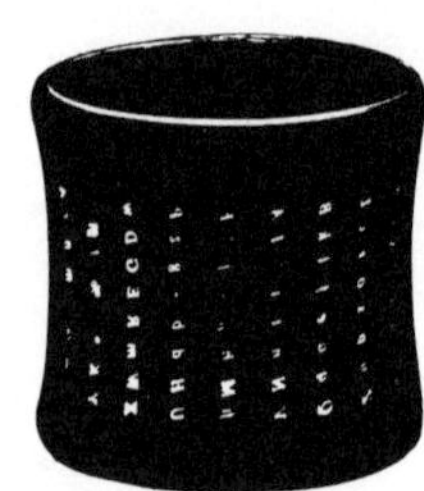

Fig. 2-29 The second generation of phototypesetters introduced the perforating keyboard, which a typist could operate to get a paper tape without regard for type specifications. These specifications are handled by a computerized unit set for face, size, measure, spacing, and so on for a second tape for the typesetting unit. The various forms of stencils shown and a light beam handle the composition on film. Most photosetting equipment in use is second-generation.

The third generation introduced the cathode-ray tube (CRT), similar to television, on which the letters are flashed for photography. This is a very sophisticated system of great speed. It has memory banks for the retrieval of old composition and inserts new material for material that has been discarded.

Fig. 2-00 Video display and editing terminal. This representative Dymo unit is using for coding (markup) and correction of computerized magnetic media, such as the diskettes and magnetic tapes, prior to use as input for phototype systems.

Fig. 2-00 A widely used form of input for phototype systems is the *diskette* (floppy disk in the trade), used by Compugraphic's EditWriter 7500 and the AlphaComp, but optional with the Linoterm. A diskette is a computerized magnetic recording disk that looks like a very thin 45-rpm phonograph record. It records, files, indexes, and retrieves up to 300,000 characters, claimed to be equivalent to half a mile of perforated tape. It can retrieve for later correction and updating.

The cassettes and magnetic cards have the same retrieving abilities. These are also used in word processing systems.

A recent development in phototype has been the conversion of word processing magnetic media—diskettes, cassettes, etc.—by means of an interface unit suitable for the phototypesetting system to be used. The converted media goes directly to video display terminal (VDT) for coding or formatting for the job. The keyboarding by the typographer is avoided and suitable input for his system is provided.

DIRECT-ENTRY PHOTOTYPESETTERS

Initially, there was only one phototype system suitable for the small printer. The year 1974 saw the introduction of several tabletop photographic typewriters termed "direct-entry phototypesetters" because no perforated tapes are necessary. In addition to the keyboard, these machines usually have facilities for viewing two lines of composition on a small viewing opening. Keys are pressed to obtain type sizes of the fonts positioned in the unit. The library of typefaces is quite large.

With prices ranging from $4,000 to $15,000, it is natural that in art departments and studios these units are taking their place beside the desk-top photolettering machines such as the Photo-Typositor. A typist operates such a unit when its services are needed.

Direct-entry systems include the Mergenthaler Linocomp typesetter (Fig. 2-35), with sizes ranging from 6 to 36 points; the CompuWriter IV, which permits virtually unrestricted mixing of eight type styles and twelve sizes in a 45-pica line; and the VariTyper Comp/Set 500 (Fig. 2-33), with a range of on-line type sizes. If various keys are pressed, the Comp/Set 500 can handle some positioning.

Today there are more than 100 models of phototypesetters, 60 keyboards, and 20 video editing terminals, as well as 10 OCR devices. Computerized systems can be programmed to position composition as specified in a layout. With the cathode-ray tube, the third generation of equipment, it is expected that page makeup eventually will be viewed on the tube (as in television) for photographing as a unit rather than letter by letter for composition.

An important economy for books arises from the fact that a perforated tape made by keyboarding for a hard-cover edition

Fig. 2-00 Merganthaler's LINOTERM typesetting system, a versatile, low-cost direct-entry machine with keyboard and video screen.

Fig. 2-00 Computerized magnetic input disks.

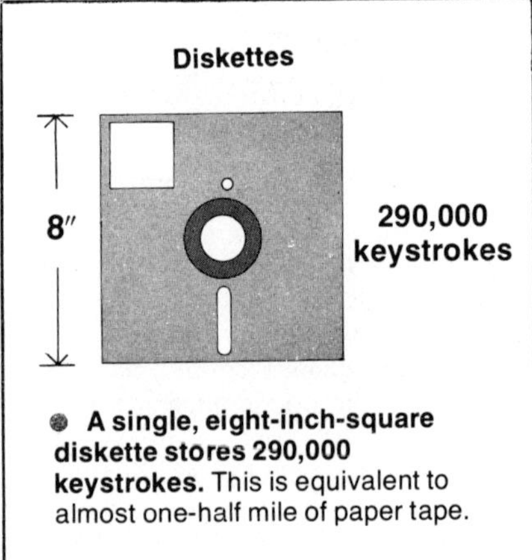

Diskettes
8″
290,000
keystrokes
A single, eight-inch-square diskette stores 290,000 keystrokes. This is equivalent to almost one-half mile of paper tape.

Input by typist using keyboard as an office function in an art, advertising, or editorial office; also from a previously prepared computerized magnetic diskette.

Manual, semiautomatic, and automatic justification models.

Video screen capacity of 24 lines of up to 80 characters.

Output—four faces and five sizes from 6 to 36 point on line; 14 sizes available, 45-pica line length; Merganthaler's library of typefaces.

Display formats: single column, 23 lines of 80 characters; dual column, 46 lines of 40 characters; split screen, 23 lines of 40 characters.

Typeset one job and edit another at the same time—even if each job requires different typefaces.

Priced within the $16,000 figure.

ABCDEFGHIJKLM abcdefghijklmnopqrstu
ABCDEFGHIJKLM abcdefghijklmnopqrstu
ABCDEFGHIJKLM abcdefghijklmnopqrstu
ABCDEFGHIJKLM abcdefghijklmnopqrstu
6-7-8-9 Times Roman

ABCDEFGHIJKLM abcdefghijklmnopqrstu
ABCDEFGHIJKLM abcdefghijklmnopqrstu
ABCDEFGHIJKLM abcdefghijklmnopqrstu
ABCDEFGHIJKLM abcdefghijklmnopqrstu
10-11-12-14 Times Roman

ABCDEFGHIJ abcdefghijklm
ABCDEFGHIJ abcdefghijklmn
ABCDEFGHIJ abcdefghijklmn
16-18-20 Times Roman

ABCDE abcdefgh
ABCDE abcdefgh
ABCDE abcdefgh
24-30-36 Times Roman

Fig. 2-00 Keyboard and typesetter.

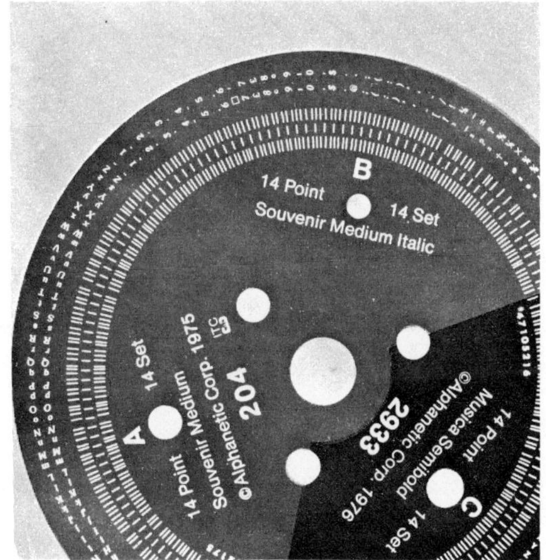

Fig. 2-00 Type font with three faces.

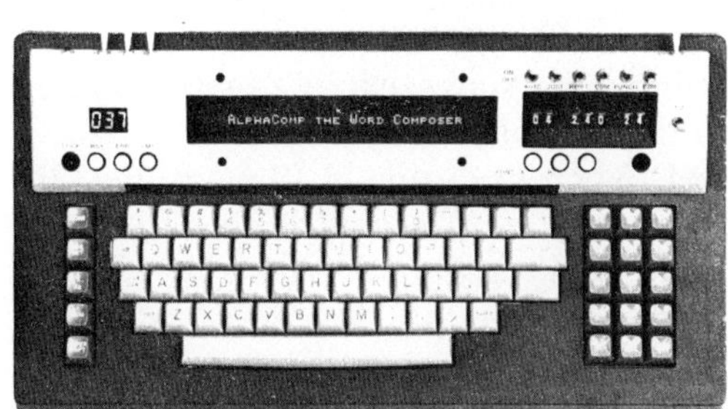

Fig. 2-00 Keyboard with visual display line at top showing what is being keyboarded.

ALPHACOMP BY ALPHATYPE

This is not a direct-entry phototypesetter but the system is so simplified that it is within the price range of most editorial or art departments, even though a minicomputer is involved to handle the problems of formatting. A visual display panel shows the operator what is being keyboarded, and corrections and changes can be made before a line is printed.

The AlphaComp keyboard, with the aid of its command keys, programs the job as well as the composition, with the help of a minicomputer, by means of magnetic coding on a diskette (floppy disk)—a thin plastic disk coated with ferric or chromium oxide. This disk is used to activate the separate phototype unit.

The phototype unit prints the type on photo paper, using a disk form of type font in the actual size instead of using lenses to change type size. A type font carries three typefaces, all the same size. The floppy disk is retained for storage and retrieval of wanted composition. Type lines can be justified or set flush left or flush right, centered. Command keys can give you a 45-pica line length, ½-point or 1-point rules, or the dot leader lines; a word or sentence can be underscored by using the keyboard. Other capabilities with type are available with the keyboard. Type sizes run from 5- to 24-point, with a maximum line width of 46 picas.

Comp/Set 500 Direct-Entry Phototypesetter

Fig. 2-37A The phototypsetter sets thirty-three type sizes and handles some positioning when keys are pressed.

33 Sizes from 5½ to 36 point are available at one time and all sizes are mexed on line to 45 picas

Fig. 2-34

can be reused for a paperback edition in a different typeface or type size merely by changing the type specifications on the control unit for the second tape. This procedure cuts costs in half.

Large-Volume Phototypesetters

Typographic services have now supplemented their metal composition facilities with the more sophisticated phototypesetting equipment, and their type catalogs also show these faces and sizes.

This type of equipment can generally print roman, italic, or boldface type in sizes from 6 to 18 points from a single type font, as illustrated by the VariTyper AM747 system Palatino face (see Fig. 2-38). The maximum measure is usually about 45 picas. Any desired letterspacing can be used. Part of a type sheet from a New York suburban phototype service using this VariTyper machine is shown in Fig. 2-39.

Phototypesetting Costs

Our inquiries show that in a metropolitan area the cost of photo straight matter runs about 15 cents per line of 10 points on 12, 18 picas wide. When volume and time permit handling the material as a "filler," the cost is much less. One New York phototypesetter using an OCR system offers 12-pica (newspaper) lines for 4 cents each and 18-pica lines, 10 points on 12, for 5¼

Fig. 2-00 EditWriter 7500.

COMPUGRAPHIC'S EDITWRITER 7500

This unit is offered as a low-cost, all-in-one, direct-entry photocomposition machine with editing, storage, and retrieval capabilities for the printing user.

Simplified keyboard layout is designed for efficient copy input and job control. Typographic pads on keyboard control automatic hyphenation logic, character fit, and copy depth for page formatting, plus size, line length, font, and line spacing, and simplify the recall and editing of stored information on a computerized diskette.

The video screen uses 12 inches of a 15-inch CRT tube and visually "talks" to the operator via two message lines. For proofing, editing, and author's alterations, the diskette storage system captures all key strokes for recall.

The phototype unit at the left produces fully mixed composition of 8 styles in 12 sizes, either 8- to 72-point or 6 to 36-point (low range). There is a large type library.

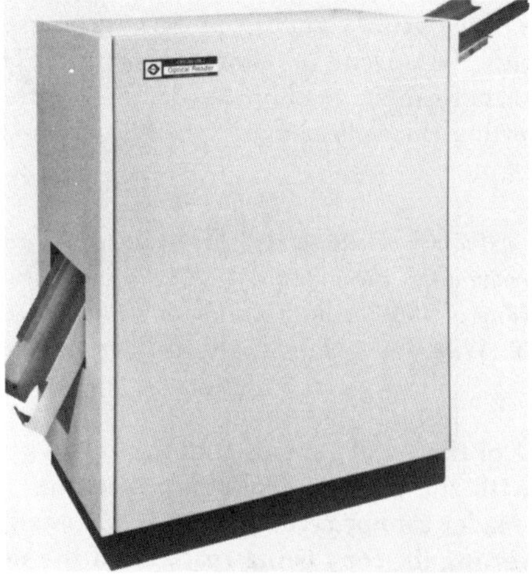

Fig. 2-00 Dymo's optical reader, Model B.

Megaron Medium	Typography is architecture, and the typographer is the architect. The building bricks he uses are the type faces, and the mortar is the spacing he selects for his composition. His blueprints are	Typography is architecture, and the typographer is the architect. The building bricks he uses are the type faces, and the mortar is the spacing he selects for his composition. His blueprints are called layouts	Times Roman
Medium Italic	*Typography is architecture, and the typographer is the architect. The build-*	*Typography is architecture, and the typographer is the architect. The building*	Italic
Bold	**Typography is architecture, and the typographer is the architect. The build-**	**Typography is architecture, and the typographer is the architect. The building**	Bold
Univers Medium	Typography is architecture, and the typographer is the architect. The building bricks he uses are the type faces, and the mortar is the spacing he selects for his composition. His blueprints are	Typography is architecture, and the typographer is the architect. The building bricks he uses are the type faces, and the mortar is the spacing he selects for his composition. His blueprints are	Bodoni
Medium Italic	*Typography is architecture, and the typographer is the architect. The build-*	*Typography is architecture, and the typographer is the architect. The build-*	Italic
Bold	**Typography is architecture, and the typographer is the architect. The build-**	**Typography is architecture, and the typographer is the architect. The build-**	Bold
News Gothic Cond	Typography is architecture, and the typographer is the architect. The building bricks he uses are the type faces, and the mortar is the spacing he selects for his composition. His blueprints are called layouts and his type rule	Typography is architecture, and the typographer is the architect. The building bricks he uses are the type faces, and the mortar is the spacing he selects for his composition. His blueprints are	School-book
Italic	*Typography is architecture, and the typographer is the architect. The building bricks*	*Typography is architecture, and the typographer is the architect. The build-*	Italic
Bold	**Typography is architecture, and the typographer is the architect. The building bricks**	**Typography is architecture, and the typographer is the architect.**	Bold

Fig. 2-40 Part of a type sheet of a small-town phototypesetter. Employing galley photoprints of text matter, the user makes up pages on the drawing board to be ready for the camera. A phototypeservice of this kind will also make up a page in paste-up form (almost all typographers will do this).

The state of the art of composition has taken great strides with the advent of phototypesetting. The average reader cannot readily identify the method used in setting the copy being read. With the need

The state of the art of setting type has taken great strides with the advent of phototypesetting. The average reader cannot readily identify the method used in setting the copy being read. With the need for speed and complete versa

The state of the art of composition has taken great strides with the advent of phototypesetting. The average reader cannot readily identify the method used in setting the copy being read. With the need

Most commercial phototypesetters of body type can produce either roman, italic, or boldface type from a single font, in sizes from 6 to 18 point by using a lens.

PT — 27 Palatino

	Reg.	Italic	Bold
6	4.0	5.0	4.0
7	3.4	4.2	3.4
8	3.0	3.7	3.0
9	2.6	3.2	2.6
10	2.3	2.9	2.3
11	2.0	2.6	2.0
12	1.9	2.4	1.9
14	1.6	2.0	1.6
18	1.2	1.0	1.2

CHARACTERS PER PICA

Fig. 2-41 This material is drawn from type sheets of the VariTyper phototypesetting AM747 system. The system can also handle intraline mixing of as many as twenty sizes.

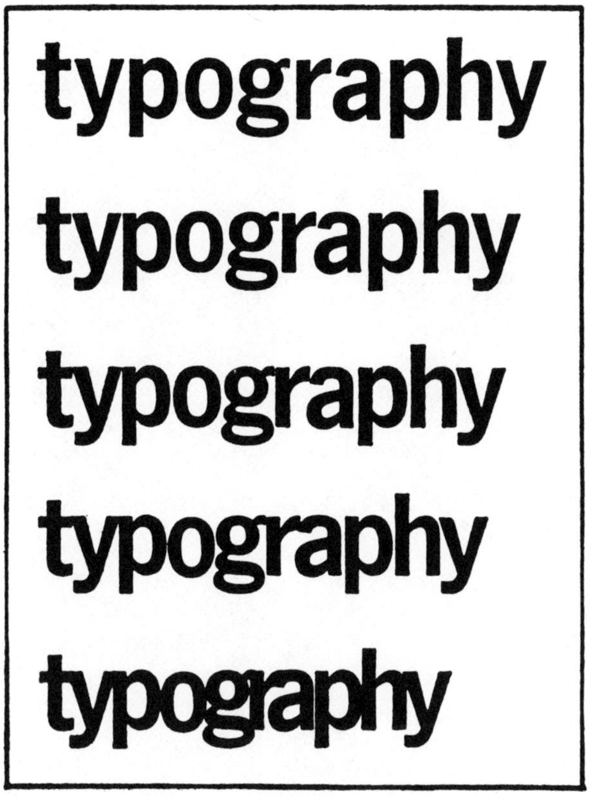

typography

typography

typography

typography

typography

Fig. 2-42 These settings, from top to bottom, are called normal, tight, very tight, very, very tight, and too tight. [*Courtesy* The New York Times]

cents each. The manuscript, of course, must be prepared for this firm's system.

In general, costs are lower for phototype than for metal composition, particularly for straight matter in volume, the equivalent of galley repro proofs used for the mechanical. Like metal typographers, phototype services will handle the paste-up of a copy unit. The extra cost appears to be in about the same ratio as that for metal typesetting.

COLD-TYPE COMPOSITION

The day-to-day printing needs of both large and small organizations present the problem of small print orders of a utility nature—price lists, parts lists, instruction

The Wondrous Flexibility of Phototypography

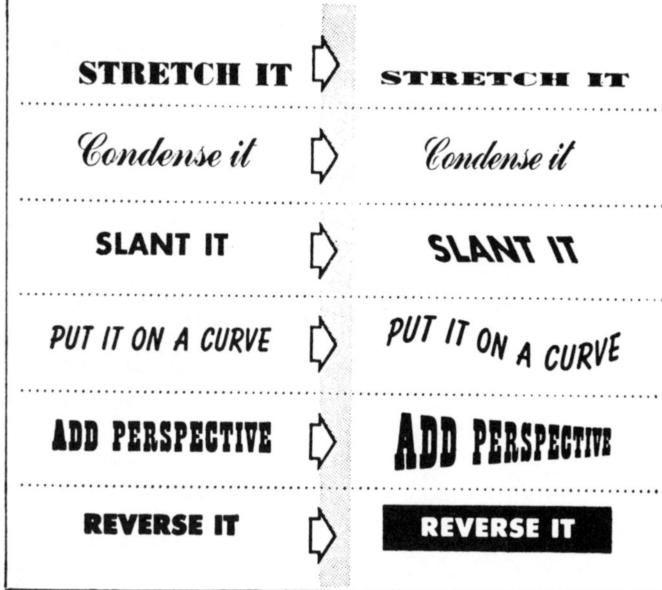

Fig. 2-43 Many typographers who are equipped for composition on film or photographic paper not only handle conventional forms of setting type but also undertake trick composition with special lenses. [*Warwick, St. Louis*]

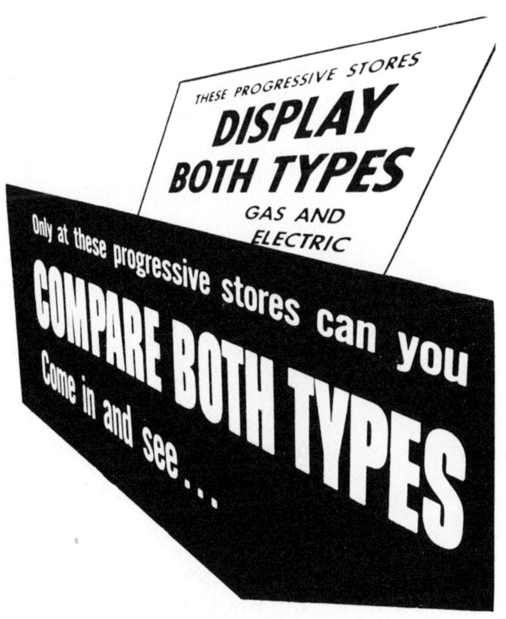

Fig. 2-44 To obtain type in perspective, a type proof and a rough pencil sketch showing the size and effect wanted are sent to a photolettering service. [*Warwick, St. Louis*]

DESIGNERS CAN USE PHOTOCOMPOSITION AS AN ART MEDIUM

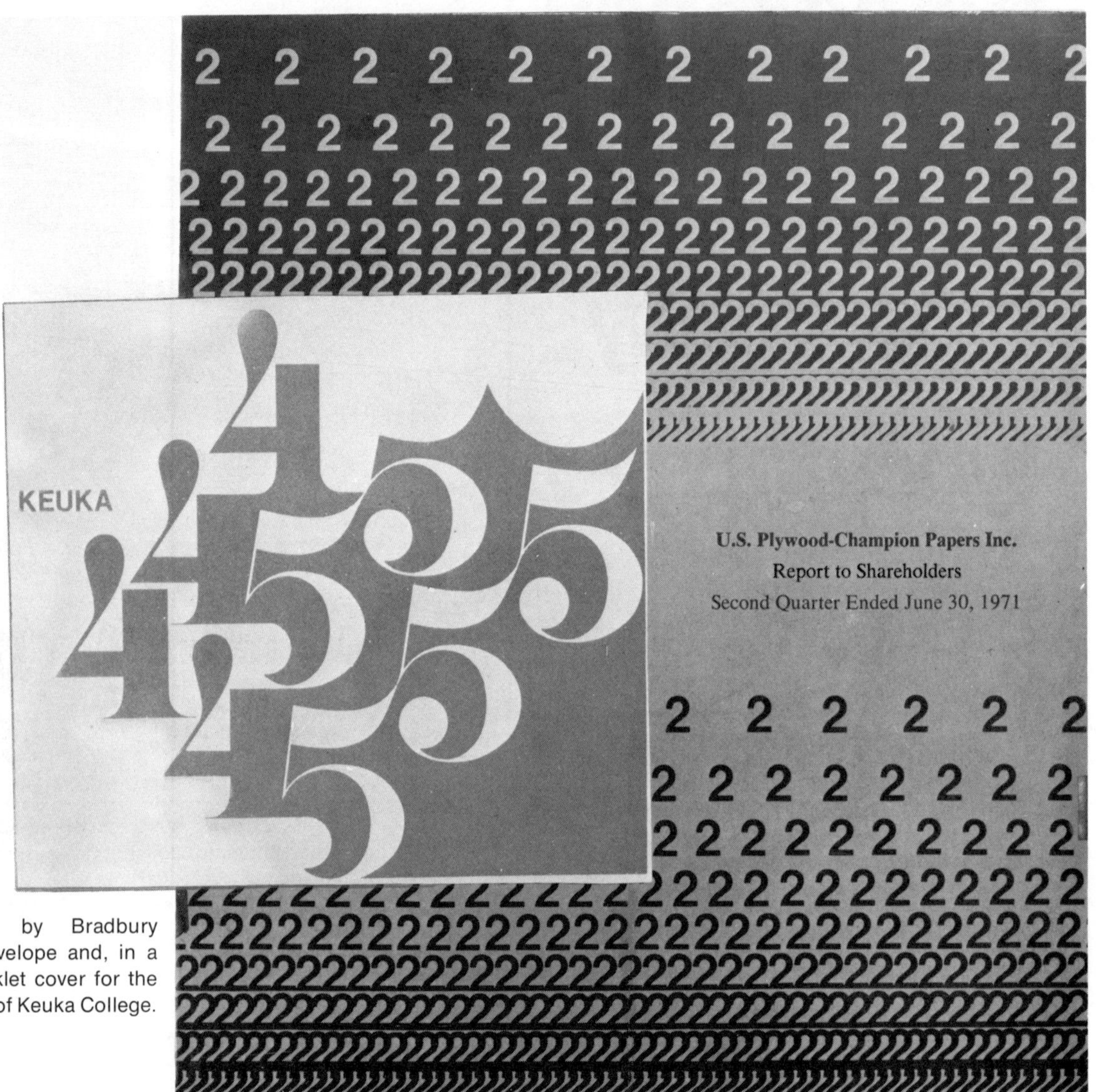

Fig. 2-45*A* Design by Bradbury Thompson for an envelope and, in a larger size, for a booklet cover for the forty-fifth anniversary of Keuka College.

Fig. 2-45*B* Cover of a stockholders' report in silver on light blue (two-thirds size).

sheets or folders, and the like—for which the end use does not require quality work. The basic problem is the cost of composition: for 1,000 copies of a Multilith job metal composition could run as high as 80 percent of the total cost. In addition, tabular composition, spaced for columns, and algebraic formulas for textbooks are particularly expensive in metal.

This short-run composition cost problem and the advantages of small offset presses using any form of composition for the camera resulted in the development of nonphotographic composition methods that do not involve hot metal. For text there are now special electric typewriters with proportional spacing and margin alignment that get the second typing automatically from a punched paper tape. Transfer letters on transparent paper are still used for display type, but mechanical lettering aids and templates are employed for larger headlines.

In a large user's production department

DISPLAY COMPOSITION METHODS USED IN THE ART DEPARTMENT

Transfer Letters

Fig. 2-46 Art supply stores carry a large selection of various forms of typefaces on paper or self-adhesive clear sheets. Some are transferred to the paste-up by pressure, while others are positioned, cut with a needle, and rubbed down.

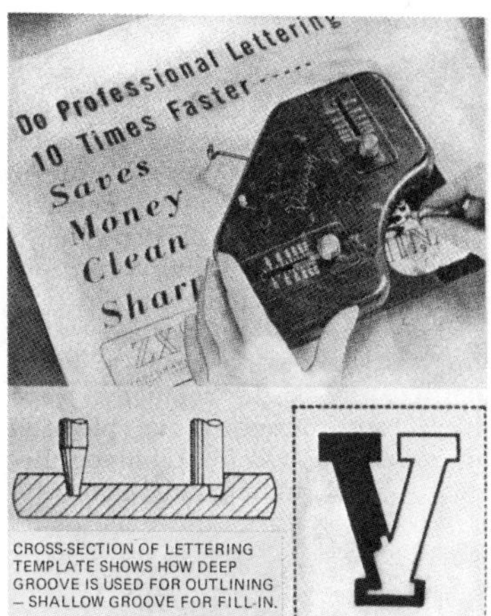

Do Professional Lettering
10 Times Faster.....
Saves
Money
Clean
Sharp
CROSS-SECTION OF LETTERING TEMPLATE SHOWS HOW DEEP GROOVE IS USED FOR OUTLINING — SHALLOW GROOVE FOR FILL-IN.

Fig. 2-47 Varigraph, a pantographic type of mechanical lettering aid widely used for display type for small print orders.

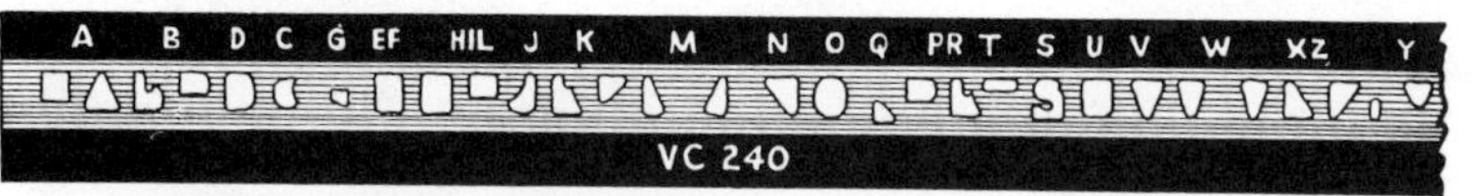

Fig. 2-48 Wrico, a stencil outline guide for drawing large letters.

Fig. 2-49 One of a number of desk-top phototypesetters.

Fig. 2-50 Photo-Typositor, a widely used phototypesetter to get any desired letterspacing for display composition. With a lens it handles sizes from 8 to 144 points.

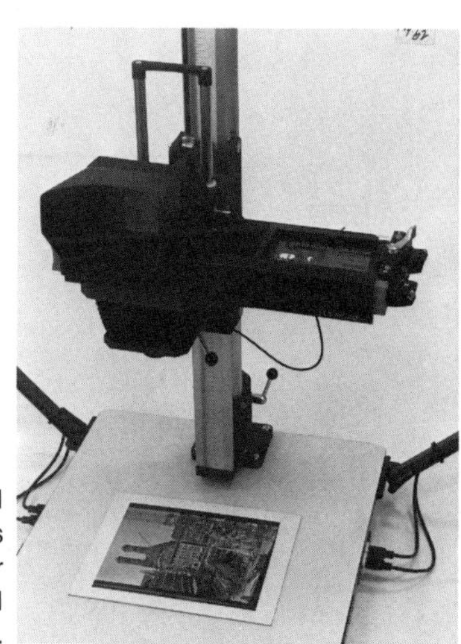

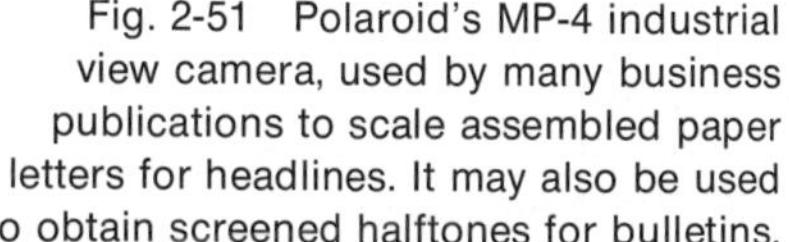

Fig. 2-51 Polaroid's MP-4 industrial view camera, used by many business publications to scale assembled paper letters for headlines. It may also be used to obtain screened halftones for bulletins.

with a large volume of small print orders, cold-type methods produced such composition for 25 cents on the dollar. Cold-type composition services estimate their selling price as 60 percent of that of metal.

Many ruled business forms, as well as tabular material, are prepared with cold-type composition. When small typefaces are not available, you should prepare a paste-up large enough to take the faces used, with vertical ruled lines in light blue, so that a negative may be prepared in the size wanted. The printer can scribe the fine rules on his negative. (The large number of pieces of paper on the paste-up prevents vertical pen ruling in black on the paste-up.)

TEXT COMPOSITION BY SPECIAL TYPEWRITERS

The VariTyper machine, the first with changeable typefaces, is now used mainly for the composition of chemical and mathmatical formulas. Two typings are

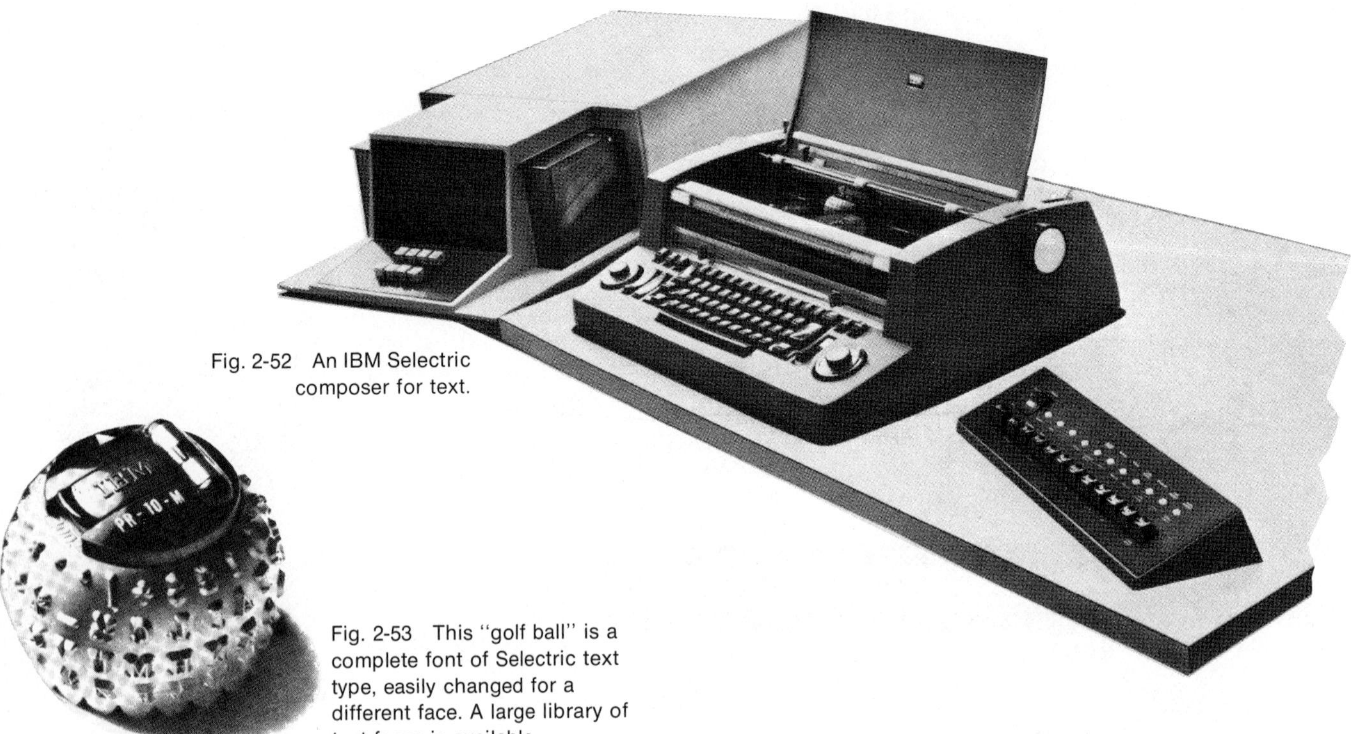

Fig. 2-52 An IBM Selectric composer for text.

Fig. 2-53 This "golf ball" is a complete font of Selectric text type, easily changed for a different face. A large library of text faces is available.

10 Pt. Medium

ABCDEFGHIJKLMNOPQRSTUVWXYZ
abcdefghijklmnopqrstuvwxyz
1234567890$.,-'':;!?*½¼¾–()[ ]=†/+%&@

Bodoni Book is an upright, well-delineated type face. It is especially characterized by distinctly contrasting thick and thin strokes. Its serifs are also distinctive, with a perfectly flat line. The strong vertical accent in the construction of each letter marks it clearly as a modern type face. Because of its easy readability, it

Bodoni Book is an upright, well-delineated type face. It is especially characterized by distinctly contrasting thick and thin strokes.

Bodoni Book is an upright, well-delineated type face. It is especially characterized by distinctly contrasting thick and thin strokes.

Fig. 2-54 Examples of IBM Selectric typefaces.

required to justify the right-hand margin.

The Justowriter, a setup with two units, a recorder machine and a reproducer machine, was the first to justify the right-hand margin automatically, with perforated paper tape produced by the recorder. Although the machines are no longer made, many are still in use. The Justowriter has some good text faces.

IBM Selectric Composer Unit

A byproduct of the IBM Selectric typewriter, which provides changeable type fonts, is the IBM Selectric composing unit, which produces a magnetic tape for an automatic second typing. The typist can make corrections by retyping over the error. Running the magnetic tape through the composing unit automatically produces corrected and justified composition for the paste-up.

There is a sizable library of text typefaces, including the popular Baskerville, Bodoni Book, Century, Copperplate Gothic, Press Roman, and Univers. Sizes range from 6 to 12 points, but most are available in 8 to 12 points in medium, italic, and bold. There are also some special newspaper faces.

Fig. 2-55 IBM electronic Selectric composer.

IBM Electronic Selectric Composer

An offshoot of the IBM composer unit, this is an electronic typewriter using the same text faces but having a memory for composition in different formats. A typist does one draft, correcting errors by backspacing and retyping over mistakes; a few buttons are pushed, and the machine is coded in the wanted format. The automatic retyping is in this format. More than 125 interchangeable typefaces are available. Format examples are shown in Fig. 2-56.

Bibliography. *Glossary of Automated Typesetting and Related Computer Terms,* Composition Information Services, 1605 North Cahuenga Boulevard, Los Angeles, Calif. 90028; Frederic W. Goudy, *The Alphabet and Elements of Lettering,* reprint of 1922 work, Dover Publications, Inc., 180 Varick Street, New York, N.Y. 10014; *Guide for Buyers of Typography,* International Typographic Composition Association, 5223 River Road, Washington, D.C. 20016, 1966.

The catalog of the Dick Blick Company, P.O. Box 1287, Galesburg, Ill. 61401, is suggested for those who live far from art supply stores.

More than just a place to sit, more than practical or comfortable, a chair is a statement of the owner's taste and personality. An arrangement of chairs, like those found in our newest collection, offers the chance to make such a statement, quiet or bold, opulent or spartan.

For dining, this year's new look is formal, but always inviting: functional chairs are covered in subtly colored cushions of crushed velvet, as easy to care for as they are to look at, from aperitif to espresso.

The arrangement for a living room can be, if you like, casual, comfortable, carefree and colorful—lavishly upholstered chairs with bold floral prints to make guests feel instantly at home. Or, for more formal entertaining, arrange our translations of the great furniture classics for a look of traditional elegance.

For informal entertaining in a kitchen or family room, the warmth of the company is reflected in the warm glow of fruitwood frames, crafted in graceful, sturdy shapes.

Employment Application				File
Last Name	First	Middle		
Street Address				Today's Date
City State	Zip	Area Code Tel. No.		SS No.
High School Attended (Years Completed)		College—Degrees		
Marital Status	Number of Children		Other Dependents	Draft Class
Previous Employer	Position		Date of Employment	
Signature		Country Cruising, Inc.		

	(In Thousands of Dollars)		
	Current Year	Last Year	Variance
Revenues	$165,203	$142,985	$22,218
Costs and Expenses	149,417	128,898	20,521
OPERATING INCOME	15,786	14,089	1,697
Other Income—Net	1,618	1,259	359
INCOME BEFORE TAXES	17,404	15,348	2,056
Taxes on Income	8,352	6,798	1,554
NET INCOME	$ 9,052	$ 8,550	$ 502
Net Income Per Share of Common Stock	$ 1.14	$ .93	$ .21

Fig. 2-56 Various formats, including vertical and horizontal ruling, produced from original typing by pressing keys.

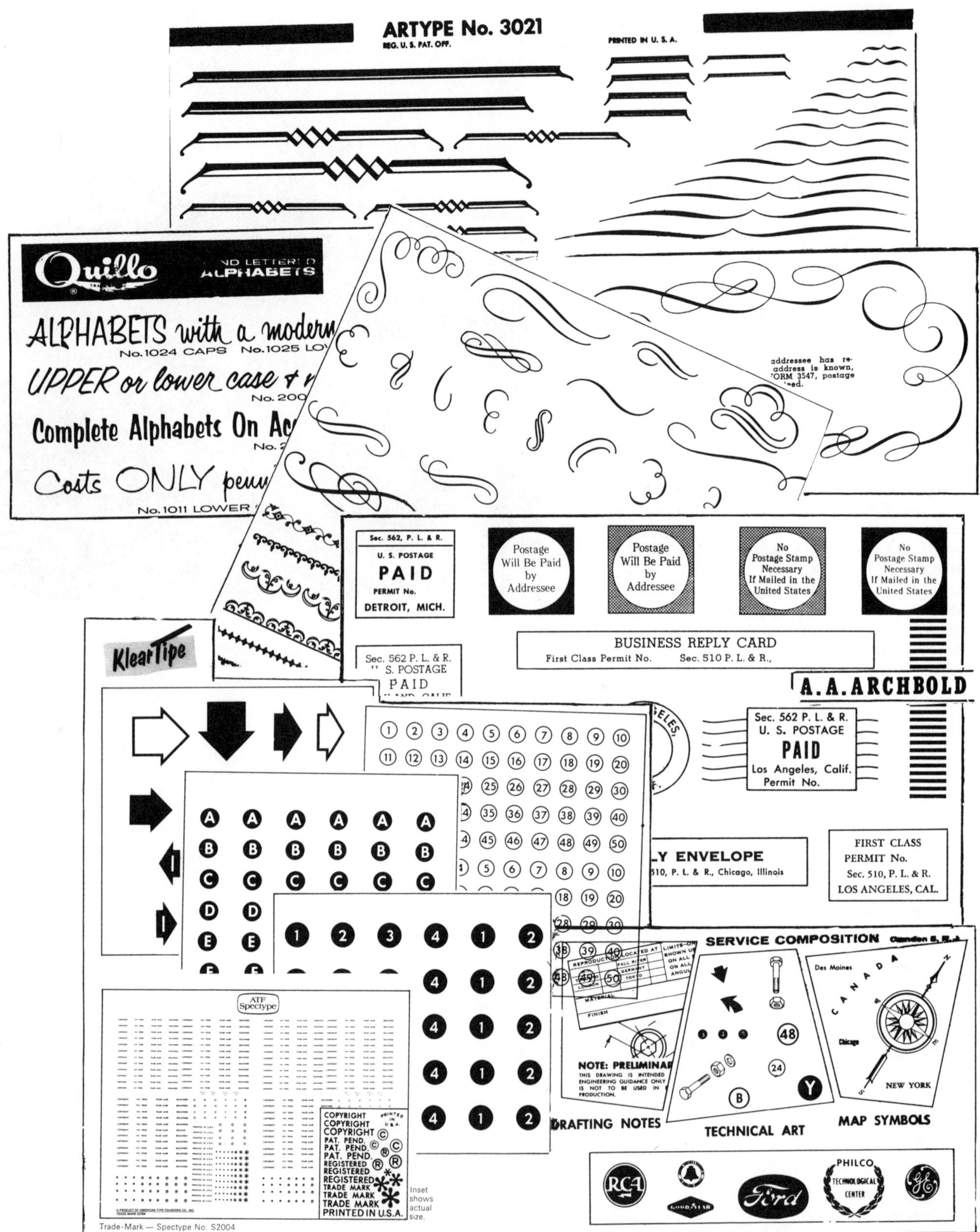

Fig. 2-57 Stock material for paste-ups, available from art stores and other sources. There are clip books, monthly services, and special proofs.

CHAPTER THREE
Camera Copy in Paste-up Form

IN FIG. 3-1 are illustrated the two methods of making up an advertisement, page, or other copy unit. On the left is the mechanical, or copy in paste-up form, and on the right are the type slugs and engravings used for making a locked-up page with metal, as is usually done by a letterpress printer. Both methods follow a supplied layout. The mechanical is prepared on the drawing board by an artist, who uses repro or etched proofs of type, lettering, Photostats, photoprints, or suitable artwork. The locked-up page of metal is prepared by the printer on a composing stone.

The example of paste-up camera copy of the Lester Bros. advertisement in Fig. 3-1 is termed "copy in one piece" for a combination line-and-tone mechanical. Tone elements have been scaled by photoprints and positioned with line elements. Camera copy in this form permits the camera operator to handle everything with one line negative and one halftone negative, which later are combined. The time that would have been required for positioning separate halftone negatives is saved under the time plate estimating system.

Some artwork, such as paintings and color transparencies, is not suitable for positioning on the mechanical, and to obtain better detail tone elements may be supplied separately in a size to permit reduction. Such subjects are outlined in red for size and position on the mechanical and keyed by letter (*A*, *B*, *C*) for identification. The printer will scale these negatives and position them on the unit line negative.

The use of the mechanical paste-up not

THE TWO METHODS OF MAKING UP A PAGE FOR PRINTING

Fig. 3-1 Copy in paste-up form is the provision of proofs of type or other composition, photos, and suitable artwork, scaled and positioned on cardboard, to furnish copy for the camera. Such copy is prepared instead of metal type and plates locked up in a printing form. [*Courtesy Intertype Company*]

only permits pages to be made up on the drawing board but also allows the use of any form of composition: paper letters, mechanical lettering aids, and display type produced by desk-top photolettering machines. The text can be handled with galley proofs of metal type, photocomposition, or special reproduction typewriters for small printing orders that cannot bear the cost of metal type or phototype.

PHYSICAL MAKEUP OF A MECHANICAL

The form of a mechanical varies with its size and the expense incurred in its preparation. Usually a mechanical must withstand considerable handling in the printer's shop as it is sent from one department to another with other copy. Ordinarily it is prepared on an illustrator's board, with a tissue overlay for instructions and a kraft paper protective cover, which is fastened to the back of the mechanical so that it can be folded back and under when the mechanical is placed on the camera copyboard.

The cover should bear the customer's name (the department and the individual if the company is large), the job identification, a list of separate elements, and the delivery date of any copy that is to come. A smooth illustrator's board is used to take ink and any hand opaquing. For paired booklet pages consisting mostly of text, 2-ply bristol board with modest margins is apt to be used so that many pages will fit on the copyboard of the camera.

Illustrator's Board with Tissue Overlay and Protective Cover

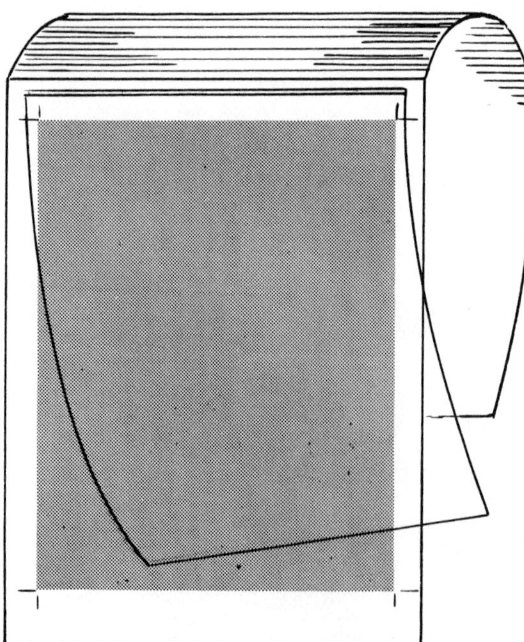

Fig. 3-2 A mechanical that entails much work is prepared on a board with a tissue overlay for instructions and a kraft cover.

There are a wide variety of illustrator's boards, surfaces, and thicknesses: the larger the mechanical, the thicker the board. Separate artwork is apt to be submitted on a rag-content surface of the cold-press type, which is not too rough for pen and ink. Plate-finished bristol board, which is available in 1- to 4-ply thickness, takes fine line detail and is frequently used in 2-ply for copy supplied as a separate element. Other types of paper and board may be used for artwork and positioned on the mechanical: kid-finish bristols, watercolor papers, Ross or coquille boards, and scratchboards.

A single copy overlay on film or parchment is apt to be fastened with tape to the top of the mechanical in such a way that the camera operator can slip paper under it to photograph it and then fold it back to show the mechanical of the key copy. If there are two or more overlays, the pin register system described in Chapter 5 is generally used so that the camera operator can take them apart and photograph all copy as a group.

For ordinary copy without pen or wash drawings, a heavy offset stock or bristol index stock is often used for the paste-up. Photos supplied as separate elements should be mounted to avoid damage and fingerprints. The job and position in which they are to be used should be identified.

Hand opaquing is being replaced by the use of red masking film, which is cut and positioned on the copy. Art supply stores sell such materials as well as colored art papers, tone sheets, and the like.

PREPARING THE MECHANICAL

Copy in paste-up form is usually prepared in the same size as a unit. It is equivalent to page makeup on the drawing board with pieces of paper (repro proofs, photos,

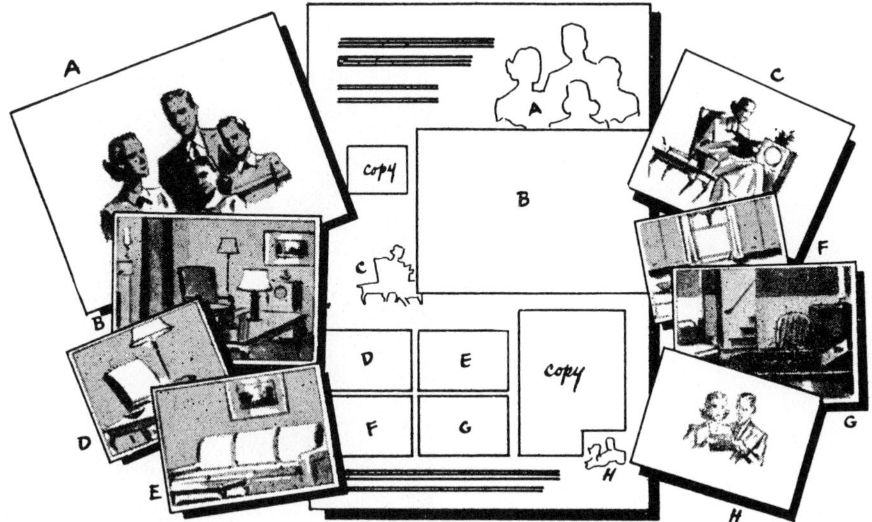

Fig. 3-3 Camera copy may be supplied in elements or as a unit. Supplying the obviously unproportioned, separate elements at the left would be the more expensive method under time estimating because of the number of camera focuses and amount of stripping required. With copy supplied as a unit (right), one halftone would handle all the tone elements without stripping, and one line negative would handle all the line copy. The two negatives would then be combined for platemaking.

scaled art, and so on) instead of on the printer's composing stone with metal type and plates. Whatever the form in which copy for the camera has been prepared (separate elements, overlay copy), the mechanical is the key copy. Various keylining techniques are used with multicolor copy to signal the platemaker to complete certain work: provide for color register, surprint on color, and the like. A tissue overlay in rough form indicates the desired results and carries any needed instructions.

When you have a line mechanical and the tone elements are supplied separately, the line negative provides the base film on which the halftone negatives are positioned to complete the unit negative. When an overlay is used for a second color with register marks, the mechanical provides the key for color register.

As a precaution in case of damage in handling, an extra set of repro proofs of type matter should accompany the mechanical. The producer can repair damage with these without holding up the job.

For all but simple jobs it is important to prepare a dummy or tissue overlay to indicate the final result wanted: color breakup, reversed elements, halftone tints, surprinting on color, lines to be held or dropped. The dummy should be sent to the producer with the camera copy.

Work Marks

From the approved rough layout of a page or copy unit the artist prepares the mechanical on smooth-surface illustrator's board or, for booklet pages, frequently on bristol board. Corner marks are drawn to indicate the work area and page size; for multicolor work center marks are added as in Fig. 3-4. These work marks guide the platemaker and the binder.

Outside the work area of the paste-up the artist indicates in light blue or in pencil the margins, column width, and height for positioning type repros and other elements, squaring them with a T square and triangle. All trim margins should be ⅛ inch. Work marks for bleed trim and folds are shown in Fig. 3-5.

Keying Separate Elements to the Mechanical

Any instructions for the keying of separate copy elements should be inserted in the work area of the mechanical, using light blue on white areas and yellow on black areas. Either initials or numbers may be used for keying. Booklet pages should always be numbered. See Copy Example *1B* (Fig. 3-9) for an illustration of keying.

Work Marks on the Mechanical

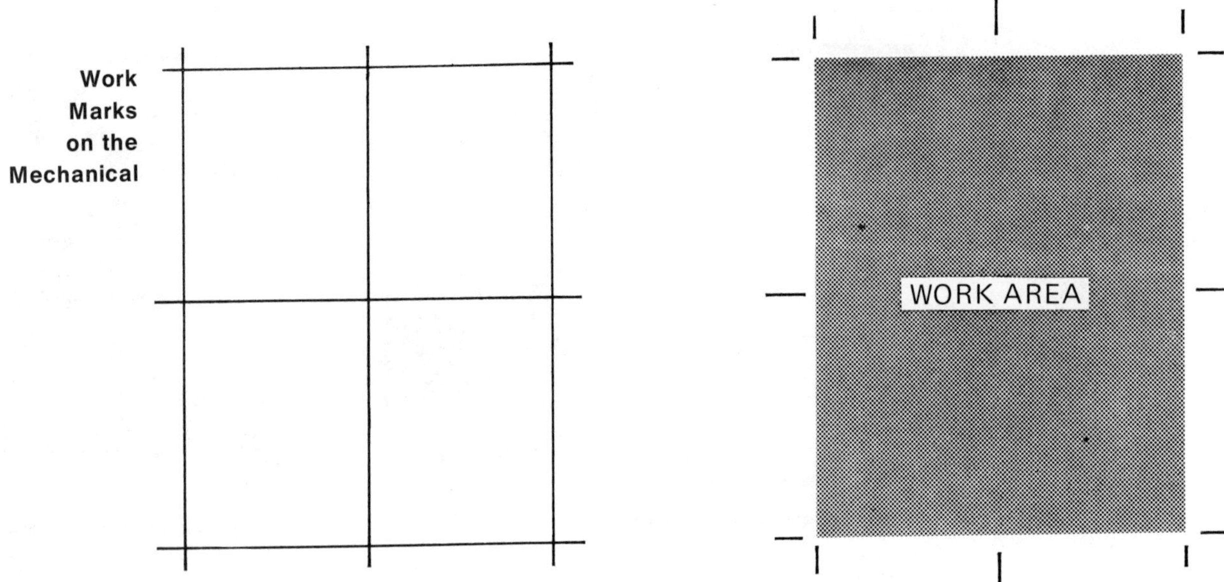

Fig. 3-4 The work, or design, area of a copy unit, such as a page, is shown at left with center lines added for possible later use. In practice, only the ends of the lines are drawn, as shown at right. Center lines are used on multicolor copy and booklet pages or for jobs on which the vertical position is not evident. Work marks are removed when the paper is trimmed or are opaqued on the negative.

Trim and Fold Marks for a Bleed Design

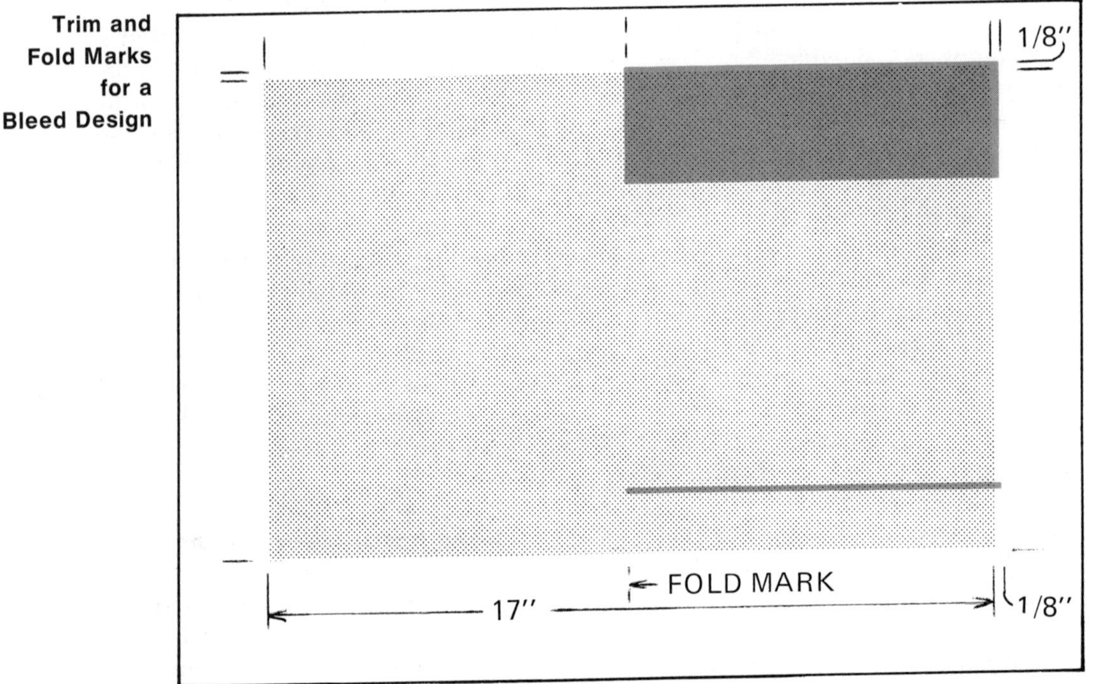

Fig. 3-5 The front and back of a four-page folder with a bleed design are shown. The shaded area is the work area of the paste-up, as indicated by corner marks. The bleed copy is extended ⅛ inch for trim with an extra work mark added. The bindery needs the fold marks (lines of short dashes) outside the work area, and after folding it will trim the page to the corner marks.

A ROUGH LAYOUT IS THE STARTING POINT FOR THE MECHANICAL

Fig. 3-6 The approved rough layout goes to the production (mechanical) artist with instructions and related data. Colors, paper, size, process, and art media have already been selected. Composition may have been ordered, or the artist may specify it. A rubber stamp indicates the delivery dates for artwork, engraving or separation, composition, and so on and the delivery date to the printer. Everything must be within the limitations of the budget and the closing dates.

Top Half of a Two-Page Spread, 10 by 7½ Inches, in Two Colors

Remodeling a smaller house

HERE'S ENTHUSIASTIC PROOF of the theory that sometimes it's wiser to buy an older house and modernize, than it is to buy a newer one roofing and siding and aluminum-framed windows and window walls, complemented by an all-brick fireplace wall. A custom-designed panel The window wall in the end gable provides enough light for a finished attic without the necessity of adding a dormer out the rear. A small front strength and sliding glass doors installed. The resulting light and ventilation for the basement area allowed it to be finished off as part of the

Fig. 3-7 The preparation of the mechanical is shown in Copy Example 15 (Fig. 5-10 in Chapter 5). Copy for the second color was produced on a clear film overlay in red with a Magic Marker. Red photographs as black and frequently is used to indicate that color will be employed.

HANDLING TONE ELEMENTS ON THE MECHANICAL

COPY EXAMPLE 1*A*

TROUBLE SHOOTING AT 611

Any customer with a problem telephone can call 611 for repair service any time, night or day. And they'll get help fast. Our cover and inside photos show how.

How long does a repair take? Usually less than four hours. But this depends on the type of problem. And on how busy our 26 local repair bureaus get.

For example, the big ice storm last December knocked out nearly 41,000 phones, necessitating longer waiting periods for some people.

Keeping SNET's 2¼ million telephones working is a big job. In 1973 there were 1,041,464 calls to 611—about 3,000 a day. This is the second lowest rate of repair calls in the Bell System.

It averages out to about one call every two years for each phone.

Of these calls, one quarter were because of no dial tone. In 22 per cent of the cases the customer couldn't receive outside calls.

Transmission noise and not being able to call out each bothered 15 per cent of 611 callers. About 10 per cent of the troubles stemmed from a physical condition—like a frayed cord a dog chewed on, coin phone vandalism, etc. The remaining 13 per cent were for miscellaneous reasons and conditions.

It all added up to a repair bill of $48 million for 1973. Repair service at no additional charge is, of course, included in the monthly rate for basic phone service.

Cover: At a repair bureau, a repair service clerk (top) takes the particulars of a 611 call and picks out the customer's card from the files. Both go to a special test position (below). There a testman electrically pinpoints the problem and dispatches a repairman to correct the trouble wherever it lies.

Inside: Repairs are made either at the customer's home (top), in the switching system itself (above left) or outdoors. The testman runs a final check to make sure the phone is working properly again before calling the customer with the news.

Fig. 3-8 Tone elements scaled and positioned with line copy for a combination line-and-tone copy unit. This form is widely used by advertising departments and agencies when the mechanical must be sent out for approval. If the tone elements are to be supplied separately for reduction or are proportioned for various pages of a booklet, Photostat copies are positioned on the mechanical, but before it is sent to the printer, *X*'s, meaning "Not for camera copy," are marked on them. It would be hazardous to use the form in Copy Example 1*B* accompanied by the art, for some pieces might be damaged or lost.

COPY EXAMPLE 1*B*

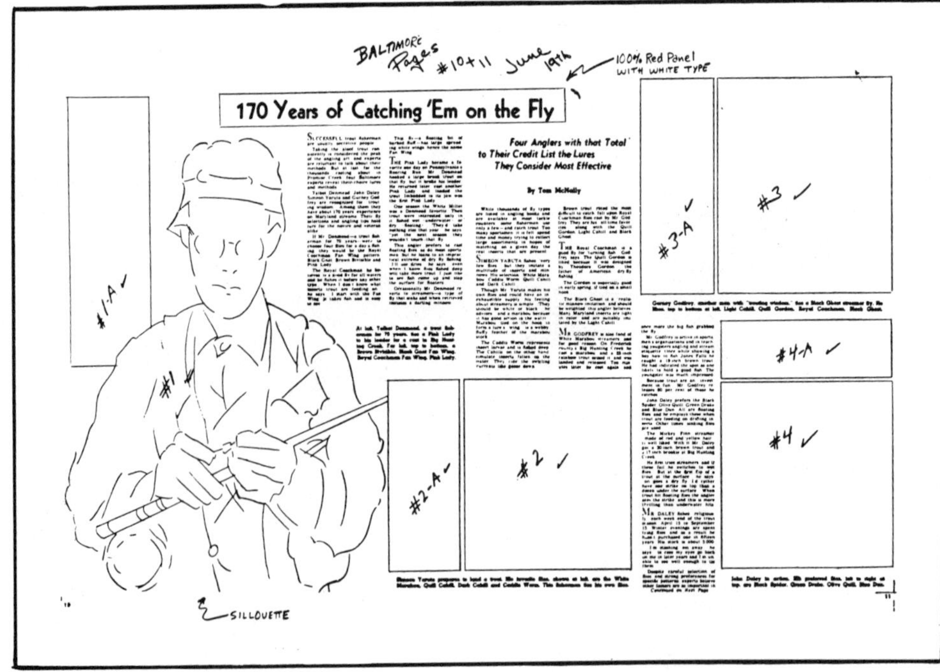

Fig. 3-9 Tone elements indicated for size and position by a red outline and keyed for identification to tone elements supplied separately. This method is often used within an organization or in cases when only departmental approval is required. For some ordinary-quality work, small halftones may cost no more than Photostat positives.

Plant's Exhaust System

The original ductwork has been retained and is used as a vent relief system discharging to the roof top penthouse and thus outdoors. The lavatories are served by this exhaust system and volume dampers and back pressure dampers in the penthouse control it. The cooling tower by which 95% to 98% of the water used for refrigeration condensing is saved is located out of sight from the street over a central stairway. This makes it possible to exhaust the building by using the cooling tower fan and closing the ouside air intake damper. Any one area can be handled in this manner by leaving its door to the stairway open and closing those for all other departments.

A view of the composing room makeup department is seen in Fig. 2, which shows the same Weathermaker unit as in Fig. 1 in the far right background plus an exhaust hood, also at the right, connected to the existing ventilating system. This view clearly shows the discharge plenum of the self-contained Weathermaker extending above the fluorescent lighting. Linotype machines are located in the left background.
ployees throughout the plant and has increased cleanliness and production.

COPY EXAMPLE 1C

Fig. 3-10 The opaquing of halftone areas on the mechanical is a photoengraver's technique (the photoengraver flops the negative to get emulsion-to-emulsion contact printing). This method is not recommended for offset for any but ordinary-quality work. In gravure it is used only for "flash tones" (tints).

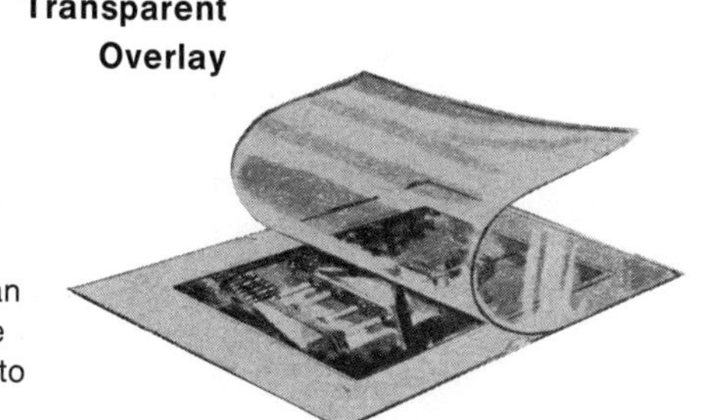

Fig. 3-11 The artist often uses a transparent film or a parchment overlay on the mechanical or on an element to separate line and tone copy that are to be combined or to carry the color copy.

TWO BASIC FORMS OF MECHANICALS

The type of an organization and the quality of a job have a bearing on the details of copy preparation for the camera. The method of estimating plate costs should also be considered. As we have explained, the purpose of the mechanical is to transfer to the copy preparation stage some of the work that otherwise would be handled by the engraver or the printer.

There are two basic forms of mechanicals for a single color. These are shown in Copy Examples 1A and 1*B*; 1*C* is a variation of 1*B*.

We have always considered that the opaquing of halftone areas on the mechanical for offset should be limited to ordinary-grade printing. The resulting "window" in the line negative makes it simple to strip a halftone negative on top, but this does not permit emulsion-to-emulsion contact printing for the offset press plate. In addition, there is some loss of tonal quality from light undercutting the dots.

If an offset printer requests the opaquing of tone areas for a long-run printing job, it will be for deep-etch press plates, which require the image reversal (mirror image) of halftones. On special thin film the printer will strip the halftone negatives under the windows of the unit negative; this gives a left-reading image as for photoengravings. If by chance a mechanical has halftone positions opaqued instead of outlined, it makes no difference to the offset printer.

For gravure monotone, tone elements should always be scaled and positioned on the mechanical or on a separate tone mechanical in position, because tone copy is photographed on a different (continuous-tone) type of film from the high-contrast film used for line copy. Copy Example 1*B* was designed for gravure in-plant editorial copy. Many gravure publications would refuse to accept this copy for an advertisement without extra charges.

HANDLING PASTE-UP COPY

As an adhesive for paste-ups, a special melted wax has replaced rubber cement for volume work. A hand applicator with an electric heating unit is sold at art supply stores, and sheet-waxing machines are available for volume use with repro proofs or galleys of metal or phototype. The advantage is that copy can be waxed in batches and positioned later; removal or repositioning is easy. Since five or ten minutes are required to melt the wax, a

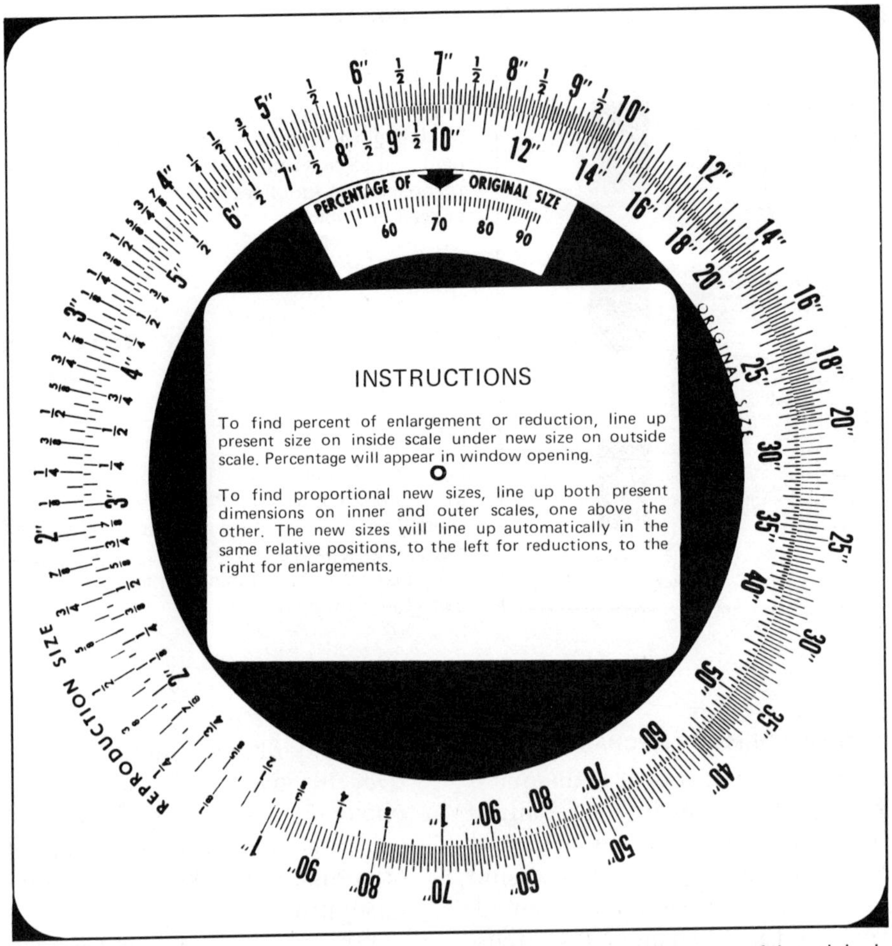

INSTRUCTIONS

To find percent of enlargement or reduction, line up present size on inside scale under new size on outside scale. Percentage will appear in window opening.

To find proportional new sizes, line up both present dimensions on inner and outer scales, one above the other. The new sizes will line up automatically in the same relative positions, to the left for reductions, to the right for enlargements.

Fig. 3-12 Proportioning a same-focus group of tone elements for 70 percent of the original size for group reduction by camera. The rough layout shows the reproduction sizes; the proportioned sizes for cropping for the group are directly opposite on the inner scale.

If, for example, a photo is to be reduced to a 4-inch reproduction width, it should be cropped for a 5¹¹⁄₁₆-inch width. Height cropping is determined in the same way. Keep the instrument at 70 percent to figure the sizes of the other subjects for the group. To handle many subjects, two or three groups may be necessary: 60 percent, 80 percent, and so on.

Proportioned tone elements can be intended for a copy unit, for various pages of a booklet, for related jobs on one order, and for process color copy.

A single tone element on a mechanical that is not part of a large job is merely marked for cropping and reproduction percentage and sent to the printer as for letterpress.

machine is not practical unless the heat is left on, as is customary in an art department. Wax stick applicators are available for corrections. Galleys should be trimmed after waxing. Always burnish down both wax and rubber adhesive.

Elements positioned on a paste-up mechanical should not be trimmed closer than ⅛ inch. Hairline rules should always be drawn on camera copy with a pen. A hairline printed from a metal rule is apt to be gray in spots, and the line will drop out in the photographic negative.

The trim size of a printed job should be able to be cut efficiently from a standard size of the paper selected (Fig. 2-3 in Chapter 2 lists the standard sizes for different kinds of paper). Neither offset nor gravure requires coated paper for fine halftone or process color printing.

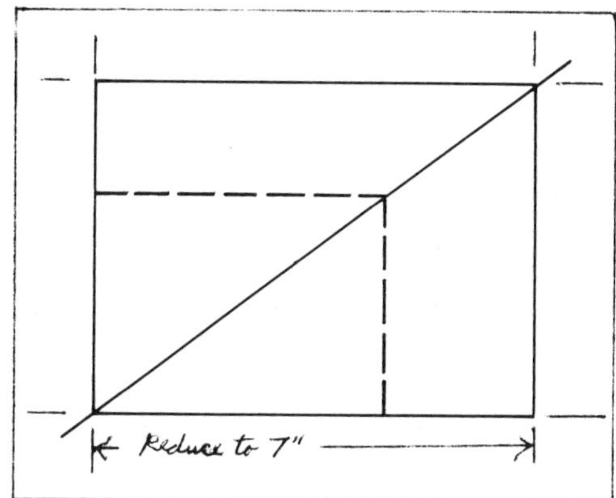

Fig. 3-13 Crop marks indicate the wanted area. The diagonal-line method of proportioning the dimensions of the cropped area for reduction to scale size is not generally used with the photomechanical process.

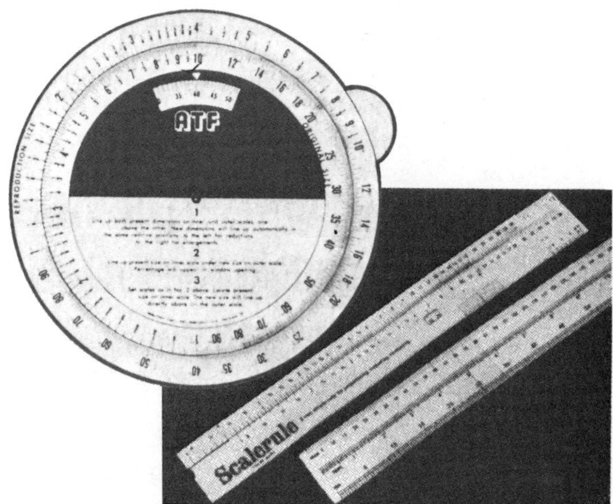

Fig. 3-14 Scaling instruments are used to determine the percentage of reduction or enlargement and to proportion multiple copy elements for same-focus economies.

When copy is sent out for photostats, prints, or composition, be sure that it is identified by the customer's name. If the customer is a large organization, add the department and the individual's name. Use a rubber stamp or a sticker label, for often work lies around for days because the studio does not know to whom it belongs.

Frequently a color subject is to be reproduced in black and white. For the mechanical it should first be photographed on panchromatic film, like that used for snapshots, to reduce the colors of the print to gray tones. If time is short, the printer can handle this job.

CROPPING AND SCALING PHOTOGRAPHS

The cropping and scaling of photographs are the same for all printing processes: the area to be reproduced is indicated by crop marks in soft pencil on the white edge of the photo for both width and height. The desired width should be indicated in inches and fractions thereof between the crop marks below the photo. For letterpress, the halftone screen should also be indicated, but this is not necessary for the other processes.

The diagonal-line method of determining proportioned height when area width is reduced or enlarged for reproduction size is used chiefly for letterpress. The reason is that there no longer are discounts for same-focus economies in camera work, that is, for proportioning two or more subjects for the same percentage of reduction so that the group can be reduced with one focus of the camera. This procedure divides the cost of the focus over the group, but the economy applies only to the photomechanical processes. The Photoengravers' Standard Scale no longer grants discounts on same-focus copy.

The commonest error with camera copy for the photomechanical processes is that the photo area and specified reduction do not fit the space provided on the mechanical, usually for height. It occurs because both scaled sizes have not been checked.

Reproduction Size as a Percentage of the Original Size

Camera operators for all the printing processes calculate the ratio of reduction or enlargement in percentages because the camera adjustment for the position of the lens is shown in that way. The size of the subject image on the ground glass in the camera back can also be seen and measured if it is wanted. Any photos or art supplied as proportioned separate elements to the printer should be marked in percentages of the original size for the reproduction size wanted.

Since a basic economy of the time plate estimating process is the absence of economic restrictions on photographing proportioned tone elements in groups (the same-focus economy), it is customary to show a change in size as a percentage of the original size. If we figure this size as 100 percent, as the process camera does, three-quarter size is 75 percent, a quarter size larger is 125 percent, and so on. Wanted cropped sizes are usually indicated in percentages of original sizes by using a scaling instrument. By positioning the reproduction size opposite the original size on the instrument, you can see at the window at the top the percentage of the original size. Economically, it is best to adjust cropping slightly to obtain a multiple of 5, for example, 70 percent instead of 67 or 72 percent. If cropping is shown in inches, the printer must convert the figures to a percentage of the original. By trade custom, cropping is tentative, but the plate size will be as ordered.

WORKING WITH THE PHOTOGRAPHER

For persons without a background in a commercial art department, the following will be helpful. In advertising, most photographic illustration is handled by professionals, much of it on location rather than in the studio, and a lot of it is produced with small hand cameras such as the 35-millimeter and 2¼- by 2¼-inch sizes for convenience. The greater part, however, will be in the form of 5- by 7-inch and 8- by 10-inch contact prints—the prints from the camera negatives. The photographer usually knows nothing about the reproduction size to be used. These contact prints (sometimes already crop-marked by the rough layout artist) go to the mechanical or production artist making the mechanical, who has the rough layout of the copy unit or dummy.

If the photos are to be scaled and positioned, as is usual with most commercial printing by offset or gravure, the contact prints are marked for cropping and size wanted and returned to the photographer, who positions the original negatives in a vertical projector, makes the projection prints in wanted sizes, and delivers them to the customer. The cost for a projection print is about $1.50.

When there are two or more tone elements on a copy unit, an art department usually positions them on the mechanical for a combination line-and-tone copy unit. Subjects in different sizes are thus reduced to one camera focus, and the printer need not strip them to position. This procedure is usual for the photomechanical processes, and agencies like to use it for letterpress in magazine ad schedules because copy in one piece reduces errors and the number of approvals by clients.

Some small offset printers and shops use a price list based on the size of negatives. Here nothing is gained by scaling and positioning; the cropped contact prints are supplied separately for camera copy.

PROPORTIONING PROJECTION PRINTS FOR SAME-FOCUS REDUCTION

When all the illustrations for a mechanical or a job such as a sixteen-page booklet are in the form of contact prints, the proportioning procedure is quite simple. Instead of ordering scaled projection prints, order size-and-one-half projection prints. Then everything will be in proportion for reduction by the printer as a group. The printer cuts the large negative apart to strip each keyed subject into position. This procedure is a major economy for offset halftones.

The photographer's contact prints from a small hand camera are usually grouped on an 8- by 10-inch print, with an enlarged duplicate for cropping on an 11- by 14-inch print. These are usually wanted in an enlarged, proportioned form.

MISCELLANEOUS TONE ELEMENTS

The original artwork in the day-to-day workload of an art department or free-lance artist includes many forms of art media: some art picked up from previous jobs, stock photos, and wash drawings as well as contact prints. To include miscellaneous tone elements in a same-focus group, an intermediate photocopy may be necessary. Special photocopy services are used to retain tonal qualities or to add contrast. The method of proportioning such elements is covered in Fig. 3-12.

Keep in mind that under time plate estimating, same-focus proportioning, also applies to process color copy. Insofar as is practical, instructions to the artist or photographer should include reproduction sizes (even a rough layout) so that work sizes will be proportioned.

COMBINING LINE AND TONE FOR A COPY ELEMENT

Quite frequently an illustration is a combination of line-and-tone copy, either a design or type matter such as a headline running across a photograph. One kind of copy, usually the line element, must go on an overlay in position to keep it separate from the other. The platemaker combines the two negatives to obtain the desired result.

In Fig. 3-15 the oval with type matter within it would print as black on the halftone. If the type or design appeared as white on the halftone, this method would not be necessary—a positive film of the type would be positioned on the tone negative for a contact print, thus providing a mask to make the type show in white on the halftone. The printer, of course, handles this work.

PREPARATION OF COPY ELEMENTS

Line copy should be prepared in the same size or be scaled to the size wanted by means of a glossy Photostat. Exceptions are art created by graphite pencil (in gravure, also pen-line drawings), which should be supplied as separate elements for special handling by the camera operator. When there are many proportioned line elements, as for an industrial catalog, the producer can make group brownline prints (blueprints chemically treated) for less cost than Photostats. When line art is prepared for reduction, it is usually executed to size and one-half.

Tone copy elements may be indicated for size and position by a red outline on the mechanical and supplied as separate proportioned elements, usually for reduction. If the copy unit has several such

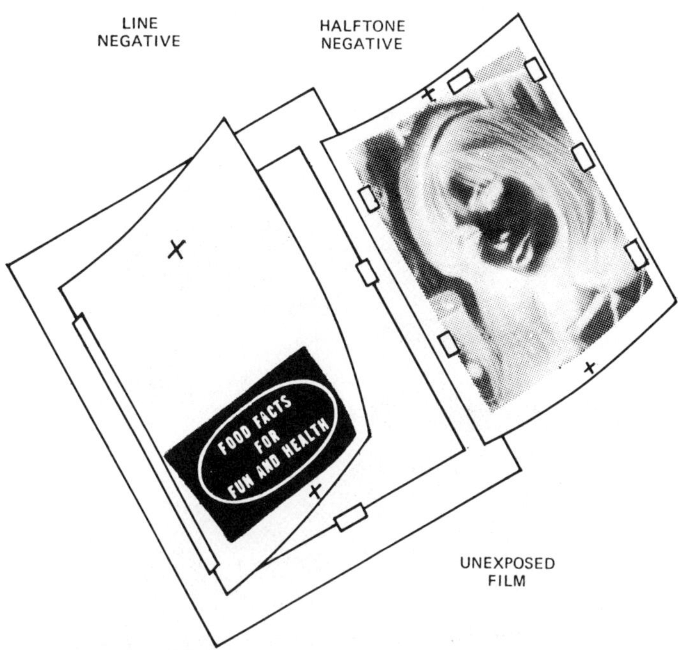

Fig. 3-15 The printing user's camera copy is the photo or art in scale with the line copy (often a headline to be reversed or printed) on an overlay. The platemaker has a film carrier to position line and tone negatives. Each is exposed separately in the dark on unexposed film, which remains light-sensitive under the black of the negatives.

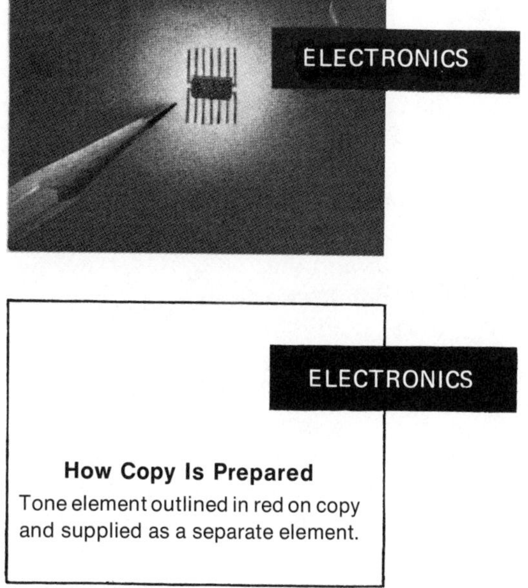

ELECTRONICS
ELECTRONICS
How Copy Is Prepared
Tone element outlined in red on copy and supplied as a separate element.

Fig. 3-16 Reversed type panel inserted into a same-color halftone. An exception to the use of a film carrier for combining line and tone copy occurs when a reversed element goes on tone of the same color. If any tone would show in the white type of the reverse, the platemaker removes the tone underneath.

Handling Type Proof or Lettering to Go on Halftones

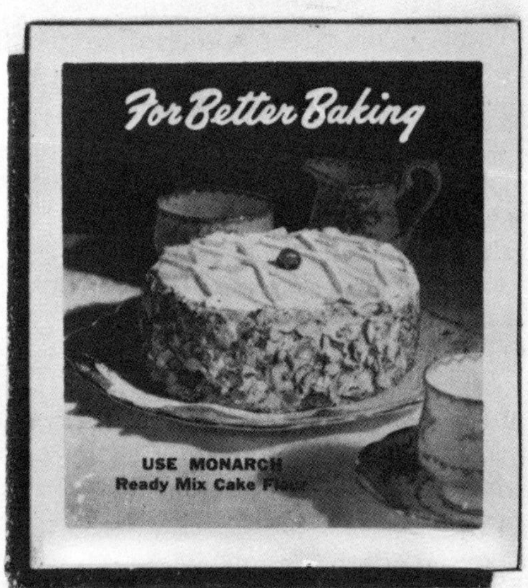

Fig. 3-17 The problem is illustrated with the artist's camera copy (left). The type proof can be attached as an overlay in position on the photo with tissue instructions for the effect wanted. The clear overlay shown here helps present the procedure plainly.

units, however, they are scaled and positioned (see Copy Examples 1*A* and 1*B*). For such printings as a booklet, all tone elements are proportioned in one or two groups; concern is with the job and not just the copy page or unit.

References to the importance of proportioning copy elements for camera copy do not apply to photoengraving, for which same-focus economies have been discontinued. For all other processes, however, these economies do apply.

PUBLICATION PRODUCTION SPECIFICATIONS

If you work for an advertising agency or an art studio or undertake free-lance work, you will find that camera copy for offset and for rotogravure publications must be supplied as specified by each publication. Offset will usually require the complete ad on film (right-reading negative, emulsion side down) ready for platemaking. Rotogravure usually will accept a completed mechanical, exactly as the ad is to appear, or perhaps copy in two pieces, a line mechanical and a tone mechanical. All work must be completed; otherwise there will be extra charges for any steps required to complete the job. Generally additional type proofs, including a transparent proof, are required.

Publication Engraving Services

For many years there have been electrotyping services that furnish electros of advertisements to the list of publications supplied by an advertising agency. Now there are similar services for gravure and offset publications. They know the specifications for each publication and forward the positives or negatives to the publication list supplied by the agency.

When such a service is used, camera copy can be submitted in any standard form. Any steps necessary to complete the copy unit to meet each publication's requirements will result in extra charges. As explained in Chapter 8, line elements for gravure are generally scaled and positioned for a line mechanical separately from the type proofs, and tone elements are handled in the same way as the copy page. This procedure avoids requiring the gravure service to do the equivalent in order to keep the series of contact prints to a minimum in preparing the complete page positives.

CAUTION ON RETOUCHING

When retouching photos to indicate highlight dropouts or outlining with Chinese white, keep the work as clean as possible and hold it to a minimum. On some photographic papers certain whites reproduce as strongly as a 20 percent tone because of the absorption of ultraviolet light. For outlining a line is sufficient, for today the platemaker generally uses masking film instead of opaquing to remove any tones close to the outline. The platemaker can even provide for flat color register as indicated.

The whites and grays used in retouching may contain pigments that absorb different amounts of ultraviolet light. When the retouched photoprint is illuminated on a process camera copyboard with ultraviolet-rich light, the retouched areas may photograph darker than the visually equivalent silver-density areas. Retouching artists should know how their white and grays photograph on different types of photographic paper. To determine how paints will photograph, the retoucher should put samples on fixed-out photographic papers and have them exposed in a process camera. The exposures will show which brand of paint is suitable for a particular paper. Or a Velox print of the halftone negative will show the result when the retouched photograph is printed.

In retouching photos it is very important not to use grays of a different cast on the same job, for example, a blue gray in some spots and a brownish gray in others. The retouched photo may look fine, but the camera operator must resort to different emulsions and a filter to get a good negative. This is a time-consuming and costly procedure. The same brand and cast of grays should be used on the same subject or on a group of photos for same-focus work.

New Technology and the Absence of Economic and Technical Restrictions

Before we continue with the preparation of copy components and the paste-up mechanical to obtain camera-ready copy and the many how-to instructions entailed, let's stand back and see things in perspective. Let's consider why the character of commercial art and its procedures have changed, the importance of time and cost factors, the need to specify type and calculate the space it will occupy, and why all restrictions on choice of art media for uncoated paper have been removed. In Chapter 7 we shall explain a new procedure, now used by all printing processes, for preparing process copy for reproduction.

There is a general impression that the form of camera copy is determined by the printing process used. Actually, it is determined by the resulting plate costs. If these costs are disregarded, copy prepared for one process can be used for either of the other major printing processes. For example, a combination line-and-tone copy unit with offset involves only the cost of the halftones in addition to the basic plate charge; and the same is essentially true of gravure because both processes use the time plate estimating method. Under the Photoengravers' Standard Scale (Item 2) the cost of both line and tone areas is double the halftone scale cost.

The reason that we discussed the proportioning of multiple tone elements was that same-focus economies are allowed under the time method. These economies also apply to process color art. For letterpress process color photoengravings, Item 2 is absent, and camera copy is frequently submitted in the form of a mechanical to take advantage of economies available. The alternative

(continued on page 62)

(continued from page 61)

is a proof of the made-up type page because photoengravers now use photocomposing methods and no longer accept type metal for combination with process engravings for electros.

Because of new capabilities and procedures in the area between the original artwork and that prepared for the camera, a category called "art production" has developed, transferring some of the steps formerly handled by the engraver to the art department in order to save time and costs. This form of production starts in the creative planning stage, which now has a wide choice of methods, particularly for process color copy. The proportioning of tone elements and composition methods are a part of art production.

Mechanical artists are now called "production artists" and are comparable to engineering or architectural draftsmen, for all prepare working drawings from designers' sketches. Just as the curriculum for graduate engineers includes mechanical drawing, commercial artists' preparation should include typography, elementary production knowledge, and the preparation of mechanicals. All will be used throughout their careers.

SIMILARITY OF MOST COPY TECHNIQUES FOR ALL PROCESSES

Since all the processes work with film, at least for platemaking, they use similar copy techniques. The reproduction qualities of artwork are the same for all the processes; the methods of providing in the camera copy for register of simple flat colors that touch each other also are the same.

From this point, in dealing with the preparation of mechanicals and their components, we shall be using the offset process, the current predominant printing method. Any variance in the form of copy will be made for economies in plate costs.

Art production has developed prepared copy for the camera. This is a means of transferring to the copy preparation stage the scaling and positioning of process color elements and their color adjustment to suit the art director instead of the engraver doing this work. Through the use of color transparencies or reproduction-quality color prints, mixed art media are reduced to a single medium, with all subjects in color balance for color separation.

PREPARATION OF COPY FOR A PUBLICATION SPREAD

When a publication spread has a design running across the gutter with single-color and simple color printing, the mechanical is prepared as two facing pages with a 1-inch space between them, as shown in Fig. 3-21. The pages will be separated when they are stripped to the binder's imposition. The space between them provides a margin for the stripper's tape; otherwise, two negatives would have to be made. Center marks should be added; the printer allows for margin creep in a thick signature.

Artists should have an elementary knowledge of bindery imposition, for in a small advertising department they often must carry a job through to completion, and with small agencies or publishers they function as a combination of art director and production head. Free-lance artists now not only design but do mechanicals. This is also true of some top designers for critical jobs; they thus have a chance to make needed changes.

PREPARATION OF SINGLE-COLOR COPY ELEMENTS

The preparation of mechanicals for single-color printing involves various techniques and methods to reduce platemaking time by the printer or to avoid extra charges by the photoengraver. The time saved by the production artist is also important. We refer to such matters as reversing type or other elements, indicating halftone tints to be applied by the

ACTUAL

A nd Watson & Boaler continues to present . . .
for the discriminating . . . individual pieces which by their own intrinsic fineness
are never "dated". Rather, with the years, they become a heritage to be used
and enjoyed. We believe that antiques . . . if preferred . . . still provide
the gracious kind of background that can be acquired in no other way,
so we continue to search the markets for unusual pieces from whatever period or place.
We also believe that it is possible to design special pieces in traditional styles
to augment these antiques and on purely contemporary lines to complement
them . . . or to stand alone. Consequently we proudly show a
custom-made piece from our own shop on the same page with collectors' items that have
survived through several centuries . . . which we have placed during our years on the Avenue.

1 Antique pottery vases and jars, which are the source of our outstanding collection of individual lamps.

2 One of a pair of very fine Adam crystal and brass sconces. Circa 1790.

3 Antique English Regency library table, of satinwood, with lyre end supports.

4 Louis Philippe painted and decorated papier-maché center table, with gleaming mother-of-pearl inlay.

5 Superb example of antique English Regency design. Coromandel wood sofa table, with ormolu mounts.

6 Late Eighteenth Century Shropshire oak dresser. Doors and drawers cross banded with mahogany. Now in the collection of the Art Institute of Chicago.

7 One of a pair of custom-made cabinets, of olive burl veneer, with ebony inlay. (One a bar, the other a radio phonograph.)

8 Delicate version of an antique Hepplewhite side chair. A noteworthy departure from his usual shield back design.

9 Very fine early Georgian reading table, with raising top, and brass candle stands.

10 Exceptional example of an English Regency desk chair. Covered in leather. Now in the collection of the Art Institute of Chicago.

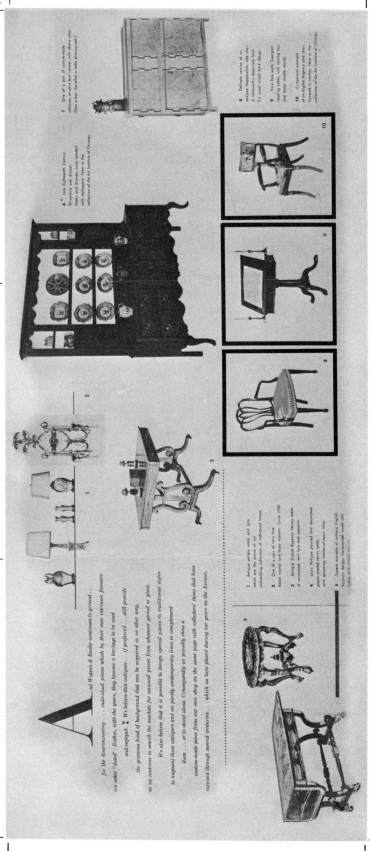

SCREEN BORDERS use 60% value

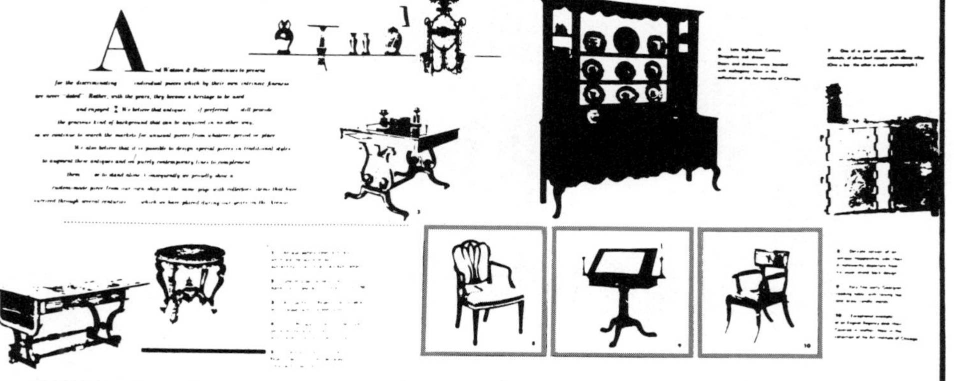

When There Are Many Small Tone Elements, Prepare a Line-and-Tone Mechanical

Fig. 3-18 Camera copy prepared as a complete unit with all copy elements scaled and positioned avoids much stripping (positioning of negatives) and the chance of error. Such a mechanical is termed "copy in one piece." The three box borders were done in black with a note requesting 60 percent tint. The copy is marked for two folds to get a six-page folder.

For a budget job, the use of screened Velox photoprints of the halftone elements would make this an all-line mechanical and thus save plate costs.

COPY EXAMPLE 3

The original ductwork has been retained and is used as a vent relief system discharging to the roof top penthouse and thus outdoors. The lavatories are served by this exhaust system and volume dampers and back pressure dampers in the penthouse control it. The cooling tower by which 95% to 98% of the water used for refrigeration condensing is saved is located out of sight from the street over a central stairway. This makes it possible to exhaust the building by using the cooling tower fan and closing the ouside air intake damper. Any one area can be handled in this manner by leaving its door to the stairway open and closing those for all other departments.

A view of the composing room makeup department is seen in Fig. 2, which shows the same Weathermaker unit as in Fig. 1 in the far right background plus an exhaust hood, also at the right, connected to the existing ventilating system.

2

This view clearly shows the discharge plenum of the self-contained Weathermaker extending above the fluorescent lighting. Linotype machines are located in the left background.
ployees throughout the plant and has increased cleanliness and production.

The original ductwork has been retained and is used as a vent relief system discharging to the roof top penthouse and thus outdoors. The lavatories are served by this exhaust system and volume dampers and back pressure dampers in the penthouse control it. The cooling tower by which 95% to 98% of the water used for refrigeration condensing is saved is located out of sight from the street over a central stairway. This makes it possible to exhaust the building by using the cooling tower fan and closing the ouside air intake damper. Any one area can be handled

15

How Book Pages Are Prepared on the Mechanical

Fig. 3-19 Camera copy for books, catalogs, and booklets is prepared in the form of paired pages according to the binder's imposition (arrangement of pages in a printing form), not as facing pages. Imposition for the same number of pages varies with the bindery equipment used, and the binder's imposition should be obtained before pasting up the pages.

If it is not practical to get the binder's imposition, position facing pages in pairs, with even page numbers on the left, numbered consecutively. The printer can then arrange the pages in imposition pairs for the camera. Use index bristol slightly larger than the page size; prepare left and right pages as a copy unit.

Artist's Imposition for Small Booklets and Four-Page Folders

Fig. 3-20 As many as four pages can be handled as a copy unit if they fill the offset press plate, but T squares are not accurate for a larger number. For short-run work, an 11- by 17-inch folder can be positioned, front and back, as a unit for work-and-turn imposition.

An eight-page booklet would be run sheetwise, front and back, with two right-hand folds. Bindery equipment is set for an ⅛-inch trim; so the horizontal fold must allow for a trim of ¼ inch, as shown. Stripper's marks have been used; ¼ inch for the fold and ⅛ inch for the trim mark.

Plant's Exhaust System

The original ductwork has been retained and is used as a vent relief system discharging to the roof top penthouse and thus outdoors. The lavatories are served by this exhaust system and volume dampers and back pressure dampers in the penthouse control it. The cooling tower by which 95% to 98% of the water used for refrigeration condensing is saved is located out of sight from the street over a central stairway. This makes it possible to exhaust the building by using the cooling tower fan and closing the ouside air intake damper. Any one area can be handled in this manner by leaving its door to the stairway open and closing those for all other departments.

A view of the composing room makeup department is seen in Fig. 2, which shows the same Weathermaker unit as in Fig. 1 in the far

4

right background plus an exhaust hood, also at the right, connected to the existing ventilating system. This view clearly shows the discharge plenum of the self-contained Weathermaker extending above the fluorescent lighting. Linotype machines are located in the left background.
ployees throughout the plant and has increased cleanliness and production.

A view of the composing room makeup department is seen in Fig. 2, which shows the same Weathermaker unit as in Fig. 1 in the far right background plus an exhaust hood, also at the right, connected to the existing ventilating system. This view clearly shows the discharge plenum of the self-contained Weathermaker extending above the fluorescent lighting. Linotype machines are located in the left background.

5

¼" Fold Trim

A view of the composing room makeup department is seen in Fig. 2, which shows the same Weathermaker unit as in Fig. 1 in the far right background plus an exhaust hood, also at the right, connected to the existing ventilating system. This view clearly shows the discharge plenum of the self-contained Weathermaker extending above the fluorescent lighting. Linotype machines are located in the left background.
ployees throughout the plant and has increased cleanliness and production.

condensing is saved is located out of sight from the street over a central stairway. This makes it possible to exhaust the building by using the cooling tower fan and closing the ouside air intake damper. Any one area can be handled in this manner by leaving its door to the stairway open and closing those for all other departments.

8

The original ductwork has been retained and is used as a vent relief system discharging to the roof top penthouse and thus outdoors. The lavatories are served by this exhaust system and volume dampers and back pressure dampers in the penthouse control it. The cooling tower by which 95% to 98% of the water used for refrigeration

A view of the composing room makeup department is seen in Fig. 2, which shows the same Weathermaker unit as in Fig. 1 in the far right background plus an exhaust hood, also at the right, connected to the existing ventilating system. This view clearly shows the discharge plenum of the self-contained Weathermaker extending above the fluorescent lighting. Linotype machines are located in the left background.
ployees throughout the plant and has increased cleanliness and production.

1

1"
Finally. A big car as
good as a Volkswagen.
ave you noticed how everyone's try-
o build a small car as good as a Volks-
en?
Vell, we think it's time someone built a
car as good as a Volkswagen.
o we did. And there it is.
he big new 411 Volkswagen 4-Door
The biggest VW sedan you've ever seen.
And the first VW with four doors.
As you can see, the 411's a new kind of Volkswagen.
With more room and comfort than you'd expect in a Volkswagen.
With more power and acceleration.
From the biggest air-cooled engine we ever
built. (Which is still very easy on gas, about 22 mpg.)
With more features as standard equipment than you'd expect in a big car:
Like an automatic transmission. Radial tires. Front disc brakes. Electronic fuel injection. Rear-window defroster. And more.
For only $2999.*
So you see, now you can drive a big car that's economical and just as reliable as our little car.
The 411 Volkswagen 4-Door sedan.
And now everyone else can start all over again.
Trying to build a big car as good as our big car.

Fig. 3-21 The two pages of a publication spread are separated in the printing form. The 1-inch space between them allows for stripper's tape and avoids making a second negative.

printer, paying proper attention to contrasting tints for the type surprinting, using an overlay to separate line from tone copy, preparing a tone mechanical to avoid much stripping to position, and reducing tone to line copy. The artist may use stock tone and pattern sheets for newspaper and rough production.

The proper use of Chinese white and retouching grays with photographs is important to save camera time. Tools, stock materials, and studio equipment also help the artist save time.

DIAGRAMS OF BINDER'S IMPOSITIONS EXPLAINING PASTE-UPS IN IMPOSITION PAIRS

SHEETWISE IMPOSITION

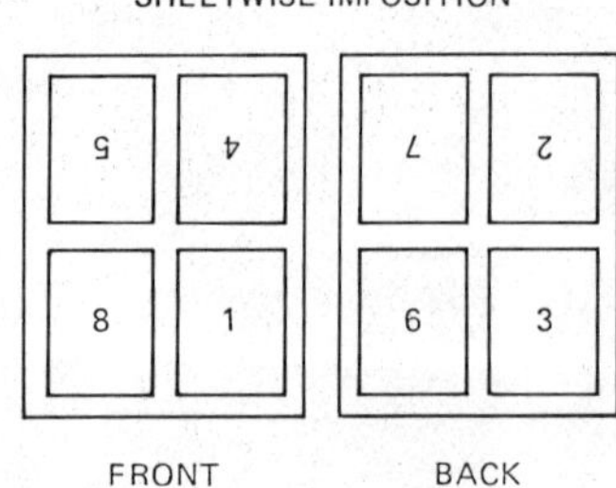

FRONT BACK

Fig. 3-22 Run sheetwise, the front of the sheet is printed. The plate is then changed for the backup, and the reverse side is printed.

WORK-AND-TURN PRESS IMPOSITION

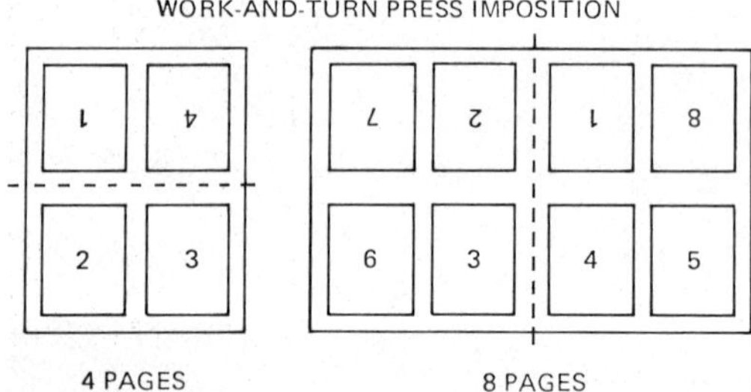

4 PAGES 8 PAGES

Fig. 3-23 Run work-and-turn on a larger press, both front and back are printed on one side of the paper; the pile of printed sheets is then turned over and run through the press again. The sheet is cut in the middle as indicated, producing two complete eight-page booklets ready for folding. This procedure saves a plate and a makeready by offset.

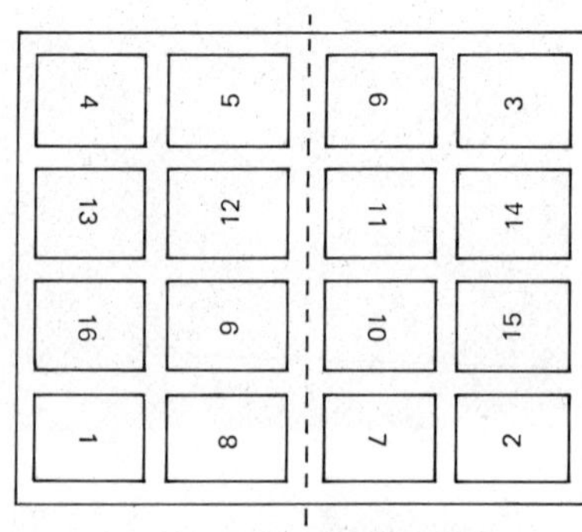

16-PAGE BOOKLET
WORK-AND-TURN IMPOSITION

Fig. 3-24 For short and medium runs, work-and-turn imposition is apt to be used, with the cut sheet folded as shown. This job could also be planned for binding two deep.

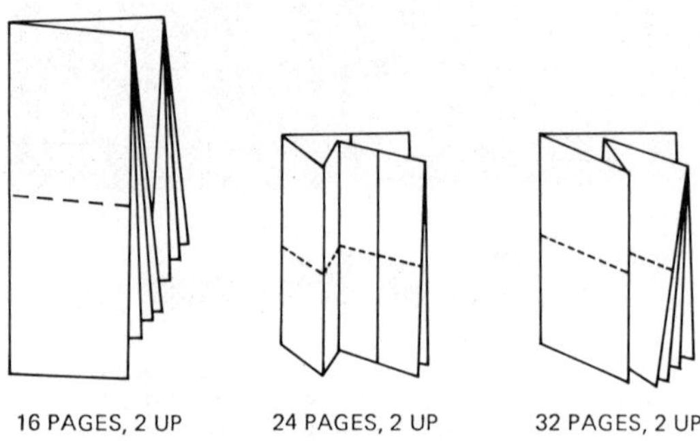

16 PAGES, 2 UP 24 PAGES, 2 UP 32 PAGES, 2 UP

Fig. 3-25 The larger the press sheet and the longer the folded section, the greater the bindery economy. Small booklets may be folded six deep.

How to Determine a Simple Binder's Imposition

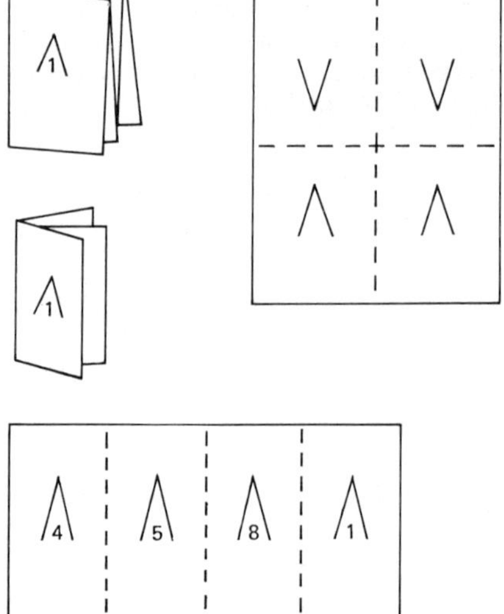

Fig. 3-26 Make a tissue dummy. With a razor blade cut a V, point up, all the way through the folded paper. Number the front and back of the V's as 1, 2, 3, and so on. Open the dummy, and you have the imposition.

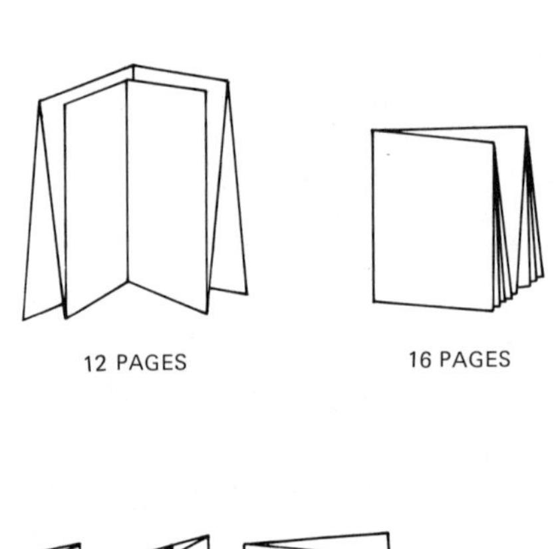

12 PAGES 16 PAGES

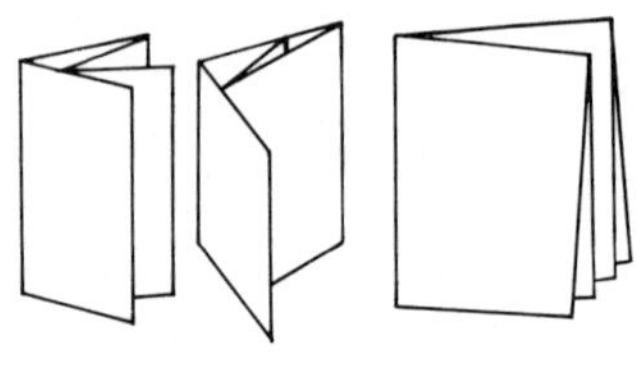

8 PAGES

Fig. 3-27 Three impositions for an eight-page signature.

PREPARING COPY FOR TYPE REVERSES

Type reverses are usually handled on the paste-up with Photostats of type proofs. If they are cut to shape, the edges of the paper should be inked with a brush or a Magic Marker, particularly if they are positioned on a reversed area. If you are pressed for time, draw the outline of the reverse on the mechanical and note on the tissue "Reverse this element" or keyline the inside outline by painting in a wavy edge. The wavy edge means that work is to be done by the platemaker.

A better method is to rule in the edge of the reverse on the type proof and add a black border measuring about ⅛ inch on the outside before the Photostat negative is made. This produces a reverse with a white margin to avoid the danger of a ragged edge and also dog-eared corners from scuffed copy.

If the reverse is to be in a tone instead of black, just add instructions on the tissue: "50 percent tint" or whatever tone is wanted.

Fig. 3-28

Irregular-Edge Reversed Element

Fig. 3-29 An element with an irregular edge that is to be reversed by Photostat should be prepared by the second method described in the text, with an ⅛-inch solid black border.

Fig. 3-30 The Photostat negative gives you the reversed-image border against a white background for trimming.

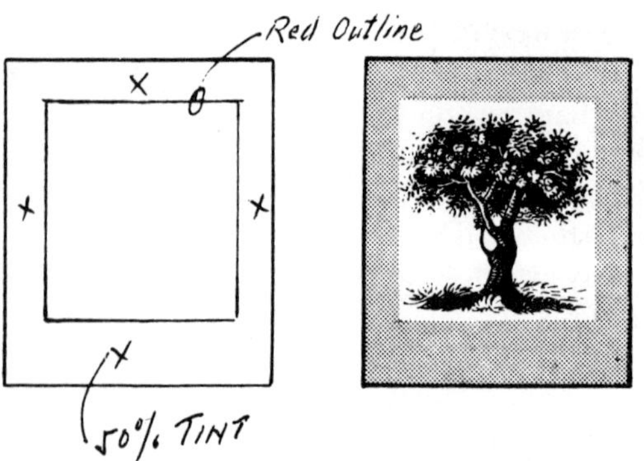

Holding Line of Tint in Red If to Be Dropped, in Black If to Hold

Fig. 3-31 The color of the holding line indicates whether the line is to be dropped or held.

INDICATION OF HALFTONE TINT AREAS AND PANELS ON THE COPY

In commercial work the artist frequently wants an area, a border, or a line of display type to appear as a tint or tone instead of white or black. A tint is less than 50 percent of a tone; a tone is 50 percent or more of a solid color. All that need be added to the copy is a boundary line for the areas in question with a note on the tissue overlay or in light blue on the copy of the tint or tone wanted: 30 percent, 50 percent, 70 percent.

If a black line is not wanted at the boundary edge of a tint area, the holding line is drawn in red. To the engraver or platemaker the red means "temporary," and the line is dropped. If the line is to be held, it is drawn in black, frequently with the notation "Hold line."

Red Outline on Overlay for Tint Area

Fig. 3-32 If the holding line for a tint runs across the design, as in this example, the line—red or black—goes on an overlay just as if you were combining line and tone copy.

Fig. 3-33 This folder was printed entirely in green. The reversed panel was dark green, and the tint area running around the top and down to the bottom was a 30 percent tint so that the design and type could be seen.

It should be understood that we have been dealing with halftone tints and tones applied by the printer or engraver in a fine halftone screen. Later in this chapter we shall take up the use of stock sheets of tints and patterns to be applied by the artist to the camera copy. These tints, which are of a coarser screen, are used mostly for newspaper production or for short-run routine printing.

Copy Example 4 (Fig. 3-35) shows the use of transparent proofs of type and symbols applied on a clear overlay to combine line with halftone illustrations. This composition is printed on the underside of thin film and then laminated to a carrier sheet. To apply these proofs to the overlay, the thin film is removed from the carrier and positioned by pressure to the illustration. Each line or symbol is cut from the film sheet with a needle and then burnished down. Thus the line copy does not mask any lines or design underneath. The method is used for maps and technical illustrations.

TONE MECHANICAL

When there are several tone illustrations in a copy unit of a catalog or booklet and reduction is desirable for holding details, a tone mechanical using size-and-one-half photos is frequently prepared. This method is more accurate than supplying keyed separate prints and avoids much stripping. The layout of the tone mechanical must provide for the reduction, either by using the diagonal-line method or by employing a Photostat to show the position of the size-and-one-half tone elements. Type proofs and other line copy go on a same-size mechanical, and the printer combines the negatives. See Fig. 3-36.

PROPER CONTRAST FOR TYPE PRINTED OR REVERSED ON A TINT OR TONE

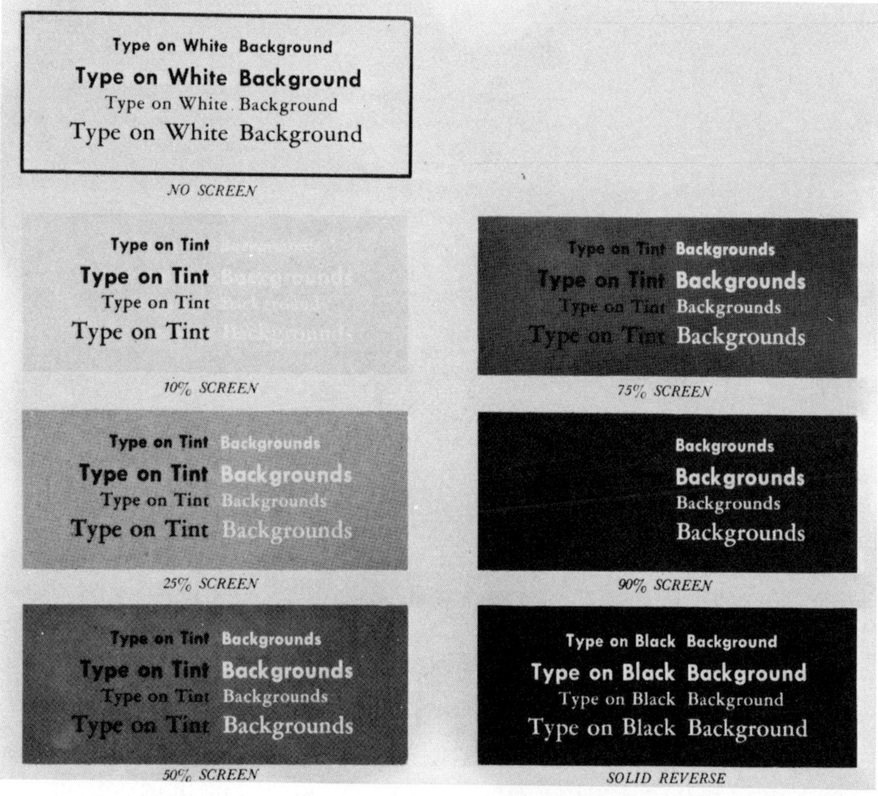

Fig. 3-34 Legibility is reduced when type is used in reverse or is combined with screen tints. These examples show the importance of selecting the proper size and style of typeface to ensure easy reading.

COPY EXAMPLE 4

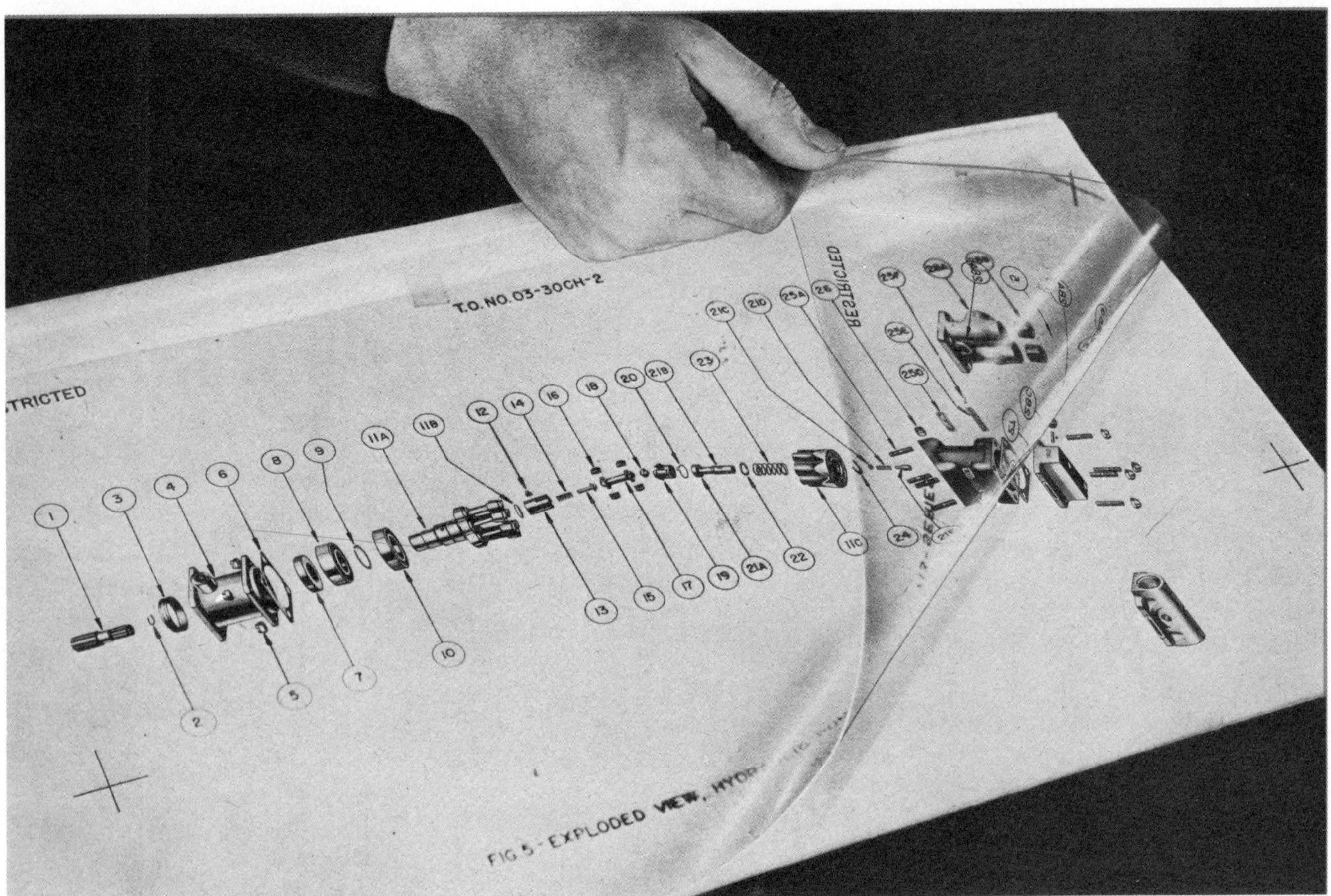

Fig. 3-35 A technical illustration uses transparent type proofs with pressure-sensitive backing on clear overlays. Halftones are on the key copy.

CONVERTING TONE COPY TO LINE

Screened Photo Prints

For budget jobs requiring many small halftones, the use of screened Velox prints of original photos or art is one solution. These prints are line copy and are scaled and positioned on the paste-up. They can be outlined with Chinese white, or the artist can add line art for a combination line-and-tone effect.

Such prints are now made by Velox specialists using the proper density for offset. Originals should be cropped and supplied in proportioned groups so that an 8- by 10-inch Velox can be cut apart for the individual subjects; the cost is about 8 to 10 cents a square inch. Prints from two-color work are also supplied by the Velox specialists, with the screen angled for color.

Making Your Own Screened Prints

If you have continuous-tone negatives, contact prints on Kodak Autoscreen Ortho film will have the halftone dots in them. Union shop regulations usually require prints of these on the paste-up. This film gives excellent definition and sharp detail. The use of a projector will permit you to change the size of the prints.

The availability of a photographic department also permits the use of anoth-

A TONE MECHANICAL IS OFTEN USED WHEN MULTIPLE TONE ELEMENTS ARE TO BE REDUCED FOR DETAIL

Tone Mechanical

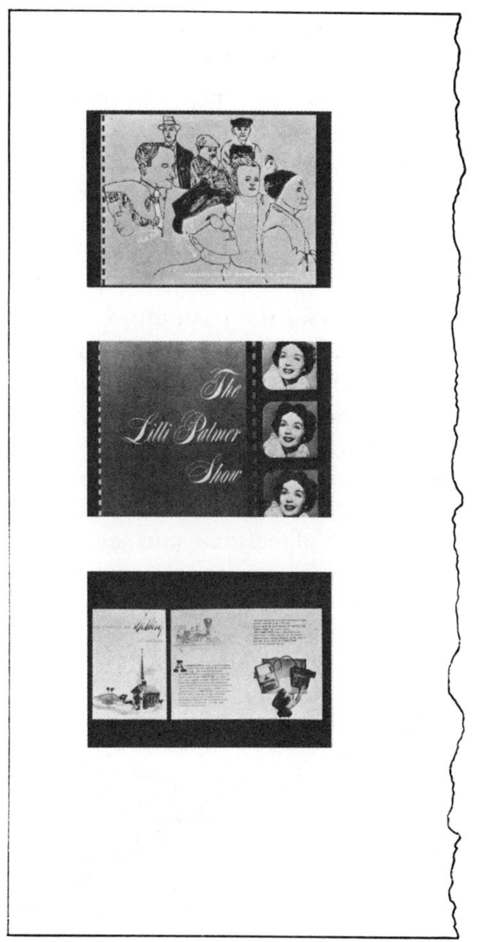

Fig. 3-36 Proportioned page tone elements are positioned so that one halftone negative will handle all of them without stripping each one into position. Gravure publications receiving black-and-white copy direct frequently specify this method to avoid a good deal of camera and contact-printing work.

Catalog Page

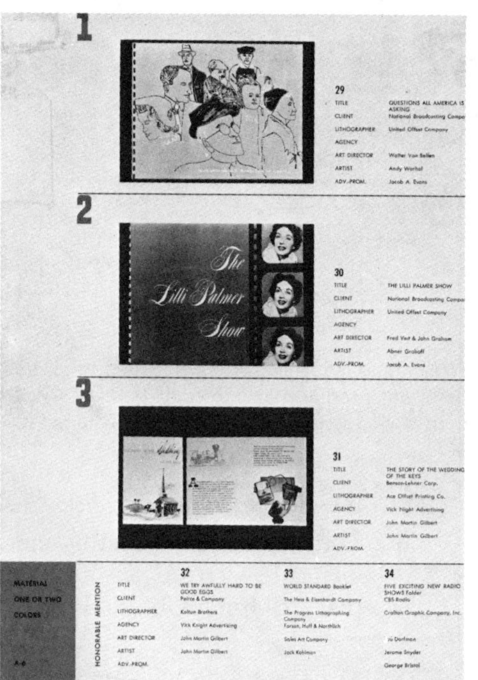

The photographer made 5- by 7-inch and 8- by 10-inch photos of winners and was instructed to make all subjects a specified size, including the black background as shown, when he made projection prints to be pasted in position. Thus many subjects could be handled in groups, and stripping time was reduced.

er method.[1] Your negative is positioned in a projector and a piece of magenta contact halftone screen is placed on top of the photo paper. The resulting print, in the size wanted, is in halftone screen ready for the paste-up. With offset, the usual 110-line screen limitation does not apply.

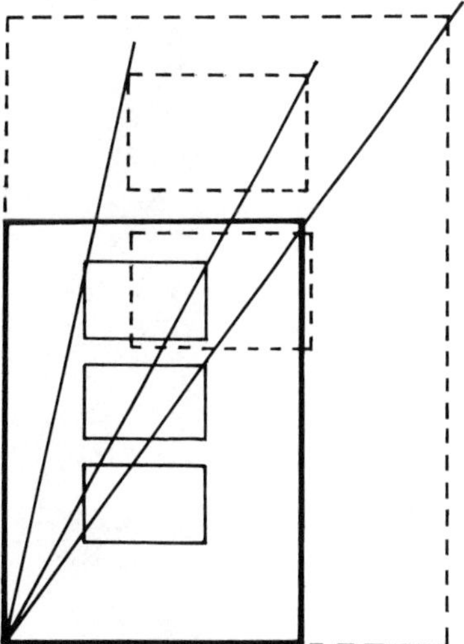

Fig. 3-37 How to get the element position on enlargement for size-and-one-half separate elements as a tone mechanical for reduction. For an irregular layout, use a ghosted Photostat as a guide to position.

[1]*Halftones and Combinations with Positive Screen Prints*, Bulletin 12, Eastman Kodak Company, 343 State Street, Rochester, N.Y. 14608.

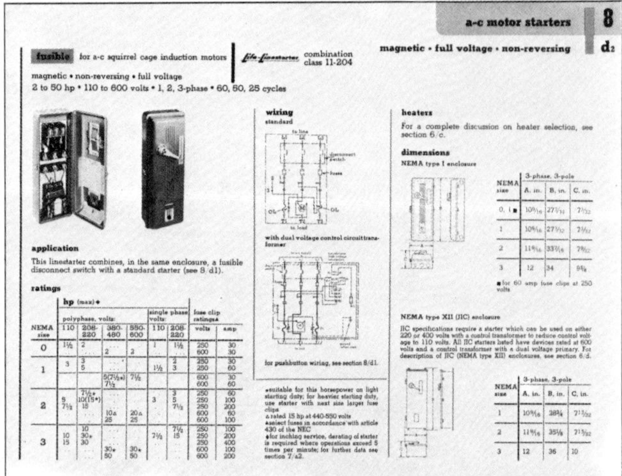

a-c motor starters 8

magnetic • full voltage • non-reversing d2

fusible for a-c squirrel cage induction motors | life-linestarter combination class 11-204

magnetic • non-reversing • full voltage

2 to 50 hp • 110 to 600 volts • 1, 2, 3-phase • 60, 50, 25 cycles

application

This linestarter combines, in the same enclosure, a fusible disconnect switch with a standard starter (see 8/d1).

ratings

NEMA size	hp (max)◆ polyphase, volts: 110	208-220	380-480	550-600	single phase volts: 110	208-220	fuse clip ratings▲ volts	amp
0	1½	2	...		1	1½	250	30
	...	...	2	2	...	...	600	30
1	3	3	...			2	250	30
		5	...		1½	3	250	60
			5(7½•)	7½			600	30
			7½				600	60
2		7½•	...			3	250	60
	5	10(15•)			3	5	250	100
	7½	15				7½	250	200
	...	...	10△	20△			600	60
			25	25			600	100
3		10	...			7½	250	100
	10	30•			7½	15	250	200
	15	30					250	400
	...	...	30•	30•			600	100
			50	50			600	200

•suitable for this horsepower on light starting duty; for heavier starting duty, use starter with next size larger fuse clips

△rated 15 hp at 440-550 volts

▲select fuses in accordance with article 430 of the NEC

◆for inching service, derating of starter is required where operations exceed 5 times per minute; for further data see section 7/a2.

wiring

standard

with dual voltage control circuit transformer

for pushbutton wiring, see section 8/d1.

heaters

For a complete discussion on heater selection, see section 6/c.

dimensions

NEMA type I enclosure

NEMA size	3-phase, 3-pole A, in.	B, in.	C, in.
0, 1■	10 9/16	27 3/32	7 7/32
1	10 9/16	27 3/32	7 7/32
2	11 9/16	33 7/16	7 9/32
3	12	34	9 5/8

■for 60 amp fuse clips at 250 volts

NEMA type XII (JIC) enclosure

JIC specifications require a starter which can be used on either 220 or 400 volts with a control transformer to reduce control voltage to 110 volts. All JIC starters listed have devices rated at 600 volts and a control transformer with a dual voltage primary. For description of JIC (NEMA type XII) enclosures, see section 6/d.

NEMA size	3-phase, 3-pole A, in.	B, in.	C, in.
1	10 9/16	28 3/4	7 13/32
2	11 9/16	35 1/8	7 13/32
3	12	36	10

Fig. 3-38 This Westinghouse catalog containing many small halftones and line illustrations was produced as line copy. Screened Velox prints of photos were positioned on the page paste-ups to get all-line copy.

Screened Prints from Polaroid Cameras

Fast prints for news bulletins and catalogs can be made with the use of a photoscreen adapter attachment for the Polaroid or any 4- by 5-inch camera that will accommodate the No. 500 Polaroid sheet film holder. High-contrast film, now available for Polaroid cameras, should be used.

New Photoprint Paper for Line or Tone Positives

A more recent development in photographic paper is a one-step method of obtaining screened prints of photographs or other tone copy that avoids the usual negative. Using a camera for a change in size or a print frame for the same size, with the new photoprint paper you get a halftone copy for the paste-up.

A different negative-positive paper is used for line copy. The method seems to have eliminated much of the Photostat volume; it was developed for offset newspapers but is suitable for much commercial printing. Several film manufacturers offer this type of material, and several daylight cameras for art departments and studios have come on the market.

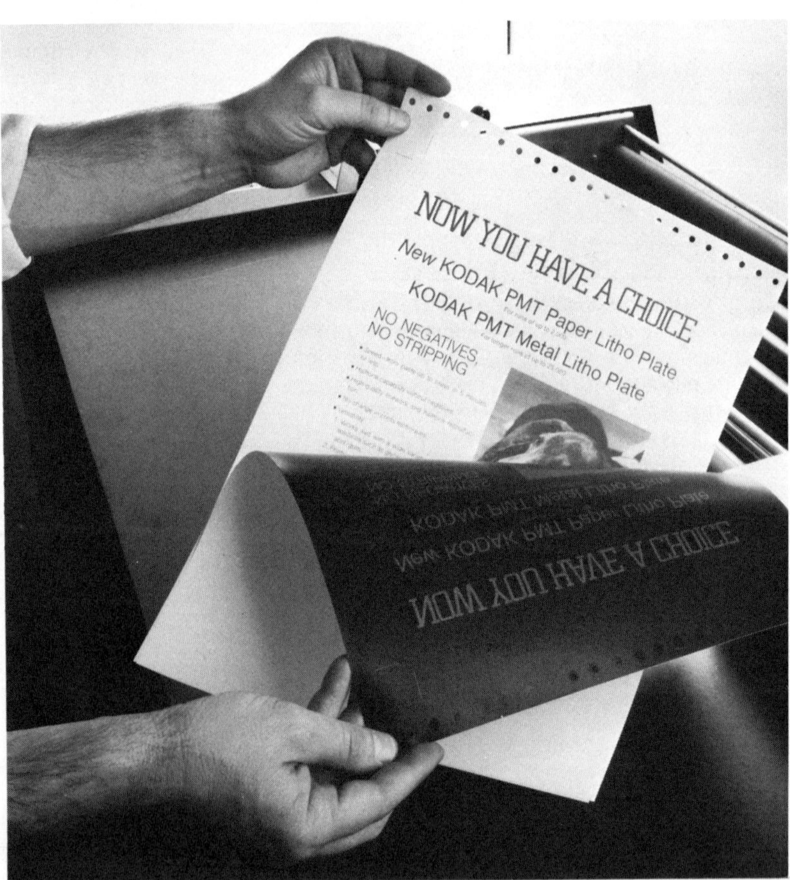

Fig. 3-39 The Kodak PMT transfer paper, a negative-positive sandwich, being peeled apart to get the screened positive for the paste-up.

Conversion of Photographs to Line Drawings

A time-saving method of preparing technical line illustrations, such as exploded views of parts, is to convert photos of equipment as well as parts to preliminary line copy to be touched up and completed by the illustrator. This method is another application of the Kodak tone-line process. Photo studios and some photocompositors perform this service, shown in Fig. 3-40. An unsharp positive mask is made and superimposed on the negative to get the line print.

Photostats Save the Artist's Time

Photostats can be made of tone art or of the actual object to serve as a base on which the artist works in black for a line drawing. Later the unwanted tones of the Photostat are bleached out. This can also be done with photoprints, using a potassium oxalate bleach.

Photostats are used so widely to help prepare illustrations that obtaining informative literature from at least one large Photostat studio is recommended. Since they are also made on acetate, they may be used as overlays for loose register.

Fig. 3-40 The Kodak tone-line process saves the artist's time when line drawings of parts are needed.

From Continuous-Tone Copy to Line Copy by the Kodak Tone-Line Process

Fig. 3-41 When line copy is preferable to a halftone, many of the larger engravers as well as specialists in metropolitan areas provide a conversion service.

A Few of the Hundreds of Tints and Patterns Available to the Artist

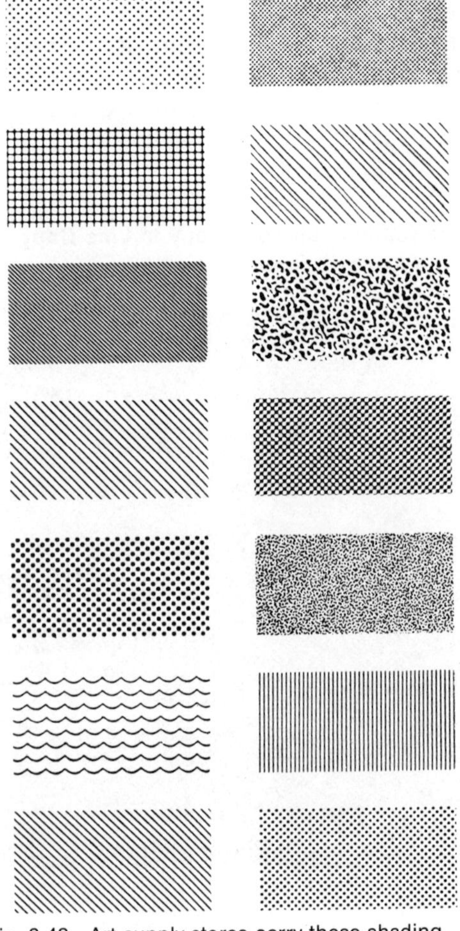

Fig. 3-42 Art supply stores carry these shading sheets on clear, self-adhesive films, ready to be added to line art for tints and backgrounds.

AIDS FOR THE ARTIST

Tints and Patterns

As we have explained, the area on the copy that is to receive a uniform tone is outlined or opaqued with instructions added for the percentage of tone wanted. The platemaker takes care of this request by stripping a piece of stock halftone film to the negative. Termed a halftone tint, it is usually in at least a 133-line screen.

When there is a large volume of routine printing, the artist adds tints and patterns to the line copy, either by pasting on the copy a piece of a stock tint sheet (Zip-a-Tone and Craftint, among others) or by working on special drawing-board material printed with an invisible tone pattern. Brushing on a developer brings out the invisible tints where desired. Tint sheets come in either black or white, white being used over reversed areas. Copy produced with these tints is classed as line copy in offset.

Peel away protective backing sheet . . . and place Craf-Tone pattern over parts of the drawing to be shaded . . .

Rub down with a cloth, starting from the bottom and rubbing from left to right, moving upward as the pattern sheet adheres to the drawing . . .

With a Craftint Cutting Needle, cut and strip away parts not desired. Rub surface with added pressure to make secure. Now the art is ready for the engraver!

Fig. 3-43

Fig. 3-44 Also available are Craftint drawing papers with tints and tones in invisible ink. With brush developers an artist obtains several tones to add to pen drawings. [*Courtesy Craftint Manufacturing Company*]

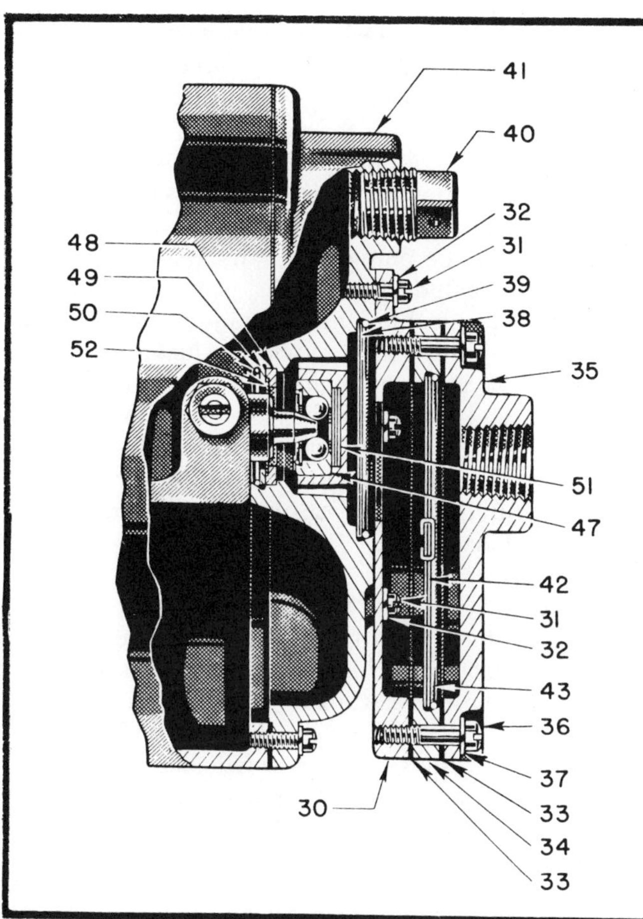

Fig. 3-45 Stock tint and pattern sheets are used to get contrast between parts in technical illustrations. The work shown uses two patterns between black and white. The work size is usually twice size.

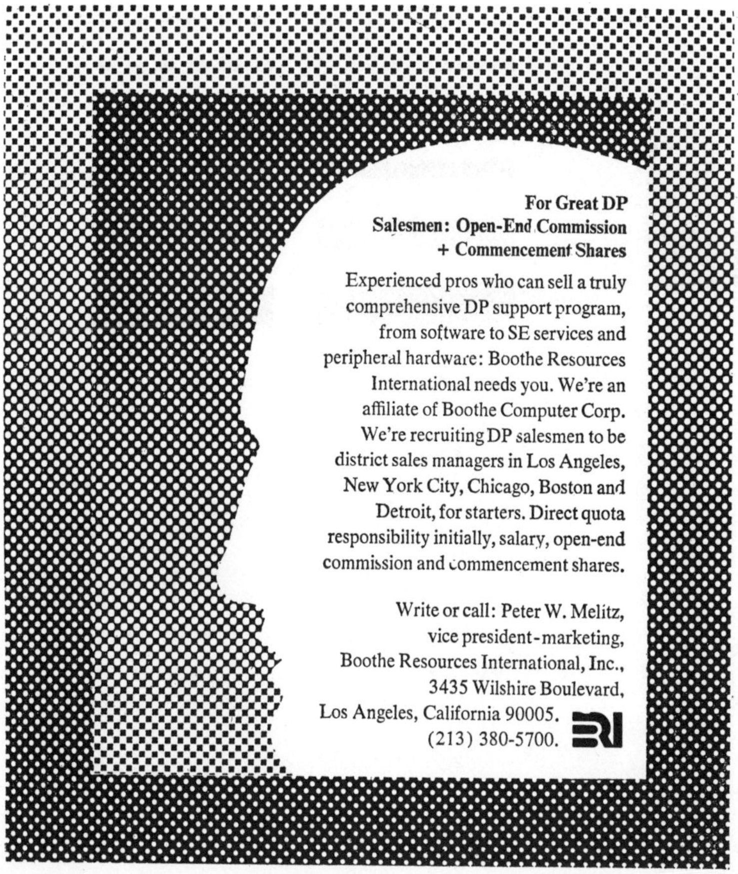

For Great DP Salesmen: Open-End Commission + Commencement Shares

Experienced pros who can sell a truly comprehensive DP support program, from software to SE services and peripheral hardware: Boothe Resources International needs you. We're an affiliate of Boothe Computer Corp. We're recruiting DP salesmen to be district sales managers in Los Angeles, New York City, Chicago, Boston and Detroit, for starters. Direct quota responsibility initially, salary, open-end commission and commencement shares.

Write or call: Peter W. Melitz, vice president-marketing, Boothe Resources International, Inc., 3435 Wilshire Boulevard, Los Angeles, California 90005. (213) 380-5700.

Fig. 3-46 To obtain the effect shown, an enlarged Velox print of a stock tint sheet is used.

Fig. 3-47 The use of the tone sheet as an art medium.

Technical Fountain Pen

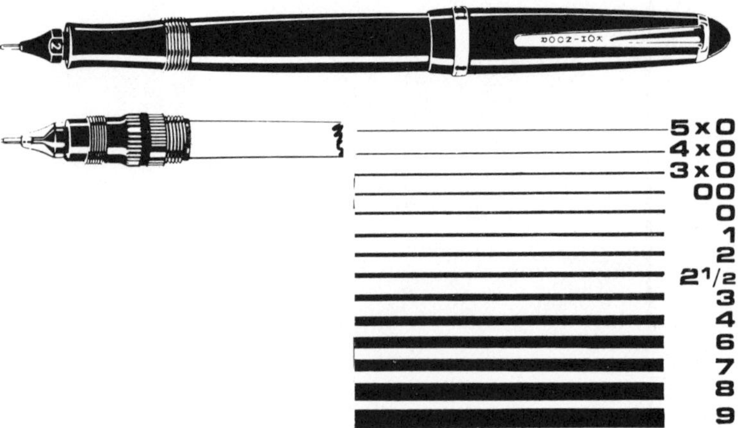

Fig. 3-48 The Koh-I-Noor Rapidograph individually interchangeable drawing point tips are designed to meet the special needs of the professional who requires frequent changes in line widths, as shown. No. 2 is widely used for commercial lap register.

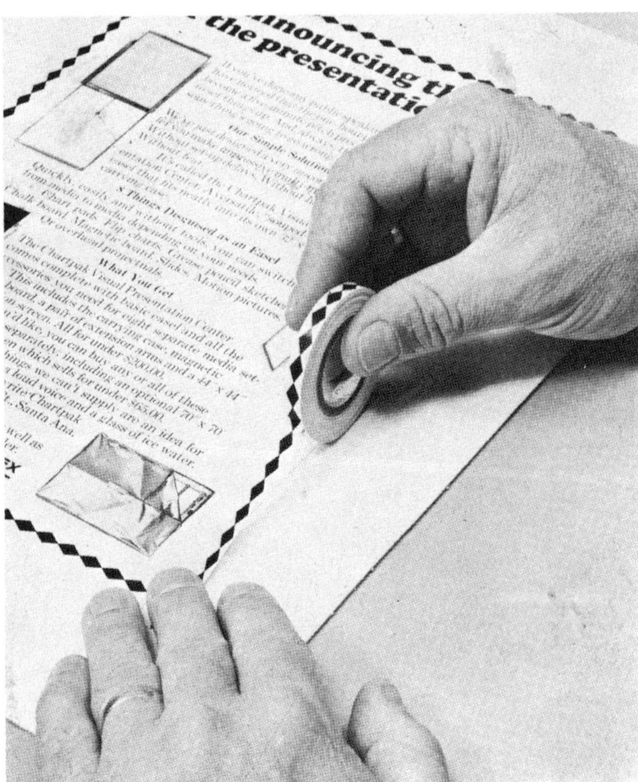

Fig. 3-49 Illustration from the Chart-Pak catalog.

Technical Fountain Pens

Technical pens, available in several brands, have largely replaced ruling pens, particularly for templates and French curves. Many pens may be used with regular drawing and writing inks for commercial and fine art techniques, or special ink may be employed. Pens are available for selected line widths; some have interchangeable drawing points for different widths. The line widths shown in Fig. 3-48 are approximate because the actual width is affected by the paper and by the speed with which the line is drawn. The No. 2 line is widely used for commercial-grade color lap register, described in Chapter 5.

Stock Art Materials

Many rules, borders, transfer letters, symbols, and characters are in constant use. These are available at art supply stores in the form of tapes or sheets with a pressure-sensitive adhesive back for easy application to the mechanical. Their use avoids a lot of handwork and inking, thus saving time.

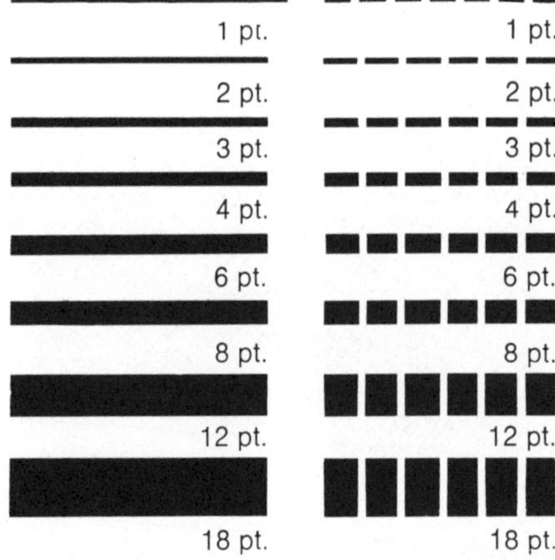

Fig. 3-50 Solid- and broken-line point size tapes.

55 line/40%

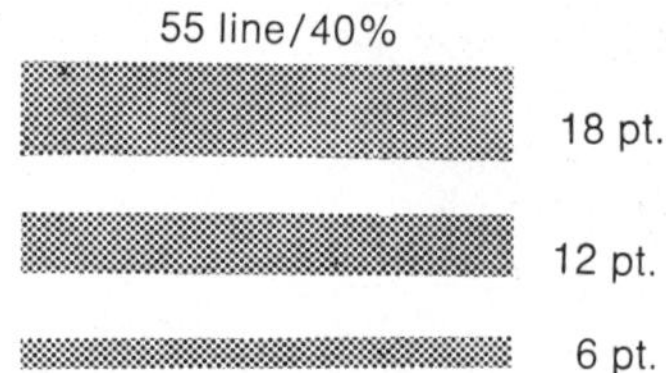

Fig. 3-51 Benday pattern tapes printed in black on transparent or opaque material.

ART STUDIO EQUIPMENT

Fig. 3-52 Photostats are giving way to photographic papers, which produce a positive copy in one step. This Visual Graphics Corporation POS ONE system camera produces any form of print, negative or positive, with a 50 percent range in size up or down.

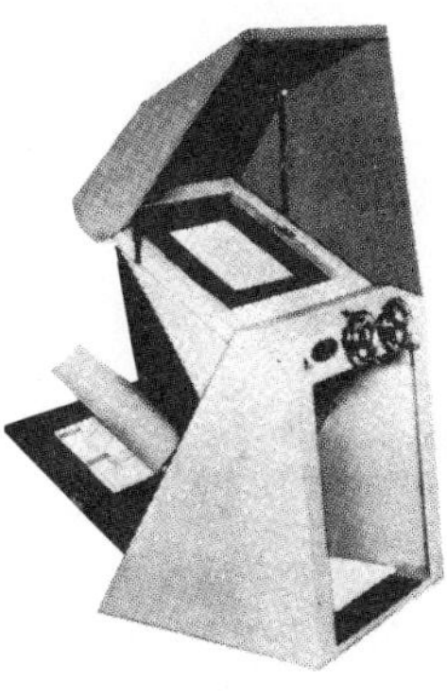

Fig. 3-53 The artist has a camera lucida instrument for tracing designs in different sizes; publications have various forms of visualizers to help scale art for page layout or to trace a design in a different size on the ground glass.

Fig. 3-54 Desk-top light tables are used to trace same-size designs.

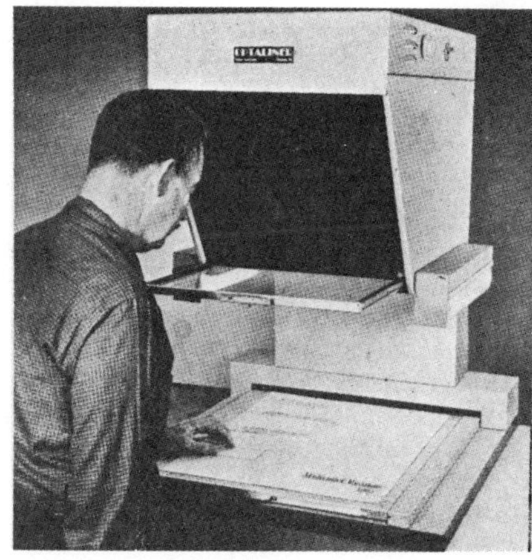

Fig. 3-55 The optical paste-up aligner, used by newspapers for fast page makeup.

Dry wax adhesive has largely replaced rubber cement for paste-up work, particularly when there are many type proofs. Galleys are waxed and set aside, to be trimmed and positioned later, even the following day. The use of wax adhesive makes it easy to reposition an element.

Fig. 3-56 Goodkin Company wax coater.

Fig. 3-57 Dry wax adhesive. [*Lectro-Stick Company, Chicago*]

SERVICES FOR ARTWORK

Listed below are the names and addresses of various services of interest to artists and art departments.

Art Supplies; Tools and Instruments; Equipment and Materials

Dick Blick Company (catalog)
P.O. Box 1267
Galesburg, Ill. 61401

Bond Borders and Backgrounds

Goes Lithographing Company
42 West 61st Street
Chicago, Ill. 60621

Clip Book Art

American Marketing Service
600 Winter Street
Waltham, Mass. 02154
Cartoon Clip Book
733 A Street
Hayward, Calif. 94541
Dot Advertising, Inc.
520 North Michigan Avenue
Chicago, Ill. 60611
Idea Art
740 Broadway
New York, N.Y. 10003
Graphics Institute, Inc.
42 West 39th Street
New York, N.Y. 10018
Clarence P. Hornung
12 Glen Road
West Hempstead, N.Y. 11552

Color Prints and Transparencies

Ray A. Atkeson
1675 Southwest Westwood Drive
Portland, Oreg. 97201
Color Masters, Inc.
143 East 27th Street
New York, N.Y. 10016
A. Devaney, Inc.
40 East 49th Street
New York, N.Y. 10017
Freelance Photographers Guild, Inc.
251 Park Avenue South
New York, N.Y. 10010
Kimberly-Clark Corporation
(positives on loan)
Neenah, Wis. 54956
Klein & Goodman, Inc.
132 South 11th Street
Philadelphia, Pa. 19107
Harold M. Lambert Studios, Inc.
2801 West Cheltenham Avenue
Philadelphia, Pa. 19150
Mueller Color Plate Company
2320 North 11th Street
Milwaukee, Wis. 53206
National Audubon Society
950 Third Avenue
New York, N.Y. 10022
Pagano, Inc.
206 East 65th Street
New York, N.Y. 10021
Shostal Associates, Inc.
60 East 42d Street
New York, N.Y. 10017

Monthly Art Services

Dynamic Graphics, Inc.
6707 N. Sheradan Rd.
Peoria, Ill. 61614
Multi-Ad Service, Inc.
100 Walnut Street
Peoria, Ill. 61602
Volk Clip Books
Box 7211
Pleasantville, N.J. 08232
Ron Yobline Graphic Studio
P.O. Box 63
Easton, Pa. 18042

Old Engravings and Prints

Argosy Gallery (old maps)
116 East 59th Street
New York, N.Y. 10022
Bettmann Archive, Inc.
136 East 57th Street
New York, N.Y. 10022
Culver Pictures, Inc.
660 First Avenue
New York, N.Y. 10016

Photo Services

Bibliography of Picture Sources
Special Libraries Association
235 Park Avenue South
New York, N.Y. 10003
Ewing Galloway
420 Lexington Avenue
New York, N.Y. 10016

Freelance Photographers Guild, Inc.
251 Park Avenue South
New York, N.Y. 10010

Kaufman & Fabry Company
180 North Wabash Avenue
Chicago, Ill. 60601

Harold M. Lambert Studios, Inc.
2801 West Cheltenham Avenue
Philadelphia, Pa. 19150

Frederic Lewis, Inc.
35 East 35th Street
New York, N.Y. 10016

Library of Congress
First Street between East Capitol Street and Independence Avenue S.E.
Washington, D.C. 20540

National Archives
Pennsylvania Avenue at Eighth Street N.W.
Washington, D.C. 20408

H. Armstrong Roberts
4203 Locust Street
Philadelphia, Pa. 19104

Shostal Associates, Inc.
60 East 42d Street
New York, N.Y. 10017

Underwood & Underwood
3 West 46th Street
New York, N.Y. 10036

World-Wide Photo
42 Morton Street
New York, N.Y. 10014

Seasonal and Special Stock Bulletins and Letterheads

Carr Spiers Corporation
Vero Beach, Fla. 32960

Idea Art
740 Broadway
New York, N.Y. 10003

National Creative Sales, Inc.
435 North Avenue
New Rochelle, N.Y. 10801

Rylander Company
111 North Canal Street
Chicago, Ill. 60606

Arthur Thompson & Company
109 Market Place
Baltimore, Md. 21202

CHAPTER FOUR
Camera Copy for Simple Multicolor Printing

THERE IS A large volume of multicolor printing, particularly printing in black and one color, for which copy is prepared as a mechanical without using a film overlay for the color copy. The tissue overlay indicates the color areas and type to surprint or to be reversed. The only lapping of touching colors is that of colors to go under the black. The engraver or printer makes two negatives, one for black and one for color, providing for any lap of color under the black or for surprinting on color (see Copy Example 8). Copy Examples 5 and 5A (Figs. 4-4 and 4-5) illustrate such camera copy. Copy for color need not be put on an overlay. However, with jobs such as Copy Example 5A and Copy Example 12 (Figs. 5-5 and 5-6), in which part of a series of mailings using the same paper and ink is printed together, color copy is frequently put on an overlay to save platemaking time. The camera copy for the series is prepared as a copy unit. Copy Example 13 (Fig. 5-7) also fell in this category, since a fine lap of inks was not necessary because of the black.

Copy Example 7 (Figs. 4-7 and 4-8) is a little more complicated, but it was handled without an overlay for the color copy. The tissue overlay indicated the reverses and surprinting on color, but the diagonal white line required a black line on a parchment overlay to knock out both the black and the color.

USE OF BOUNDARY LINES FOR COLOR AREAS

Copy Example 8 (Figs. 4-17 and 4-18) is representative of the longer press runs of national advertising printed matter, for which the print orders may run in the millions. A different type of offset press plate is employed for such printing, resulting in the use of keylining for boundary lines of color areas instead of brush-opaquing such areas on an overlay of the mechanical. The important advantage is accuracy of color register when colors other than black touch, for the line is common to both colors, and its width determines the amount of ink lap wanted. The lap ranges from 1/32 to 1/64 inch. This lap is required because the paper may shrink.

For larger orders of color printing the deep-etch press plate came into use because of its longer life. This type of plate, which requires photographic positives, is termed a "positive-working plate." The action of light through clear film results in a temporary resist coating. The black image on the positive film (lines, dots, or solids) holds back the light from the plate coating, permitting the image to be dissolved and uncovering the metal for etching. The ink-receptive image is developed, and the temporary resist coating of the non-image areas is then washed off.

MASKING FILM REPLACING BRUSH-OPAQUING

Thin, translucent red masking film with an adhesive backing on a heavier clear film carrier sheet was first developed to avoid brush-opaquing by platemakers on their positives. The platemakers positioned a carrier sheet over the wanted color area on a light table, cut the film into the boundary, or holding, line, and then

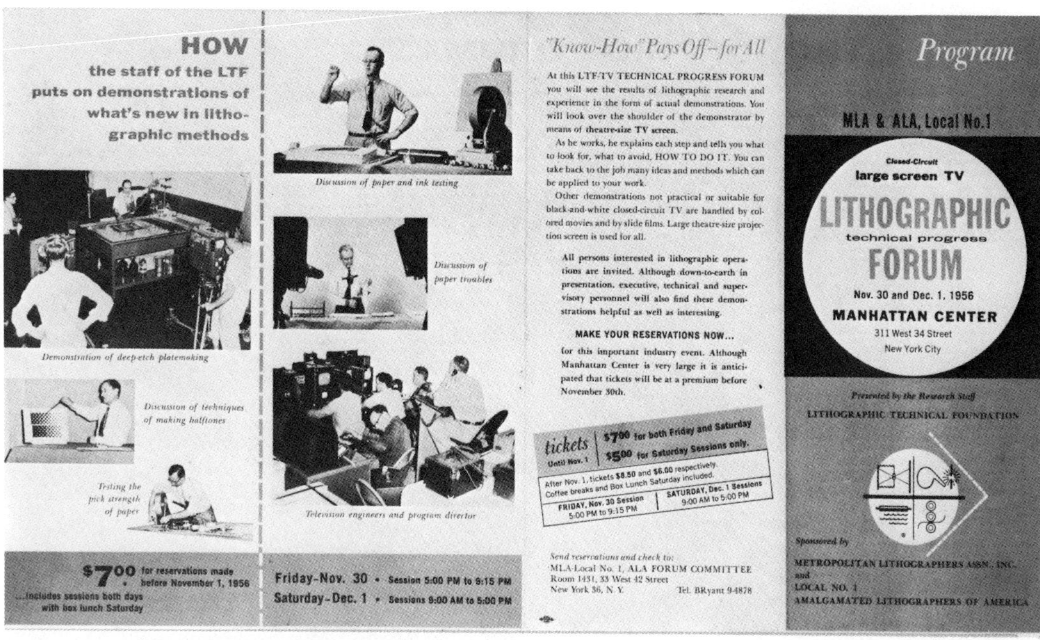

HOW
the staff of the LTF puts on demonstrations of what's new in lithographic methods

Demonstration of deep-etch platemaking

Discussion of techniques of making halftones

Testing the pick strength of paper

$7.00 for reservations made before November 1, 1956 ...includes sessions both days with box lunch Saturday

Discussion of paper and ink testing

Discussion of paper troubles

Television engineers and program director

Friday-Nov. 30 • Session 5:00 PM to 9:15 PM
Saturday-Dec. 1 • Sessions 9:00 AM to 5:00 PM

"Know-How" Pays Off—for All

At this LTF-TV TECHNICAL PROGRESS FORUM you will see the results of lithographic research and experience in the form of actual demonstrations. You will look over the shoulder of the demonstrator by means of theatre-size TV screen.

As he works, he explains each step and tells you what to look for, what to avoid, HOW TO DO IT. You can take back to the job many ideas and methods which can be applied to your work.

Other demonstrations not practical or suitable for black-and-white closed-circuit TV are handled by colored movies and by slide films. Large theatre-size projection screen is used for all.

All persons interested in lithographic operations are invited. Although down-to-earth in presentation, executive, technical and supervisory personnel will also find these demonstrations helpful as well as interesting.

MAKE YOUR RESERVATIONS NOW...

for this important industry event. Although Manhattan Center is very large it is anticipated that tickets will be at a premium before November 30th.

tickets Until Nov. 1 | $7.00 for both Friday and Saturday | $5.00 for Saturday Sessions only.
After Nov. 1, tickets $8.50 and $6.00 respectively.
Coffee breaks and Box Lunch Saturday included.
FRIDAY, Nov. 30 Session 5:00 PM to 9:15 PM | SATURDAY, Dec. 1 Sessions 9:00 AM to 5:00 PM

Send reservations and check to:
MLA Local No. 1, ALA FORUM COMMITTEE
Room 1431, 33 West 42 Street
New York 36, N. Y. Tel. BRyant 9-4878

Program

MLA & ALA, Local No.1

Closed-Circuit
large screen TV
LITHOGRAPHIC
technical progress
FORUM
Nov. 30 and Dec. 1, 1956
MANHATTAN CENTER
311 West 34 Street
New York City

Presented by the Research Staff
LITHOGRAPHIC TECHNICAL FOUNDATION

Sponsored by
METROPOLITAN LITHOGRAPHERS ASSN., INC.
and
LOCAL NO. 1
AMALGAMATED LITHOGRAPHERS OF AMERICA

Fig. 4-1 Folder in two colors prepared from copy in one piece. No overlay was used for color. See also Copy Example 8.

peeled off the red film and positioned it on the color area of the positive. If there was a second color touching, they did the same on that positive, the common line giving the ink lap. This method is far more accurate and faster than brush-opaquing two films.

Naturally, the use of masking film was adopted by the copy preparation department; instead of opaquing a color area on an overlay, a mask was cut to register with the key copy underneath. When it was practical to do so, the unwanted red film was peeled off, and the carrier sheet served as the overlay material.

If boundary-line copy is supplied to printers who do not make deep-etch plates, they simply position masking film on the copy to opaque indicated areas.

Ulano[1] and other brands of masking film are sold by art supply stores.

FORMS OF SIMPLE COLOR COPY

At this point it is well to explain that there are two forms of copy for handling colors:

[1]*Collection of Time and Cost Savers for the Artist,* Ulano Products Company, Inc., 210 East 86th Street, New York, N.Y. 10028, 1971.

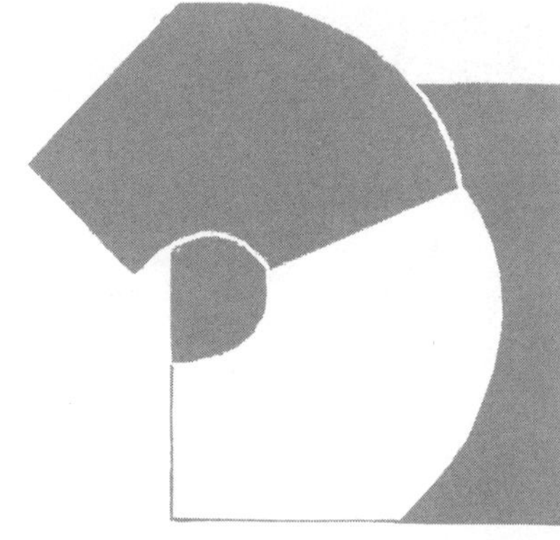

Fig. 4-2 Masking film replacing brush-opaquing. This film, made by Ulano and others and sold by art supply stores, may easily be rubbed down on the mechanical by the artist. It is also used by the platemaker to strip in color and reversed areas on photographic positives.

Fig. 4-3 This Ulano short-axis swivel-tip knife can follow an irregular holding line to cut masking film.

COPY EXAMPLE 5

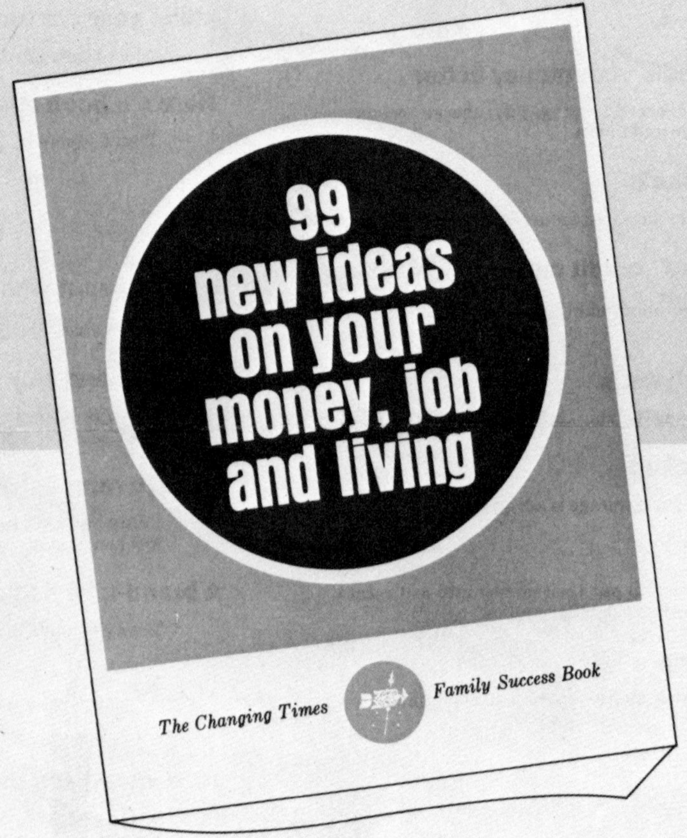

Get This Valuable New Book FREE
99 new ideas on your money, job and living
The Changing Times Family Success Book
The latest edition of Kiplinger's Family Success Book
"99 New Ideas on YOUR MONEY, JOB & LIVING"
with your new subscription to
CHANGING TIMES
The Kiplinger Magazine
The new edition of this valuable book will help you do a better job of managing your personal and family affairs. It will show you how to get more for your money . . . how to increase your earnings and get ahead . . . and how to build security for the future.

Fig. 4-4 This two-color example illustrates the handling of simple "loose," or "spot," register. The copy is prepared as for a single color, but the tissue overlay indicates work to be in color or in black to surprint on color. It is a simple matter for the engraver or platemaker to make separate black and color negatives.

the *one-piece* method, demonstrated in this chapter for simple work, and the *overlay* method. Copy in one piece is preferred by producers because of its accuracy and by advertising agencies because it avoids the chance of error and reduces the amount of approval required from clients. However, the overlay method must be used to handle some copy problems, as explained in Chapter 5.

COPY EXAMPLE 5*A*

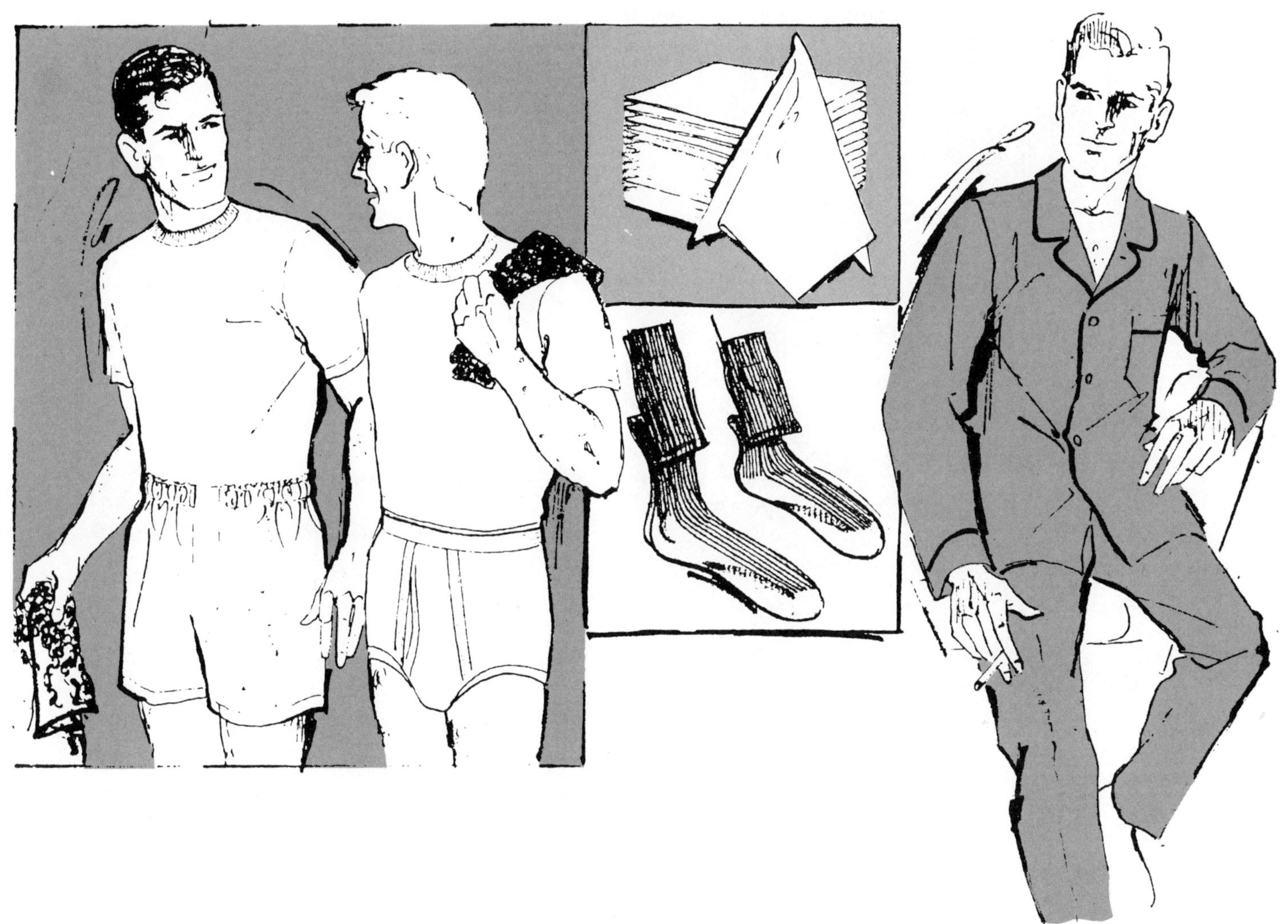

Fig. 4-5 There is a type of line illustration in which a light color is used as a tint for contrast but which does not require accurate register since "leaks" or overprints are not important. The copy for color is apt to be prepared as an overlay, using red masking film cut along the holding lines. The platemaker can also handle this job.

COPY EXAMPLE 6

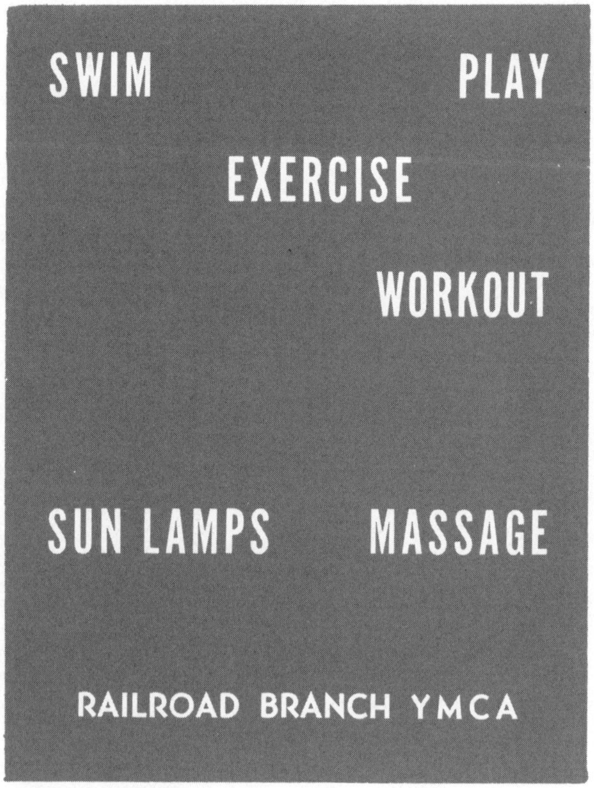

SWIM PLAY

EXERCISE

WORKOUT

SUN LAMPS MASSAGE

RAILROAD BRANCH YMCA

PLEASE POST

SWIM THE YEAR 'ROUND. PLAY

HANDBALL, BADMINTON, BASKETBALL, VOLLEYBALL. EXERCISE THROUGH BOXING, BAG PUNCHING, WEIGHT LIFTING AND CALISTHENICS. WORKOUT ALONE OR WITH OTHERS = ROWING MACHINE, MEDICINE BALLS, BICYCLE, WEIGHTS, BAR-BELLS, STALL BARS, ETC.

SUN LAMPS AND MASSAGE

Membership Rates and Payment Plan on Request

If you are interested in any of the above or in residence, social activities, cultural programs, clubs, write or call

GRAND CENTRAL

RAILROAD BRANCH YMCA

224 East 47th St., New York 17 PLaza 5-2410

From Type Proof,
a Second Color with Reversed Type,
Surprinted Black

Fig. 4-6 Using the repro type proof with color-broken tissue overlay as camera copy, the platemaker makes a negative, opaques the type matter for black, and from this makes a contact positive. This produces a film for the red plate with type reverses. The opaque on the original negative is then washed off, and the words to be reversed (red plate) are opaqued. The platemaker now has a negative for the black type to surprint on the red background.

COPY EXAMPLE 7

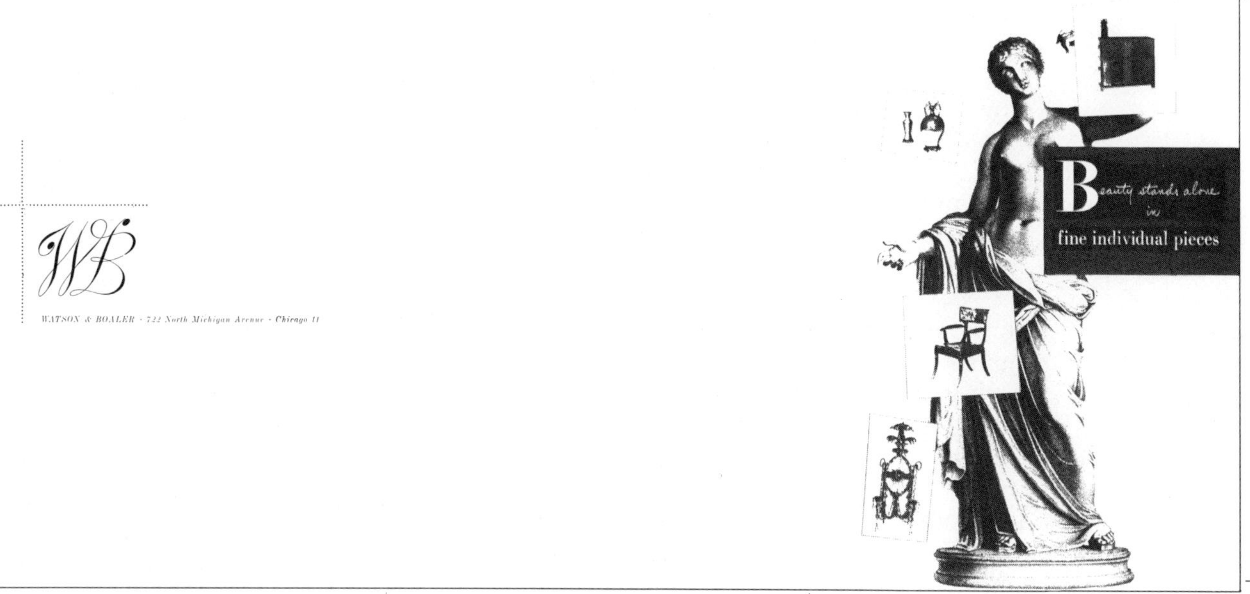

Fig. 4-7 The mechanical shown above is for one side of a folder to be printed in a light tan color on two of the pages with type reverses and black surprinting. The *WB* script and the horizontal dotted line, plus the merchandise boxes to be knocked out by the platemaker as directed on the tissue overlay, were to show as white. The diagonal white line on page 1 was handled by a 2-point black ruled line on a parchment overlay (not shown). The positive film of this as contact-printed on both negatives for black and color resulted in the white line showing. The platemaker knocked out the color of the *WB* and the horizontal type line to show as white. To hold better detail in the small furniture illustrations the mechanical was prepared in an 8⅞₁₆-inch page width and reduced to a 6¾-inch width when printed. Windows were cut in the parchment overlay to show corner marks so that these could serve as register marks.

Mechanical: Front Side of a Six-Page Folder; Two Colors from One-Piece Copy

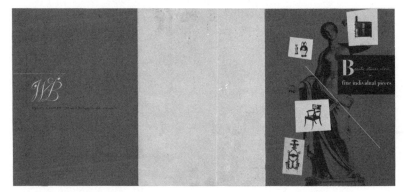

Fig. 4-8

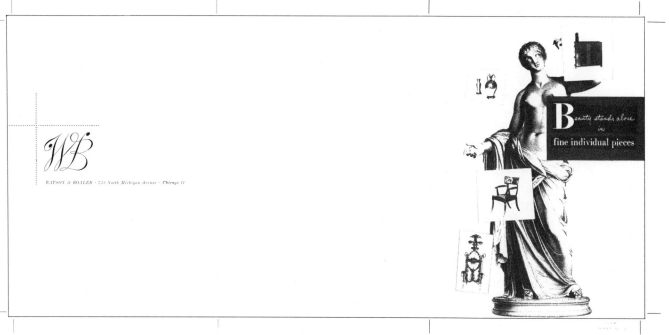

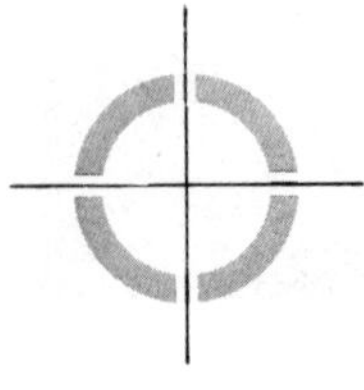

Fig. 4-9

COLOR REGISTER

Thus far we have been dealing with black and one color. Opaque black ink masked ink lap where it touched color, and the register was handled by the platemaker. Now we are dealing with true colors that touch, and the resulting secondary colors may be undesirable. Too much lap of a blue and a yellow with transparent inks, for example, will result in a noticeable green line.

Under time plate estimating, a major purpose of the mechanical and the various methods of preparing copy for multicolor work is to save platemaking time, which now costs about $20 an hour with minimum charges. Under the Photoengravers' Standard Scale, there are special charges and Note E, which concerns operations of a hand nature. These entail costs in addition to the unit scale cost. Today the large printing user checks extra charges very closely, for these can be due to inaccurate or incomplete mechanicals.

In the material that follows, the three types of simple color register are demonstrated, frequently with both one-piece and overlay copy forms as well as with copy examples to help clarify the application of the method. Provision for simple color register in the copy is usually for opaque inks, and the lap, or "trap," of inks is about 1/32 inch in commercial-grade printing. However, when printing includes a process color subject, transparent inks must be used, and any supplementary simple color work—backgrounds, panels, color spots—will require a different color register method to avoid the formation of a noticeable secondary color. Color register for the process subject itself is handled by the platemaker.

COLOR REGISTER DETERMINED BY INKS AND DESIGN

Depending on the type of pigment used in their manufacture, printing inks are either transparent or opaque. Process color inks—yellow, blue, and red—are examples of transparent inks. When two such inks overprint or lap, a secondary color results: yellow on blue produces a green color because the light passes through the ink film and is reflected back to the eye from the paper. Black is an example of opaque ink; practically any color can be made with opaque pigments.

When a dark opaque ink is printed on top of a light-color background, usually there is no perceptible change in the dark color, but when a light color is printed on a dark background, it loses color strength. If necessary, the printer will knock out the background so that white paper will reflect color surprinting. When two light opaque colors lap too much, the lapping is frequently noticeable.

In preparing copy for touching colors, therefore, you must consider the amount and accuracy of the ink lap for color register and for surprinting on a color and prepare the copy accordingly except for type matter. The closer the color register required, the more expensive the printing operation.

MECHANICALS FOR BLACK AND TWO OR MORE COLORS

There are two kinds of multicolor printing: *simple color*, for which copy for the camera is prepared in black or gray tones; and *process color*, which requires finished art and photographic color separation, usually for the four-color process (paintings and color transparencies). This second form of color printing is covered in Chapter 7.

Many mechanicals are prepared for more than two colors, raising the problem of providing for the proper register of touching colors other than black. In addition, the kind of ink to be used in the printing (opaque or transparent pigments) must be considered. Most simple color printing is done with opaque inks because of their color strength and ability to provide the exact color wanted, but much advertising printing, particularly for collateral material, is done with transparent inks because the main publication advertising illustration consists of process artwork.

TYPES OF COLOR REGISTER

With all the printing processes three types of simple color ink register are used:

Overlay Method

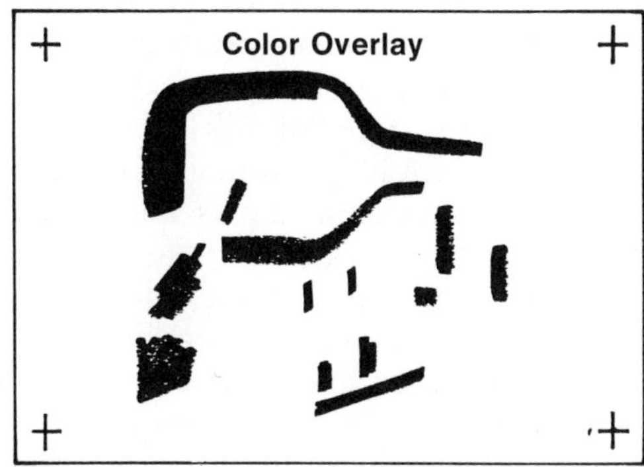

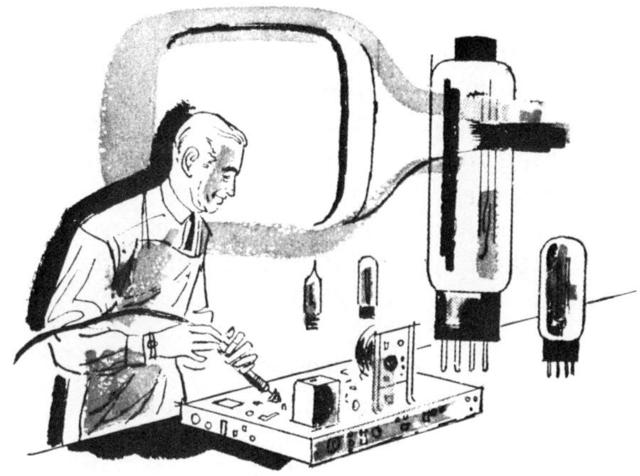

Fig. 4-10 With an irregular design and black surprinting color, an overlay is used for the color copy, registered to the key copy. It is not necessary to provide for ink lap. The overlay method is also used for widely scattered color elements if some of them are surprinted.

Copy in One Piece

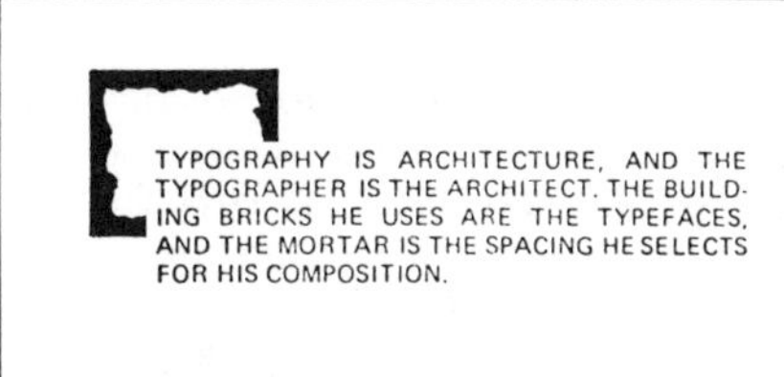

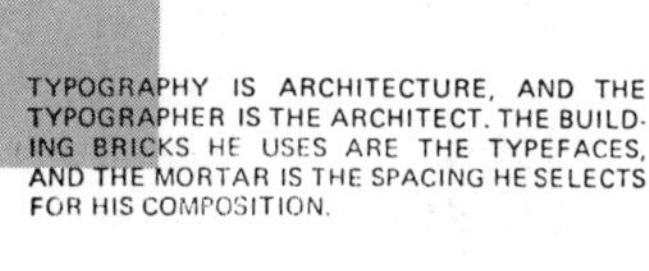

Fig. 4-11 With regular-shaped color designs formed by using a straightedge or a compass, copy can be prepared in one piece with a gap. The platemaker makes two negatives or positives, one for each color. Guided by a tissue overlay or dummy, the platemaker completes each of them, masking unwanted images or type.

Color Areas Outlined; Edge Surprinted

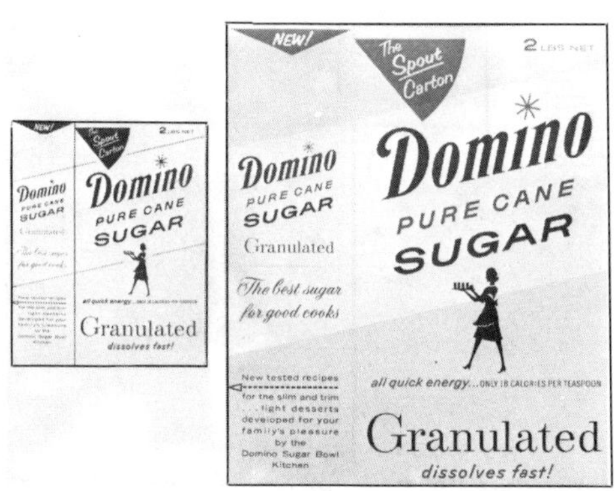

Fig. 4-12 With larger color areas, boundaries are frequently outlined without opaquing. If surprinting extends outside a regular-shaped boundary, a gap in the line permits camera copy for the image surprinting in dark color. On the negative of the background color, the platemaker completes the line as illustrated with the woman and the reversed element above.

Platemakers now use masking film instead of opaquing an area. In this case, copy permitted reverses in red, the type and the woman in dark blue, and the background color in yellow. The yellow would probably be handled with masking film on the positive, and from this the contact negative. Color boundary lines should be in red or be marked: "Drop line."

1. Loose register, which is used for spot color (not touching) and for surprinting black on a color area.

2. Lap register, which is used for register of touching flat color opaque inks. For the better grades of printing the lap is about 1/64 inch, and for commercial-grade printing 1/32 inch in offset. For letterpress and rotogravure, the lap is generally 1/32 inch and 1/16 inch respectively.

3. Hairline register, used when simple color transparent inks touch in color register. A form of keylining provides a fine line common to both touching colors, resulting in a very fine lap of inks. The width of the line determines the ink lap.

The methods of preparing copy for each of the three types of flat color register are discussed and illustrated below.

Loose Register

This type is illustrated in the examples of the overlay and copy-in-one piece methods shown in Figs. 4-10, 4-11, and 4-12.

Lap Register

This is the most widely used type of color register for commercial printing. The width of the ink lap of colors that touch depends on the type of ink used, the colors, and the grade of printing. For commercial-grade work the lap is about 1/32 inch.

With lap register of touching colors, the production artist begins to show his skill and knowledge, for his job is to prepare camera-ready copy in such a form that for most work platemaking costs will be held to a minimum. This means that, insofar as is practical, the artist's camera copy should avoid the need for manual operations by the platemaker or engraver.

If the overlay method is handled accurately, it saves money. Often, however, the work is not accurate. Sometimes a nonstable film has been used, and it shrinks. This usually entails extra charges not provided for in the quotation for a job—trouble the producer does not want.

LAP REGISTER

Overlay Method

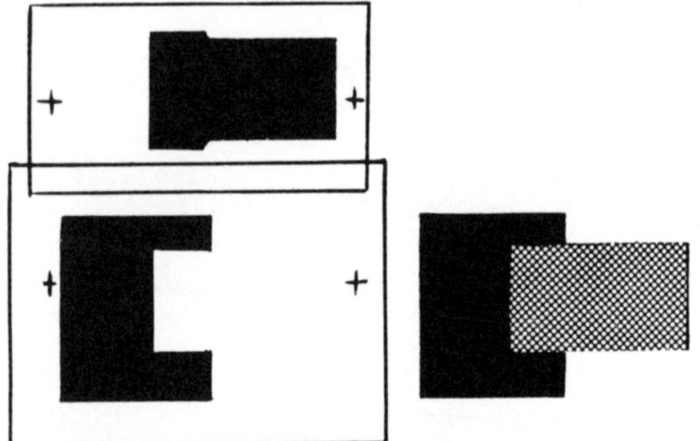

Fig. 4-13 Lap register by the overlay method is used mostly to save money on plate costs, since register of touching colors is provided for in the camera copy. For copy involving more than black and one color, this method requires accuracy to avoid leaks where colors do not lap because of the shrinkage of paper or overlay material. Its use is generally confined to small-size jobs printed in groups, as in Copy Examples 12 and 13 in Chapter 5.

The artist handling preseparated colors for illustrations uses the overlay method but generally works in 2 to 4 times size. This procedure gives a holding line of at least 1/16 inch, making it easy to bring color images into the line for irregular register.

Copy in One Piece

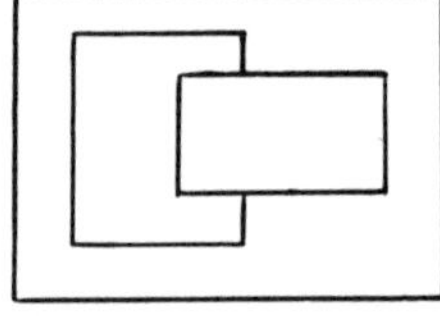

Fig. 4-14 The copy above in regular-shaped register of touching colors just gives the boundary, or holding, lines of two touching color areas; composition and Photostat reverses can be positioned within them for any surprinting or reversed elements. On the photographic positive film, the platemaker strips in the red masking film for the flat color areas for each color press plate. The holding lines where the two colors touch are common to both colors and determine the width of the ink lap. The register is very accurate.

Fig. 4-15 The example with a woman introduces a keylining technique used for colors registering in an irregular shape or for a reversed black into color. The background color is opaqued (or masking-filmed) to 1/8 inch of the inserted image; this signals the platemaker: "Colors touch; provide for register." Keylining is covered in Copy Examples 9 and 10.

The overlay is safest when a dark color or black laps a light color with opaque inks because the lap can be broader without showing. Copy Example 8 (Figs. 4-17 and 4-18) could have been prepared with an overlay, but the experienced designer used copy in one piece for accuracy, and the platemaker did not require much time to prepare the positive for blue with masking film on the positive. Copy Examples 9 and 10 (Figs. 4-37 and 4-38) were also handled with lap register, the former in three colors and black requiring surprinting of type on red and register of colors inserted into red. Opaque inks were used.

In national advertising, all parts of an advertising campaign should be integrated with the publication ads. A standard method uses one or two key illustrations from the full-color publication advertising to make it pay off to its fullest extent. As a result, all incidentally illustrative treatment of collateral printing—window displays, posters, direct mail, informative literature—must be printed with transparent inks. These inks require a different form of color register even though the incidental color treatment may be simple color work. This treatment is covered below in the section on hairline register.

One-Piece Copy Advocated by Platemakers for Simple Color

Offset printers with color strippers advocate avoiding the use of an overlay when practicable for simple color work. Copy Example 8, like Copy Example 7, illustrates the method of merely drawing boundary lines for color areas and tints in red (temporary holding lines). If a line is drawn in black and is not to be held, note on the tissue: "Drop line." The opaquing of copy to ⅛ inch of the holding line is discarded. Copy to appear in black, such as the "Lithographic Forum" square reverse on the mechanical, is done in black.

From the mechanical shown, the printer

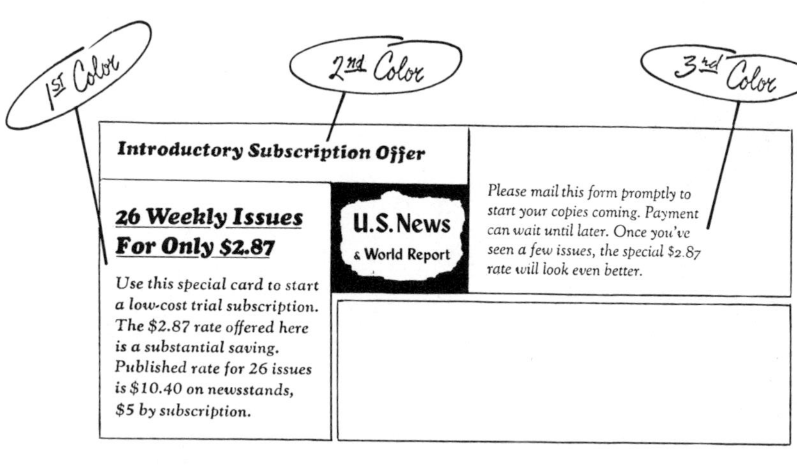

Lap Register Provided on Copy Merely with Lines

Fig. 4-16 This very simple example shows how lap register is handled merely with holding lines: the artist cuts the masking film halfway into the line for both touching colors. The width of the line determines the width of the ink lap. To lap the color under the reverse, the artist cuts the masking film for a 1/32-inch lap. If the mechanical artist does not use masking film, a tissue overlay shows what is wanted, and the printer's stripper will use the mask on the color positive.

Type to surprint is trimmed with a wavy edge and pasted in position on the mask or area. For a reverse a Photostat negative is trimmed with a wavy edge and positioned by the artist.

COPY EXAMPLE 8

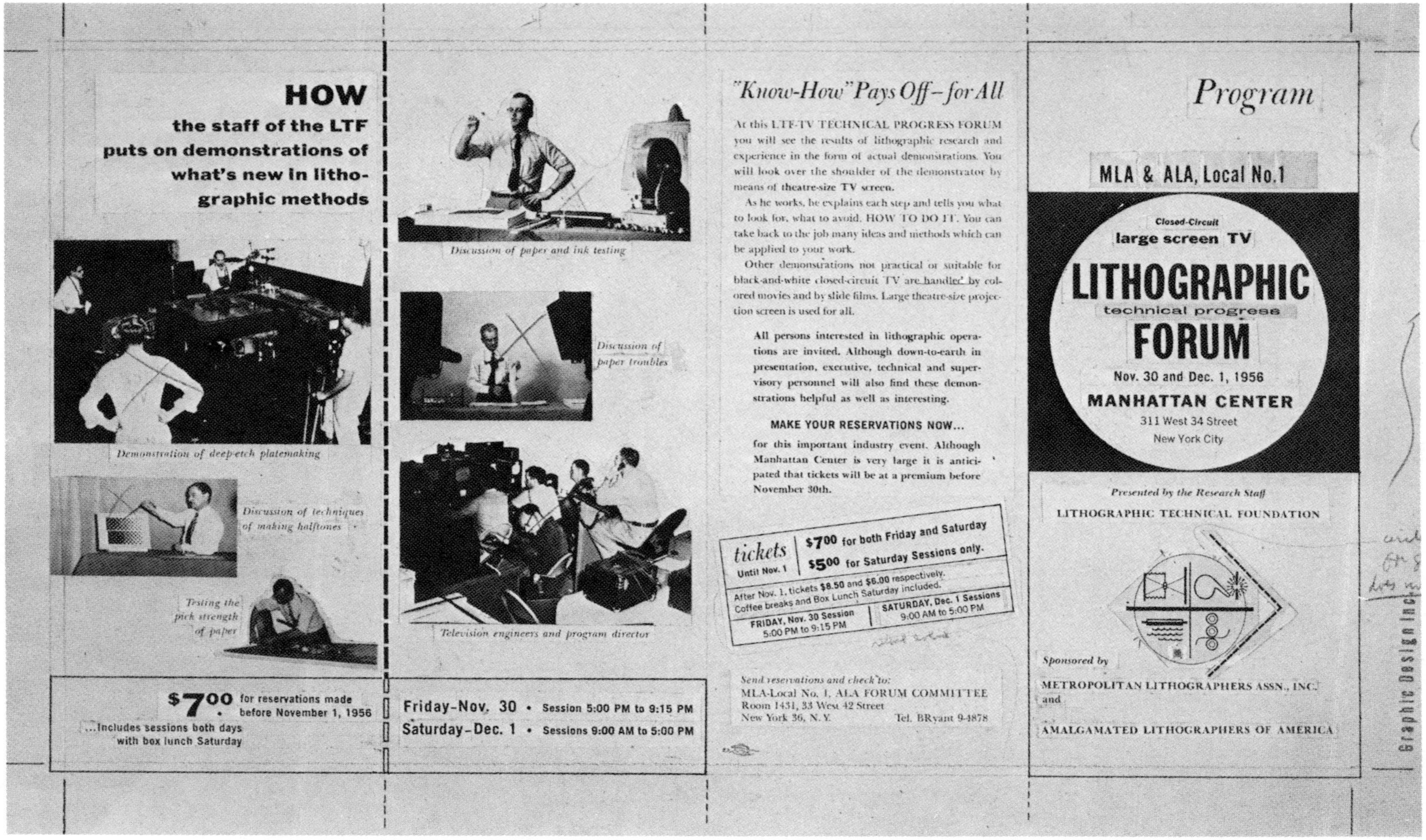

HOW
the staff of the LTF puts on demonstrations of what's new in lithographic methods

Demonstration of deep-etch platemaking

Discussion of techniques of making halftones

Testing the pick strength of paper

$7.00 for reservations made before November 1, 1956
...Includes sessions both days with box lunch Saturday

Discussion of paper and ink testing

Discussion of paper troubles

Television engineers and program director

Friday-Nov. 30 • Session 5:00 PM to 9:15 PM
Saturday-Dec. 1 • Sessions 9:00 AM to 5:00 PM

"Know-How" Pays Off–for All

At this LTF-TV TECHNICAL PROGRESS FORUM you will see the results of lithographic research and experience in the form of actual demonstrations. You will look over the shoulder of the demonstrator by means of theatre-size TV screen.

As he works, he explains each step and tells you what to look for, what to avoid, HOW TO DO IT. You can take back to the job many ideas and methods which can be applied to your work.

Other demonstrations not practical or suitable for black-and-white closed-circuit TV are handled by colored movies and by slide films. Large theatre-size projection screen is used for all.

All persons interested in lithographic operations are invited. Although down-to-earth in presentation, executive, technical and supervisory personnel will also find these demonstrations helpful as well as interesting.

MAKE YOUR RESERVATIONS NOW...

for this important industry event. Although Manhattan Center is very large it is anticipated that tickets will be at a premium before November 30th.

tickets Until Nov. 1 | $7.00 for both Friday and Saturday | $5.00 for Saturday Sessions only.
After Nov. 1, tickets $8.50 and $6.00 respectively. Coffee breaks and Box Lunch Saturday included.
FRIDAY, Nov. 30 Session 5:00 PM to 9:15 PM | SATURDAY, Dec. 1 Sessions 9:00 AM to 5:00 PM

Send reservations and check to:
MLA-Local No. 1, ALA FORUM COMMITTEE
Room 1431, 33 West 42 Street
New York 36, N. Y. Tel. BRyant 9-4878

Program

MLA & ALA, Local No. 1

Closed-Circuit
large screen TV
LITHOGRAPHIC
technical progress
FORUM
Nov. 30 and Dec. 1, 1956
MANHATTAN CENTER
311 West 34 Street
New York City

Presented by the Research Staff
LITHOGRAPHIC TECHNICAL FOUNDATION

Sponsored by
METROPOLITAN LITHOGRAPHERS ASSN., INC.
and
AMALGAMATED LITHOGRAPHERS OF AMERICA

Graphic Design Inc

One-Piece Mechanical for Two Colors, with Tissue Overlay Indicating Color and Surprinting

Fig. 4-17 Here is another example of camera copy for black and one color prepared without the use of an overlay for color copy, as is typical of contemporary procedures adopted to avoid bad register and hand opaquing. The boundaries of color areas and tint panels were drawn in red, indicating: "Drop line." Lines to be held, such as the box under the blue "ticket" panel, were drawn in black. The circle around the offset symbol was marked "Drop line" on the tissue overlay. *X*'s on the tone elements (Photostate) mean "For position and subject only." Photos were supplied as separate elements for reduction.

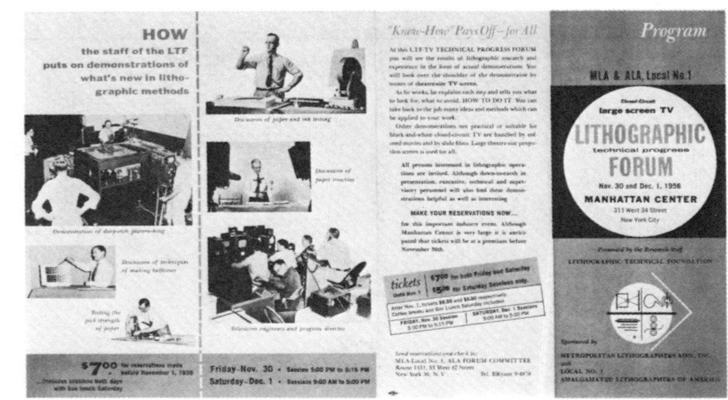

Fig. 4-18

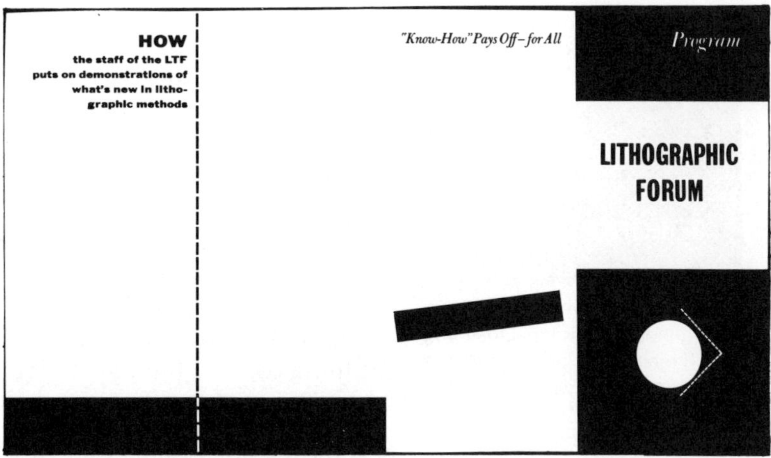

Fig. 4-19 Positive prepared for blue.

Fig. 4-20 Positive prepared for black.

The two positives made by the printer from the mechanical of Copy Example 8.

made two negatives. Guided by the tissue overlay for color breakup, the printer prepared one for the color and the other for the black and also provided for reverse or surprinting of type. The two films shown are positives used for deep-etch press plates. A contact print of a positive gives a negative film.

With this particular example—black and a light blue—the only touching colors were the blue above and below the square reverse. For color register the stripper merely provided for a 1/32-inch lap under the black when the masking film was cut. For the tint areas on the ticket information, the stripper cut along the line when preparing the positive for blue.

There are copy problems that require the use of the overlay method; these are described in Chapter 5. If the overlay method is accurate, however, it can reduce plate charges. It is often used for a series of small pieces printed as a unit, as in Copy Example 13.

A Keyline Technique Is Used for Hairline Register

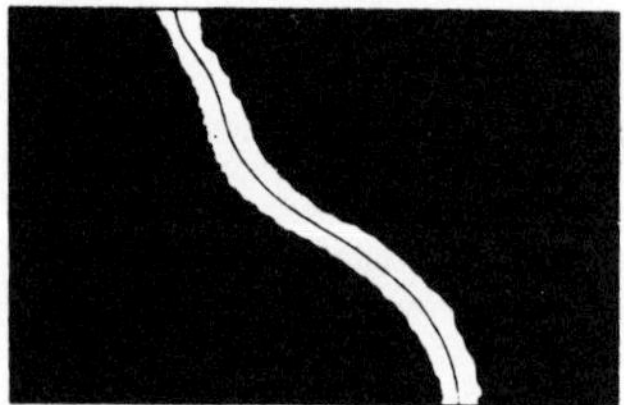

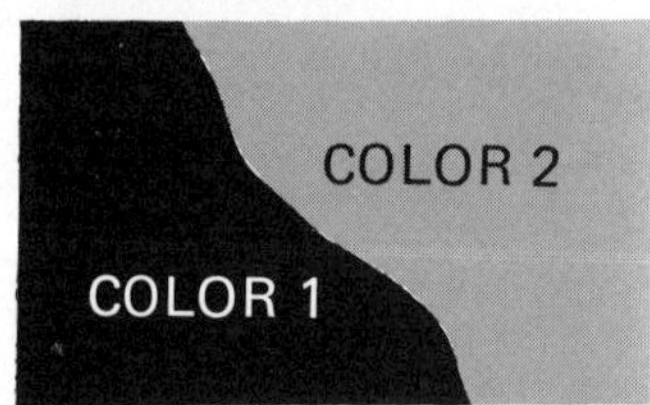

Fig. 4-21 A fine line is drawn where two colors touch; its width determines the ink lap. Opaquing with a wavy edge to ⅛ inch of the line signals the platemaker: "Colors touch; provide for register." (See also Copy Example 11.) Masking film has largely replaced brush-opaquing.

Copy Prepared for the Use of Photographic Spread or Masking Film

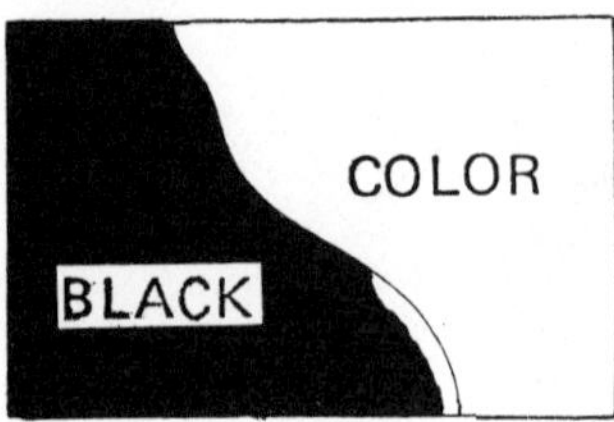

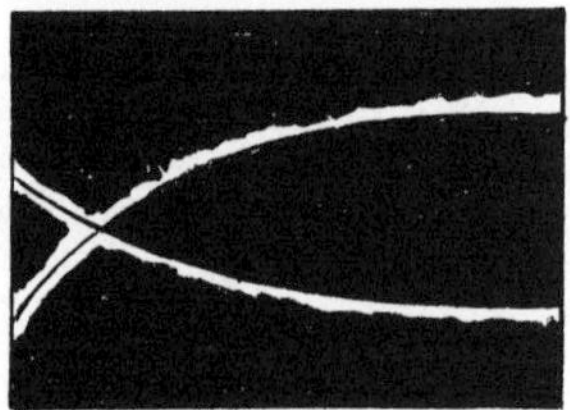

Fig. 4-22 Camera copy is prepared here in a variation of hairline register. For black or a dark color, paint or mask up to the line, and merely outline the boundary of the color area if there are only two colors. If more than two colors are to register, mask or opaque each up to ⅛ inch of the line, as shown.

This form of copy is suitable for the platemaker's use of either "photographic spread" or masking film. The platemaker will paint up to the line of selected color areas, depending on which color is to lap under, according to the sequence of printing the colors.

Provision for Color Lap Unnecessary for Type Matter

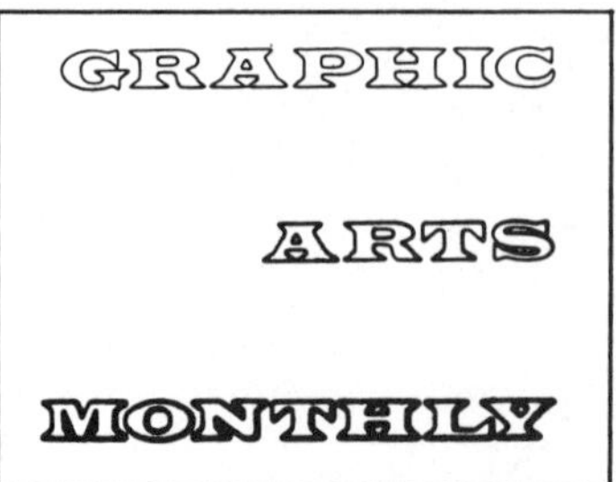

Fig. 4-23 This example illustrates how type can be "spread" by the camera to give a lap for color register. Other methods are used by the printer for some types of production.

Hairline Register

This type of register, which is required with transparent inks, uses only the one-piece copy method. When simple color printing is handled with transparent inks, often because the main artwork of a campaign is in process color, the lap of registered colors must be very fine to avoid a noticeable secondary color from the lap. To get such a fine lap of touching colors, particularly for an irregular shape, a keylining copy technique is used, as illustrated in Fig. 4-21. The fine holding line is common to both colors in this example, and its width therefore determines the amount of ink lap.

Headlines in Color on a Dark Background

Frequently display type or lettering in color is placed on a dark background color. To get contrast for visibility and to avoid a possible secondary color by surprinting, a silhouette of the type or lettering is removed from the background by the printer so that the type color will go on white paper to get the reflection for contrast. Any necessary lap of inks is handled by the platemaker, who takes care of this problem in the camera operation or in exposing the flats for the press plate. The type matter is handled on an overlay for position.

KEYLINING COPY TECHNIQUES

"Keylining" is a rather ambiguous term that refers to methods of preparing copy for the camera in one piece—techniques that not only provide the camera copy but avoid complicated copy preparation by indicating and facilitating operations to be completed by the platemaker, usually for flat-color work. Keylining is used by all the printing processes for copy in paste-up form. We shall see how these copy methods signal the platemaker: "Colors touch; provide for register," "This element surprints," or "Reverse this element."

Keylining is actually an old trick of the trade. The techniques go back to early stone color lithography in which outlines of the art to be reproduced were traced and then transferred to the various litho

Fig. 4-24 The line element is positioned, and the background is opaqued to ⅛ inch of the element with a wavy edge to the opaquing. This provides camera copy for the element and signals the platemaker: "Colors touch; provide for register."

stones to key the design for each color. A black crayon transfer key was reproduced; the width of the line was common to both touching colors and provided the amount of color lap desirable for register. A red key outline, made with dragon's blood powder, was not reproduced and so served only as a temporary guideline for the litho artist, a copyist. Today, therefore, in copy preparation a line in black is held, while the platemaker understands that a line in red is a temporary guideline. Although the red line is picked up by the camera and shows on the negative, it is not held after work has been completed.

The litho artists and transfer men completed the work indicated for each color stone; they reversed elements, touched in backgrounds, completed work for the key lines, provided for type and designs to surprint, and so on, using their craft skills in the steps between the designer's stones and transfer proofs and the large press stones.

When process photoengraving first came into commercial use, lithographic craftsmen were hired by the engravers because they were the only printers experienced with color. These men naturally applied many of their litho techniques to the new photographic methods, working on negatives or positives instead of on stones. Work was added or removed to complete the images for each color.

The preparation of copy in paste-up form for the camera gradually moved from the art department of the litho producer to the user's advertising and production departments, and the keylining copy techniques accompanied the transfer of this

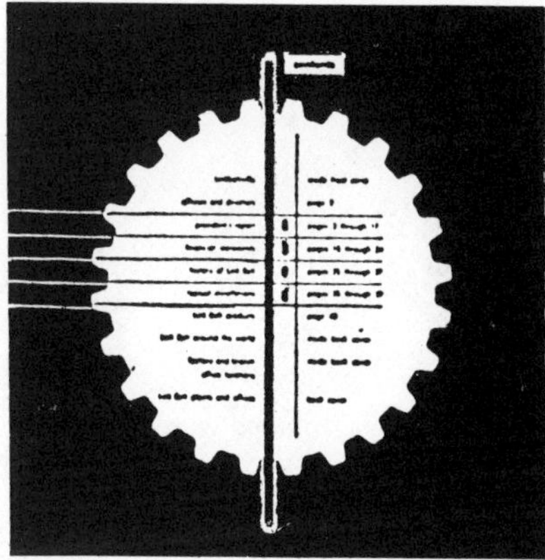

Fig. 4-25 This keylining technique was used in Copy Example 10 to handle the vertical black bar extending into the light blue background. Actually, the platemaker used a loose register and merely surprinted the black on the blue. If the choice of inks had made it necessary, copy provided for lap register.

Fig. 4-26 Another application of this keylining technique is shown in Copy Example 9 to register the woman's head and shoulders into a red background. The tissue overlay indicated that the woman's dress was blue; the keylining also registered this.

A negative is made for each color, and the platemaker provides for the color register.

Keylining around Type Matter on an Opaqued Area Means "Surprint on the Color"

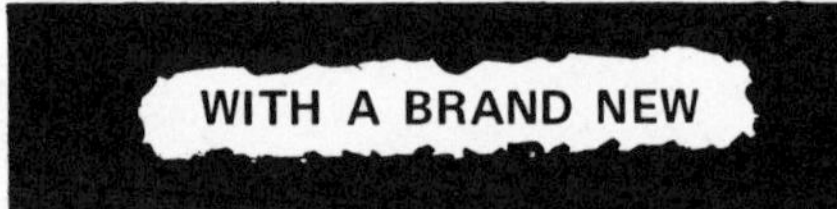

Fig. 4-27 Copy Example 9 contains the line "With a brand new" in black on a red background, with the copy handled as shown here. This provided camera copy for the type in black, and the platemaker merely filled in the white area when completing the negative for the red plate.

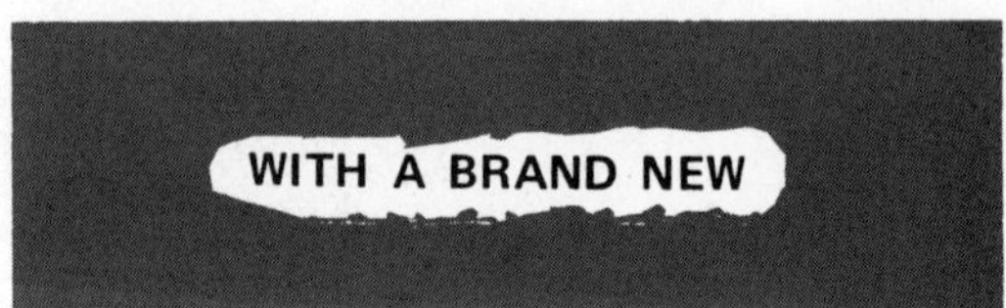

Fig. 4-28 When masking film is used instead of brush-opaquing, the type to surprint is merely pasted on the film.

A Reversed Element to Go on Color Is Keylined as Shown

Fig. 4-29 A reversed design with an outline in white is trimmed with a wavy edge as shown and positioned on the color area, thus simplifying the provision for color register. See also Copy Example 10.

Both Reversing and Surprinting Are Handled by Copy in One Piece

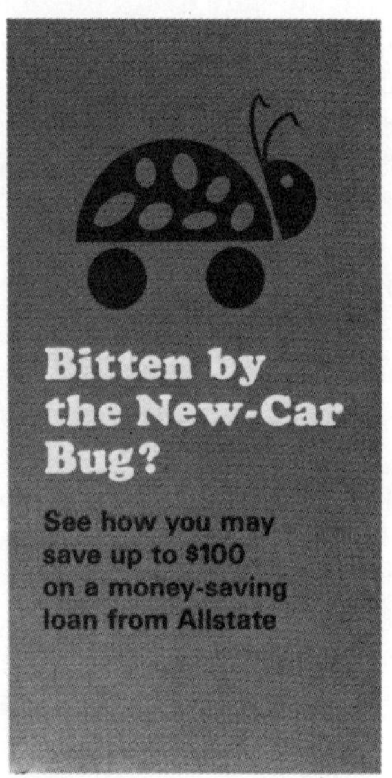

Fig. 4-30 The camera copy on the left will be sufficient for the platemaker for both black and a second color with reversed type. Such copy may be handled in several ways. In the simplest way the negative for black would have the reversed type masked, and for the color a strip masking film would be placed over the whole area to the boundary lines, the film being removed from the reversed element (positive of type). If the holding line is in black, note: "Drop line."

ORDER YOUR COPY NOW!

These actual pages serve as your introduction to the new, 1971 Ayer Directory — bigger, more complete than ever before!

● If you have never used the Ayer Directory you owe it to yourself, and to your organization, to buy one now.

● If you have an old copy of the Directory, update your Information Center now with the new, 1971 Ayer Directory.

$42 plus 63c postage and handling, within the U.S.

Fig. 4-31 Color or tint panels can merely be drawn with red boundary lines, but sometimes they are keylined inside lines as shown here. The tissue overlay gives the instructions. A Photostat negative can handle the reverse.

Surprinting or Reversing Type or Design on a Color Panel

Keylining Used Occasionally to Indicate a Reversed Headline

Fig. 4-32 Most reversed copy elements are handled on the mechanical by positioning a Photostat negative or ruling in the edges and marking: "Reverse this element."

A Keyline Technique Is Used to Insert a Regular-shaped Color Element into a Halftone Area

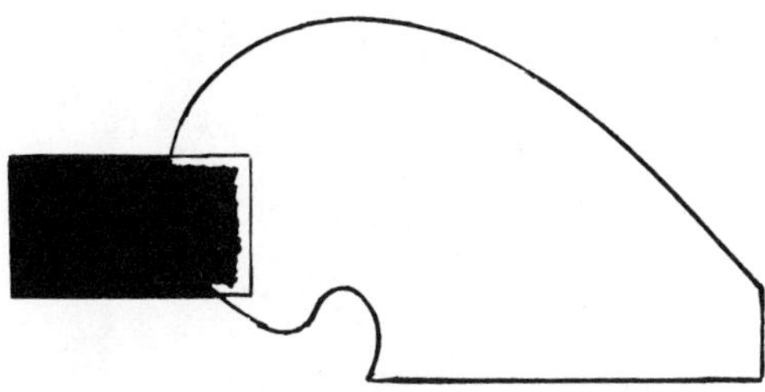

Fig. 4-33 Where color touches a halftone, draw a fine line on tone copy; insert color element, keylined on the color side of the line.

work to the user. In some areas the producer still does the copy preparation for many of his customers or for specialized forms of production.

The techniques described below demonstrate the usual keylining applications, with reference to copy examples in which these techniques have been used. As mentioned in the section "Color Register," the kind of ink and its color have much to do with the provision for color lap and have a bearing on the preparation of keylined copy.

INSERTING A LINE ELEMENT INTO FLAT COLOR

The artist should understand that the keyline technique is used for accuracy in color register and that the time will be charged. When registering color to a black line, such as the dome in Fig. 4-24, keyline copy and the platemaker will provide for register. No keylining is necessary to register to black reverse, but the artist can cut the masking film for flat color and allow 1/16 inch to lap under the reverse.

How to Handle Copy for Shadow Lettering

RIGHT   WRONG

Fig. 4-34 A common error with headlines in color, whether type or lettering, is to outline the black shadow areas. Just the opposite should be done. If the shadow is also a color, keyline where the colors touch.

What Is a Knockout?

The Overlay

The Knockout

Fig. 4-35 One form of what a platemaker terms a "knockout." A knockout may be just a line, as in Copy Example 7, or reversed type or lettering, but usually it is an irregular tone element to be inserted into a background—flat color or halftone. A scaled positive of the element contact-printed with a negative of the background gives the platemaker an exact outline for color register.

A dropout is an area of copy not wanted in the reproduction and not replaced.

An Irregular Tone Element Inserted in a Color Background; No Provision for Register Required

Pencil sketch on tissue overlay for size and position.

Fig. 4-36 Scaled tone element positioned on an overlay. Usually the tone element is not in scale; so a pencil sketch is used for size and position.

COPY EXAMPLE 9

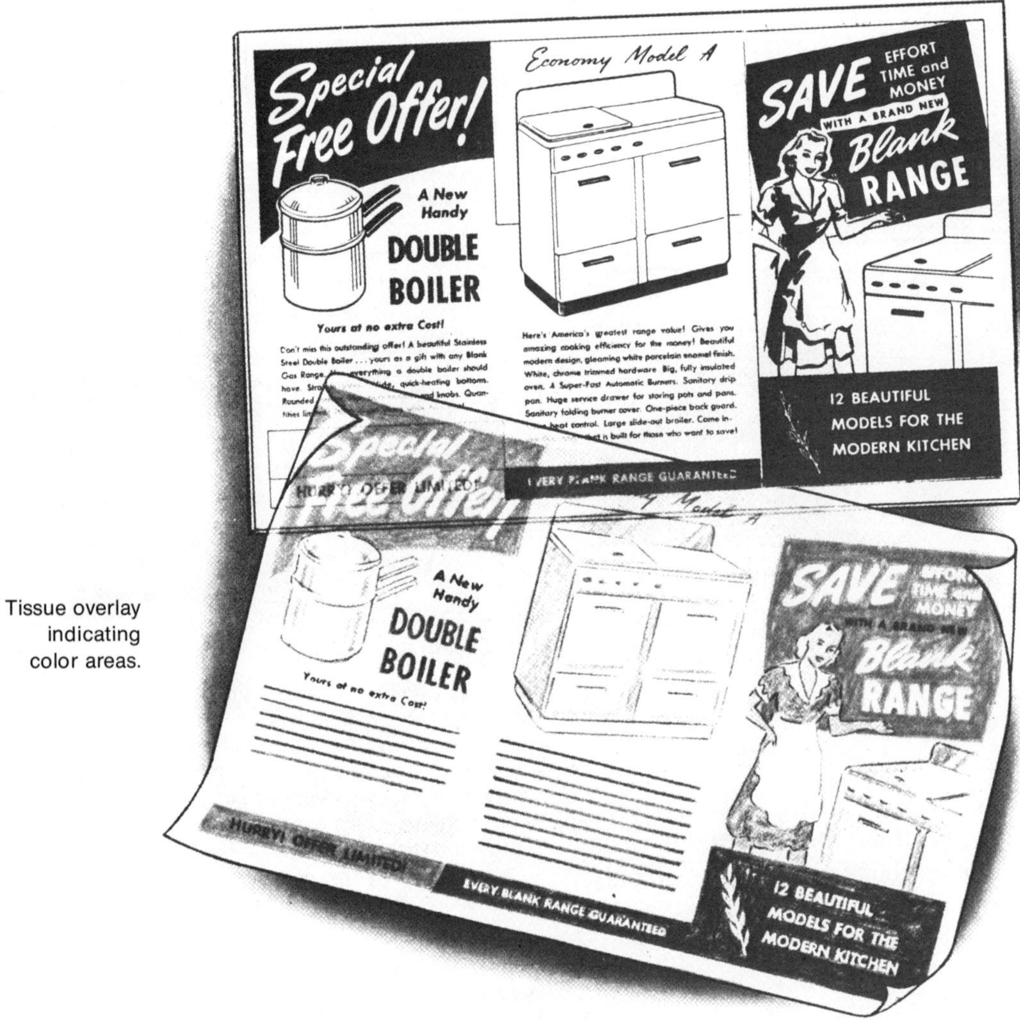

Tissue overlay indicating color areas.

Fig. 4-37 [*Courtesy Stecher-Traung Litho. Corp.*]

SIMPLE FOUR-COLOR PRINTING PREPARED WITH COPY IN ONE PIECE

Copy Example 9 (Fig. 4-37) shows how copy for four color's can be prepared in one piece, using Photostat reversed panels and a red outline for color boundaries. The reversed panels, "Free Offer" and "Save," and the strip outlined at bottom left were printed in red. The background behind the stove, woman, and "Save" panel and the panel just above the red at bottom left were printed in yellow. Type for "12 Beautiful Models for the Modern Kitchen" was also printed in yellow against the blue of the panel at bottom right. Notice how the "With a brand new" type in the "Save" panel was keylined to indicate that it was to surprint, and observe the keylining technique used for registering the woman's head and shoulders and the blue of her dress to the red panel.

This method of preparing simple three- and four-color copy for commercial printing is more accurate for color register than the overlay method, and it avoids the cost of artwork and expensive process color separation.

COPY EXAMPLE 10

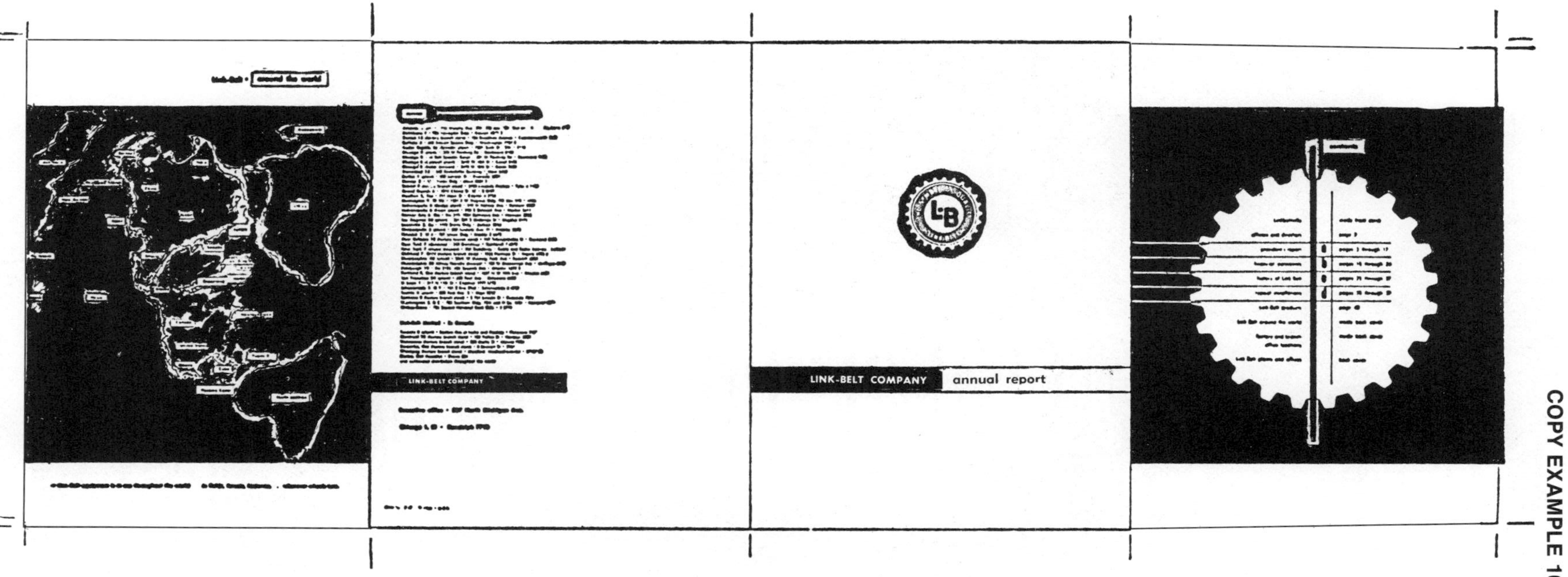

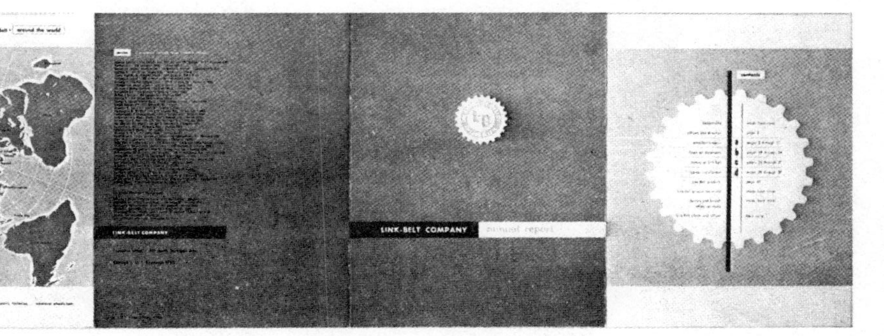

This Example Uses Many Previously Demonstrated Techniques

Fig. 4-38 This gatefold cover in black and two colors was prepared as copy in one piece by using keylining for color register and surprinting type on color. The reversed line element was handled against the color background. Radial white lines on the ocean were handled by a knockout overlay (not shown). A brown-red background was used in front and back; blue was used for the ocean on the left gatefold and for background on the right gatefold. The vertical black bar on the right was keylined for lap register to light blue. Actually, the printer used a loose register and surprinted the black on color to achieve the same result.

COPY EXAMPLE 11

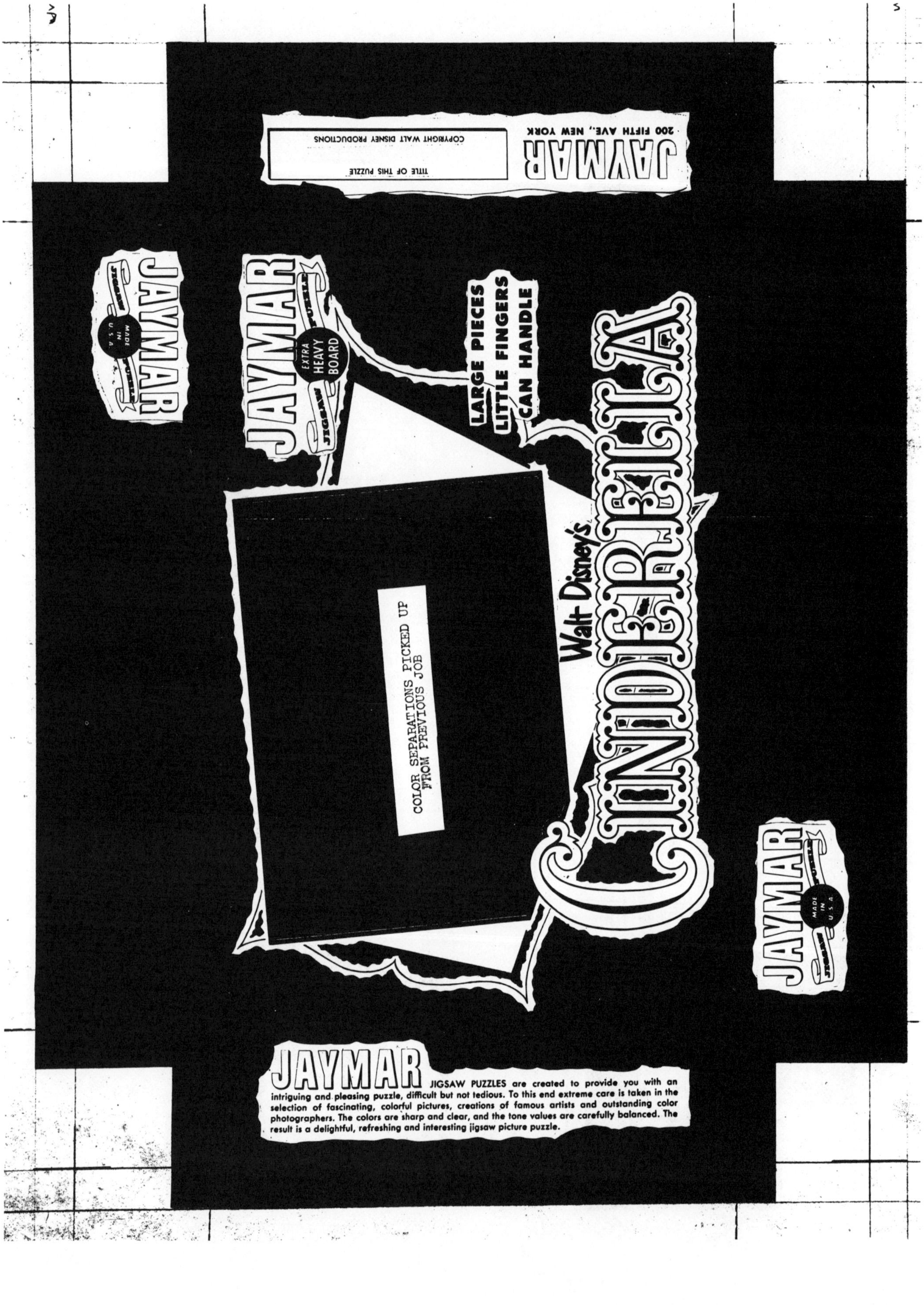

JAYMAR 200 FIFTH AVE., NEW YORK

COPYRIGHT WALT DISNEY PRODUCTIONS

TITLE OF THIS PUZZLE

JAYMAR JIGSAW PUZZLE MADE IN U.S.A.

JAYMAR JIGSAW PUZZLE EXTRA HEAVY BOARD

LARGE PIECES
LITTLE FINGERS
CAN HANDLE

Walt Disney's CINDERELLA

COLOR SEPARATIONS PICKED UP
FROM PREVIOUS JOB

JAYMAR JIGSAW PUZZLE MADE IN U.S.A.

JAYMAR JIGSAW PUZZLES are created to provide you with an intriguing and pleasing puzzle, difficult but not tedious. To this end extreme care is taken in the selection of fascinating, colorful pictures, creations of famous artists and outstanding color photographers. The colors are sharp and clear, and the tone values are carefully balanced. The result is a delightful, refreshing and interesting jigsaw picture puzzle.

Fig. 4-39 Box wrap: hairline color register by keylining.

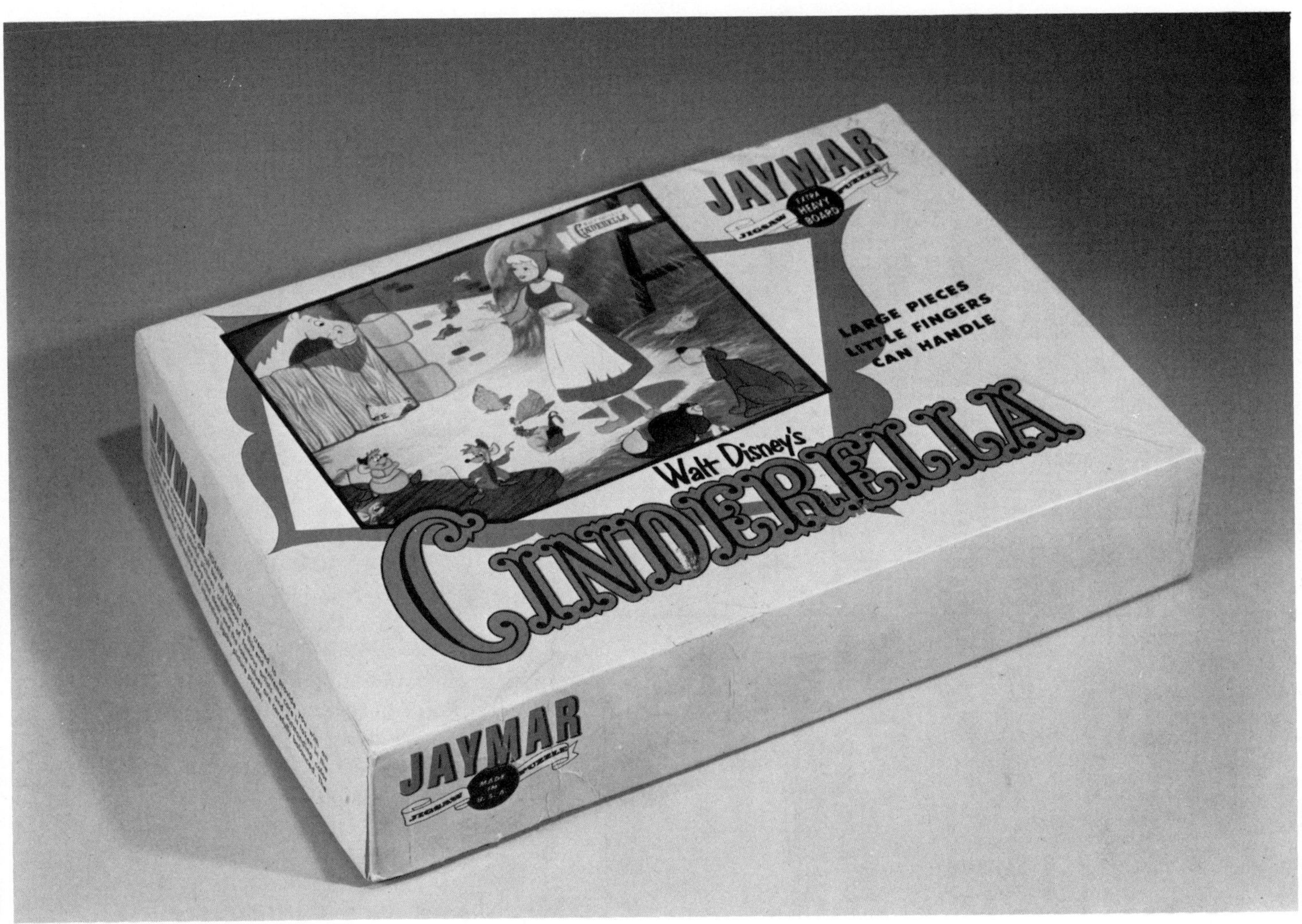

Simple Color Design Often Supplements Process Art or Plates on Hand

Fig. 4-40 Hairline register used for transparent inks; overall color a light yellow, surprinted and registered for both hairline and lap of "Cinderella" in dark color; surprinted with black.

This example happens to be a box wrap that used a pickup of color separations from a previous job. Hairline register is used principally for collateral advertising materials that are integrated with publication ads by means of key process color illustrations—a standard and effective method. The offset process is generally used because of its capability of enlarging or reducing and converting process photoengravings and gravure separations, thus avoiding duplication of process color costs. Collateral materials usually require supplementary simple color design.

CHECKING PRINT PROOFS BEFORE PLATES ARE MADE

The paste-up artist should see proofs of unit negatives before press plates are made. In offset printing, various types of photoprints—blueprints, brownline prints, diazo prints, silver prints from halftone negatives for black dots—are made from the negatives and positives of copy units or of a complete job so that the work may be checked before plates are made. Brownline prints are chemically treated blueprints, made if reproduction copy is wanted.

Ink Rollers

Black

Split-Color Roller

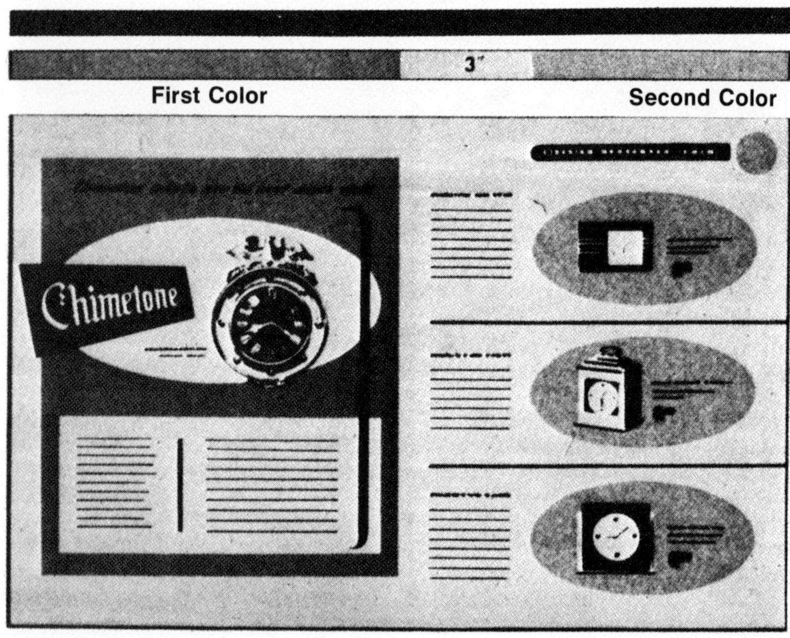
3"
First Color
Second Color
Chimetone

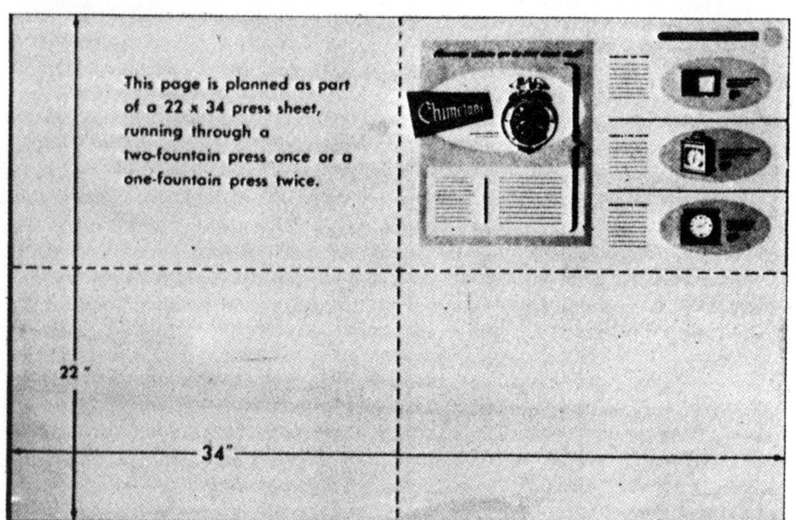
This page is planned as part of a 22 x 34 press sheet, running through a two-fountain press once or a one-fountain press twice.
22"
34"

DESIGNING FOR SPLIT-FOUNTAIN WORK

Fig. 4-41 In this illustration the bars at the top represent the ink rollers of the press. The separation between ink colors never need be more than 3 inches; for color tints, the separation can be as narrow as 1¼ inches. [*Information from Dayton Rubber Company, Dayco M-C Division, Dayton, Ohio*]

For all but the simplest work blueprints should be ordered and checked by the paste-up artist to make sure that no elements have been detached from the paste-up, that separate elements are positioned correctly, and that reverses and other work have been carried out by the platemaker. If the proof is correct, plates are made.

For booklets, catalogs, and the like photoprints of the flat are made and folded into a dummy to check imposition, margins, and simple color breakup, particularly subheads in color. Two colors on the same photoprint are handled by separate exposures of each flat: a longer exposure for a dark print and a shorter exposure for colors. To check exact measurements or fit, as for a book jacket or catalog cover, wet blueprints are used, for the paper shrinks when it is dried.

Prints of separate copy elements, termed "loose" blueprints, are sometimes used by the layout artist to determine position, for example, the placement of a title or headline on a design. The pages of Christmas or fashion catalogs may be laid out with the loose prints of illustrations and type blocks, and the flats stripped to the paste-up of prints as the layout.

To check the quality of a halftone negative made from doubtful copy, a silver print (black on white) is used. A Velox print also is suitable but is more expensive.

PARTIES ARE MORE FUN WITH NO-CAL BEVERAGES

A glass of any of the No-Cal flavors is refreshing and festive. For those who prefer a highball or cocktail, No-Cal makes an extra-dry and tastier mixed drink. The thoughtful person who serves sparkling, delicious No-Cal will soon become the most popular hostess in town.

NO-CAL HIGHBALLS

Prepare 7 or 8 oz. highball glass with ice cubes. Pour 1 oz. rye, bourbon, scotch, rum, brandy or gin over the ice. Serve with twist of lemon, lemon peel and stirrer. Fill with No-Cal Ginger.

NO-CAL SOUR

1 oz. fresh lemon juice; 1 oz. vodka or rye, bourbon, etc.; 1 dash bitters. Shake well and strain into whiskey sour glass. (4 oz.) Fill with No-Cal Ginger. Garnish with cherry and slice of orange.

NO-CAL FRUIT PUNCH

Put cracked ice into 12 oz. goblet. Add: 1 oz. fresh lemon juice, 1 oz. fresh orange juice, 1 oz. pineapple juice. Fill up with No-Cal ginger. Decorate with fruits.

NO-CAL LEMONADE

4 or 5 ice cubes, 1 oz. fresh lemon juice, 1 oz. fresh orange juice. Put above into tall 12 oz. glass and fill with No-Cal ginger. Decorate with fruits. Sip with straws.

Why No-Cal Makes This Valuable Booklet Available to You

The bottlers of No-Cal sincerely hope that this little book will help in bringing you well-being and happiness. You may be assured that we will continue to supply the public with the best in beverages for pleasure and health.

For a complete set of cocktail and highball recipes write to:

SOUTHERN BEVERAGES, INC.
3601 Northwest 55 Street
Miami 47, Florida

16

FOOD FACTS
FOR
FUN AND HEALTH

By **LUCILE H. PARKER**

NATIONALLY KNOWN NUTRITIONIST

Prepared and produced for NO-CAL Beverages

TWO-COLOR PRINT PROOF; TWO EXPOSURES OF A BLUEPRINT

Fig. 4-42 A blueprint used to check imposition and color breakup. Two flats were exposed on the same blueprint paper. A shorter exposure for the color permitted color identification of the elements.

CHAPTER FIVE

Applications of the Copy Overlay

WE HAVE TOUCHED on the use of the overlay: for combining line and tone copy in a single-color printing; for providing camera copy for a knockout, with the film positive serving as a mask when positioned on a negative for contact-printing; and for handling a design in color that is to be surprinted with black type or design. Figure 4-10 is an example of the last of these uses. Because the black surprints or does not touch the color, color register is not a problem.

The major use of overlays is to provide separate camera copy for color, usually for the copy unit when opaque inks are employed. However, you will find that some mechanicals can be prepared either by the overlay method or by the one-piece–copy method. The overlay method is chosen if plate economies are important, particularly if several small printed pieces are to be prepared as a copy unit, as in Copy Examples 12 and 13 (Figs. 5-5, 5-6, and 5-7), but the artist's work must be accurate; otherwise, charges for corrections will cancel much of the economy.

COLOR REGISTER AND INK LAP

You may recall from Chapter 4 that the overlay method is used only for loose register and lap register. With lap register there must be some ink lap because the paper may expand or shrink in printing. Details for the provision of proper lap in the overlay were presented.

Later in this chapter, in the section "Preseparated Color by the Artist," the use of the overlay in a standard method employed for book illustrations is discussed. In this case there is usually just a holding line, and the lap is halfway into the line. The mechanicals are prepared 1½ to 4 times size to facilitate provision for the lap.

USES OF OVERLAYS WITH COLOR

Generally speaking, overlays with color are employed for the following purposes:

- Irregular color design to be surprinted by black or a dark color (Fig. 4-10). Overlays are not used with transparent inks unless special watercolors keyed to certain inks are worked on thin overlays to obtain secondary colors in design, as in greeting cards.
- Handling color in tone to be surprinted with black or another color (Copy Example 15; Figs. 5-10, 5-11, and 5-12; also Figs. 5-13, 5-14, and 5-15.
- Handling a reverse design or type running across touching colors (Fig.

A carefully prepared layout as rendered by the creative artist.

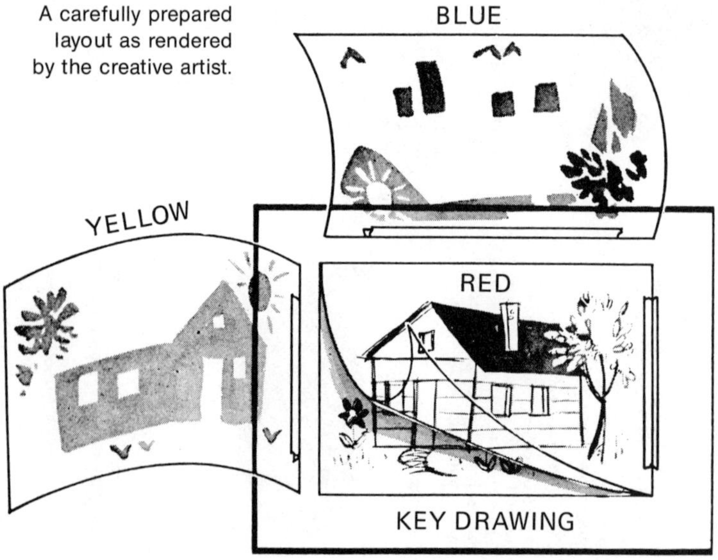

Fig. 5-1 The old flap method of handling overlays shows how copy for each color is prepared on a separate overlay by the artist, who works in black or in grays for tones.

USE OF INDIVIDUAL ELEMENT OVERLAYS

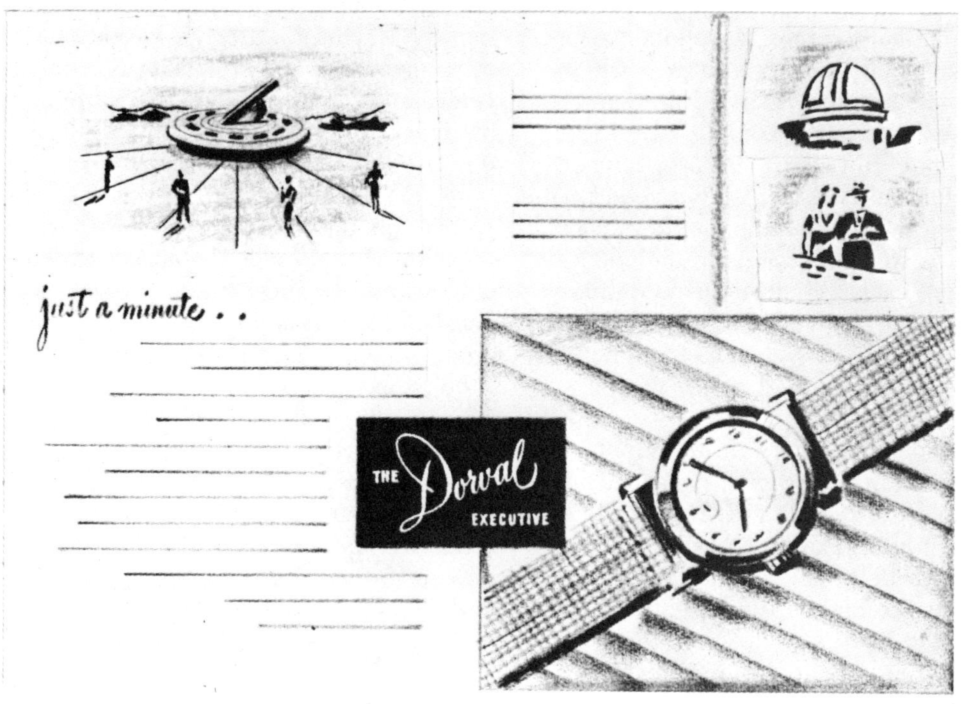

Overlay

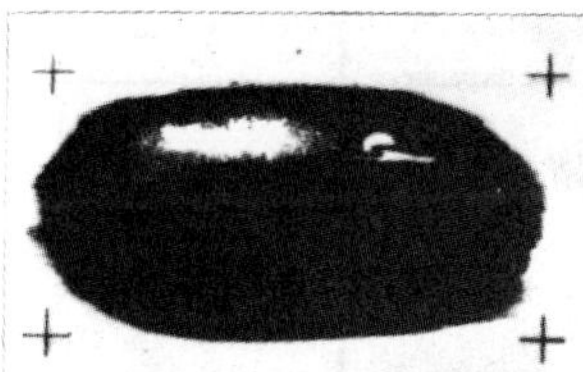

Fig. 5-2 When a color mechanical is large, as for a 25- by 38-inch broadside, separate overlays are usually made for each element carrying a second color. This procedure avoids the danger of the film overlay's shrinking. The platemaker detaches the overlays to photograph them as a group, and the stripper positions them by register marks. [*Courtesy of authors of* How to Prepare Art and Copy for Lithography]

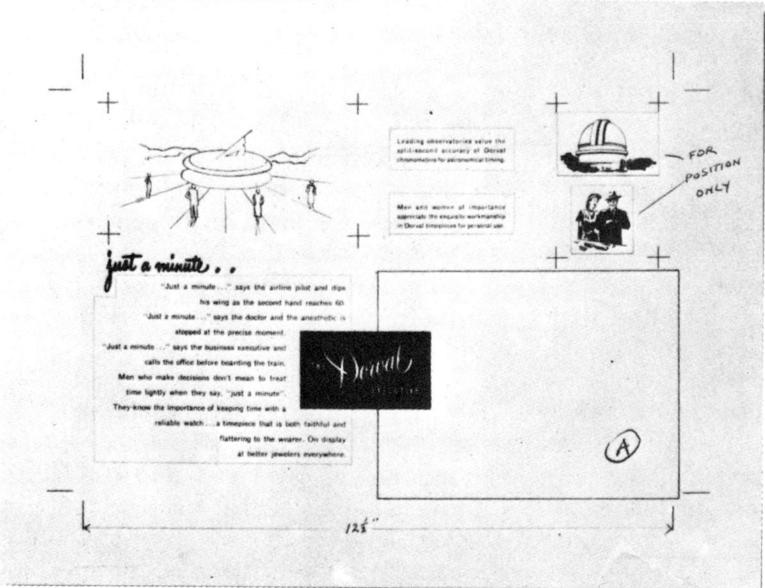

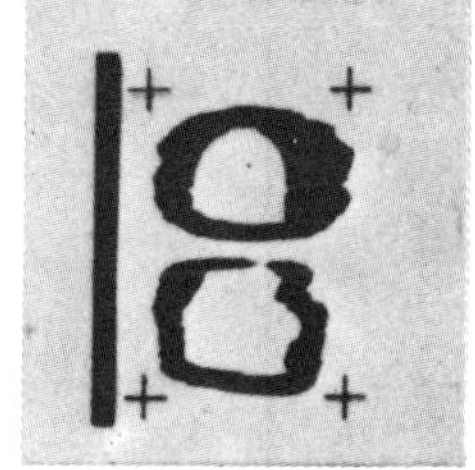

Overlay

Note that register marks are kept close to the copy to save film in group camera work. Two register marks are sufficient with small elements.

5-9). The overlay provides copy for a knockout.

- Individual overlays on elements for large open designs, some of which may be surprinted (Fig. 5-2).
- Supplying camera copy for a multiple halftone tint area: for offset when there is less than 1 inch between two or more tint strengths to allow space for the stripper's tape; for gravure, for which each tint strength is outlined on a separate overlay (Copy Example 21; Figs. 8-6, 8-7, and 8-8). Single tint strength is opaqued on the mechanical.
- Preseparated colors by the artist for illustrations, particularly for children's books and greeting cards. A blueprint of key copy on the film overlay helps to get good lap register (Copy Example 16; Fig. 5-20).
- Saving money on plate costs with loose and lap color register when several small jobs are prepared as a unit on the mechanical (Copy Examples 12 and 13).

Element Overlays

With a large mechanical, such as a 28- by 35-inch broadside, individual overlays on elements are generally used to avoid misregister caused by a shrinkage of the overlay. Keep register marks close to the subject to save film. See Fig. 5-2.

Color Areas on One-Piece Copy

When an artist opaques color areas with copy in one piece, he frequently works in red. Red, which photographs as black, indicates a color area.

Copy Example 14 (Fig. 5-8) includes type overlays for surprinting and reversing type on tone, as handled for gravure. This copy could be used for offset, but usually one positioned type proof would be supplied with the reversed type circled. The producer would make two negatives, opaquing one to leave only type to surprint. On the other negative the producer would opaque all but the type to be reversed and from this make a knockout positive by contact. The rough tissue overlay indicates the final result wanted.

PRESEPARATED COLOR BY THE ARTIST

The principle of mechanical color separation by placing the design for each color on a separate overlay (black or gray tones) is also used by the creative artist for simple forms of color illustrations. The major purpose, particularly for book illustrations, is to avoid the cost of process color plates. Since only a rough color sketch is required for approval, the artist's expense may also be smaller. The procedure goes back to the days of stone lithography, when all paintings were reproduced by litho artists (copyists) who made a key outline of the design, which was transferred to many litho stones, one being required for each ink color in the painting. Guided by the original artwork, the litho artist worked on each stone with litho crayon, tusche, and ink to get the tones and details in black. Many ink colors were necessary because all the pigments were opaque. The Metropolitan Museum of Art in New York has a lithographed reproduction of a watercolor with a proof book showing the nineteen different inks used in its preparation.

The modern procedure, of course, uses separate overlays instead of separate litho stones. Alternatively, an artist using the original stone techniques makes a keylined mechanical signaling the platemaker to complete indicated work and to provide a negative for each color, as shown on the tissue overlay or the dummy.

Procedures in Use

Most colors preseparated by the artist are prepared on film overlays for opaque ink by line copy, including tints and patterns applied by the artist. Any tone copy is put on the mechanical or on a separate overlay. For the illustration in Figs. 5-3 and 5-4, there were a mechanical for the tone and a line overlay for the color.

Guided by the approved rough color sketch, the artist prepares the key copy for the black on illustrator's board, usually proportioning it for size and one-half, a practical work size that facilitates the provisions of any needed color lap. If the illustrations are to be small, as in Copy Example 17 (Fig. 5-21), the work is fre-

PRESEPARATED LINE AND TONE IN COLOR BY THE ARTIST

Book Illustration

Fig. 5-3

Brown (Tone)

Green (Line)

Fig. 5-4 A two-color illustration by Roger Duvoisin for *Bhimsa* by Christine Weston (Charles Scribner's Sons, New York, 1945) was done in watercolor for the brown and with an overlay in flat color for the green. The resulting illustration is shown in a black-and-white halftone. The method used avoided the cost of separating the colors photographically.

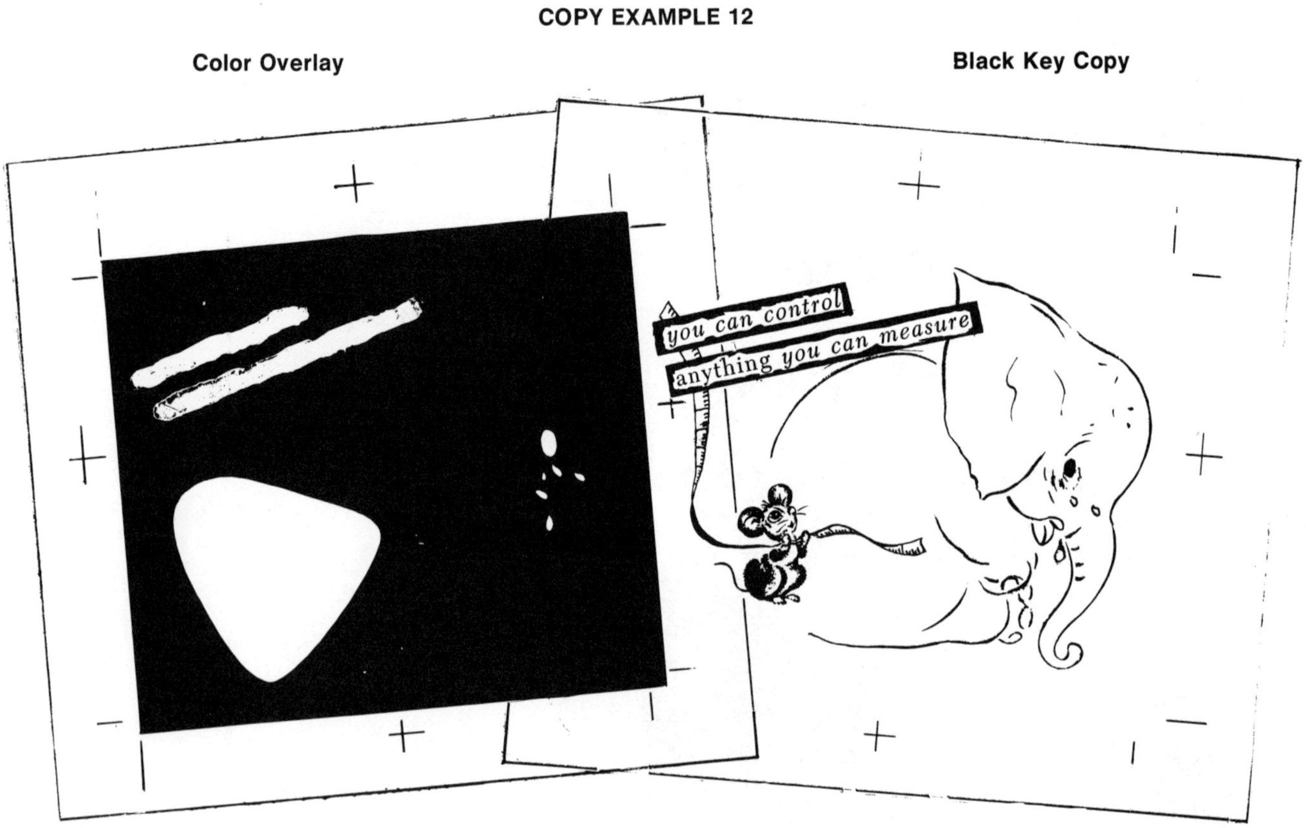

COPY EXAMPLE 12

Color Overlay | **Black Key Copy**

Fig. 5-5

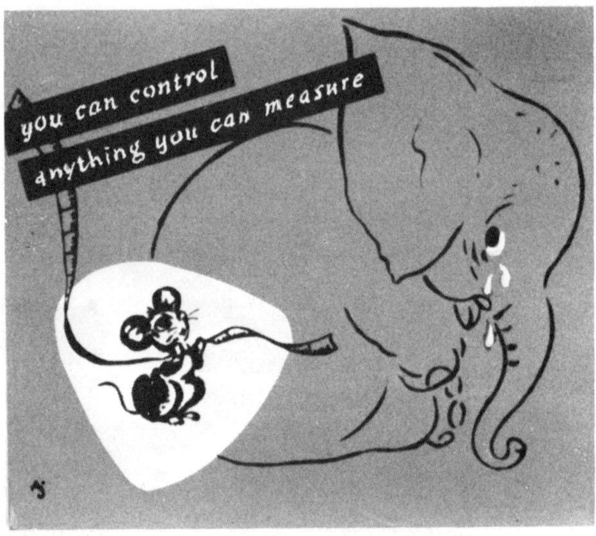

Fig. 5-6

Four Folders Prepared as a Copy Unit; Overlay for the Color

This very simple illustration in line with a background in light green was handled with an overlay for the green. It could have been executed with the copy in one piece and a tissue overlay to show the color area and handling of reversed-type panels, but the four overlays for the color avoided handwork in the platemaking. Since there were four folders, each with the same layout and color and only the front illustration different, the four subjects were handled as a group, and the saving was multiplied by more than 4 times. If the color had been in tone, however, the use of the overlay would have been the only method of handling the job.

COPY EXAMPLE 13

COPY FOR FIVE SMALL FOLDERS PREPARED AS A UNIT

Second imposition on this half of the press sheet.

The five folders, measuring 5½ by 3⅜ inches with one fold, were printed in black and yellow on one side and in black and red on the reverse side of the sheet.

Half of 17- by 22-Inch Press Sheet, Two On; Flat Made from Copy Unit of Multiples

Copy: Paste-up with Overlays, One for the Color and One for Halftone Tints

Fig. 5-7 An example of copy preparation that handled five small folders. It provided the flats for black and color, run two on the press plate without stripping.

The job run was black and red on one side and black and yellow on the reverse side of the sheet. Overlays were used for colors and halftone tints; lap register was provided in copy for touching colors, and black was surprinted on color.

When there are a series of printed pieces, they usually are planned for a combination run using the same stock and colors. Note that by planning the single fold on the side of the piece instead of on top, ten pieces were cut from the sheet instead of eight. This is an example of good planning for ordinary quality at a minimum cost.

COPY EXAMPLE 14

Overlay diagram illustrates the general assembly of paste-up and overlays. (*a*) The original paste-up carries all type that can be pasted down and will not interfere with the art. (*b*) Overlay with all type that will be overprinted on art or photograph. This type is pasted in the proper position. (*c*) Overlay with all type that will be reversed on art or photograph. Do not fail to mark overlay "Reverse." (*d*) Color guide tissue that will carry a rough guide, for the printer to use visually, of all flash-in colors such as type, panels, and backgrounds. Colored pencil or pastel media are suitable. (*e*) Assembly diagram of the type and color guide overlays is shown although this sequence of overlays is not important. (*f*) Photograph of the final reproduction with all type and color in their proper places according to instructions.

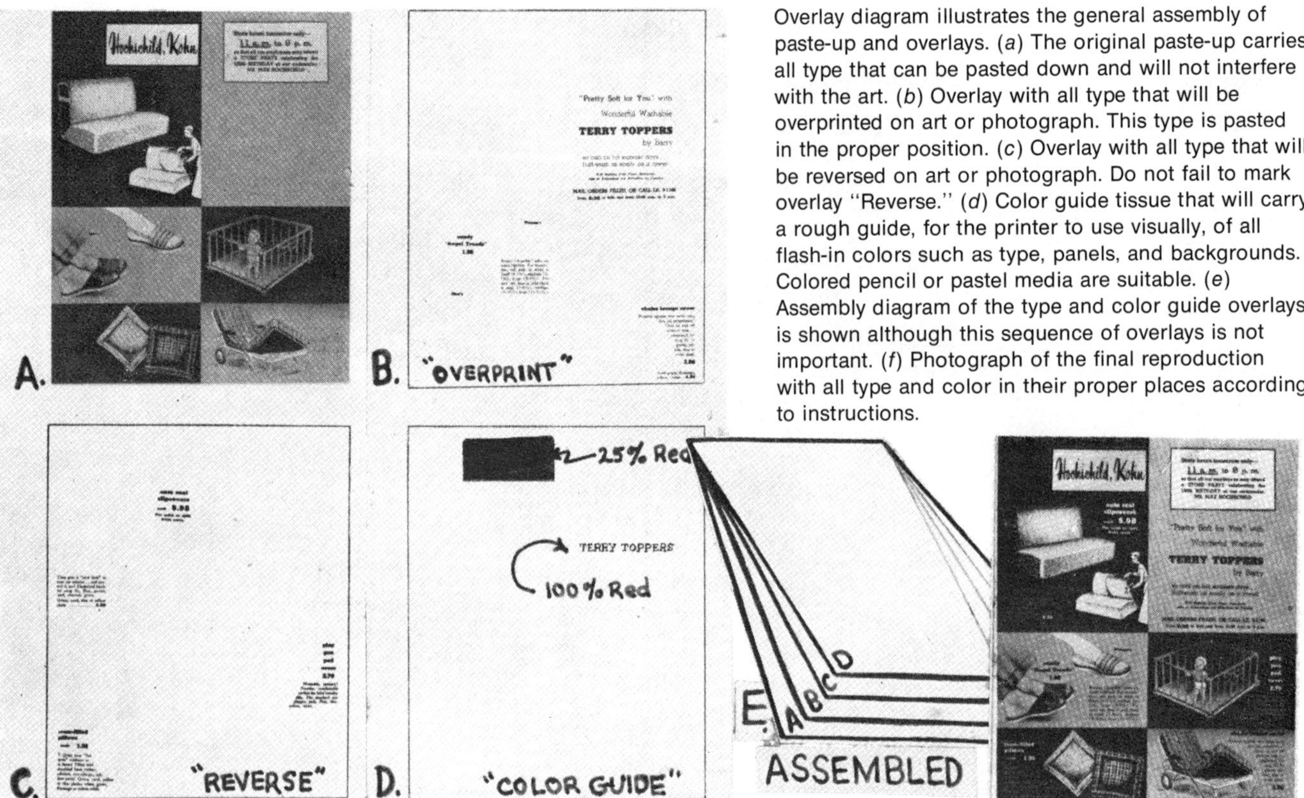

Fig. 5-8 This example uses separate overlays for surprinted type and reversed type, both of which are positioned. The two can go on the same overlay with the reversed type circled. [*Courtesy* Gravure *magazine*]

When an Element Runs across Two or More Colors, It Is Handled on an Overlay

Fig. 5-9 In this illustration the "Swift's Premium" cartouche oval reverse running across two touching colors would be handled on an overlay. The stripper would position the two negatives (colors) and then with a positive of the overrunning design knock out the reverse image to get a proper fit on the two colors.

Use of a Knockout Overlay

Since a photographic positive is required to knock out an image, a Photostat negative of the design is often used for the overlay to get the needed positive, thus saving an intermediate step by the platemaker.

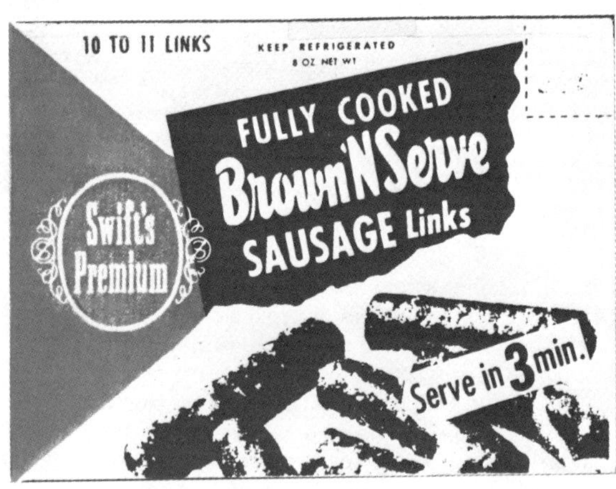

COPY EXAMPLE 15

Remodeling a smaller house

HERE'S ENTHUSIASTIC PROOF of the theory that sometimes it's wiser to buy an older house and modernize, than it is to buy a newer one

roofing and siding and aluminum-framed windows and window walls, complemented by an all-brick fireplace wall. A custom-designed panel

The window wall in the end gable provides enough light for a finished attic without the necessity of adding a dormer out the rear. A small front

strength and sliding glass doors installed. The resulting light and ventilation for the basement area allowed it to be finished off as part of the

Fig. 5-10

Top half of a two-page spread, 10 by 7½ inches.

Fig. 5-11

Fig. 5-12 A Magic Marker tone in red and black on the overlay supplied camera copy for both color and black in tones.

How Color Art Was Prepared

The planning for several million booklets in color called for minimum cost. With the use of offset, an inexpensive uncoated stock permitted fine halftone work. The thirty-three illustrations in two, three, and four colors required the use of an inexpensive art medium and freedom from process color costs.

The job was planned for keyline drawings in black with a tone overlay for each color. Working on clear vinylite material with felt tip applicators (red, yellow, and blue), the artist got both the primary and the secondary colors. For example, viewing the blue and yellow overlays in contact, he saw the green that would be obtained. (These colors are transparent and produce the tonal qualities of watercolors, avoiding any "mechanical" tonal qualities.) Handling the color copy in groups of the same focus reduced plate costs.

Tone in black was obtained from overlay duplicate halftone negatives by opaquing unwanted color design.

Eleven illustrations were in four colors, five in three, and twenty-two in two. Planning saved both time and money. [*Client: Aluminum Limited Sales, Inc. Agency: J. Walter Thompson Company Art: Alfred Avison Studio, New York*]

AIRBRUSH ART FOR COLOR REQUIRES BLACK SURPRINTING FOR SHADOW DETAIL

Fig. 5-13 Two original photoprints of this tool, one in normal tone and one in high key to surprint color, were cut and combined. The normal print was greatly retouched for black with highlights, and the light half was retouched for shadow detail to surprint color.

Color copy was prepared in black on a film overlay, the unused half of the normal photoprint being retouched for highlights. Camera copy was slightly more than twice size.

Black Key Copy

Fig. 5-14 Copy prepared twice size, with part surprinting in high key and providing shadow detail on color.

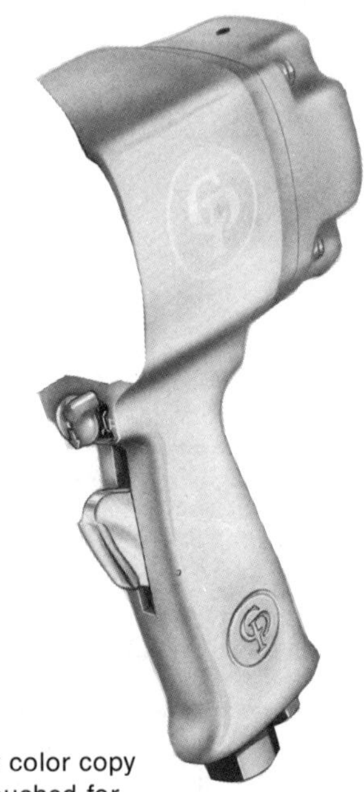

Fig. 5-15 Overlay color copy in dark tones, retouched for highlights of color.

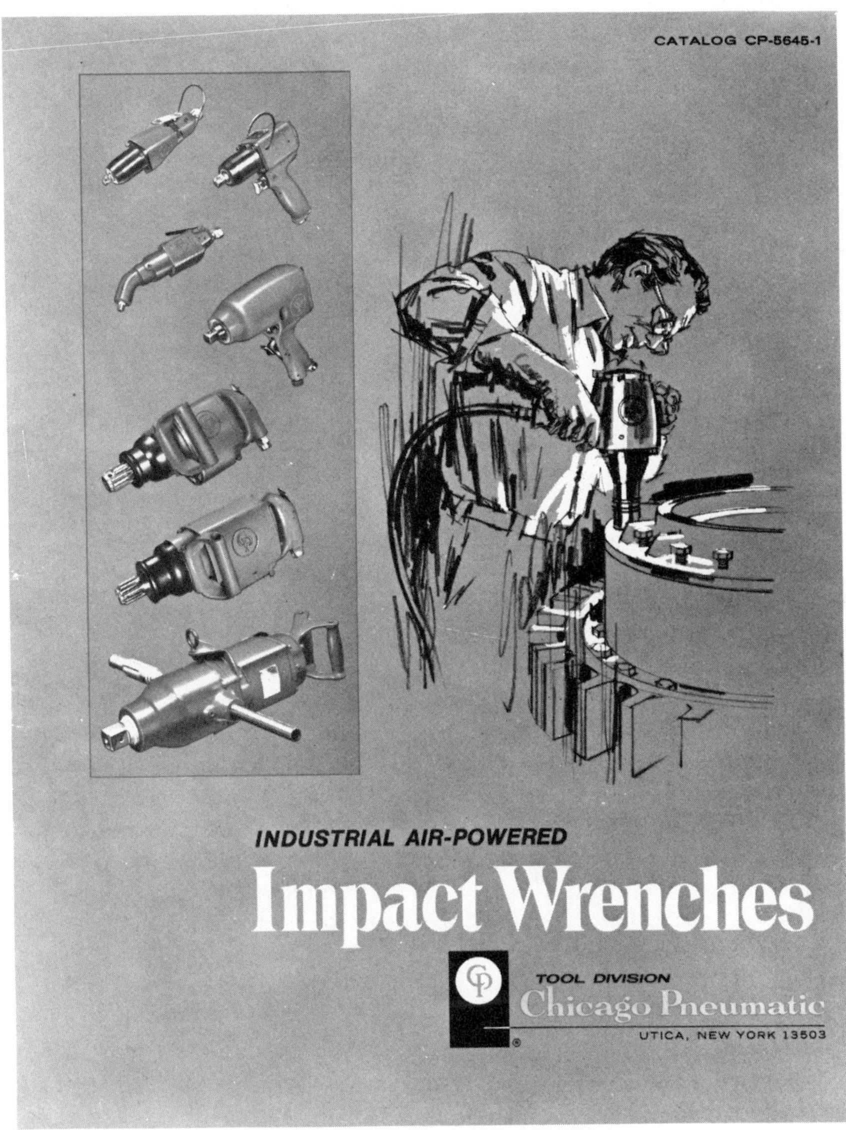

Fig. 5-17 Key copy: black.

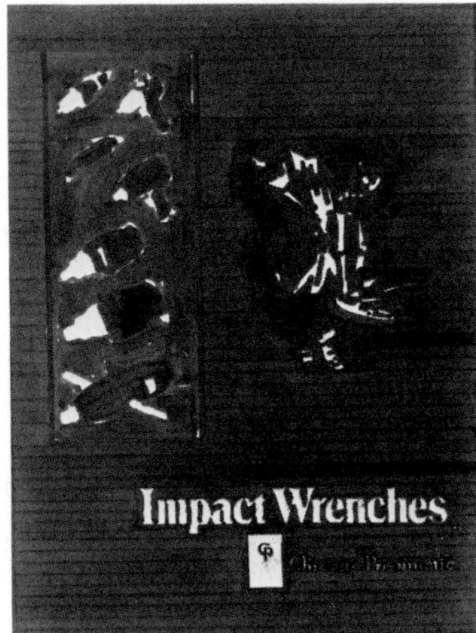

Fig. 5-18 Red plate.

Highlight Dropout Overlay
Prepared by Artist with Illustration

Fig. 5-16 The illustration of the tool operator in scale on the key copy was prepared separately in 120 percent of scale size with a dropout mask overlay on clear film, in register, to be contact-printed on the red negative for the result shown in the cover reproduction. The panel background with pictures of tools and the company name were printed in a light olive green (not shown).

Fig. 5-19 Highlight dropout mask overlay for white areas of red plate, prepared on separate art for tool operator. Rough layout (Fig. 5-18) indicated reversed type and effect wanted.

quently done 4 times the reproduction size. All camera copy is executed in black or gray tones. When the copy is in line with only a few tone elements, these are scaled and positioned as Velox screened prints, which are classed as line copy. Such prints are also available for two-color work, screen-angled and registered. Copy Example 16 (Fig. 5-20) is all line copy.

Prescreened tint areas (Velox and artist's tint sheets) should not be used for rotogravure because of the risk of a moiré or star pattern resulting from the gravure rescreening. If use in rotogravure is absolutely necessary, employ a coarse screen such as 55-line.

The use of preseparated color with opaque inks can be almost an art technique in itself because of the extra color strength as compared with the process inks used for flat-color printing.

Preseparated Color for Transparent Inks

To handle a volume of artwork requiring the usual secondary colors with process inks, such as art for greeting cards, special art techniques are available. With special watercolors keyed to standard process inks the artist, guided by a rough color sketch, works each primary color on a separate thin film overlay. Positioned in register sandwich-style, the secondary colors thus formed can be seen. The printer photographs batches of same-color overlays in groups. All the colors have been separated, and no color correction is required.

Bourges Color Corporation's Colotone sheets perform the same function except that unwanted color areas are removed by brushed solvent or a scraper. Tone art can be added with special colors. Each colored sheet comes in five different tone values: 10, 30, 50, 70, and 100 percent. Besides the standard process colors, the standard (opaque) poster red, yellow, orange, and green ink colors of the business paper associations are available.

Supplementing Process Subjects with Preseparated Color Design

Frequently with collateral printed material and sometimes with publication ads, the key illustration is in full color and so must be printed with regular transparent process inks. Often the key illustration is picked up from another job, and the separations are available, or conversions of color photoengravings may be used for offset production.

Incidental illustrative color treatment such as color spots, backgrounds, and tints is often added. To avoid additional process color expense, preseparated color camera copy is prepared. Remember that hairline register must be employed because of the transparent inks being used.

LOW-BUDGET COLOR COPY

Every artist runs into situations in which little money is available for artwork or in which much is expected for the money allotted, particularly in book design. These needs created the "contact autopositive technique," of which an example in single color is shown in Fig. 5-22. The artist works with a dark pencil on the rough side of frosted film overlay material and by the pressure of the pencil stroke on the abrasive texture obtains the desired tones. The pencil should be hard enough not to smear: the jet-black extra-smooth Ebony Pencil 6325 is recommended and was used for this illustration.

Note that there is no halftone screen and that the result approaches the texture of stone lithography. The artist works in the same size in the usual right-reading manner, and from his artwork a contact negative is made and positioned as a halftone negative would be. The reproduction will also be right-reading. Since camera expense is avoided, you can't get much lower plate costs.

Tissue Overlays in Pencil

It is quite simple to take a black-and-white photo and add one or two colors for a Multilith job. The artist merely uses the broad strokes of a graphite pencil or crayon on tissue overlays to add tone color where it is wanted.

For commercial work you can add color to a black-and-white photo by sending the photo to an offset producer with instructions to make a halftone negative and

COPY EXAMPLE 16

A PICTURE IN FOUR COLORS IN "THE FOUR CORNERS OF THE WORLD" (Knopf)
Written and illustrated by Roger Duvoisin

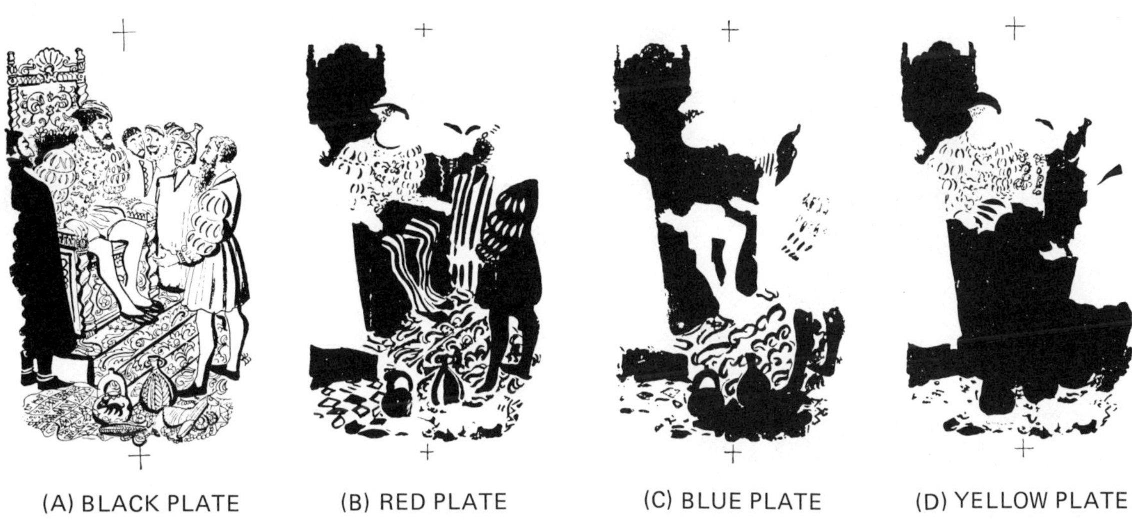

Fig. 5-20 The cuts on this page demonstrate the usual procedure of a book illustrator when he is required to make separation drawings for a picture to be reproduced in several flat colors. The upper-right cut is a halftone reproduction of the printed picture in black and three colors. When the artist made his key drawing for the black plate (*A* is a line cut from this drawing), he placed transparent overlays on the key copy and on one overlay painted in black the areas to be in red (*B*), on another overlay the art for the blue areas (*C*), and on a third overlay the art for the yellow areas (*D*). Since the artist worked in black while doing the overlays, this copy did not require the use of filters when it was photographed. There was considerable surprinting of colors with this subject: the chairback required three colors to get a reddish brown.

COPY EXAMPLE 17

PRESEPARATED COLOR TECHNIQUES AS USED BY THE READER'S DIGEST

Fig. 5-21 A large portion of the editorial content is offset on uncoated paper. Until the present use of process color most of the color illustrations were prepared by artists as shown here.

A comprehensive sketch is planned on the basis of a key plate (usually black) and three or four *Digest* colors selected from twenty-eight special hues and supplied to the selected artist with instructions to render an overlay for each color on textured Vinylite or on matte-finish acetate in register on the key drawing. The art shown here was prepared 4 times scale size. [*Illustrations from an article by Robert H. Blattner in* Art Direction *magazine*]

(A)

(B)

(C)

(D)

(E)

(F)

A. Jordan plate is bluish green.

B. Mountain plate is purple blue.

C. Key plate is black.

D. Cameo plate is a dark flesh tone.

E. Pink plate is a light coral red.

F. Finished proof with all colors in register.

Fig. 5-22 Example of the contact autopositive technique by the artist, using a graphite pencil on grained acetate. A contact negative made from this produces a right-reading reproduction.

blueprints on overlay material that you supply. Each blueprint supplies the holding lines for a color as you work in black or wash for the color.

The availability of four-color offset separations for less than $100 has largely replaced the use of fake process color in four colors by the preparation of wash overlays.

PIN REGISTER SYSTEMS

When the camera operator photographs key copy and overlays, the usual practice

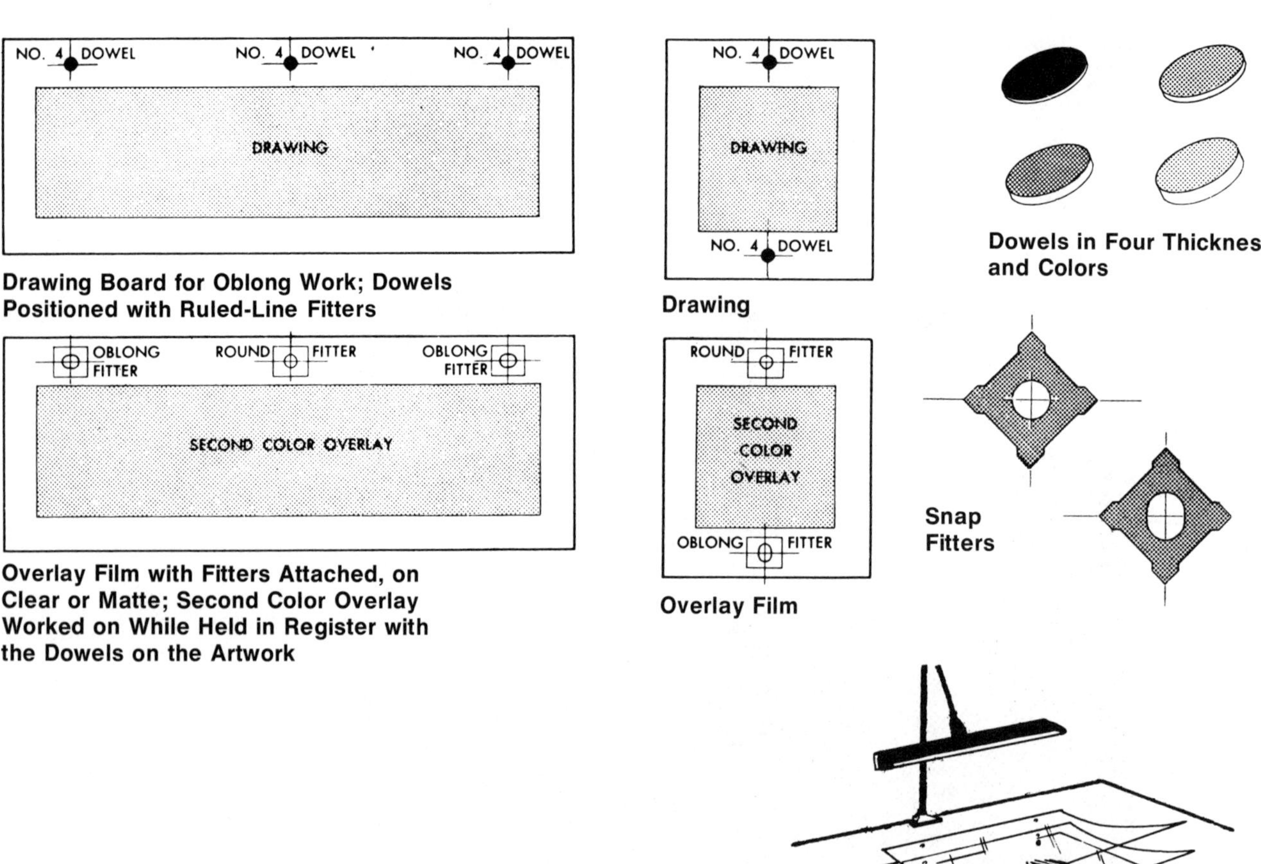

Drawing Board for Oblong Work; Dowels Positioned with Ruled-Line Fitters

Overlay Film with Fitters Attached, on Clear or Matte; Second Color Overlay Worked on While Held in Register with the Dowels on the Artwork

Drawing

Overlay Film

Dowels in Four Thicknesses and Colors

Snap Fitters

Fig. 5-23 [*Accurate Step & Repeat System, Inc., 858 Sussex Boulevard, Broomall, Pa. 19143*]

is to handle all copy as a group. This requires flap overlays to be torn apart.

Various makes of pin register systems are coming into use. Snug-fitting holes in the overlays fit over pins or dowels fastened to the key copy on illustrator's board.

Rapidly superseding the old flap acetate overlays and more recent pin register and punched hole method is the use of round "button" dowels on the black key copy and fitters on the overlays, as shown in Fig. 5-23. This patented method avoids the awkward flaps (which in any case the producer frequently removes for photographing all copy as a group) and the punching of illustrator's board and the acetate.

Register marks are placed on the key copy. The overlay is frequently notched as shown or cut to give clearance for the dowel button. With the overlay in place, the notched fitters are positioned to register lines and taped to the overlay. An adhesive-backed dowel is then placed through each fitter to stick to the key copy sketch; the oblong fitter should point toward the round dowel to allow for expansion or contraction. Additional overlays have fitters positioned on the dowels of the key copy before they are taped in place.

The fact that illustrator's board expands and shrinks 1/16 inch or more in large sizes is the reason for the use of oblong fitters. It takes time to get overlays and key copy back into register. It is suggested that old aluminum press plates be obtained from a regular producer. These can be cut to the desired size with scissors and laminated to drawing paper, with shellac to get a dimensionally stable illustrator's board, or Precision Art Board can be purchased. It is important that the overlay material used be dimensionally stable; ordinary acetate dries and shrinks.

Caution: For Acetate Overlays Use a Dimensionally Stable Material

There are many types of acetate material, both matte and clear-finish. The type used for copy overlays should be of a quality that will not shrink from drying out or expand from moisture. Work is held up when the platemaker finds that the overlay copy has shrunk 1/16 inch and does not fit the key copy. Dimensionally stable brands include Vinyline and Cronar; art supply stores usually also offer other brands. A thickness of 0.005 inch is generally used. Acetate inks, opaque, thinner, and opaque removable solution are available.

MATERIALS THAT FACILITATE PREPARATION OF OVERLAYS AND MECHANICALS

The volume of artwork on overlays, as well as the use of coated sheets of acetate in colors, has resulted in the development of dimensionally stable materials and a variety of surfaces and coatings, ranging from clear, transparent sheets that take ink or wash to removable opaque coatings and colors.

Some of these materials avoid brush-opaquing by the artist, and others permit the artist to see the black key underneath as he works the color area on the overlays. Standard color sheets that permit seeing the results of combining colors are available, and yet the artist can remove unwanted areas and even add tone with color and brush.

Continuous-tone illustration is obtained by contact negatives from pencil on grained acetate. The result resembles stone lithography.

The larger art supply stores sell many of the materials listed below. The number at the end of each paragraph is the key to the name and address of the manufacturer offering informative literature.

Clear Acetate Sheets

These take all types of inks and colors and pen, brush, or airbrush. They will not chip or crawl. (1), (2)

Matte-Surface Acetates

There are many types and degrees of roughness; the acetates take pencil, pen, brush, and blueprint coating. They are used for scribing. The underside is opaque, and the top is white. (3)

Masking Film

This film is translucent but photographs as black. Mounted on a base, it can be hand-cut for a clean line and removed if desired. It is used for opaque areas and adheres to illustration board with rubber cement. (4), (5), (6), (10)

Transopaque Overlay Sheets

They have a red coating that photographs as black; it is removed by scraping small areas and by dissolving large areas. The sheets are widely used for design in black and white on a colored background; also with adhesive tape for cutting and positioning. There is a liquid coating for corrections and added pen or brush detail. (2)

Bourges Colotype Overlay Sheets

These are transparent plastic sheets that match twelve basic standard transparent inks in five different values. By working each color as an overlay, the artist can visualize the result of combining them for secondary colors. The artist removes unwanted color and adds with pencil, pen, or brush. (2)

Colored Acetate Sheets

These come in transparent colors, grays, and black to match standard inks and are used to visualize results in flat colors with secondary colors; they have an adhesive backing. Reds are used for overlay sheets;

there are also pattern sheets in color applied by the artist. (2), (7), (9)

Blueline Emulsion Film

Dinoblueline prints of the black key provide an overlay on which detail for color can be turned to black in selected areas by applying a chemical with a brush; the rest of the design in blue will not photograph. After a print has been made, hydrogen peroxide applied to black lines turns them back to blue for reuse for a second color. Brush-opaque areas for solids; the film is accurate for color lap. (8)

Tints and Patterns

These provide invisible tones on either film or drawing paper that are developed chemically where wanted by brush application. Multicolor types are also available. (9)

Sources for Materials If Art Supply Stores Are Not Available

(1) Abraham Seltzer & Co., Inc.
231 West 54th Street
New York, N.Y. 10019

(2) Bourges Color Corporation
20 Waterside Plaza
New York, N.Y. 10010

(3) Henry P. Korn Associates, Inc.
300 Park Avenue South
New York, N.Y. 10010

(4) Ulano Products Company, Inc.
210 East 86th Street
New York, N.Y. 10028

(5) Morley Associates
273 Columbus Avenue
Tuckahoe, N.Y. 10707

(6) Separon Co.
56 West 22d Street
New York, N.Y. 10010

(7) Cello-Tak Manufacturing, Inc.
35 Alabama Avenue
Island Park, N.Y. 11558

(8) Di-Noc Division, 3M Company
1700 London Road
Cleveland, Ohio 44112

(9) Craftint Manufacturing Co.
18501 Euclid Avenue
Cleveland, Ohio 44112

(10) Serascreen Corp.
5-25 47th Road
Long Island City, N.Y. 11101

CHAPTER SIX
Artwork for Letterpress Printing

As WE POINTED out in Chapter 1, the artist is concerned chiefly with copy *elements* when preparing artwork, including photographs, for the photoengraver. To work intelligently the artist should know the kind of letterpress printing and the type of paper to be used: commercial, magazine, or newspaper printing. The paper and the printing method affect the choice of a suitable art medium and determine the tonal qualities required for good reproduction. The rougher the paper surface, the coarser the halftone screen used, resulting in a loss of some details and tonal quality. For example, the quality of 65-line newspaper halftones does not equal that of 133-line halftones on coated paper. Part of the artist's job is to anticipate any loss of details and, in executing the work, to accentuate details and add extra tonal qualities.

THREE CATEGORIES OF LETTERPRESS

From the artist's point of view the three forms of letterpress printing are distinguished by the kind of printing press used, the type of printing plate, and the conditions under which the printing is to be used by the reader. Design and layout are adjusted, and artwork prepared, to suit each kind of printing.

Commercial (Job) Printing

In this type of printing each job is printed individually with a free choice of paper and colors. Accurate color register and extra pressure for halftone areas (lockup and makeready) can be provided for the particular job. Such individual attention produces the best quality of letterpress printing.

Magazines and Other Periodicals

The larger consumer publications are printed on special large rotary presses using publication-quality coated paper and usually 120-line halftones. The limitations on suitable artwork are those of standard process inks, as specified by the Magazine Publishers Association. The hues of some colors can only be approximated. The smaller periodicals are printed on flatbed presses and usually do not go beyond two-color work. The Standard Rate & Data Service publishes the production specifications of all publications.

Since better illustrations and process color are available in the larger magazines and since readers tend to spend more time in reading them, layout and design differ from those of newspapers. Moreover, bleed design is available.

Newspapers

Because the cheapest kind of uncoated paper and a fast but rough type of standardized printing are used for newspapers, there are limitations on suitable artwork, and extra contrast is required for tone. Design and layout are aimed at catching the attention of the reader, who goes through a newspaper in a short time.

ARTWORK FOR COMMERCIAL PRINTING

The creative concept has full rein in commercial printing, with cost and time the only limiting factors, for reproduction requirements can be adjusted to the needs of the artwork. Better grades of coated paper can be used. In addition, most process color printing is done with 133-line halftone screens, and 150-line screens are available if needed for finer details. Vignette halftones and subtle tonal gradation are practical, and any of the special types of halftones can be used.

PRACTICAL CONSIDERATIONS

Most printing that involves the use of illustration and color is the result of preliminary planning and of cooperative work by the copy and art departments to execute the plans. Approved rough layouts for printed pieces are really blueprints for work to be done by artist, photographer, engraver, typographer, and printer. Ordinarily all decisions have been made as to size, paper, colors, printing process, composition, and the art medium to be used (the budget is the determining factor). A rubber stamp on the layout includes delivery dates for art, composition, engravings, and so on.

SELECTING PAPER

The kind of paper to be used for the reproduction, that is, coated paper of a particular quality or a smooth or textured uncoated paper, largely determines the choice of a suitable art technique and its preparation to ensure good reproduction. Coated papers can take 120-line or finer halftone screens, and smooth uncoated papers frequently can take 100-line or coarser halftones, but most rough-textured papers are suitable only for line art techniques in commercial letterpress printing.

Chapter 2 listed the standard sizes of the various types of letterpress printing papers. The size of a printed piece should be chosen to cut efficiently from a standard size of paper without excessive waste; about 1 inch should be allowed in both dimensions for printing margins and trim. Any departure from this rule should be made for a good reason, for almost 25 percent of the cost of printing is attributable to the paper stock.

PHOTOENGRAVINGS

As you will recall from Chapter 1, the reproduction qualities of camera copy are the same for all the major printing processes. There is a variation in the negatives, but that is under the control of the camera operator, and any difference in the form of camera copy supplied to the printer or engraver is due to plate costs, as determined by the process being used. There are considerations, such as large quantities and plates for magazine schedules, that may nullify the importance of plate costs.

As an example, you might want 1,000 flyers, consisting of composition and a small halftone, in a single color. The printer would set the type, allowing space for the halftone, and either you or the printer would order the halftone to be inserted in position with the type. For a large halftone covering most of a page, the engraving would be ordered with a mortised area in which the metal type would be inserted. The plate cost would be for the engraving, plus a small charge for the mortise. If type matter was to be part of the engraving, making it a combination line-and-tone engraving, plate costs would be more than doubled under Item 2 of the Photoengravers' Standard Scale. For publication schedules this extra cost would be insignificant, and the combination engraving would reduce errors and the number of approvals required.

Photoengravers no longer accept metal type to be combined with process engravings for electrotypes. This means that either a repro proof of the made-up type page or a mechanical with the type matter must be supplied. Under the scale called Color Process Engravings, however, there is no premium charge for combination line-and-tone engravings. Because of the use of photographic composition methods for both display and text type and of repro galley proofs of text (a major economy), art departments now usually supply the photoengraver with a mechanical of the whole page or ad. Process elements are indicated with Photostats. The mechanical also frequently serves as a comprehensive layout for the client's approval.

LINE PHOTOENGRAVINGS

With letterpress there is no base plate charge that includes line illustrations, and there are no same-focus discounts on either line or tone photoengravings. This

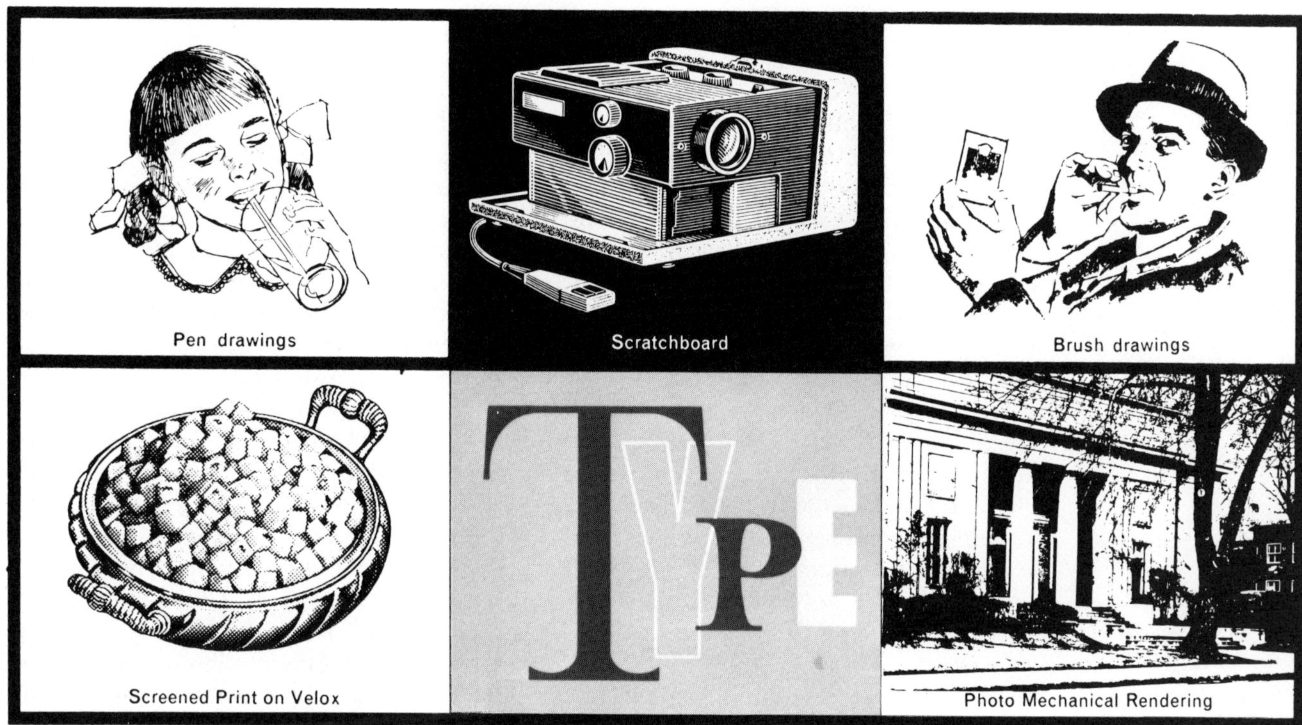

Fig. 6-1 Types of line photoengravings.

means that elements are not proportioned unless they are positioned to go on one engraving. A group of small halftones is frequently so positioned because a large engraving costs less than four or five separate halftone engravings.

Some kinds of paper—text, antique-finish, bonds, newsprint—are best suited to line photoengravings because of their rough texture. Any halftones for use with these papers must be in a coarse screen (65- or 75-line). Line artwork should be 100 percent black, such as drawings with a pen, dry brush, crayon, or carbon (Wolff) pencil on textured board. A graphite pencil drawing requires a halftone. Pen-line cross-hatching should not intersect at angles of less than 30 degrees to avoid the danger of the ink plugging up at the point of intersection, and the amount of reduction should be kept small.

Tone copy is sometimes converted to line by a photomechanical rendering, a tone-line process available from engravers. Screened Velox prints of photos, which are made by specialists, also are used, particularly in newspaper production. Reverses and tint panels should be opaqued on copy to avoid extra charges, but they can be indicated in light blue. For newspaper production and some rough commercial printing, stock tints and patterns from pressure-sensitive sheets are applied by the artist to line drawings for tonal effects. Cost is assessed on the benday Photoengravers' Scale.

The cost of line art depends on who does it. Although the engraving cost is lower than for halftones, the principal economy is effected in the press operation: much less makeready time is required for adjusting pressures to achieve a good impression.

HALFTONE PHOTOENGRAVINGS

Tone copy—any artwork involving shades of gray or colors such as photographs, wash drawings, watercolors, paintings, pastels, and graphite pencil drawings in gray tones—must be photographed through a halftone screen in the camera back. The amount of light reflected from minute individual areas of the artwork on the copyboard through the camera lens and halftone screen results in large or small clear halftone dots on the film negative. Even a white background will be reproduced with very small halftone dots (about a 5 percent tone); dark areas will be reproduced with dots so large that they run together, leaving only very small white specks in the reproduction (about an 80 or 90 percent tone). Thus the tonal qualities of artwork are reproduced by the halftone method, which is used by both letterpress and offset.

The engraver's halftone screens range from 55 to 150 lines to the inch. The finer the halftone screen used for engravings, the better the details in the printing. Most commercial halftone printing on a good-quality coated paper is done with a 133-line screen.

With smoother uncoated papers like machine-finish paper, coarser halftone screens such as 100- or 85-line are required, and the engravings may have to be deep-etched to lessen the possibility of ink filling in the plates. An antique wove-finish book paper can take a 65-line newspaper halftone, but generally only line copy is used on this paper. The same holds true for uncoated cover stock, bristol board, and the bond papers.

Today many special-effects screens—linear, circular, mezzotint types, and so on—are in use, mostly for newsprint stock. A consultation with your photoengraver on the use of such a screen instead of the conventional halftone screen might help to solve the problem of tone on an antique-finish paper. The usual solution, however, is to switch to the offset process, which can print fine halftones on this paper.

Copy for Halftones

The bulk of the tone copy used in commercial printing consists, of course, of photographs, but there are large numbers of wash drawings with black lines for details and contrast. Some carbon pencil, crayon, and charcoal drawings also are used, generally in combination with other techniques for details, shading, and backgrounds. Various felt-tipped daubers have come into use for tint areas, prepared on film overlays, when the artist wishes to avoid the mechanical appearance of the halftone tint applied by the engraver.

Most tone copy is prepared to be reduced in size for reproduction. Photographs are cropped to indicate the area to be included on the engraving. Crop marks in soft pencil on the edges of a photo are sufficient; plate size and halftone screen should be indicated on the bottom between vertical crop marks for width. Always check the height of the engraving, using either the diagonal-line method or a scaling instrument, to make sure that the engraving will fit the layout space. The copy should be marked for the halftone screen to be employed, and the engraver's proof should be on the stock used. Areas for halftone tint panels should be opaqued for photoengravings or indicated in light blue.

When there is to be an assembly of tone elements for a halftone, engravers recommend that copy be supplied in loose form with a layout. The paste lines and the uneven edges of a copy assembly would show on a halftone.

Retouching Photos

The same brand of retouching grays should always be used on a single photograph or group of photographs. The use of different brands with slight differences in the color cast of the gray could produce a bad negative. Employment of a good Chinese white made from titanium is important, for ultraviolet absorption causes some whites to reproduce as a tone. Keep to a minimum the use of white to indicate highlight dropouts and outline halftones.

Coarse-Screen Halftones

When coarse-screen halftones are to be used, prepare copy for minimum reduction, for the screen dot formation tends to obscure details. Tone copy should have greater contrast to offset the lower light reflection from uncoated paper: accentuate details in both light and dark areas. Extra contrast is frequently required with

TYPES OF HALFTONE PHOTOENGRAVINGS

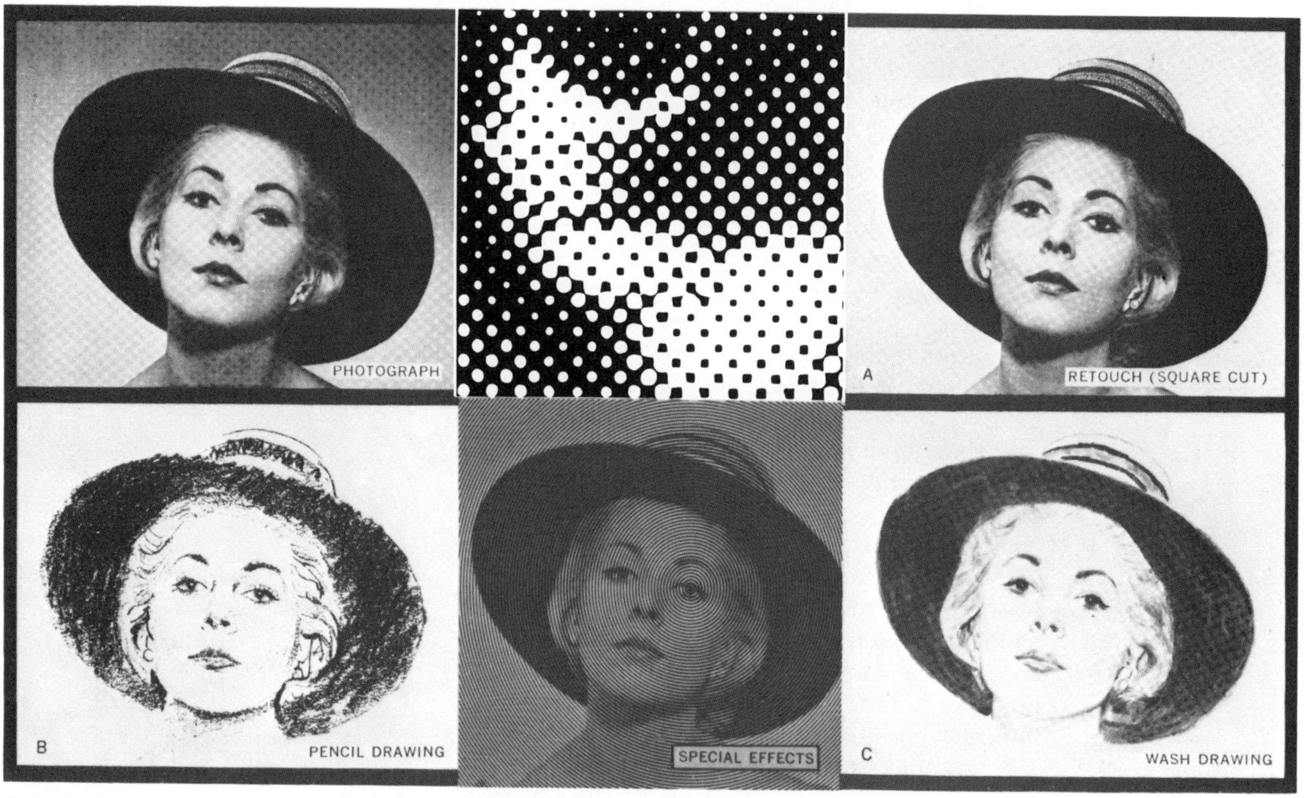

PHOTOGRAPH
A RETOUCH (SQUARE CUT)
B PENCIL DRAWING
SPECIAL EFFECTS
C WASH DRAWING

Fig. 6-2 There are three basic halftone types: square-cut (*A*), dropout (*B*), and outline (*C*). Vignette and silhouette types are variations of *C*. Halftone engravings are made from copy in which tone is represented in a continuous (unbroken) manner: photographs, wash drawings, graphite pencil drawings, tints prepared with felt daubers. The number of scale units for a given plate size is based on the square-cut type. The other types shown as well as the silhouette and vignette types are termed special types and carry a premium charge over the scale cost. [*Courtesy Rapid Grip and Batten, Ltd.*]

photographs and may be provided by retouching. In the section "Artwork for Newspapers" we shall discuss the use of extra lighting in studio photography to get details and contrast between subject and background.

Types of Halftones

There are three basic types of halftones: the square-cut type, in which there are dots in all areas, even for white paper; the outline type, in which the dots outside the subject have been removed by the engraver; and the dropout type, in which the engraver has been instructed to remove dots inside the subject. The third type is usually achieved by painting dropout areas on a photograph in Chinese white and for other artwork by outlining the areas on a tissue overlay. The silhouette and vignette halftones are variations of the outline type. It is on the square halftone that the Photoengravers' Standard Scale units are based. Outline, silhouette, and vignette halftones involve a minimum premium charge of 50 percent, and the dropout type costs 3 times the copper scale figure.

COMBINATION ENGRAVINGS

You will frequently have occasion to combine line and tone copy to get a line-and-tone photoengraving. Camera copy must be prepared in such form (an overlay is used for line) that the engraver can handle each kind of copy separately and then combine them for the combination plate. A type headline in black or white (reverse) on a tone background is the commonest subject of a combination plate.

There are two accepted methods of preparing copy:

1. Prepare a working drawing on which all tone copy is scaled and positioned or a paste-up of photos. On an overlay (paper, parchment, or film) position all line elements (lettering, type proofs, design); register them to the drawing or paste-up.

2. To permit reduction of tone copy, prepare a working drawing of all line copy, including type proofs, in position. On this drawing indicate in pale blue wash the exact position of the various tone elements, which should be keyed. Supply tone elements separately so that the engraver can reduce and strip them to the indicated position. This tone assembly will be contact-printed with the line copy separately on unexposed film to produce the combination.

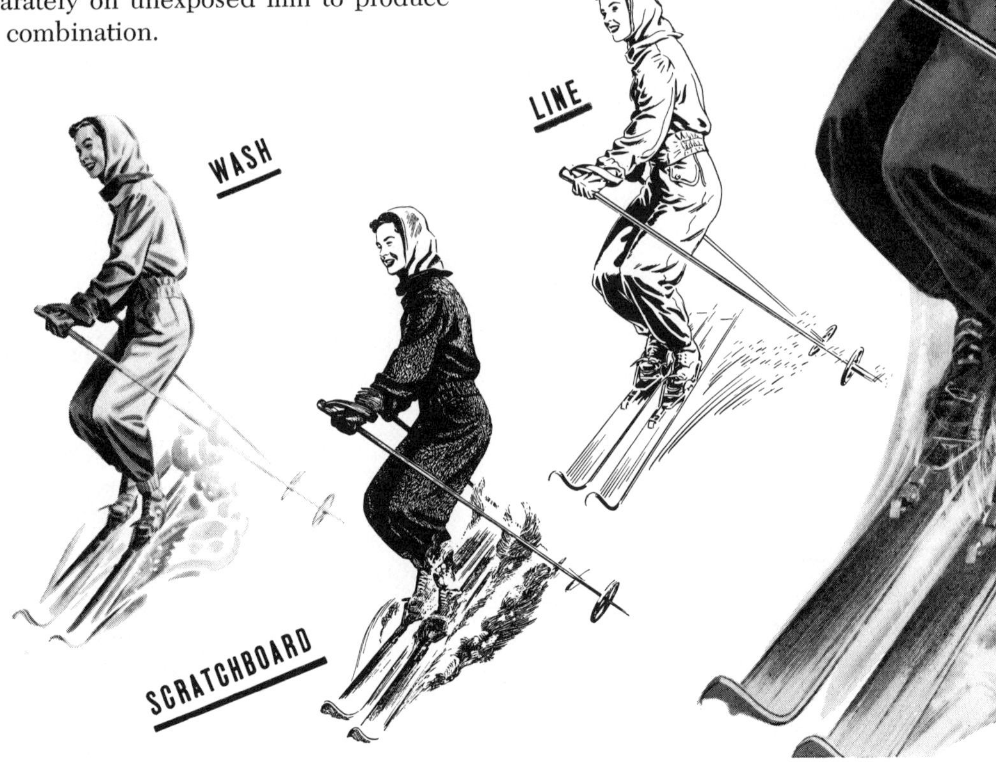

Fig. 6-3 Reproductions of various art media, including some of the special types of halftones.

Estimating Photoengraving Costs

Since photoengravings are the only kind of printing plates whose cost is not estimated by the time required to make them, a detailed explanation is in order. The basic cost is for the size in a rectangular shape for a particular kind of plate—copper, zinc, or process color plate—each of which has a different cost scale, as indicated in units on a large form ruled in squares of inches and quarter inches with the number of units shown. The larger the plate, the greater the number of units. Each engraving firm has its own unit value, which varies to some extent with the kind of service required by the customer. The number of units times the unit value gives the scale cost of the engraving. Added to the scale cost may be premiums for special types of halftones and extra charges for stripping, handwork, and so on, all set forth in detail in the scale form.

Same-focus discounts are no longer allowed. One-piece process color photoengravings are limited to a maximum size of about 15 by 17 inches because of the difficulty of the etching operation.

The charts shown in Fig. 6-4, which are based on the number of units at a unit value of 8.9 cents converted to square inches, may be helpful in approximating photoengraving plate costs. Obtain the unit value prevailing in your area.

USE OF COPY IN PASTE-UP FORM FOR LETTERPRESS

In our brief description of the three major printing processes we mentioned the fact that Item 2 of the Photoengravers' Standard Scale approximately doubles plate costs when line copy and tone copy are combined in the same engraving and that this is the reason that single-color copy for the engraver usually consists of *elements*. We also stated that offset and gravure both use line-and-tone copy for the *unit* because under time estimating of plate costs this cost does not apply to combination plates, which are charged merely for the extra time.

However, when full-color ads are prepared for publications, a different scale, Color Process Photoengravings, is employed, and use of a combination plate does not double scale costs. The photoengraver wants either repro proofs of the made-up type page or a mechanical of the advertisement, for electro duplicates will be needed for each publication. The mechanical has certain advantages: not only the use of galley repros of type but photocomposition and photolettering for display and reverses. The chances of obtaining the wrong copy and the number of approvals are reduced.

When a single-color advertisement is to appear in a number of publications, the extra cost of a combination line-and-tone plate is unimportant, and its use assembles all the elements of an advertisement: heading, subheading, illustration, body type or text, and logotype. Such plates also permit the use of certain combination line-and-tone treatments that otherwise might be difficult to execute. A line-and-tone mechanical is prepared for the engraver.

Flexography and Plastic Relief Plates

The flexographic printing process employs a rubber relief plate wrapped around the cylinder of a rotary press. It is used mostly for very thin materials, which tend to puncture on metal plates. Copy in paste-up form is prepared for a zinc line engraving of the copy unit, and from this a matrix of special cardboard is made to serve as a mold for the rubber.

Many newspapers are now using photography and a photomechanical plastic relief plate. This, of course, requires paste-up copy. If laser relief plates are developed, these too will require copy in paste-up form.

CAMERA COPY FOR COLOR PRINTING

For commercial letterpress printing as well as for most national consumer magazines there are two forms of color printing, *process color* and *simple color*. Process color is used for paintings and color transparencies, the colors of which are separated photographically by means of color filters in the camera. Separate filters are used to get each of the three primary colors—red, blue, and yellow—and black.

The particular filter holds back all colors except the one wanted, and separation negatives are thus obtained for the four engravings.

Since photoengravers get their final tones by etching the copper engravings, a process that requires a uniform metal temperature, a set of process color engravings is limited to a maximum size of about 14 by 17 inches for practical use. Because there is a lateral reduction in the size of halftone dots in the etching, the enlargement or reduction of process plates usually is not satisfactory.

An important problem of commercial letterpress is the cost of press lockup (positioning plates for register) and makeready (adjusting plate areas—printer's overlay and underlay—for extra pressure) with process printing. Since this cost is the same for a short or a long press run, the size of a practical minimum print order is affected.

Almost all process color printing is done from electros of the original process engravings to avoid possible damage to and wear of the originals. The cost of these electros must also be considered.

As with all photoengravings, the cost of a group of individual small process engravings on a square-inch basis is much higher than that of handling all the elements on one large engraving. For example, four individual 2- by 3-inch process engravings would scale at 428 units, whereas if the elements were proportioned and positioned with a ¼-inch gutter between them, the resulting 4¼- by 6¼-inch engraving would scale at 152 units. There would also be an economy in press lockup.

Prepared Camera Copy

A new standard procedure of handling process copy is the use of prepared camera copy instead of the original color transparencies or paintings. The original artwork, together with layout and directions, goes to a color preparation studio (color photo laboratory) instead of to the photoengraver. The studio reduces mixed art media to a single medium (transparencies or reproduction-quality color prints), with all elements in tonal balance, scaled and positioned, and color-adjusted to suit the art director. "Assemblies" (two or more process elements) are usually emulsion-floated transparencies on film, scaled and positioned, and suitable for color separation and correction by electronic scanning machines to obtain continuous-tone separation negatives for the photoengraver. This method saves much time and cost and is widely used for magazine ads.

A recent development, the invention of the laser scanning machines, gives screened color separations for any of the processes in a matter of hours.

This procedure would not be used for a single process copy element unless it were a 35-millimeter or 2¼- by 2¼-inch transparency. Such process copy is too small for color correction and must be enlarged as either a transparency or a color print so that this work can be done.

Limitations of Process Reds and Blues

Regardless of the printing process used, some colors, among them Persian blues and emerald greens, can only be approximated with the four-color process. Process red is a cold red; so a warm Christmas red must be faked with a black tint. A royal blue is darkened in the same way. The artist should obtain color charts showing the colors obtainable on coated and uncoated paper. For letterpress these charts are available from photoengravers and from the Magazine Publishers Association. Magazines all use standardized process inks.

Simple Color

For this second kind of multicolor printing the colors are separated mechanically either by the artist or by the engraver. The great bulk of this printing is in black and one color, but more than one color can be used. Book illustrations are frequently done in several flat colors, as demonstrated in Copy Examples 16 and 17 (Figs. 5-20 and 5-21), showing preseparated color by the artist.

For black and one color a mechanical paste-up is often prepared as for single color, and the elements that are to appear

SCALE ESTIMATED PHOTOENGRAVING COSTS CONVERTED TO SQUARE INCHES FOR COMPARISON OF COSTS OF DIFFERENT KINDS OF PHOTOENGRAVINGS

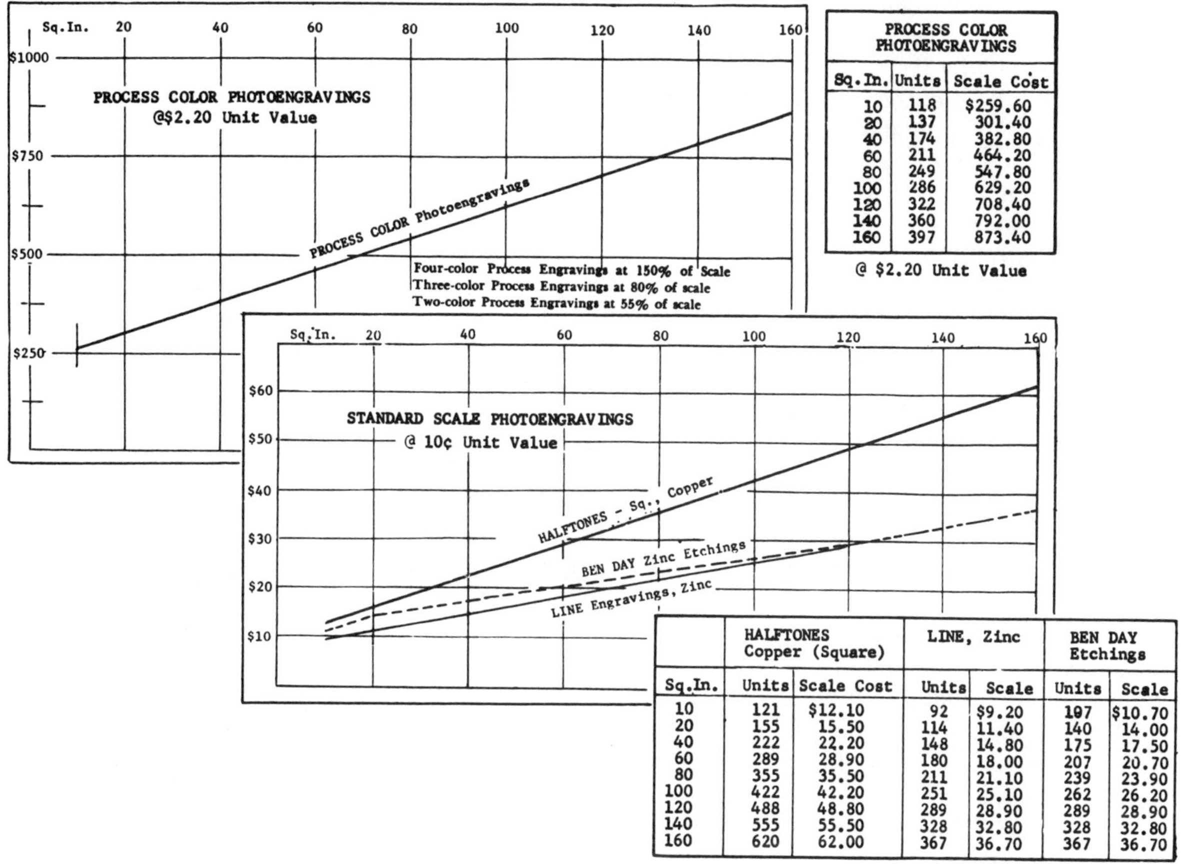

PROCESS COLOR PHOTOENGRAVINGS		
Sq. In.	Units	Scale Cost
10	118	$259.60
20	137	301.40
40	174	382.80
60	211	464.20
80	249	547.80
100	286	629.20
120	322	708.40
140	360	792.00
160	397	873.40

@ $2.20 Unit Value

	HALFTONES Copper (Square)		LINE, Zinc		BEN DAY Etchings	
Sq. In.	Units	Scale Cost	Units	Scale	Units	Scale
10	121	$12.10	92	$9.20	107	$10.70
20	155	15.50	114	11.40	140	14.00
40	222	22.20	148	14.80	175	17.50
60	289	28.90	180	18.00	207	20.70
80	355	35.50	211	21.10	239	23.90
100	422	42.20	251	25.10	262	26.20
120	488	48.80	289	28.90	289	28.90
140	555	55.50	328	32.80	328	32.80
160	620	62.00	367	36.70	367	36.70

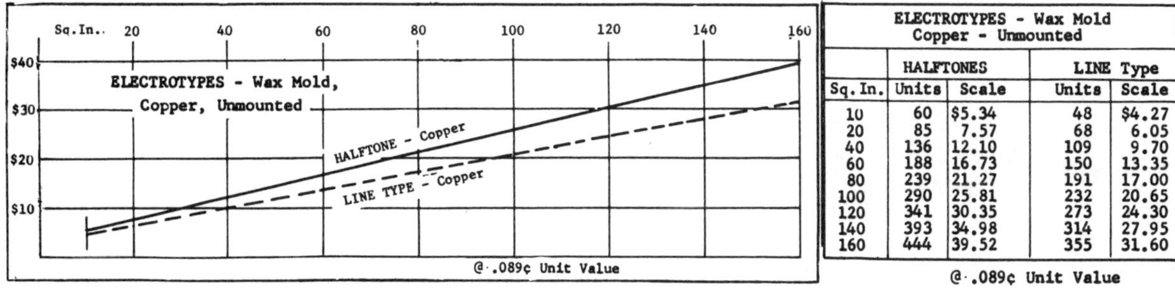

ELECTROTYPES - Wax Mold Copper - Unmounted				
	HALFTONES		LINE Type	
Sq. In.	Units	Scale	Units	Scale
10	60	$5.34	48	$4.27
20	85	7.57	68	6.05
40	136	12.10	109	9.70
60	188	16.73	150	13.35
80	239	21.27	191	17.00
100	290	25.81	232	20.65
120	341	30.35	273	24.30
140	393	34.98	314	27.95
160	444	39.52	355	31.60

@ .089¢ Unit Value

Fig. 6-4 If you multiply the maximum width and height of an engraving to obtain the number of square inches, you may find these graphs helpful in approximating the scale, or basic, plate cost. For halftones this cost is based on the square halftone. Any additional operations required to produce special types of halftones or to position, remove, or combine elements and the like involve extra charges, as listed on the three photoengravers' scales. Your photoengraver can supply copies of these scales, or you can write the American Photoplatemakers Association, 166 West Van Buren Street, Chicago, Ill. 60604. Each photoengraving firm sets its own unit value, which varies with the area and the kind of service required.

The scale cost of electrotypes, like that of photoengravings, is indicated by the number of units in the plate size. The unit value is set by each electrotyper, often on a contract basis.

in color are indicated on the tissue overlay. This is sufficient for the photoengraver, who makes two negatives, opaquing unwanted work in each. Copy Example 8 (Figs. 4-17 and 4-18) is an instance of such two-color copy.

Much collateral printed material makes use of available magazine process color plates for key artwork, while incidental illustrative treatment—backgrounds, tint panels, color spots—is prepared by the artist on the mechanical. Since the process art will require the use of transparent inks, hairline register should be provided for touching colors in the collateral material. This is demonstrated in the box wrap in Copy Example 11 (Figs. 4-39 and 4-40).

For some flat-color printing you may choose either copper or coarse-screen zinc halftones. Copper is used for better quality because of the control made possible by hand operations, whereas zinc is employed for speed. With zinc the camera copy must be of good quality, for there are no hand operations.

Since previous chapters on the preparation of mechanicals and other camera copy dealt with offset printing, it is well to remind the reader that the reproduction qualities of artwork are the same for all the printing processes and that all use the same keylining and other copy preparation methods. The original photoengraving craftsmen came from lithographic plants; today all the photomechanical workers—photoengravers, gravure engravers, offset lithographers—belong to the same union.

ARTWORK FOR MAGAZINES AND OTHER PERIODICALS

In general, the preparation of artwork for the periodical division of letterpress printing is the same as for commercial printing. However, the limitations of reds and blues in the four-color process are increased by the use of standardized process inks, as specified by the Magazine Publishers Association for wet printing on the four-color magazine presses.[1] These inks must be used so that an advertiser's color plates will be suitable for a list of consumer publications. Each publication issues color charts printed on its paper to show the results of combining colors in 10 percent steps. Because inks cannot be changed as in job printing, an artist doing finished art must know what shades of color to avoid.

The Standard Rate & Data Service[2] and each publication publish production specifications for advertisers. The "class" magazines use 120- and 133-line halftones; general and business publications tend to use a supercalendered paper and 100- and 110-line halftones. Since the advertiser may be spending a great deal of money for space in several national magazines, the cost of color plates and the absence of press lockup and makeready for job printing do not have the same importance, there is a wider choice of design and art media.

Publications with a circulation of less than 50,000 usually are not printed on the large rotary magazine presses because of the costs of preparation and of curved electros. Most farm and trade journals are printed on two-color flatbed commercial presses using opaque inks for black and one color. Machine-finish book paper and halftone newsprint requiring coarser-screen halftones such as 100-line and 85-line are frequently used. Printing is handled directly from the advertiser's plates—originals, electros, or plastics. Any process color is supplied by the advertiser as an insert.

CAMERA COPY FOR THE PHOTOENGRAVER

There is a wide choice of art media for advertising. Photographs are often taken on location with small hand cameras on 35-millimeter and 2¼- by 2¼-inch color films, which are too small for color cor-

[1]Inks for offset publications, both two-color and four-color, have also been standardized. New standards are contained in a fourteen-page booklet, *Recommended Standards for Advertising for Web Offset Publications.*

[2]*Print Media Production Data,* Standard Rate & Data Service, Inc., 5201 Old Orchard Road, Skokie, Ill. 60076, annually.

rection. Various forms of prepared copy are used to save time as well as plate costs. Regardless of the original art media or size, assemblies of process copy (two or more subjects) for an advertisement or editorial copy are usually prepared with reproduction-size, positioned color transparencies on film. With this form of copy the photoengraver can make color-corrected separations with an electronic scanning machine, can make contact separations with a vertical enlarger for the best quality, or can color-separate with a camera and filters.

Agencies frequently use color prints instead of transparencies if an illustration consists of components, if changes or additions must be made, or if considerable color adjusting is required in a short time. Clients sometimes specify prints because the visual quality is closer to the possible reproduction quality.

Since electros of process plates are always supplied for consumer magazines, mechanicals are prepared for the whole ad being sent to the photoengraver, process copy being indicated by scaled and positioned Photostats. Process camera copy is supplied as a separate element or as an assembly of two or more elements.

When the mechanical for a process color magazine ad is prepared, incidental flat color copy is frequently prepared in color and positioned with the process art if it will not unduly increase the number of scale units. If flat color art in black is widely separated from the process color copy, it is handled on the mechanical of the page by the artist, who may use overlays for colors.

DESIGN AND LAYOUT

Design and layout have undergone many changes since scientific marketing and advertising techniques were adopted. The test of worth is not appearance but results: does the advertising sell the product or service? *Advertising Service for Students*,[3] a portfolio of outstanding advertising case histories of successful campaigns published every other year, is the link between theory and practice. For two decades these portfolios have shown how strategy, creative planning, and copy keep changing.

Advertising design for magazines must carry out the advertising theme, which is based on market research. As for a choice between hand illustration and photography, the general feeling is that hand illustration is preferable for interpretation, in situations in which people are to be shown rather than individuals, or for a situation or condition not available for photography. Hand artwork is often the best choice for human-interest appeal. Photography is generally used for realism in representation and hence is widely employed for specific audience appeal and for depiction of the product itself, particularly in full color. Small hand cameras with a motor drive (eight frames per second) are widely used in advertising to achieve believability; 100 pictures may be taken to get the exact expression wanted. Photography is apt to be used for a descriptive article, and hand illustration for fiction.

Magazines are selected by advertisers for their appeal to a specific market or type of reader. Layout and text are designed accordingly: the copy can go into greater detail, and with full color the layout frequently bleeds over the page edge. Color backgrounds, or allover background tints, are often used for attention value, particularly with rotogravure. A complementary background in a contrasting lighter color can help make an illustration stand out.

ARTWORK FOR NEWSPAPERS

The third form of printing by the letterpress process is rather rough in comparison with commercial printing and that done on coated paper on large rotary magazine presses. Newspaper pages are made up with type and plates; usually the plates are stereotypes made from paper mats of the advertiser's original photoengravings in a coarse screen. A stereotype mat of the made-up page is rolled, and from it is made a curved press plate to be clamped to the press cylinder for the printing.

[3]*Advertising Service for Students*, Margaret Maytham, Southport, Conn. 06490.

Improperly Lighted

Fig. 6-5 Only one very harsh and improperly placed light was used to illuminate these vegetables. As a result, there are dark shadows distorting the shape of the vegetables and extreme highlights minimizing details.

Properly Lighted and Retouched

Fig. 6-6 A backlight and a fill light were added to open up the shadows and give form to the vegetables. A fill light should be placed as close to the lens as possible so that every crevice may be seen. As shown here, retouching should be kept to a minimum for the best photographic reproduction.

Improperly Lighted

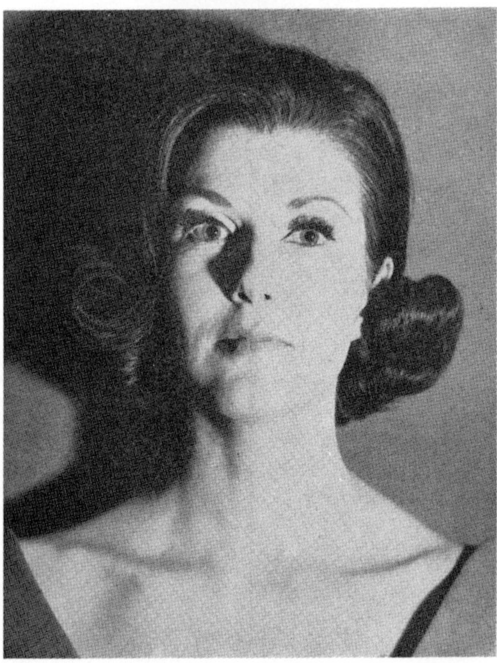

Fig. 6-7 This subject lacks contrast to the background because it is lit by only one poorly placed light that casts ugly shadows.

Properly Lighted and Retouched

Fig. 6-8 Four lights were used on this portrait, with a backlight spilling on the background to outline the model's hair, give contour and depth to her features, and fill in harsh shadows. Retouching may be necessary to add subtle highlights.

Newsprint is the cheapest printing paper and requires the use of coarse halftone screens—55- to 75-line. An advertisement originally made up with 65-line halftones is apt to be supplied to a large list of newspapers in mat form. Thus additional tonal qualities will be lost because two intermediate stereotypes are made to get the press plate.

These mechanical limitations restrict the choice of artwork suitable for newspapers, and for conventional newspaper reproduction artwork falls into three general categories: photography, wash drawings, and line drawings.

Tone Value for Newspaper Illustration

Fig. 6-9 There should be an approximate 25 percent difference in tone values from white to black. The gray scale reproduced here shows the approximate minimum tonal difference between adjacent areas. It is not intended to preclude the numerous in-between values but can be used as a guide.

PHOTOGRAPHY

The following recommendations are useful in preparing photographs for newspaper reproduction:

- Extra contrast, obtained by correct illumination of the subject for details, definition, and focal depth of background, is desirable. Glossy Velox prints are the best. Details should be accentuated.
- Necessary retouching should be kept to a minimum. Use one type and brand of retouching grays, particularly on photos for one job.
- Use a good brand of Chinese white (titanium pigment), for some whites reproduce as gray. Avoid fluorescent whites. Tones next to highlight dropout areas should be a little darker than usual.

Kromo-Lite Process

Fig. 6-10 A combination highlight dropout engraving produced by conventional photoengraving requires time and money. Most metropolitan newspapers make their own engravings for advertisers and include the cost in their advertising rates. Their photoengraving departments use the Kromo-Lite process for highlight wash-and-line drawings, which are widely used for fashion illustrations. The artist executes his drawing in the usual way but adds Kromo-Lite solution to his wash water. For airbrush work, lampblack is used with the water and the Kromo-Lite solution. [*Dorothy Hood for Lord & Taylor Newspaper wash-and-line highlight dropout art prepared by the Kromo-Lite process*]

WASH DRAWINGS

Like the photographs, wash drawings show the subject in a continuous range of tones from white to black. For fashion illustrations particularly, they often include line work. Adjacent tones should have good contrast. Wash drawings are frequently highlighted in part, as shown in Fig. 6-11. Areas of a design that are not to be highlighted can be indicated by light blue on the overlay. The engraver can then make a highlight dropout mask.

Wash Drawing

Fig. 6-11 Wash drawing with highlight dropout areas. The wash drawing, like the photograph, shows the subject in a continuous range of tones from white to black. Good value contrast between adjacent tone areas must be maintained. Extremely dark areas should generally be used for accent and not as a main portion of the illustration. The wash drawing may have an overall tone or be highlighted, as in this illustration. Areas of a design that are not to be highlighted can be indicated by light blue on an overlay, and the photoengraver can make a highlight dropout mask to drop the halftone dots for the white.

The following recommendations are useful in making wash drawings for newspaper reproduction:

- Light tones should be painted slightly darker to stand out against the off-white newsprint. The edges of a light wash should be slightly accentuated.
- Avoid using two kinds of black such as lampblack and india ink, for the resulting dull and bright blacks register differently on the engraver's negative.
- Avoid vignettes, which print poorly in newspaper reproduction.

LINE TECHNIQUES

Fig. 6-12 Pen-line drawing used for shading and values.

Fig. 6-13 Pen-line drawing excessively reduced.

Fig. 6-14 Pen-line drawing with solid blacks.

Fig. 6-15 Drybrush is an exacting medium. Its successful use depends upon moving a nearly dry brush across a textured surface, leaving black only on the top of the texture with white in the depressions to create varying values.

Fig. 6-16 Drybrush technique employed with a Magic Marker on textured paper.

Fig. 6-17
Carbon pencil drawing.

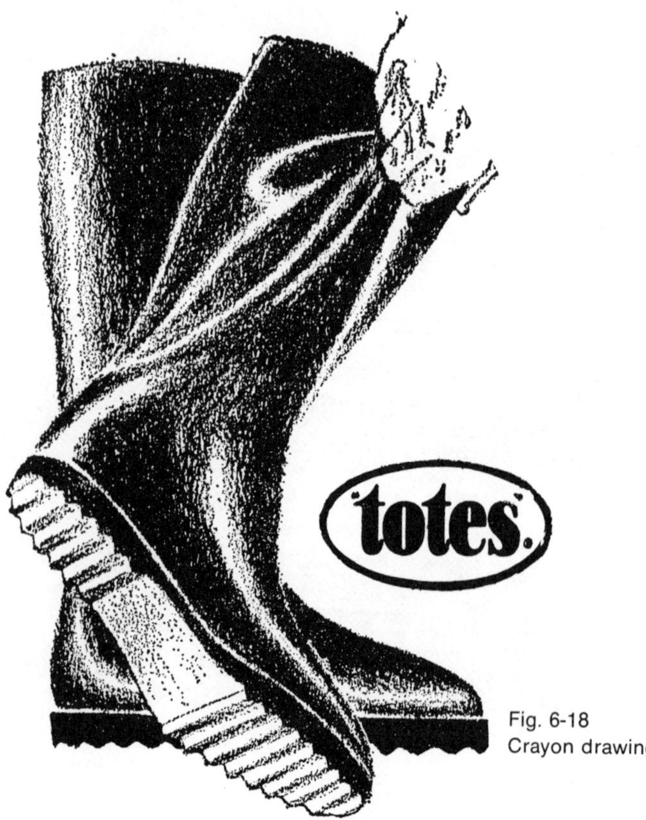

Fig. 6-18
Crayon drawing.

Fig. 6-19 Felt and nylon tip drawing. Never use a nylon tip on film or paint over the drawing.

USE OF PATTERN AND SHADING SHEETS BY THE ARTIST

Line drawing using transparent pattern sheets.

Line drawing using transparent pattern sheets exclusively.

Fig. 6-20

Pen-line drawing without shading.

LINE DRAWINGS

As you will recall, line art does not involve the use of the halftone screen when engravings are made. Line drawings are prepared by using a pen, a nylon-tipped pen, or a felt-tipped applicator with black ink on suitable smooth paper or board or by drybrush or artist's carbon pencil on a textured board. Graphite pencils should not be used for line art because the gray tones do not reproduce; the graphite crystals reflect light when photographed. The artist's work size for pen-line drawings should not be greater than size and one-half because excessive reduction causes pen-line shading to fill in and reproduce as a solid.

Tints and Patterns by Artist

The artist's work in pen-line newspaper illustration is frequently supplemented by stock tint sheets, which are used to apply tone to selected parts. This material, which is available at art supply stores, is applied as shown in Fig. 6-20.

Screened Velox Prints

Wash drawings and photos are sometimes converted to line copy by means of screened Velox photoprints. Backgrounds or highlights can be painted out to remove the halftone dots, and pen-line drawings can be added. This form of copy produces an inexpensive line-tone engraving by the benday Photoengravers' Standard Scale. For newspaper photoengravings the coarse-screen zinc halftone scale (75-line screen or coarser) applies.

The informative literature usually available from the larger Photostat services offers many cost- and time-saving tips to the artist.[4]

OFFSET-PRINTED NEWSPAPERS

The restrictions on the tonal qualities of art and photos and on the use of halftone screens finer than 75-line do not apply to offset newspapers. Screens of 120 lines and even finer screens are in common use with these papers.

Kodak, Agfa, and others have developed special photographic papers and processes—the Kodak PMT papers (see Fig. 3-39) and the Agfa PP proof-positive method—to speed up newspaper paste-up work. The basic idea is to obtain scaled screened prints or line prints in one step, avoiding the intermediate negative, or to obtain same-size prints with a print frame. Such special papers produce copy for the paste-up—halftones to a 100-line screen. Special daylight cameras are also being used.[5]

CAMERA COPY FOR THE FLEXOGRAPHIC PROCESS

The use of molded rubber printing plates cast from a matrix, reproduced from either a zinc or a magnesium photoengraving, presents special requirements in the preparation of a mechanical. When the assembly of copy elements is completed, a rectangular border about ¼ inch wide should be added about ½ inch from the copy on all four sides. In addition to carrying center marks and relevant bearer data, this border acts as a retaining barrier to impede the flow of rubber as it is pressed into the matrix and thus to help produce an accurate rubber printing plate. This restrictive action tends to maintain the thickness of the rubber plate, thus ensuring greater accuracy. The border is removed before the rubber plate is mounted on the press cylinder.

[4]Some of the line illustrations and related material in this section are drawn from Report 10, *Black-and-White Newspaper Reproduction*, an excellent booklet prepared by the American Newspaper Publishers Association–American Association of Advertising Agencies Joint Committee. Consult your local newspaper.

[5]*Kodak Handbook of Newspaper Techniques*, Eastman Kodak Company, 343 State Street, Rochester, N.Y. 14608, 1968. It covers the subject from composition methods and copy preparation to newspaper color methods.

A separate plate is required for each color. The plates are registered color to color by the center marks in the border (see Fig. 6-21).

PRECAUTIONS FOR FINE LINES AND TYPE

In printing from rubber plates the impression squeeze tends to spread the ink slightly. For this reason fine line work should be prepared a little lighter than the desired reproduction, and reversed elements should be prepared slightly heavier. Thus the fine lines do not fill in.

For the same reason precautions should be taken in selecting typefaces. Type 14 points or smaller should be lighter in weight than the desired reproduction. For a reversed-type element use boldface type to obtain a lighter weight such as a medium face. In general, avoid fine serifs and lines in typefaces, and do not use a size smaller than 6 points (if a reversed type, not smaller than 8 points).

CRITICAL MEASUREMENT: COMPENSATING FOR DISTORTION

Flexography is widely used in packaging printing, in which die cutting and scoring for folding make the measurement of designs and backgrounds critical. The artwork and the layout for packaging are prepared to compensate for the distortion that takes place both in the molding of the rubber plate and in the printing operation.

When the rubber plate is molded, the vulcanizing causes it to shrink 0.020 inch for each inch in both width and length. When the plate is fastened on the printing cylinder, the circumference increases, the amount of the increase depending on the cylinder diameter. For example, on a 2-inch plate cylinder 3 inches of rubber plate increases to 3.225 inches, but on a larger cylinder the increase is smaller (on a 7-inch cylinder the plate increases only to 3.006 inches). With a cylinder diameter of 16.650 inches there is no change in the plate circumference.

Obviously, when the measurement of a design is critical for die cutting or folding, the artist must consult the printer for instructions on the allowance to be made for the distortion. The printer supplies a

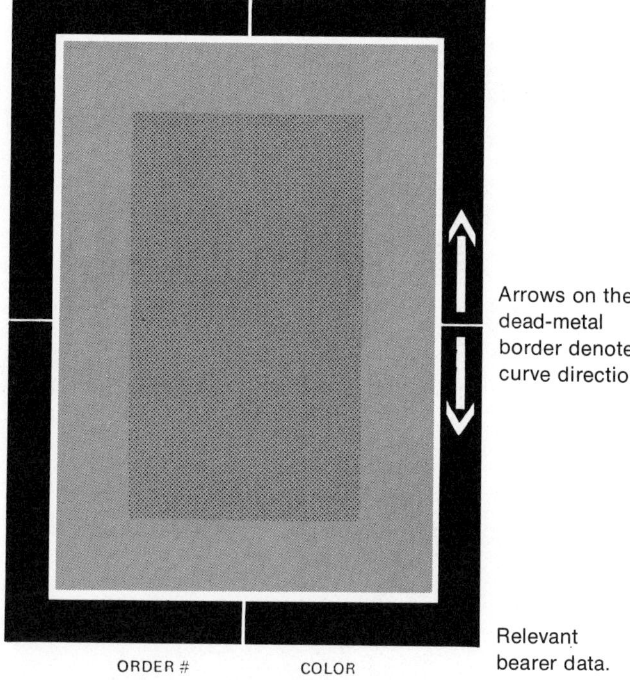

Fig. 6-21 A mechanical for flexography should carry a dead-metal border about ¼ inch wide, placed ½ inch outside the work, or copy, area. Fine center marks on the border are extended into the dead area to permit accurate positioning on the press.

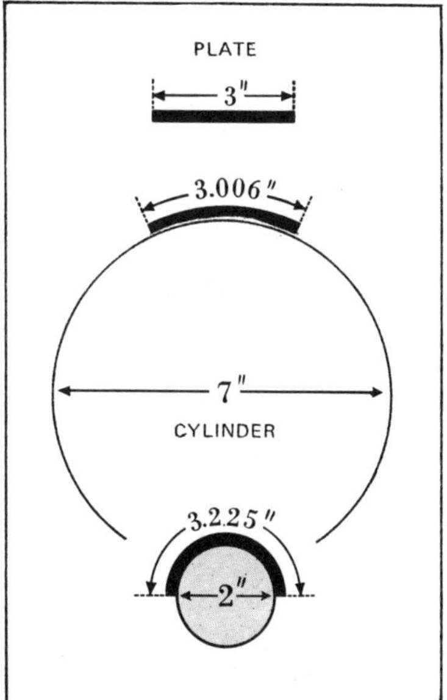

Fig. 6-22 When a rubber printing plate is mounted around the plate cylinder, the printing surface is lengthened, but to a greater extent on a small-diameter cylinder than on a larger one.

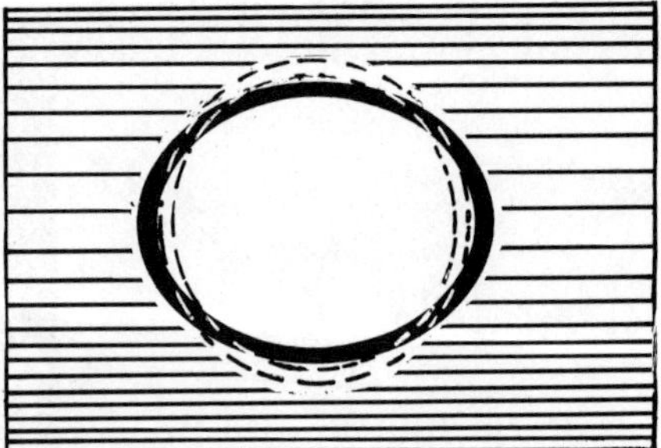

Fig. 6-23 Since the image size around the cylinder will increase slightly, art should be executed to allow for this distortion. There is plate shrinkage across the cylinder, and the art should be extended slightly. The printer supplies the artist with a distortion chart for the stretch factor to be used. For critical measurement only, a circle would be slightly elliptical on the copy prepared for the camera.

distortion chart for the cylinder size to be used and information on which dimension will go around the cylinder. The chart shows the artist what to allow for stretch around the cylinder; the usual allowance across the cylinder is an addition of 0.020 inch per inch. Thus the art for a circle would be prepared to be slightly elliptical (Fig. 6-23 is exaggerated).

In compensating for distortion in some critical flexographic printing the type matter and angled artwork present a problem. In such cases copy is prepared as for other printing, and the flexographic platemaker uses special lenses to make a negative for the zinc engraving that compensates for the distortion. Copy prepared originally for another printing process can usually be handled by this photographic method to avoid remaking the mechanical. However, there is an extra charge for the photographic method.

CHAPTER SEVEN

Process Color Copy: Its Preparation

To REPRODUCE MOST color artwork such as paintings and photo color transparencies and prints, all the major printing processes employ the four-color process method. With the camera copy placed on the copyboard of a process camera and a proper color filter used with the lens, color separation negatives are made for the three primary colors and black by the subtractive color method. To get the yellow negative, the filter being used holds back the blue and the red; then other filters are used to get the red and blue negatives. The filter for the black is used essentially to accent details and darken color tones. Secondary colors are obtained by adjacent halftone dots of the primary color inks, in an optical illusion. With just three color ink pigments, the four-color process does not have the range of the artist's palette or of the dyes in a color transparency, and some colors can only be approximated unless a fifth or a sixth color is used.

LIMITATIONS OF THE FOUR-COLOR PROCESS

When working with colors, the artist should be aware that there are limitations to the colors that can be reproduced, imposed mainly by the process red and blue. For example, you cannot get a good Persian blue or emerald green. Since both the process red and the process blue are cold in hue, you cannot get a warm Christmas red or a royal blue; the red and blue can only be darkened with a black tint.

These limitations are particularly stringent in publication printing, for which standardized process inks are used. Various publication associations publish color charts showing the results of combining

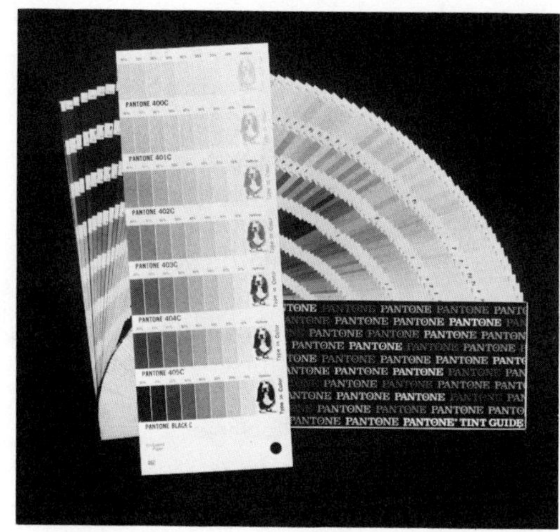

tones of color on both coated and uncoated papers. Most of the larger consumer magazines also publish their own color charts on the paper they use.

In commercial printing process inks can be changed to suit job needs, or a fifth or a sixth color can be used to meet exacting requirements. In the cosmetic industry as many as eight colors are used to match hair tints and the colors of lipsticks and nail polish. Some fine arts reproductions are printed in ten colors.

A commercial artist working in color should understand that his or her artwork must be suitable for reproduction by the four-color process. If the work requires six colors, it may be rejected. Here are some tips for the artist:

Process Red

To reproduce purples, dark blues, cold browns, and cold pink tones, the ink must

[1]Pantone, Inc., 55 Knickerbocker Road, Moonachie, N.J. 07074.

be close to the magenta or cold red, whereas to get clean oranges, warm Christmas red solids, and extremely clean flesh tones, the ink should be cleaner or toward the warm red. The artist should avoid mixing any of the two groups of colors in the same painting. For example, if there are clean oranges, avoid purples, dark blues, and so on.

Process Blue

To get the dark blues, purples, and royal blue tones of a painting, the printer's ink should be of a reddish cast, but if the subject has much clean green, the blue ink used should be closer to peacock or greenish blue. If the artwork contains both clean greens and cold purples, one of the two colors must be sacrificed if only one blue is to be used in the printing. Otherwise, either the greens would be too olive, or the purples would be too dirty.

Other Problems

The few limitations of process red and blue inks mentioned here do not cover all the problems of four-color reproduction, but they do point the way to closer cooperation between the creative artist and the reproduction technician. When on unfamiliar ground, consult one of your producers for guidance and procedure before artwork is prepared. This is standard procedure in the book publishing field, in which time and budgets are always tight. Get the producer's recommendations on problems: there are art techniques and color processes that save time and money and may be suitable for the desired quality. In advertising production time and cost usually have priority over quality.

ADVICE ON PAINTING AND PIGMENTS

Avoidance of Overpainting

To make a correction or a change in an oil or opaque watercolor painting the artist should remove the old work first. Otherwise some of the rays of the copyboard arc lamps will penetrate the paint and bounce back from the canvas to register on the color separation negatives. This produces a muddy spot on each of the four color separations that must be corrected by hand, resulting in extra charges.

Do not letter on top of artwork. Position lettering or type proof on an overlay; it will be handled by the platemaker.

Choice of Pigments

Almost any form of art can be color-separated photographically, but the platemaker's charges may vary greatly with the pigments used and the secondary colors required. Transparent pigments are the simplest to color-separate. There are watercolors keyed to standard process colors, and if these particular colors are suitable, no color correction will be required.

Color reproduction is frequently unsatisfactory when an artist varies the type of paint. The change may not be apparent to the eye, but when the colors are separated photographically, each type of paint—acrylic, tempera, casein, and so on—may require special handling with filters and different developers. The same type of paint should be used throughout the subject or group to be color-separated.

Both type matter and lines reproduced in process colors should be limited to one or two colors. The use of all four colors causes unnecessary register problems with a large press sheet.

White pigment should be used sparingly to lighten colors, and the same brand should be used throughout a painting or group. Different brands may reflect different light rays from the arc lights and add to the correction time because different filters and developers are needed to get good separations. You will find that the work of the best artists saves several hundred dollars in plate costs because they know the requirements for four-color reproduction and the methods to be used for different grades of quality.

WORKING WITH THE PLATEMAKER

Notification of Paper Choice

Engravers or platemakers should be informed of the kind of paper to be used for the reproduction of tone work, for they adjust the allover tonal contrast in accordance with the choice of a coated or an uncoated paper. It is best to send a swatch of the paper along with the artwork and also the paper mill brand for process color.

Color samples should appear on the kind of paper to be used. In particular, don't send a color sample on coated paper if uncoated paper is to be used. Even with the same ink, the colors on the two kinds of paper will differ because of light reflection from the paper.

Dispatch of Artwork

Color separations or process color photoengravings take time. To avoid the extra cost of overtime to meet a specified delivery date, send artwork to the platemaker before the mechanicals are finished. This is also the case with coloraphoto laboratory preparing camera-ready copy.

NEW PROCEDURE WITH PROCESS COPY

Prior to World War II reproduction color photography was generally limited to 35-millimeter Kodachromes or their equivalents, which were too small for color correction, and for all printing processes the color cameramen had to follow an involved procedure to obtain scaled color-corrected separations. The results were not seen until color proofs of the plates were made. Carbro prints (enlarged as desired), forming a sandwich of special tissues with each color on a separate tissue, were the only form of reproduction color prints. Duplicates could not be made. The available photo color prints were not of reproduction quality.

DEVELOPMENT OF ART PRODUCTION

In Chapter 1 we discussed the transfer of advertising production from the production department to the art department of the user or to the art department of the user's agency because of the application of new technology to photomechanical methods, particularly under the advantages of time plate estimating. The use of color photography by art directors in advertising and for magazine editorial pages, together with the development of color photo laboratories to handle the intermediate steps in obtaining camera-ready copy, is the major factor in the development of production procedures in the art department. Today process artwork does not go directly to the engraver or platemaker unless there is only a single process subject. Even in this case, however, art consisting of a 35-millimeter or 2¼- by 2¼-inch transparency is too small for color correction by either the engraver or the platemaker, and a larger transparency or print is made and supplied.

When the offset process, with its wider choice of paper and composition methods and a different cost system for engravings, began to be used in volume for advertising, for a time approved layouts first went to the production department for recommendations to the art department on process, paper, composition, art media, and so on, to keep the job within the limitations of the budget and closing dates. It was the art department that made the paste-up mechanical and other forms of copy for the camera. Previously the user's production department had taken the rough layout, artwork, and copywriter's text and purchased photoengravings, composition, and printer's services.

Naturally, it was not long before art directors and assistants learned production for graphic reproduction, with the extra capabilities and economies made possible by offset. The new technology, which was a result of research on faster methods and lower costs, was applied principally in the preparation stage of camera copy. The purpose was to transfer to copy preparation the equivalent of some of the engraving and typesetting operations and so save time and costs.

Color Prints and Transparencies

The first major development was reproduction-quality color photoprints, even in sizes as large as 16 by 20 inches. Their use permitted mixed art media to be reduced to a single medium, usually scaled and color-adjusted and sometimes positioned for an assembly. Very important to nation-

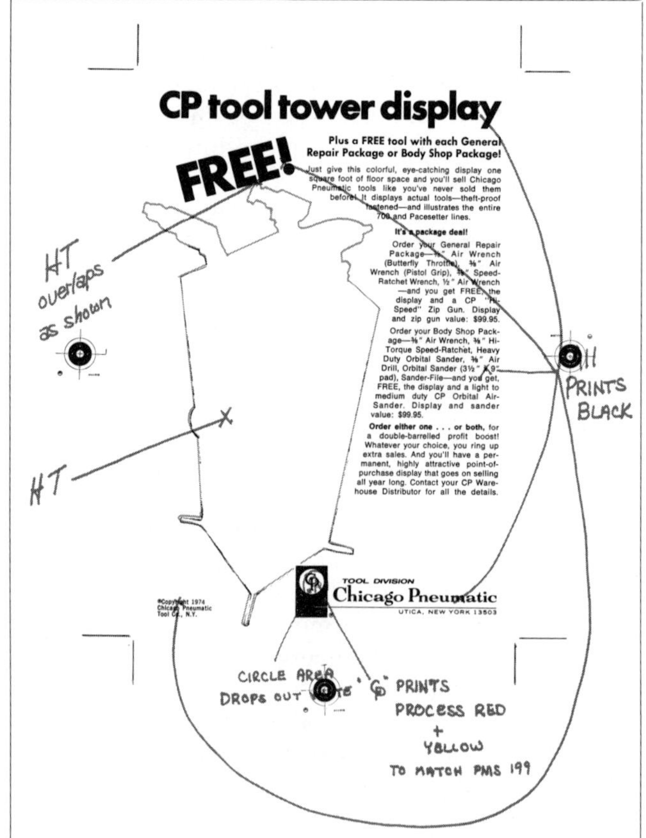

Fig. 7-2*A*. Mechanical with a single process color element. This Chicago Pneumatic mechanical gives a good idea of how instructions are handled on a tissue overlay. The single process color subject was merely outlined in red for size and position: the artwork was a 3¾- by 4¾-inch transparency supplied as a separate element.

Fig. 7-2*B*. The completed advertisement.

al advertisers was the fact that inexpensive duplicate color prints could be made. The duplicates are usually needed for simultaneous production at different printing plants as well as for different processes.

A few years later photographic technicians could handle color transparencies in the same way, even inserting components without expensive featheredging to hide the edge line. Now there are color photo laboratories or studios that undertake all such work with either prints or transparencies. The original artwork and a layout are sent to a color laboratory, which prepares camera-ready copy exactly as wanted. This copy then goes to the engraver or printer, depending on the printing process being used. For same-focus economies, which are available with all processes except letterpress, these intermediate photo steps produce the proportioned process elements.

With the use of such forms of camera copy, particularly transparencies, electronic scanning machines were subsequently developed to obtain color separations in hours rather than days for any of the printing processes. The machines can take even a 35-millimeter transparency and enlarge and color-separate it. This procedure for producing prepared camera copy is now standard for all printing processes.

Composition Methods

With the photomechanical printing processes there is no need for metal type.

When metal type is used, it is ordered in the form of galley repro proofs to make up a page on the drawing board, with a choice of a variety of display type for headlines. Such composition now is usually handled in the art department for reasons of economy and speed. Composition costs with these methods are only half of those of a made-up advertising page type repro proof.

SHIFT OF ADVERTISING PRODUCTION TO THE ART DEPARTMENT

With the explanation of these developments our understanding of why much of advertising production was shifted to the user's art department, not only for the photomechanical processes but to a more limited extent for photoengravings, becomes clearer.

Now when rough layouts are approved, decisions have also been made on colors, printing process, paper, art medium and its preparation, and, usually, composition. The roughs go to a production (mechanical) artist, who by means of a paste-up mechanical proceeds to make up the page or copy unit on the drawing board, scaling and positioning copy elements including Photostats or outlines for the size and position of process elements. A member of the art department, probably an assistant art director, will already have turned over some of the process art to a color photo studio, with instructions to produce the prints or transparencies wanted. This prepared art is sent to the production artist, and everything is then put in shape for the printer.

Extent of Change: TAPPI Survey

As mentioned in Chapter 1, a survey[2] of 2,400 art directors that had been made in 1968 by the Technical Association of the Pulp and Paper Industry (TAPPI) revealed the changed character of the work of their departments. It disclosed that 76 percent of the art directors worked directly with graphic arts suppliers instead of through the production department, that 62 percent specified and bought plates and separations, and that 66 percent bought or specified printing and binding. Art directors now have the authority to operate as they think best and usually take charge of certain production men to determine cost and time factors. Production still handles agency "traffic": the shipment of clients' plates and mats to magazines and newspapers and production details that are not the concern of the art department.

Although the agency production department does not produce the camera copy, we are told that the department is responsible for extra engraving charges if it places the order. Production people, too, must be up to date on the new production procedures and techniques and know camera copy.

REPRODUCTION-QUALITY COLOR PRINTS

A few years after World War II there were many new developments in color photography and in photomechanical equipment and methods. Reproduction-quality photo color prints, first the dye transfer and a little later the Type C color print, introduced prepared process color camera copy. This meant that mixed art media could be reduced to a single medium: color prints scaled, positioned, and color-balanced for an assembly on a copy unit or proportioned for same-focus economies time plate estimating. Almost any operation can be handled as described below under "Services of Color Photo Laboratories or Studios": preparing an illustration of components, making a transparency from a color print, or vice versa, changing a color or a shadow, and so on.

Previously, the only reproduction quality print used to scale and position process color elements was the carbro print, a hand operation of combining colored tissues, but duplicate copies were not possible.

In the early years dye-transfer prints were widely used because they were

[2]CA Report 16, Technical Association of the Pulp and Paper Industry, One Dunwoody Park, Chamblee, Ga. 30338.

best for changing and adjusting of colors, or for combining or inserting other process elements by photocomposition. But since the methods used are largely manual, their cost for 8 × 10-inch to 16 × 20-inch sizes runs around $250. Today they are used largely for critical color matching.

TYPE C COLOR PRINTS

The Type C print has endured because of its relatively low cost and availability in at least two quality grades, having to do mainly with delivery time—overnight or in two to three days. The cheapest—"presentation" grade—ranges in cost from about $20.00 for the 8 × 10-inch size to around $50.00 for the 20 × 24-inch size. Reproduction quality Type C prints cost from around $50 (8 × 10-inch) to $100 (20 × 24 inch). Additional copies are about half cost, but lower in quantity, such as $6.00 ea. for 25 copies.

The standard sizes are 8 × 10, 11 × 14, 14 × 17, 16 × 20, and 20 × 24 inches. Some studios also supply 24 × 30-inch and 30 × 40-inch sizes.

C prints are made from copy in negative form. With the higher prices there may not be an internegative charge; but with a price studio there may be an extra $5 charge if the copy is in positive form.

Many color photo studios have perfected their own reproduction-quality prints which are not Type C.

COLOR TRANSPARENCIES

Small photographic color transparencies were used for printing before color prints were developed. Such transparencies went directly to the engraver or platemaker to be scaled, color-corrected, and positioned to the layout. The procedure was so complicated that photoengravers charged a premium over the cost of reflection camera copy. If copy components were to be inserted or combined for an illustration, expensive featheredging was required at the joining line.

With the postwar development in color photography came color film in larger sizes such as 8 by 10 and 11 by 14 inches. It was not long before duplicate transparencies became available for scaling to size and positioning to layout. The same color photo studios usually produced these in the size wanted from 35-millimeter color originals, or to reduce mixed art media to transparencies to get better highlights. Later on, some of the new plate-making techniques required transparent camera copy.

Reproduction-quality duplicate transparencies are usually made in just two sizes—8 by 10 and 11 by 14 inches—for pricing. Any size up to these costs the same. They are made from any size original transparency or art work. Some studios offer a good discount if the original art is a Type C print.

Transparencies frequently require color adjustment to suit the art director or client, and retouching is in order. If the retouching is poorly done, a transparency can be ruined. With a costly transparency, engravers advocate using a duplicate for retouching. They use the original to make the color separations and the duplicate for any necessary color adjustment and correction.

Printing technicians seem to agree that a good color transparency in proper register for sharpness and with proper focal depth will give the best reproduction, particularly in the highlights. However, many camera operators will tell you that a print is better to hold important details in shadowed areas.

If the transparency on hand is too strong or too weak in a color, it can be color-adjusted by using Bourges color masking filter overlays, even for spot areas such as a fashion model's dress against a background. The filter overlay that makes the desired adjustment is fastened to the transparency.

It should be understood that color adjustments made to suit an art director alter camera copy. It is the producer's problem to use color correction to duplicate the colors of the adjusted original. The producer increases or reduces color tones on the separations or on the copper engravings to obtain the wanted result.

Advertising photographers work closely with art directors in the creative stage either in the studio or on location. In the field 35-millimeter and 2¼- by 2¼-inch hand cameras are widely used for convenience; some have motor-drive attachments for eight frames per second. To get the expression or element of believability wanted by the client, 100 or more pictures may be taken.

The brilliance and purity of colors of a transparency cannot be reproduced with four-color printing by any process, for the color quality of three pigments on paper cannot match the qualities of dyes on transparent film with transmission lighting. For this reason some printing users prefer color prints, the qualities of which are closer to the reproduction on paper.

Use of a Viewing Light

The color values seen in a transparency depend on lighting conditions. These conditions must be the same when user and producer judge the color values; the same type of viewing light should be used by both. At least one brand of light has a dial control; when the user obtains the desired result, the dial setting is noted on the edge of the transparency so that the engraver can duplicate the lighting. Official standards have been established.[3]

MEASUREMENT OF TONAL QUALITIES BY INSTRUMENT

A major reason for the improvement of process color reproduction is the use of the densitometer to measure the density, or tonal qualities, of selected areas at both ends of the gray scale on reflection or transmission copy. A reflective type of densitometer is used to measure art and prints and the reproduction. A transmission type measures transparencies and photographic negatives and positives. With a viewing eye on the end of a cord, tones on the ground glass of a process

[3]These are contained in a folder obtainable from the American Association of Advertising Agencies, 200 Park Avenue, New York, N.Y. 10017.

Color Prints Can Be Used for Assemblies

Fig. 7-3 The problem in handling the Betty Crocker spread was to obtain favorable perspective for each element and avoid shadows of one element falling on another. Separate color prints were made of most of the elements and then were stripped in the form of a one-piece montage copy for the platemaker. [*Courtesy* Art Direction]

Fig. 7-4 The subject with its lilliputian scale obviously involved scaling and combining several color elements. Such preparation work to obtain copy in one piece for the camera is usually handled by a color photo laboratory.

MASKING ALONE IS USED FOR SOME COLOR CORRECTION

Don't be a week behind.
Order your own copy
of Electrical World
and get the news fresh.
Reading a crumpled, dog-eared copy of Electrical World is better than nothing.
But it's not better than reading your own copy. Fresh and up-to-date. Addressed to you personally. Because there are a number of things wrong with a routing list.
By the time your copy gets to you the news may be stale. And so may you.
How many times have you wanted to clip an article? And didn't because you were afraid to incur the wrath of the next guy on the list.
Don't put it off any longer. Subscribe now. For 8 dollars a year (or less if your company has a club plan) you can have your own copy every week. That's less than 16 cents an issue.
You'll like being a week ahead for a change.

Fig. 7-5 Low production cost for a full-color page. To promote the economy of full-color production costs for advertising in the offset section of *Electrical World*, a promotion to agencies showed that costs for this house ad were less than $275. The costs included separations and Color Key print proofs as well as photography and composition.

camera can also be measured. Science has replaced the human eye in judging tones because visual perception varies widely from person to person.

PHOTOGRAPHIC MASKING FOR COLOR CORRECTION

Formerly the engraver or platemaker handled most color correction on the color separation negatives; this was a hand operation. With offset, at least 60 percent of the work was done on the continuous-tone negative separations, and the rest by dot-etching the screened positives. New technology substituted photographic masking for hand tonal changes on the negatives and made possible a greater degree of correction. Such masking is now widely used by all three major printing processes. A rush photoengraving set of color engravings can thus be made in two days instead of the usual ten days.

With offset, masking not only has reduced the number of hours required for color correction but has opened the door for short-run process color (1,000 sales portfolio sheets in full color for $200) and permits pleasing picture-quality separation (limited color correction) for less than $100. An example is the *Electrical World* ad promoting the magazine's offset section (*see* Fig. 7-5).

Choice of Reflection or Transmission Copy Determined by the Masking System

Five different masking techniques are used in offset; some require reflection, or opaque, camera copy, and others need transparencies. Art production therefore ascertains from the engraver or producer which form of copy is desired.

The degree of color fidelity required also has a bearing on the form of camera copy. For example, medical literature directed to doctors that shows the color of diseased tissue must be exact. A microphoto in color would be converted to a large dye transfer print, the visual quality of which would be closer to the printed reproduction than a transparency. Moreover, the print could be color-adjusted to suit the requirements of all concerned and would provide for reduction. Accurate color is the objective.

DEVELOPMENT OF COLOR PHOTO STUDIOS

Printing and related costs almost doubled after World War II. The introduction of dye transfer prints of reproduction quality stimulated research aimed at lower costs and faster methods. New photographic processes, materials, and equipment caused the printing user to adopt new procedures in the area between the original artwork or transparencies and copy prepared for the camera. These resulted in prepared camera-ready copy, a development that transferred the scaling and positioning of process copy elements from the engraver or platemaker to the copy preparation stage in the user's art department. Time and costs were substantially reduced. For example, the use of color prints on the mechanical for a small travel folder reduced the cost by $1,800.

It was the user who developed prepared copy, principally to save time. In advertising, delivery is wanted "yesterday," and it is not unusual for a laboratory to complete a rush job overnight so that the client can inspect it the next morning. An agency often has its own free-lance color correction artist so that it can have a job done quickly rather than wait its turn at a studio service.

Services of Color Photo Laboratories or Studios

By means of transparencies or color prints

- Mixed art media can be reduced to a single medium or to two media, with all subjects put in tonal balance.
- Original process copy can be scaled or proportioned.
- Color can be removed, changed, or added. Backgrounds and shadows can be strengthened or adjusted, and contrast added.
- Colors can be added to black-and-white photos (a form of the Flexichrome method).
- Assemblies of process elements can be scaled and positioned, either as transparencies on film or as color prints on a mechanical in a very large size.
- Reflective (opaque) copy can be converted to transparencies, or vice versa.
- Duplicates of transparencies and color prints can be made.
- An illustration can be photocomposed of separate components—superimposed, inserted, combined, and so on. Type or lettering can be added or surprinted.
- The 35-millimeter and 2¼- by 2¼-inch color transparencies from small hand cameras can be enlarged to suitable color correction size, and multiples color-balanced.

ELECTRONIC SCANNING MACHINES FOR PROCESS COLOR SEPARATIONS

The invention of electronic scanning machines, or scanners, to make process color separations for any of the printing processes is an example of new technology related to the development of reproduction-quality color transparencies and photo color prints. The purpose of these machines is to automate the manual methods of photoengravers and other platemakers, particularly the scaling and positioning of process elements in an assembly for a copy unit as well as necessary color adjustments for the art director. Their use avoids most of the extra cost of mixed art media.

The mechanical principle of a scanner is similar to that of a machinist's lathe. The transparency is wrapped around a glass cylinder that revolves, but instead of a cutting tool a light beam inside the cylinder passes through the transparency, and the colors are separated for each of the four color separations as the revolving transparency moves laterally, several hundred lines per inch. Pushing buttons determines the suitability of the continuous-tone separation negatives for the different processes. For the halftone method, the platemaker formerly made the final screened halftone negatives or positives, but now laser scanners (a new development) can make these for any printing process. Some scanners utilize the contact halftone screen; others do not.

The maximum size of the screened separations is about 24 by 24 inches. For larger-size work, large process color cameras may have a 58-inch circular screen; projectors handle twenty-four-sheet poster work.

Special Transparencies for Assemblies for Use by Scanning Machines

Many full-color advertisements contain several process color illustrations. Under standard production procedures the engraver would scale and position these elements on all four process engravings. At $20 an hour the job would be quite expensive. Today special camera copy is prepared for the use of scanners, which are almost standard for full-color magazine ads. The original artwork goes with the layout to a color photo studio, which reduces all elements to scaled transparencies. Each transparency is emulsion-floated to position on clear film for the assembly. The result is good copy for scanning machines under any of the printing processes. The platemakers handle all the color elements as one transparency, avoiding time-consuming scaling and positioning.

REFLECTION AND TRANSMISSION COPY NOT GROUPED FOR THE CAMERA

In art production you must not overlook the fact that reflection (opaque) camera copy goes on the camera copyboard and transparent copy goes into a transparency holder in the copyboard for backlighting. For offset and rotogravure, to which same-focus economies apply, do not supply a transparency and a watercolor for group separation, for they must be photographed separately. A color photo laboratory can convert the watercolor to a transparency, or both can be converted to color prints, scaled and positioned or proportioned for reduction. If there are a number of process subjects, you can plan for two groups, one of transparencies and the other of reflection copy, to obtain same-focus economies.

WORKING WITH COLOR PHOTO STUDIOS

Informative literature obtainable from the larger color photo studios is recommended. A list of such studios follows.

Authenticolor
227 East 45th Street
New York, N.Y. 10017

Berkey K & L Custom Services, Inc.
222 East 44th Street
New York, N.Y. 10017

Color Central, Inc.
612 North Michigan Avenue
Chicago, Ill. 60611

The Color Wheel, Inc.
227 East 45th Street
New York, N.Y. 10017

Robert Crandall Associates, Inc.
(Sales representative of
Color Corp. of America)
306 East 45th Street
New York, N.Y. 10017

Evans-Avedisian Color Lab, Inc.
342 Madison Avenue
New York, N.Y. 10017

Kurshan An'Lang Color Service, Inc.
222 East 44th Street
New York, N.Y. 10017

Newell Color Laboratory, Inc.
816 Seward Street
Hollywood, Calif. 90038

Pic Color Corp.
25 West 45th Street
New York, N.Y. 10036

Rapid Color, Inc.
1236 South Central Avenue
Glendale, Calif. 91204

Stewart Color Labs, Inc.
563 Eleventh Avenue
New York, N.Y. 10036

Stowell Studios, Inc.
11 West Illinois Street
Chicago, Ill. 60610

Streisand, Zuch & Freedman, Inc.
40 East 49th Street
New York, N.Y. 10017

The table on page 151 was prepared by Robert Crandall Associates.

LARGE PROCESS COLOR MECHANICALS

We have mentioned assemblies of transparencies on film made by color photo studios. Usually the studios are not equipped to handle anything larger than a standard large magazine page with such camera copy. With color prints, however, they frequently fill requests to make up a color mechanical in a larger size.

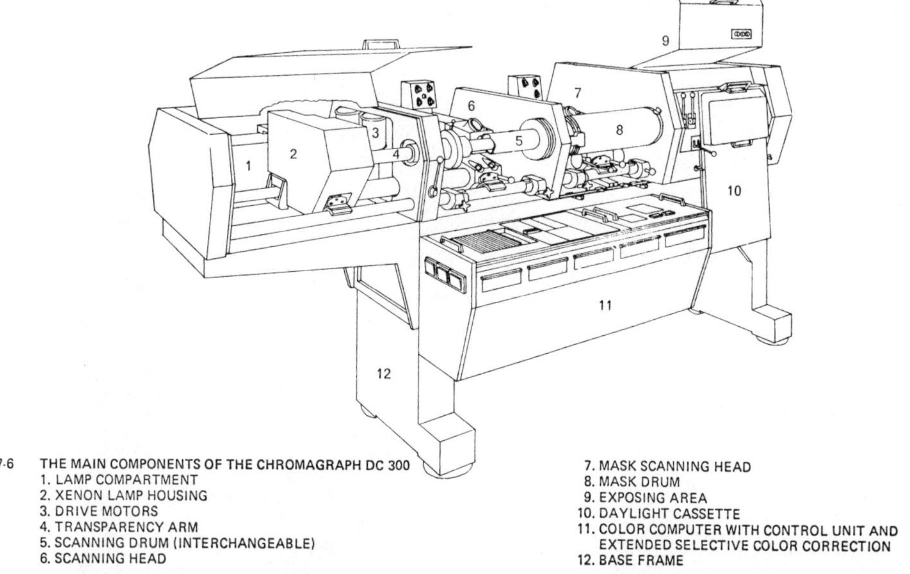

Fig. 7-6 Schematic drawing of the Chromagraph DC300 laser scanning system.

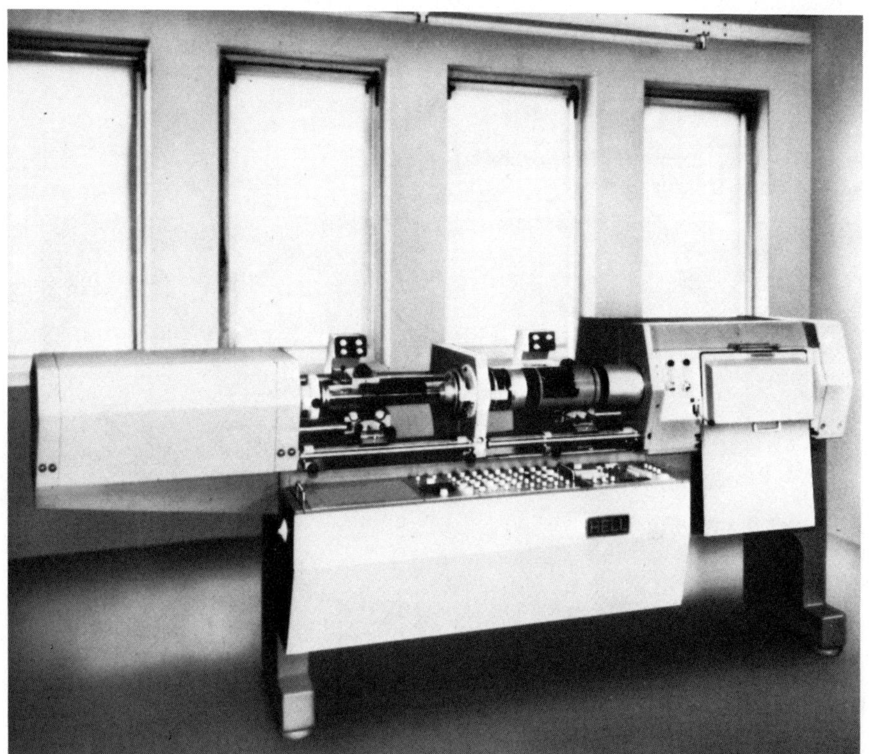

Fig. 7-7 The Chromagraph DC300, a daylight-operated electronic scanner to produce color-corrected continuous-tone or direct screened separations from various color originals. The scale of reproduction in relation to the original is continuously adjustable between 33.33 and 1600 percent. Any portion of the original can be selectively enlarged. The scanner has a separate programming mask cylinder to combine pictures, lettering, backgrounds, and so on. The maximum original and recording size is 16 by 20 inches.

Color Transparencies and Reflective Artwork Cannot Be Color-Separated Together

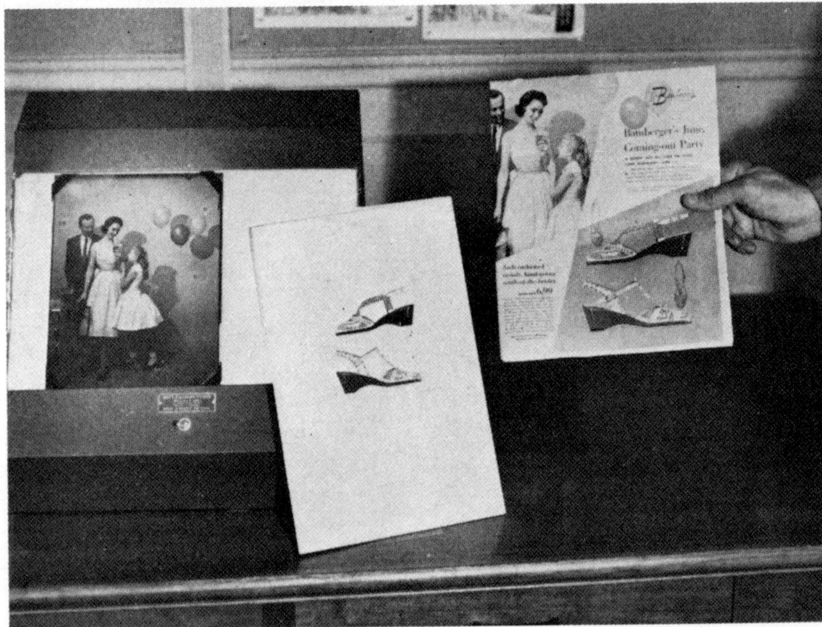

Fig. 7-8 A combination of opaque art (direct lighting of the copyboard) and a transparency (backlighting) requires two sets of color separations and extra color stripping to obtain the ad shown at the right. A proportioned transparency of the shoe artwork positioned with the transparency of the people would permit both elements to be handled by one set of color separations.

Process Color Elements Proportioned for the Copy Unit or Job

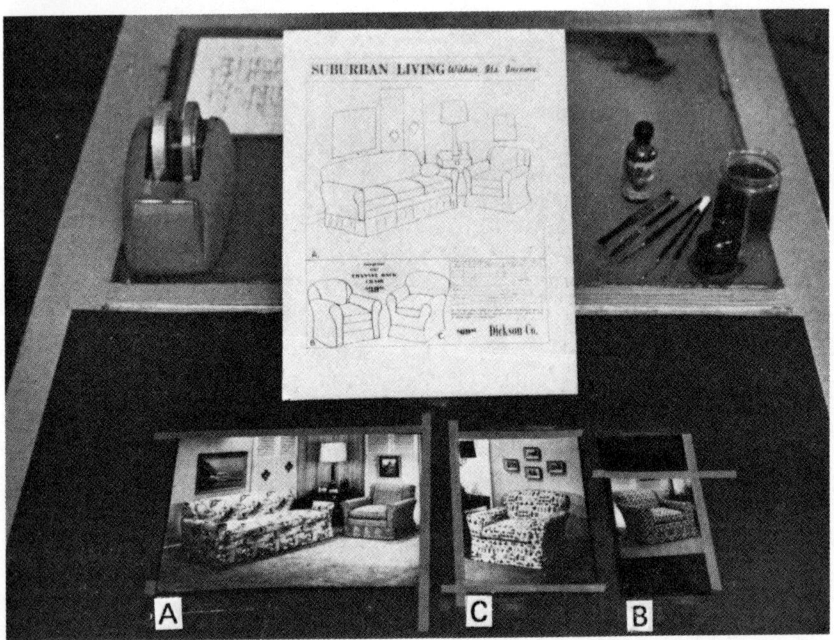

Fig. 7-9 If process color elements are not scaled or proportioned for gravure or offset (time method), extra color separations will be required. For this layout only the *A* and *B* elements were scaled; the *C* element had to be color-separated separately.

PHOTO COLOR TRANSPARENCIES AND PRINTS

If you want	And you have	Order
A color print or color transparency for reproduction (one or several)	Color transparencies Color negatives	Repro dye transfer prints Repro duplicate transparencies Repro Type C prints or duplicate transparencies
To make a selection from a number of color originals to preview an ad	Color transparencies Color negatives	Internegatives and Type C prints Type C prints
To produce a color assembly ready for reproduction	Color transparencies and color artwork	Color-corrected duplicate transparencies of all, scaled and positioned on film
A color layout for presentation	Color transparencies and color artwork Color negatives	Presentation dye transfers plus Type C prints or Ektachrome paper prints Type C prints
Finished artwork for reproduction, needing retouching and correction	Color transparencies Color artwork Ektacolor negatives	Retouched repro duplicate transparencies; in extreme cases, repro dye transfer prints plus retouching
To produce color plates for an ad in several places simultaneously or by more than one process	Color transparencies Color artwork Ektacolor negatives	Repro duplicate transparencies or repro dye transfer prints Repro duplicate transparencies or Type C prints
To present a new advertising program or idea to a client or to reproduce an ad or ad campaign in jumbo size for sales presentation	Color transparencies, finished art, tear sheets, or proof Ektacolor negatives	Comprehensive dye transfer prints; Ektachrome paper prints Type C prints
Display pieces for point of purchase or exhibit	Color transparencies Color artwork Ektacolor negatives	Color "printparencies" Color display duplicates (Print on translucent base)

Courtesy Robert Crandall Associates, New York.

Advertising collateral material often requires folders and broadsides that are much larger than a magazine page. For such materials the user's or the agency's art department makes the mechanical. The department must take into account not only the binder's imposition because of folding but technical details such as whether negative- or positive-working press plates are to be used. Here we are

An Illustration Made Up of Components

Fig. 7-10

referring to offset, which is the practical process for large process plates and the usual one for the print orders involved.

Of great importance is the fact that the producer who made the separations for the advertising campaign has already made multiple plate sizes, as ordered in the creative planning stage. The producer, of course, does almost all the related printing. For exceptions such as twenty-four-sheet posters, the customer's order to the producer should specify which separations are to be supplied to another shop.

There is also the matter of converting magazine color plates. These plates are constantly used for collateral pieces, usually in a larger size, of the color artwork in a different layout. This procedure avoids duplicating process costs. Conversions cost only about 25 cents on the dollar. Separations in the same size are often picked up from other offset jobs and can be enlarged or reduced within reasonable limits.

An offset color shop can also make assemblies of transparencies in a large size. The shop wants the transparencies in a scaled size and a tissue tracing of the layout. It will strip them to position on Mylar film, with the emulsion side up if deep-etch plates are to be made. This procedure saves much time.

If this type of job is to be handled by letterpress or gravure, you should obtain instructions on the maximum size of process copy unit to prepare. The photoengraver is apt to be limited to a 14- by 17-inch process unit, and the gravure printer by the largest chase on his step-and-repeat machine.

POSITIONING OF TYPE MATTER ON THE OVERLAY

Whether it is a question of an assembly on film or of reflection copy on a process color mechanical, all the printing processes want type matter and other black elements kept separate from the process color copy, usually on an overlay. A mechanical with all line copy positioned on it is suitable if process artwork is merely indicated and supplied separately, as in the Chicago Pneumatic mechanical (see Fig. 7-2). The platemakers photocompose the black line work with the black separation negative or positive of the process separations.

COPY EXAMPLE 18

The Preparation of an Assembly

Fig. 7-11 Instead of having the photoengraver carry out the scaling, positioning, and combining of elements, art production and the color studios now handle the equivalent of this work and supply the photoengraver or the offset or gravure platemaker with copy in one piece in the form of transparencies on film. Much time and costs are saved. [*Photos by Robert Crandall Associates, Inc., New York*]

COPY EXAMPLE 19

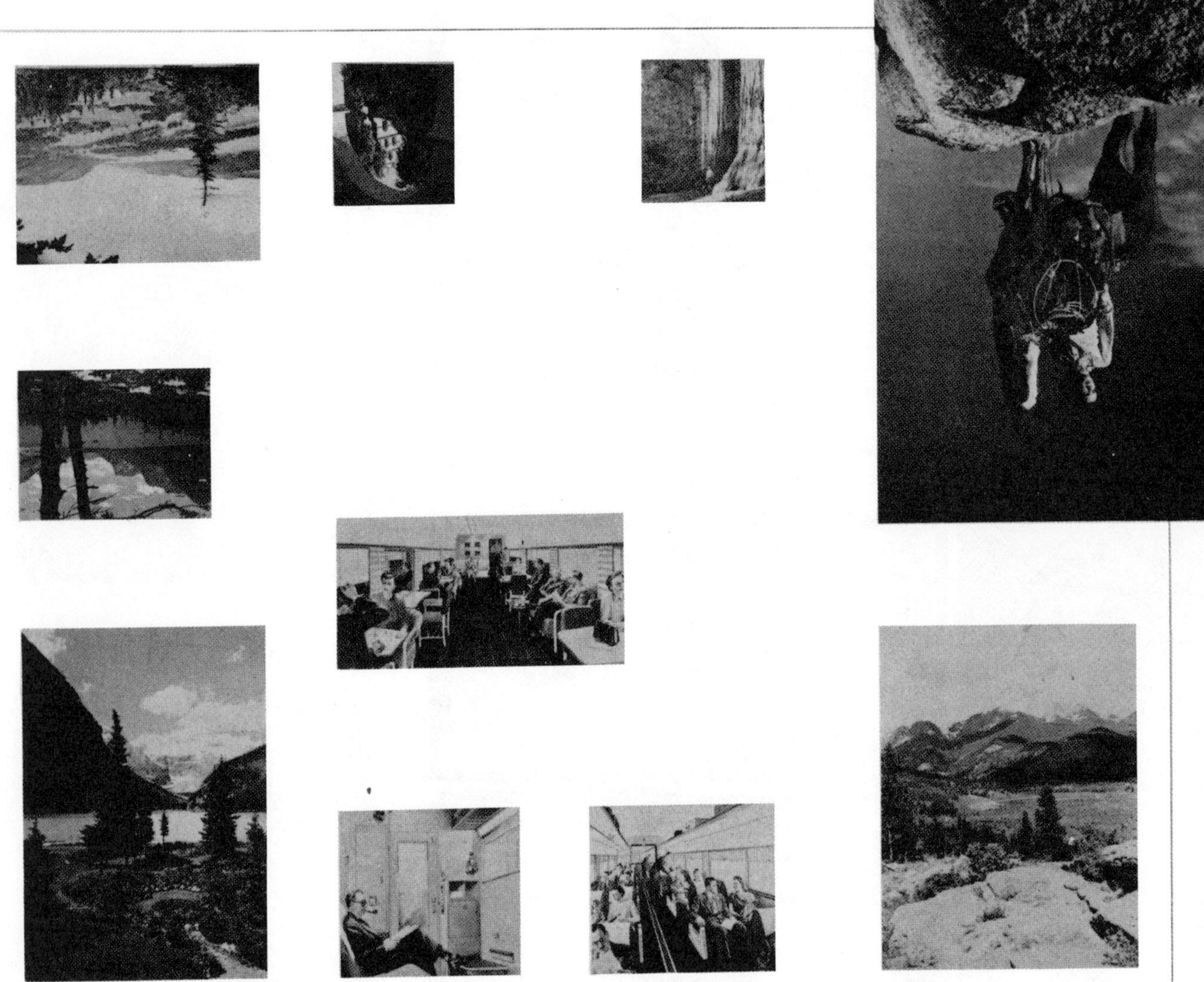

COLOR PRINTS SCALED AND POSITIONED FOR CAMERA COPY

Fig. 7-12 Mixed art media reduced to a single medium for a mechanical. The use of one set of color separations avoided stripping the four color plates. The original art included three 35-millimeter Kodachromes, one 8- by 10-inch and three 4- by 5-inch transparencies, and three 16- by 20-inch paintings. This color mechanical was made with color prints, color-adjusted to suit the art director. It could have been made with transparencies on film. This form of camera copy with ten elements eliminated the stripping of forty halftones to register on the set of four color forms for offset printing. Large process cameras (60-inch circular screen) can easily handle a 25- by 38-inch broadside. Composition and black design are positioned on an overlay to keep black separate from the color copy.

2A. Fly front bow blouse in polyester crepe by Gregory & Goldberg. Off white, seafoam or pink. 10-16. **17.00**
2B. White dotted Arnel® triacetate shirt in dusty green or pink by Sybil. 10-18. **15.00**
2C. Fur collared sweater. Natural or black dyed American lamb on basket weave 100% Wintuck® Orlon® acrylic. By Herald House in black or natural. S,M,L. **50.00**
2D. Tweed turtleneck by Jane Irwill. Camel, rust or green polyester-acrylic. S,M,L. **13.00**
2A
2B
2C
2D
3A
3B
3C

Fig. 7-13 An assembly of process color elements: a spread in full color from a department store booklet. The multiple components of a process copy page are termed an "assembly." Art production sends the original art with the layout to a color laboratory, where all process elements are reduced to a single art medium (usually transparencies, but color prints can be used), scaled, positioned, and color-balanced. This method includes all process copy on one set of separations.

ENLARGEMENT OR REDUCTION OF PROCESS PRINTING

Fig. 7-14 A calendar in several sizes, such as this one with twelve pages of color, is a standard item with many companies. Offset is the logical process because it can handle all sizes from the original separations and, with a large press sheet, print all as a gang run. Jumbo wall calendars are usually blowups. TWA specified that all process color was to be in a 150-line or finer screen.

ENLARGEMENT OR REDUCTION OF PROCESS ELEMENTS OR SEPARATIONS

We have mentioned the fact that in both offset and gravure color correction to obtain the final tonal qualities wanted is handled on the separation films instead of on the copper plates of the engravings as in letterpress. A halftone negative of a subject or the reproduction can be reduced to about 75 percent of size before filling in, or it can be enlarged. In the enlarging process the halftone screen starts to get coarser in the larger size. To exceed the practical limits of reduction or enlargement, a special camera filter is used to rescreen the subject in the normal halftone screen.

When collateral advertising material is integrated with full-color publication ads, a standard method employs a key illustration. The size range is apt to be extreme. In such a case the producer can put the continuous-tone color separations of the illustration in the transparency holder of the camera and make the various screened sizes needed, all in a fine halftone screen regardless of size. The Johnson Outboard collateral pieces are an example of this procedure (see Fig. 7-17).

Fig. 7-15

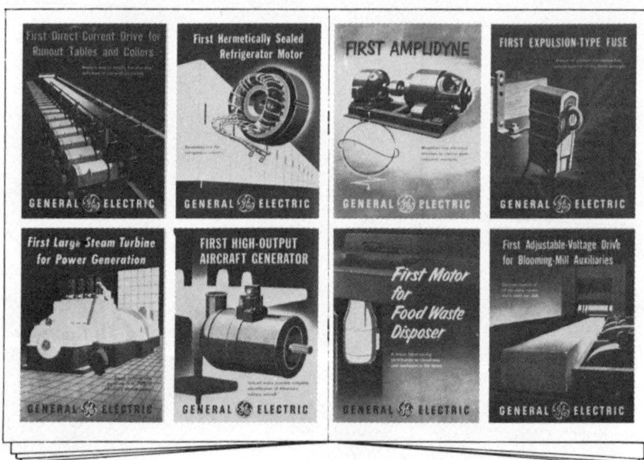

Fig. 7-16 The General Electric pages are center spreads of a sixteen-page full-color magazine insert. The problem was plate costs for the two sizes needed: *Business Week* has a smaller page size than *Fortune.* Offset handled both sizes from the original stripped separations.

OBTAINING MULTIPLE PROCESS PLATE SIZES FROM ONE SET OF COLOR SEPARATIONS IS A MAJOR PLATE ECONOMY WITH OFFSET AND GRAVURE

Color separations, 16 by 12 inches.

Yellow Red Blue Black

Half-page magazine ad.

Dealer folder.

Annaul report, 8½ by 11 inches.

Postcard.

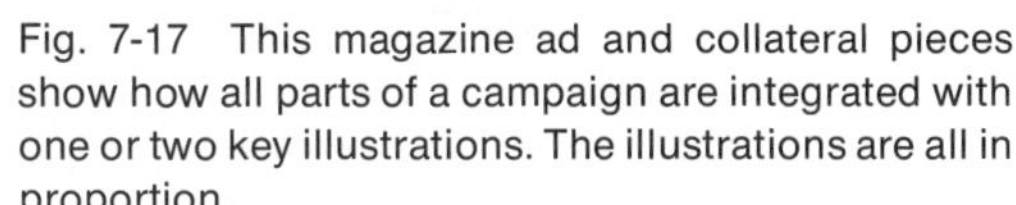

Fig. 7-17 This magazine ad and collateral pieces show how all parts of a campaign are integrated with one or two key illustrations. The illustrations are all in proportion.

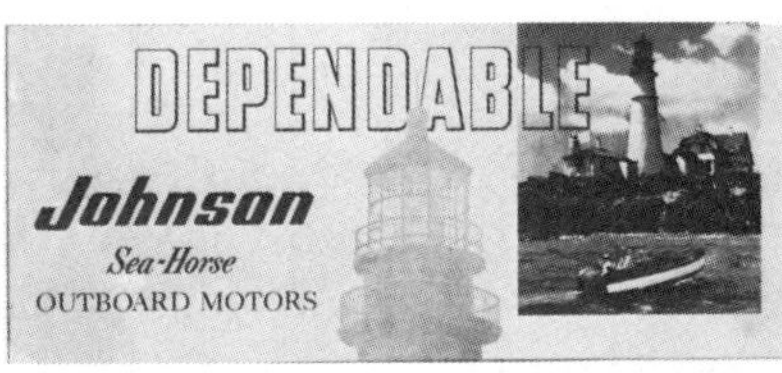

Small window strip.

Window display, 21 by 31 inches.

At the top of the page are the four color separations and under them the various pieces of collateral material for the dealers. All the pieces are in proportion, and all but one of the various illustration sizes were made from the one set of color separations. The exception was the large window strip, which was a blowup of the smaller size. [*Lamport, Fox, Prell & Dolk Inc. Western Printing & Lithographing Co.*]

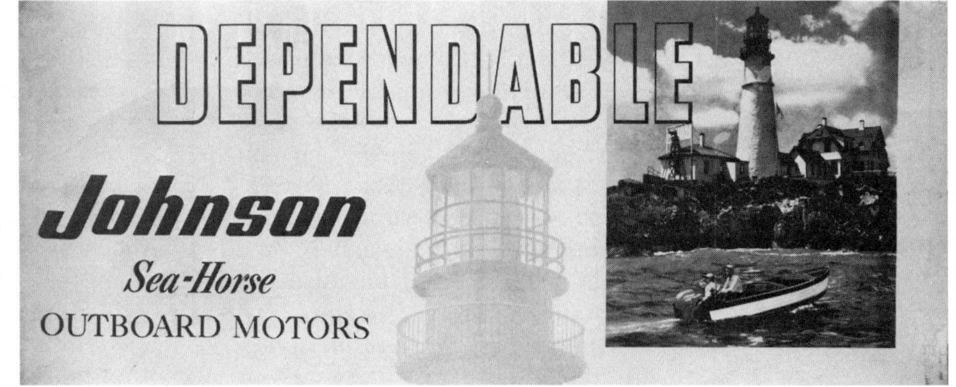

Large window strip, 41 by 17 inches.

FULL-COLOR MAGAZINE PLATES CONVERTED FOR OFFSET PRODUCTION OF COLLATERAL MATERIAL

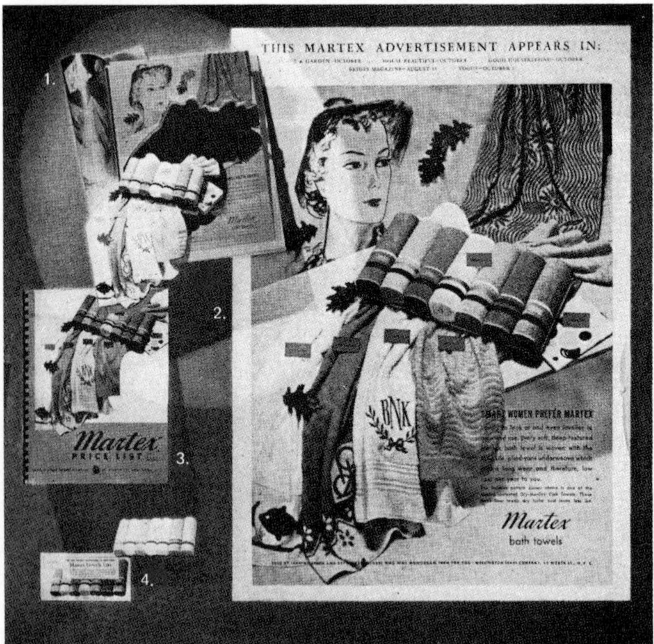

Fig. 7-18 Conversion of magazine color plates to obtain separations for collateral pieces by offset: (1) original four-color process advertisement that appeared in magazines; (2) blowup of the ad for use as a mailing piece, window display, or poster; (3) featured subject lifted from the original background and inserted in another background for the front of a catalog and price list; (4) another use of this feature, as an envelope stuffer.

Fig. 7-19 Conversion of separation positive from the full-color gravure magazine ad provided offset separations for the two dealer display pieces.

PROCESS CONVERSIONS

In national advertising all three of the major printing processes are used. Obviously, it is desirable to avoid the duplication of process plate costs in reproducing the same illustrations by the different processes. Today the engravings or separations of one process can be "converted" for either of the other two processes by the larger engravers or color producers. Offset conversions from process color photoengravings cost about 25 cents on the dollar, as compared with duplicating color plate costs from the original artwork.

In the simplest form of conversion, photoengravings are converted for offset by pulling clean black proofs of the four color plates and photographing them to obtain screened offset positives. If the client wishes, the size can be changed and color strength can be adjusted. Ludlow's Brightype method is used for offset positives, and Minnesota Mining and Manufacturing's Scotchprint and Du Pont's Cronapress process for same-size conversions, in which special film and pressure are used instead of the camera. For rotogravure, "split-dot" positives are made from the screened positives of the halftone processes.

To convert gravure to either of the other two processes, the camera operator handles the continuous-tone positives as transparencies to obtain screened negative halftones. To convert offset screened positives for photoengravings, negatives are made with a slightly larger halftone dot to permit lateral reduction of the dots in the

COPY EXAMPLE 20

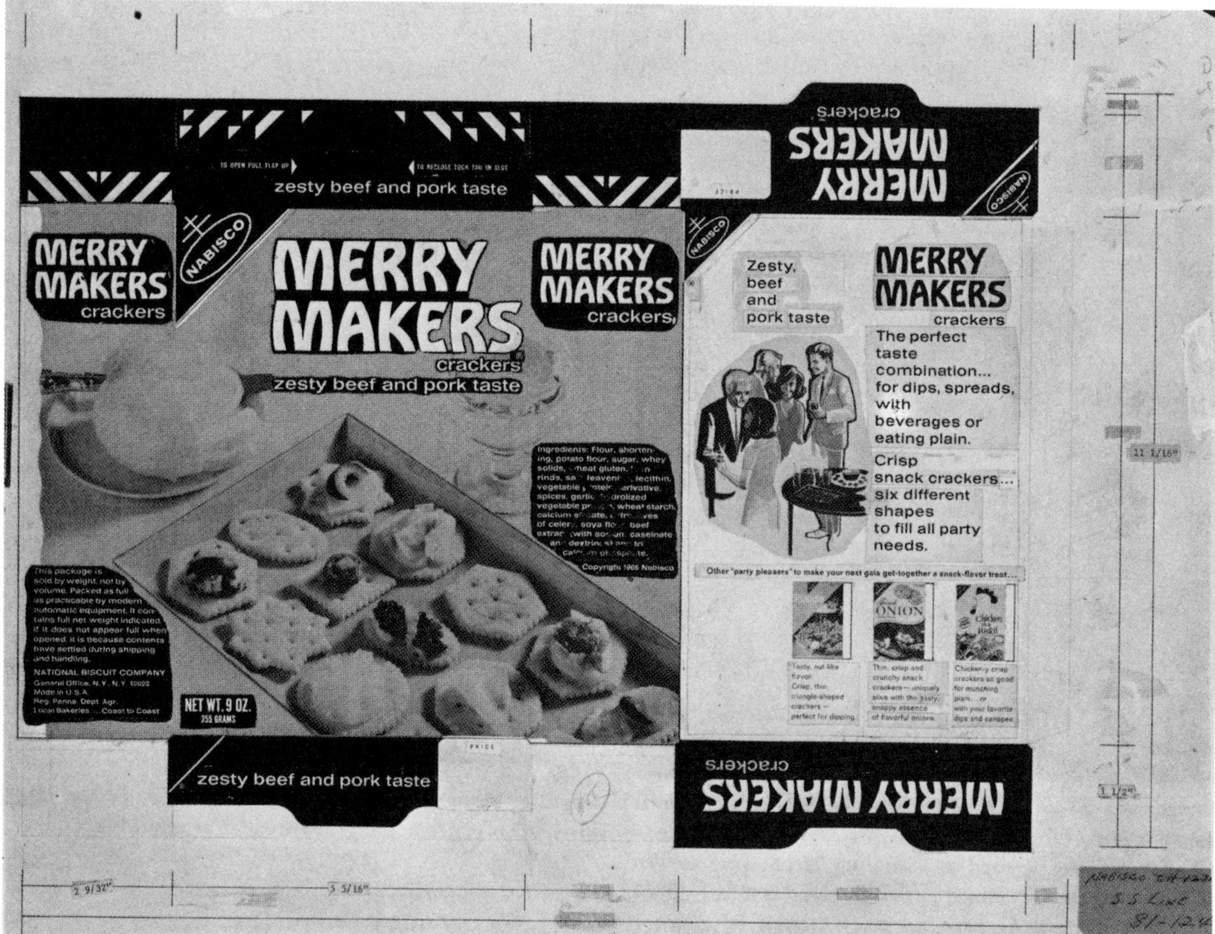

Folding Carton Mechanicals Require Extreme Accuracy

Fig. 7-20 Packages, especially folding cartons, are produced in the millions. Particularly for food and cosmetic packaging, no expense is spared for the camera-ready copy and the printing, which is often in more than four colors; 200-line halftones are frequently used on boxboard.

As in this example, the lineup of the folds, proper bleeds, and glue pattern areas makes the preparation of folding carton art one of the most specialized fields. Color register is in 0.001 inch to assure accurate cutting and scoring operations.

The usual mechanical is frequently equivalent to a comprehensive layout for the platemaker. From this and the specifications the platemaker produces the final camera copy, often using photomechanical equipment. The cost is about $500.[4]

acid etching. Regular screened offset separation positives are used to obtain the split-dot gravure conversions.

Possible economies are considered during the creative planning process. In planning a Father's Day promotion for a shaving lotion, for example, a full-color magazine advertisement was executed in an open design to make the artwork suitable for a dealer display background, thus integrating the display with the magazine ad. Conversion of the magazine plates for the blowup of the art saved $1,000 in plate costs.

[4]Consult *Packaging Printing,* North American Publishing Company, 134 North Thirteenth Street, Philadelphia, Pa. 19107.

SPECIAL PROCESS COLOR METHODS

When many full-color subjects are to be reproduced, it is best to consult a large color lithographer or photoengraver specializing in process color about a process or method of preparing camera-ready copy that will save time and costs. There are timesaving process color and nonprocess methods that are used by all the printing processes. Many platemakers have their own special methods or are familiar with methods in general use.

The separation of any black from the original color art simplifies color separation and usually reduces time charges with all the printing processes. For example, the artist does the black on a film overlay positioned on his color art. For photoengravings, the Color Process Photoengravings scale would apply: the three-color discount (80 percent of the scale cost), plus the engraving for black (frequently line) figured under the Photoengravers' Standard Scale. The saving thus obtained runs from $100 to $400 for large-size engravings. If four-color process engravings are used, the cost is 150 percent of scale in New York. This method was used for the *Reader's Digest* advertisement in Fig. 7-21. With offset, this kind of color reproduction would be handled with inexpensive color separations (masking only used), as illustrated in Fig. 7-5.

Eastman Fluorescent Process, Used for Watercolors

Still used for children's picture books because of the number of subjects and the character of the illustrations, this fast and economical process employs special fluorescent colors to simplify color separation. The artist should have some experience with the process because some of the paint colors differ from the reproduction colors. Artwork should be proportioned for group photography, and arrangements made with a printer who has the special lights required for the camera.

Large Subjects (Posters and Similar Items)

The artist's sketch size is usually 16 by 36 inches for twenty-four-sheet posters. Instead of illustrator's board, a grained plastic sheet with some opacity can be used. For each color separation the printer handles art on the copyboard as reflection copy but also backlights it as for a transparency. The backlighting exposure burns out the highlight areas, just as with the patented fluorescent process. With an average of forty-five plates being needed for posters in full color, savings can be substantial.

Flexichrome Process

This process is a method of adding colors to a black-and-white photo for process color separation. The original special film is three-dimensioned after exposure and developing, the thickness of the emulsion providing the tonal qualities to the roughly applied dye colors. Color photo studios produce Flexichromes, but the nature of the film used at present is much more critical for color application. However, the process is still used, particularly for two colors keyed to special ink colors.

SPECIAL FORMS OF COPY FOR VOLUME WORK

When a given kind of artwork is to be reproduced in quantity, consult a large engraver or offset color printer for recommendations. For example, greeting card production may use special watercolors keyed to process inks and work each separate color on thin overlays. When these are placed in register, the resulting secondary colors can be seen. The printer incurs no costs for color separation but merely photographs each color group separately with the proper filters.

Noncritical four-color elements, such as color spots, printed with transparent inks because of process color illustrations formerly were handled as preseparated art by the artist or by a variety of special artwork. Such procedures have been replaced by very low-cost offset process color separations, as demonstrated in Fig. 7-5. These are produced solely by photographic masking; no handwork is involved (originally litho artists did this work by hand on the continuous-tone separations). Much time is saved.

ADVERTISEMENT

Buy-Words from Carolyn Davis®

Bring the world a little closer. With a **Bausch & Lomb Reader Magnifier,** you'll easily read print that seems small to you . . . do delicate hobby work . . . even thread a sewing machine presto! You'll never know how useful a magnifier can be until you own one. Bausch & Lomb makes magnifiers from clear ophthalmic glass, or optical plastic, with the same care they give prescription eyewear. There's a round model, a rectangular reading model, and a reading model with a built-in light, priced from $5.59. Ask to see **Bausch & Lomb Magnifiers** (Rochester, New York 14609).

Good news for your pet. Bad news for your pet's fleas. **Sergeant's®, the pet care people,** have come up with "a whole new breed" of flea collar—Sentry® IV with Sengard™. Sentry IV kills fleas on your dog or cat for 120 days, not just 90. It's the only collar with Sengard, an exclusive new time-release flea-killer. Instead of telling your pet to go scratch after only 90 days, the new Sentry IV Collar goes right on killing fleas for another whole month. Get the first four-month flea collar, new **Sentry IV with Sengard** from Sergeant's. They've been taking care of pets for over 100 years.

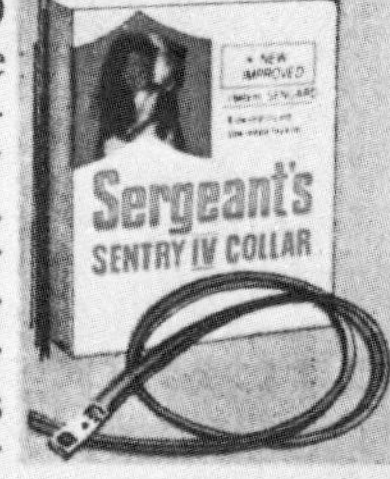

The longer a spot "sets" when something spills, the harder it will be to get out. So don't wait till you can get it dry cleaned: Lift the spot out quickly with **K2r Spot-lifter.** It's the home dry cleaner that's so easy to use. Just spray K2r on, let it dry, then brush K2r and the spot away. For only about a penny a spot, K2r lifts most any spot out of non-washable fabrics in seconds. Before spaghetti spills on a lap again, or gravy drips on the carpet, get a spray can of **K2r Spot-lifter** for the house and keep it handy. You'll save yourself a lot of spots . . . and a lot of cleaning bills.

Introducing Nesco's **Pot Luck,** the slow/fast all-purpose electric cooker. Pot Luck has a thermostatically controlled temperature range of 200° to 500° with special slow cook settings. Because it's oval-shaped with a 6-qt. capacity, Pot Luck holds almost anything, up to an 8-lb. roast. Set temperature "high" to brown or saute; set on "slow/cook" for your favorite pot roast, or to simmer a stew all day. Cookwell removes for easy cleaning (it's dishwasher safe) or refrigerator storage. Spring green or persimmon red to look pretty in your kitchen or on a table. See them at your **Nesco** dealer.

It's easy to recognize poison ivy—but somehow not so easy to keep everybody away from it because it's everywhere. So for the times when someone in your family meets poison ivy, keep soothing **Ivy-Dry** on hand. A family favorite for over 25 years, Ivy-Dry relieves itching from poison ivy, oak or sumac and dries up blisters. You can also use it to relieve itching from insect bites, sunburn, minor skin irritations. And it's safe and effective for children and adults. Now that the outdoor season is here, pick up some **Ivy-Dry** lotion or cream. You can get it at leading drug counters.

Three-Color Process Photoengraving with the Black on an Overlay

Fig. 7-21 Some of the less exacting process color work can be handled as in this advertisement, with economies ranging from $100 to $400, depending on the plate size. In this case, the black was a line engraving. The process work was priced at 80 percent of the Color Process Photoengravings scale, whereas four-color process color is priced at 150 percent of the scale. [*Courtesy* Reader's Digest]

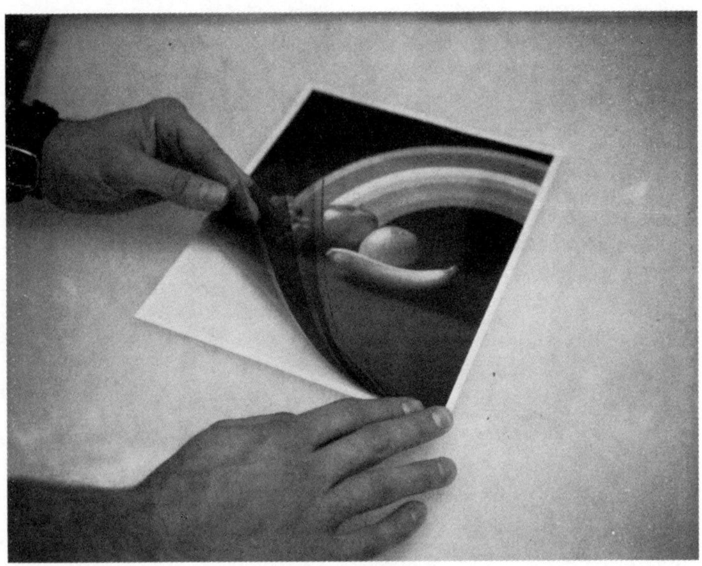

Prepress Color Proving

Fig. 7-22 Color proof made from Minnesota Mining and Manufacturing's Color Key sheets in the form of transparent sensitive material (one sheet for each color), placed on top of each other for final viewing of color break and register.

ALTERNATIVE COLOR METHODS

Budget restrictions on much of the advertising material in color will not permit the use of process color, and for some work not even the cost of the original art. Ingenuity in planning, coupled with the economies of time plate estimating, has provided many solutions to the cost problem. Most of the nonprocess color techniques were covered in Chapter 5, under the heading "Preseparated Color by the Artist." Because of its wide use, we shall cover here a two-color tone process that works from black-and-white photographs to add color and obtain greater detail in both light and dark tones.

DUOTONE PROCESS

In making a halftone negative it is not possible to get all the detail in both ends of the gray scale; so the camera operator compromises by exposing the film for the middle tones. Alternatively, to hold details in both light and dark areas the camera operator makes two negatives, one of which is focused to get details in the light areas and the other to get details in the dark areas. The first negative is usually printed in a color, frequently a light blue or tan, and the second negative in black for details in the dark areas. Thus the photo is printed with a broader tonal range, and a second color is introduced. A modified duotone has just a part of the subject in color—a fashion model's dress, for example, against a background.

VELOX PRINTS FOR TWO-COLOR PROCESS PRINTING

For low-cost commercial-quality work, you can send two-color process art to a Velox print specialist, specifying the printing process to be used. The Velox specialist will make two process screened prints, one for black and one for color, properly angled and scaled to the size ordered. The cost is by the square inch, but $30 or $40 will cover most of the smaller-size illustrations, as compared with 55 percent of the Color Process Photoengravings scale.

COLOR PROOFS

For commercial-grade process printing by offset, various forms of photographic print proofs in color are made from the screened negatives on very thin films to check layout and register and to approximate the quality of results. If further color correction is wanted, it can be made. The cost is about 10 cents on the dollar in comparison to plate proofs in ink. This type of proving is often used for work of known producers when color accuracy is not critical.

THE TWO AREAS OF ART PRODUCTION

Since most art production procedures are used with process color artwork, a summary of the major procedures may be helpful. There are two fields of art production, creative planning and the preparation of camera-ready copy.

CREATIVE PLANNING STAGE

Avoidance of Cost Duplication of Color Separations

The engravings or color separations of any major printing process can be converted for either of the other two processes. The most widespread use is the conversion of magazine color engravings for collateral material by offset. The cost is about 25 cents on the dollar.

Mixed Art Media

Mixed original artwork frequently cannot be avoided. Prepared camera copy can reduce all the elements to transparencies or color prints, scaled, positioned, color-adjusted, and balanced.

Multiple-Purpose Design

A full-color magazine page may be executed in an open design so that the artwork is suitable for a dealer window display.

Gang Press Run

Creative planning considers the use of the gang press run for suitable collateral material such as a series of mailings or dealer material. Use of the large printing form is a basic advantage of offset because of the absence of press lockup and the usual makeready time.

Multiple Plate Sizes

From one set of color separations (continuous-tone negatives) both offset and gravure can make positives for the different plate sizes needed for various layouts. This procedure is also used when conversions are not practical (for a reduction greater than one-third). See Fig. 7-17.

Enlargement or Reduction of a Full-Color Piece

A full-color piece may be enlarged or reduced for window strips and dealer material, calendars, and so on with offset. See Figs. 7-14 and 7-15.

Large Process Mechanicals

Offset and gravure can exceed the limits of the maximum process photoengraving size. A mechanical for a 25- by 38-inch size can be prepared with process copy elements (color prints or transparencies), all to be included on one set of color plates. There are economies in both platemaking and press lockup.

Alternative Process Color Methods

Under time plate estimating there are various forms of camera copy and of color separation methods that are less expensive than the conventional color correction procedures. Their use has reduced the amount of preseparated color work by the artist.

Preseparated Color by the Artist

These techniques are generally used to save costs by avoiding the need for finished art and the expense of process color, but they are also used for color strength when required. They are frequently employed with a process color illustration for incidental color treatment and backgrounds.

Composition Methods

Any form of composition—photographic or mechanical lettering aids, cold-type methods—can be used but the most important is phototypesetting. Pages are now made up on the drawing board, and typewriter typesetting is handled in the art department.

Choice of Paper

Paper often determines the printing process. Offset can use any type of paper except cellophane or wax for fine halftones with available economies; rotogravure requires a smooth paper; and with letterpress paper determines suitable typefaces and the choice of suitable art media (this is not the case with photomechanical processes).

PREPARING CAMERA-READY COPY

The work in the creative planning stage, particularly for advertising, amounts to rough layouts for publication and newspaper ads and for collateral material. These layouts are the designer's drawings. As we have indicated, a considerable knowledge of printing production is involved, and some orders are issued for intermediate photo steps between the original art and that prepared for the camera.

The second area of art production consists of preparing working drawings for the engravers and platemakers for the different methods of printing and, in so doing, carrying out some of the platemaking and typesetting operations, such as scaling and positioning copy elements and handling page makeup on the drawing board.

At this stage of the work, copy elements are assembled and prepared for camera-ready copy as described in Chapters 3 to 6, due attention being paid to the form in which camera copy should be prepared under time plate estimating or the Photoengravers' Standard Scale method of estimating plate costs. The production (mechanical) artist preparing the mechanical paste-up should endeavor to avoid some of the usual platemaking and typesetting operations, provide for the right form of simple color register in the copy, or keyline and signal work to be completed by the platemaker.

The skills involved and the new technology of the photomechanical printing processes have developed a new job classification equivalent to that of the draftsman in engineering or architecture. This is a new employable job skill that pays well for qualified beginners, and it is an ideal entry to a commercial art career.

The diversified use of the printing processes for all types of layouts on many different kinds of paper, with periodicals and newspapers shifting to offset and gravure, naturally requires artists and designers to have a fair knowledge of printing production as it relates to their work. Otherwise, much of their time will be wasted. Top-pay artists, with their knowledge of printing production, have developed techniques that save money on plate costs.

The almost-universal use of the mechanical has created thousands of new jobs in commercial art. An indication of the importance of good work is the fact that in New York experienced mechanical artists are offered as much as $15,000 a year. This is the trained beginner's job, from which a person moves up to boardman and starts making layouts and comprehensives and the more complicated illustrative treatment. Ability cannot be hidden and is well rewarded.

Since art now selects and specifies typefaces, art education should include this subject and, of course, copy fitting. The higher-paid mechanical artists are frequently called on to specify much of the typography for their work.

If by chance one of your early jobs is that of a one-person art department, more of your time will be spent on production than on artwork. You will have to see your jobs through to completion. When you start to work for a small advertising agency, you probably will have to wear two hats, that of art director and that of production manager.

INFORMATION FOR THE TECHNICALLY MINDED

The following article by John Deurwaarder, chief of the Graphic Arts Department of Clark College, Vancouver, is published by courtesy of *Printing Magazine*.

A Short Course on the Theory and Control of Color in Print

Neutral white light contains all the colors of the spectrum. We can conveniently divide the visible spectrum into three primary colors: red, blue, and green, and when the primaries are combined in proper proportions, the result is white. We also can isolate the colors in "white light." A red tomato is red because it reflects that color while absorbing all the other colors from white light. A piece of blue glass is that color because it passes or transmits blue and absorbs the other colors.

To reproduce color accurately, proper proportions of the three primary colors must be contained in the light presented to the ink film. The most efficient colors for controlling the primaries are the pigments, cyan (blue/green), magenta (blue/red), and yellow (red/green). When yellow and cyan, for example, are overlapped, we see green because that is the only color that each does not absorb. We have produced green by controlling, or in this case eliminating, red and blue.

What happens when the three pigment colors are overprinted? First, when the yellow and cyan overlap, the yellow absorbs the blue ray from the white light and the cyan absorbs the red ray, leaving only the green ray to be reflected by the combination. In much the same manner, when these pigments are mixed, they retain their light-subtracting qualities so that in the mixture the yellow absorbs the blue ray, leaving only the green ray to be reflected by the mixture. Note that in color-process printing, the primary pigment colors are generally "transparent." The light passes through the pigment film to the white paper beneath and then it is reflected back through the film to the eye.

There are a number of ways by which light waves reach our eyes. Indirectly, as when light passes through a transparent object held between our eyes and the source of light (called transmission) or directly, as when we stare into the sun or a light bulb or when light bounces from an object to our eyes (called reflection). In printing, we are basically concerned with transmitted and reflected light waves.

The surface of a red tomato has the faculty of absorbing all light waves that hit it except those that correspond to red. We might say that an opaque substance appears to be a particular color because it reflects the wave lengths corresponding to that color and absorbs those that do not. When all wave lengths are reflected and one does not dominate another, the substance would be perceived as white. Transparent substances absorb some wave lengths and transmit others.

Pigments, ink, and almost anything else you can think of are perceived as a certain color because we "see" the wave length they reflect or transmit—we cannot see those that are absorbed. Color that results from adding light energy is called additive color. Color that results when an object subtracts wave lengths is called subtractive color.

INTERPRETATION OF COLOR

In the graphic arts we are concerned with such light absorbing materials as film, pigments, and the surfaces of paper. All materials that are not sources of light energy operate by the subtractive method. Each of the process printing inks, cyan, magenta, and yellow, ideally transmits ⅔ and absorbs ⅓ of the spectrum; that is cyan (blue-green) absorbs red; magenta (blue-red) absorbs green; and yellow (red-green) absorbs blue.

Our brain interprets color sensations in three dimensions: hue, saturation, and brightness. Hue is that characteristic of color by which we distinguish red from green, yellow, blue, etc. Saturation is often called purity of color or chroma, and is often expressed as the strength or amount of a given hue in a color, or the intensity of that hue. Brightness is that quality by which we express similarity to a series of grays, ranging from black to white, such as the difference between a strong red and a light pink.

A change in the environment in which a color is inspected will influence the discrimination of color. Color is influenced by light under which it is observed and its relationship or proximity to other colors. It is affected by changes in the darkness or lightness of background materials.

Colors are observed under differ-

(continued on page 166)

(continued from page 165)
ent varying light conditions. White light, such as daylight, differs, for example, from the color quality of an incandescent light bulb. Daylight at midday, for example, is energy rich in the blue of the spectrum, while incandescent lighting is predominantly rich in the yellow-red end of the spectrum. Candlelight is also distinctly yellow.

LIGHT AFFECTS COLOR

Because of the variation of light sources, color matching and color comparisons become difficult unless such observations are made with the same lighting conditions. Light source has a dramatic effect on color observation. When we view a blue object under a pure red light, the object will appear black. This is explained by the subtractive color phenomenon.

The influence of the proximity of some colors to others and their background brightness affect perception of color. The color of a transparent subject, for example, may be distinctly or dramatically influenced by background color. The value and saturation of color decrease as the value of the background decreases. Color may also be influenced by the quality of reflected light, as when we view a transparency against an opaque background, such as a sheet of paper.

When ink is printed on a rough surface, the surface scatters white light in much the same way as do bits of broken glass. This, in turn, adds white light to the printed area and the color appears to be diluted, washed out, or impure. Conversely, when printing on a smooth glossy surface, the ink appears purer and distinguished in hue.

Inks may be either opaque or transparent. Opaque pigments reflect light at their outer surface and have the property of covering or hiding the background on which they are printed. Opaque white pigments generally produce a light top-tone, and the bulk ink is likely to appear the same as the color which it will print. Transparent pigments do not reflect light at the surface, but rather "transmit" light, or allow the light to pass through the film of the ink and be reflected from the surface on which it is printed. Transparent ink films change the light passing through them by absorbing the color(s) that "aren't there" and passing the color(s) that "are there"—just as a red tomato absorbs blue and green and transmits the red to our eye.

REPRODUCTION OF COLOR

Transparent pigments lie flat against a sheet of paper which, in turn, becomes the (reflecting) light source for the ink placed on it. Overlapping transparent inks produce intermediate colors as each film layer allows light, though altered, to pass through it. Conversely, overlapping opaque inks reflect light and do not transmit or pass light; therefore, they do not produce intermediate colors when overlapped.

There are as yet no perfect inks. However, theoretically perfect process ink (subtractive) primary colors, which are able to reproduce most of the colors in the spectrum, are:

Cyan—absorbs all red and transmits blue-green.

Yellow—absorbs all blue and transmits green-red.

Magenta—absorbs all green and transmits blue-red.

To compensate for ink variation to obtain the most accurate result, it becomes necessary to make additional corrections and adjustments when preparing the inks.

When we introduce halftone screening, we compress the tonal range or range of values available in a printed reproduction, because the small unprinted areas of the white paper reflect white light and dilute the print. When we add white light, we raise the value of a color and decrease its purity. It becomes apparent therefore, that paper is the reflective light source for transparent inks.

PAPER SOURCE OF ILLUMINATION

The color judgment of any subject, be it a tomato or a film, is wholly dependent on the quality and quantity of the light which illuminates it. The sheet of paper becomes the source of illumination for transparent ink film. A truly cyan ink film will absorb (subtract) all the red wave lengths from white, which is one-third of the spectrum, and pass the green and blue wave lengths, which are two-thirds of the spectrum.

Neutral white paper has the characteristic of reflecting the same kind (quality) of light that it is illuminated by, although a certain amount may be absorbed. When paper reflects all wave lengths equally, meaning its characteristics do not alter the quality of light—it is a neutral white sheet. A tinted sheet absorbs some of the wave lengths. A paper that does not reflect any light is black paper. A neutral gray sheet is one that absorbs a part of the quantity of light that strikes it. You can say that ink colors become duller and less brilliant as the brightness of a sheet decreases. The brightest portion of the over-all printed page is the unprinted area of the sheet of paper. The reason for the printed areas being less bright is because they have absorbed part of the light. A paper with low brightness will correspondingly print low in brightness.

The most accurate color reproduction is obtained on papers that reflect the light that strikes them without changing its quality; correspondingly, most brilliant color reproduction can be arrived at on papers with high balanced reflectance. Rough surfaces scatter light. When light strikes the multitude of uniform reflecting surfaces and debases the print with white light, it becomes grayed because of the addition of uncontrolled and unwanted white light.

Smooth paper surfaces minimize troublesome light interference, giving uniform directional reflection of light. An open surface paper tends to absorb both ink vehicle and pigment, which in turn leave dull pigment particles on the surface. Measuring "paper surface efficiency"—with limitations—is today one of the many valuable means to ascertain the color printing possibilities of paper.

Accurate color results are arrived at by printing on a finish which will retain the vehicle and pigment on the surface. Only enough vehicle permeates the surface to provide good bonding of ink to paper. Glossy inks enhance purity of printing in color.

CHAPTER EIGHT
Camera Copy for Rotogravure

MOST OF AN artist's copy preparation for gravure will be intended for advertisements in publications: large consumer magazines and Sunday color supplements to newspapers. Later the artist may do some catalog or packaging work. We have said that camera copy is the same for the processes using time plate estimating. This is essentially true, but there are slight variations in copy that are required by publications to save preparatory costs when they do not charge for the engraving. Gravure catalog producers may recommend procedures to cut plate costs, such as the use of phototype on film, that are not advocated by publications. Packaging printing is technical because of the close register requirements and the use of flat color backgrounds for which copy providing for color register is prepared, as with offset.

SENDING CAMERA COPY TO A GRAVURE ENGRAVER OR DIRECTLY TO A PUBLICATION

When an advertisement is to appear in a group of publications, the mechanical and related copy are sent to a gravure engraving service with a list of the publications that are to receive the advertisement. Copy is prepared in essentially the same manner as for offset except that pen-line art is treated as tone copy. Moreover, halftone tints applied by the artist or screened copy should not be used because of the danger of a moiré pattern resulting (see Fig. 8-1).

For full-page ads, either color or monotone, the gravure service sends positive films directly to each publication on the list, just as electrotypers do for letterpress publications. For fractional-page ads in monotone, a rotoprint (a glossy photo) of the advertisement is sent exactly as it is to be reproduced. Some specialized photoprint services also prepare rotoprints. Many gravure publications give a rebate to the advertiser when page positives are supplied.

If only one or two gravure publications are used, however, camera copy is usually sent directly to them. The gross advertising rate generally includes the engraving cost for monotone, but copy must meet the production specifications of each publication; otherwise there will be extra charges. One-piece copy, with all elements scaled and positioned as they are to be reproduced, may be specified; or copy may be acceptable in two pieces, a line mechanical and a tone mechanical. The form of acceptable color copy is specified: generally process copy must be prepared so that one set of color separations will handle all color elements as wanted. Such copy is usually prepared as an assembly by a color laboratory. If two gravure publications are to be used, the advertiser makes an arrangement with the first publi-

From photograph.

From halftone copy.

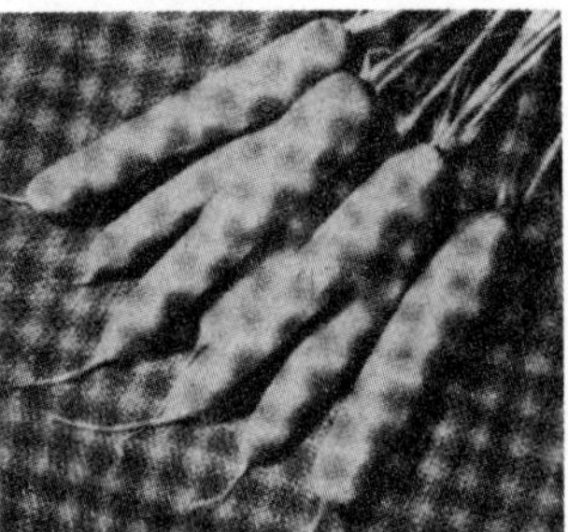

Fig. 8-1

cation to send duplicate positives to the second one. There is, of course, a charge for this service.

Obviously the art department must know whether a gravure engraving service is to be used or camera copy is to be sent directly to the gravure publication. If printing is to be on uncoated paper, particularly newsprint, tonal detail should be accentuated for wash drawings and photos. Production specifications usually give the minimum type sizes for newsprint: 6 points; 8 points if reversed. Agency art departments usually have the Standard Rate & Data Service production standards for all publications as well as color charts showing color qualities on the paper used.

Gravure color proofing is quite expensive. It is not generally ordered unless several publications are to be used.

PROCEDURES OF THE GRAVURE PRINTER

A printer's production procedure varies with the kind of job and equipment. Plants tend to specialize—in publications, packaging, catalogs, direct mail, and so on, for large quantities using multiple imposition. The objective of the printer is to get a continuous-tone unit or page positive on film. This positive is obtained by a series of contact exposures to negatives of the line copy (high-contrast film) and the tone copy (continuous-tone film). Care is taken to prevent the unit piece of film from being light-struck except for the image to be contact-printed. Like the other printing processes, gravure uses overlay copy to combine line and tone and to knock out reversed type or design on tone. Except in packaging, little flat color is used by gravure, which is essentially a tone process. The industry recommends the use of the photographic-spread register technique (see Fig. 4-22) on the mechanical for touching flat colors in packaging backgrounds.

Most gravure color plants other than those handling publications are reported to use the step-and-repeat photocomposing machine for positioning unit positives on film to make up the printing flat, or form, that later is contact-printed on a carbon tissue plate coating. Gravure engraving services also use the step-and-repeat machine. But for the large gravure publication presses using standard page sizes, page positives are pin-registered to a metal jig for positioning in strips to be contact-printed on the carbon tissue (plate coating on a carrier sheet), which is later applied to the copper-surface printing cylinder. The etching operation produces ink wells of varying depth to give light or dark tones.

THE GRAVURE CAB, OR CABRIOLET

Because gravure uses two kinds of photographic film for its element negatives—high-contrast film for line (100 percent black as in type, rules, and reverses) and continuous-tone film for tone, pen-line drawings, and tints—a rather complicated procedure is used to assemble and position the copy elements to make up the complete unit on film. A pin register film carrier, the cabriolet, or cab, is used for a series of contact prints to combine and position the various negatives for the unit positive. It is impractical to strip pieces of film to make the unit positive, as is done with the halftone process, which uses the same kind of film for both line and tone negatives.

With the usual line-and-tone mechanical the gravure engraver will mask the tone copy and make a line negative, then mask the line copy and make a tone negative. Copy should be designed to keep engraving operations to a minimum. Costs are much lower with a tone mechanical than with separate proportioned elements, and unproportioned elements are the most expensive camera copy.

USE OF FLASH TONES INSTEAD OF HALFTONE TINTS

All copy for gravure is reproduced in a 150-line screen. For this reason halftone tints such as Zip-a-Tone and screened prints such as Velox should not be applied on copy by the artist. With their use a moiré pattern (see Fig. 8-1) might result from rescreening. If a screen pattern is necessary, keep it large and angle it at

Fig. 8-2

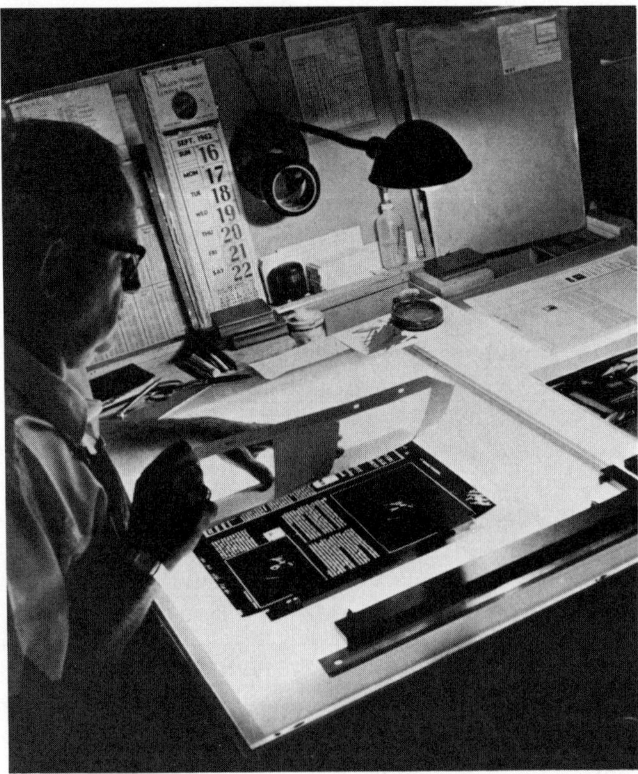

Fig. 8-3

The Gravure Cabriolet:
A Film Carrier for Photocomposing Pages

On the left the layout man is positioning pieces of goldenrod masking paper over the two tone areas of the line negative, and to his left is the tone flat. On the right he is positioning the tone flat; the tone negatives have been removed to show you that the goldenrod paper underneath has been cut away to let light through for exposure to the positive film underneath. This view also demonstrates how the line elements are masked during the tone exposure. [*Courtesy Standard Gravure Corp.*]

45 degrees to match the angle of the gravure screen.

For tint panels and backgrounds, gravure "flashes" in the tone wanted: 30 percent, 60 percent, and so on. If there is only one tone, it can be handled in black or just outlined in red on the mechanical, with a notation of the strength wanted on tissue overlay. If a copy unit is to have two or more tones, a separate overlay should be prepared in black for each tone strength, and all should be registered to the copy unit (see Copy Example 21; Figs. 8-6, 8-7, and 8-8). Tone areas executed in solid black on the overlays produce windows in the negatives. The indicated tone is flashed (exposed to arc lights) onto the unit positive, the length of exposure determining the strength of the tone.

Gravure makes wide use of tint backgrounds in monotone and of color backgrounds. These need only be indicated on the mechanical instructions; if the background color is uniform, a color swatch is sufficient.

MONOTONE GRAVURE ON NEWSPRINT

Many of the precautions regarding tone reproduction on newsprint by the letterpress process also apply to rotogravure camera copy. The artist should keep in mind that newsprint lacks the light reflection qualities of a coated paper. This means that tonal details should be accentuated in the light and dark areas of both wash drawings and photos, subtle contrasts in tone should be avoided, and the edges of a light wash should carry extra contrast to make them stand out against the oyster white of the paper. Your artwork should be slightly darker than the reproduction wanted.

Small type with fine serifs and lines should be avoided on newsprint, and the minimum size set at 6 points (8 points if reversed), because of the danger of the type filling in. The medium and bold faces of such type as the Gothics and Twentieth Century (square or sans serif) are recommended. Flash tones that are to be surprinted or have type reversed should provide the necessary contrast: surprint on a 30 percent tint, and reverse on a 60 percent or darker tone.

Press proofs for gravure are fairly expensive and generally are not ordered unless an engraving service is preparing positives for a list of publications. Print proofs from the positives permit checking.

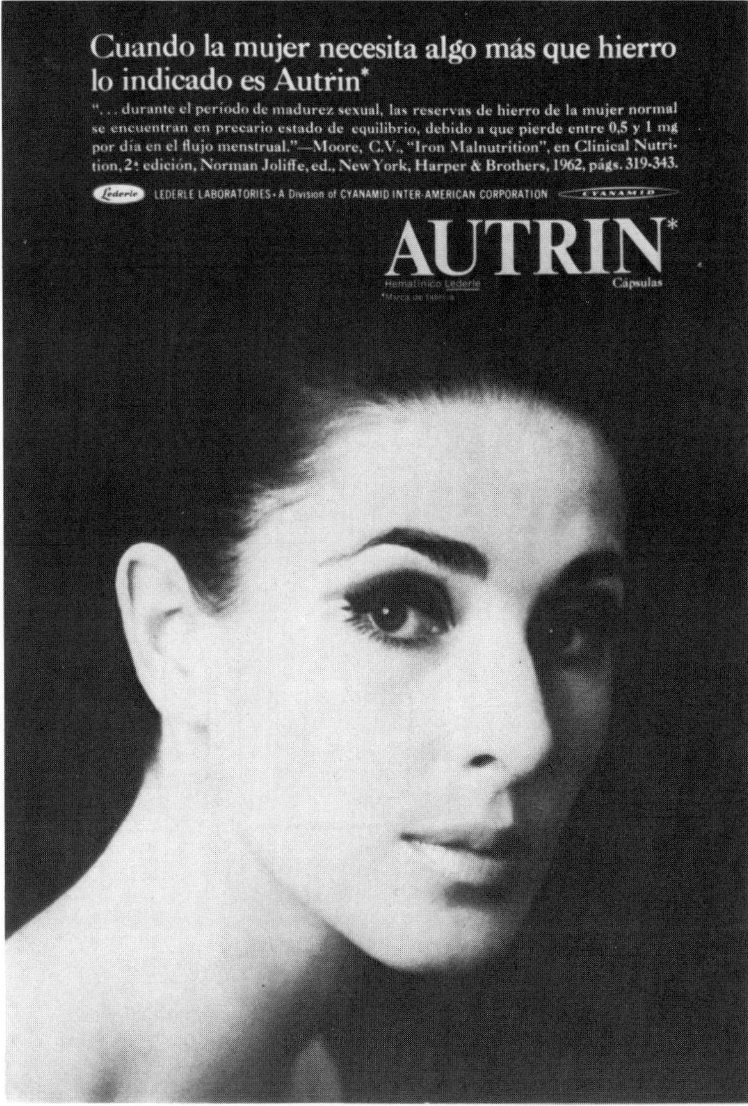

Fig. 8-4 With gravure, a type reverse (Photostat negative) to go on the black background of a photograph should be placed on an overlay, not on the photograph. This precaution must be taken because the black reproduced from high-contrast film differs from that obtained from continuous-tone film. A Photostat negative gives the engraver the positive he needs for the type knockout.

PREPARATION OF CAMERA COPY

Line-and-Tone Wash Drawings

Since pen-line drawings are photographed on the same continuous-tone film as tone copy, pen details can be executed right on a wash drawing instead of on an overlay, or wash can be added to a pen-line drawing if it has been made with waterproof ink. When a 100 percent black line is required with tone copy, it should be put on an overlay. This stricture applies to all gravure work.

Reversed Type on Tone

A glossy Photostat negative of type goes on a positioned overlay for a knockout. When a photograph has a black background, do not paste a Photostat on it, for the difference in the two blacks will be noticeable. Continuous-tone film gives a black that is 80 or 90 percent.

Wash Drawings

Avoid using both lampblack and india ink in a wash drawing: the resulting dull and shiny blacks do not photograph in the same way. It is preferable not to mix wash drawings and photos in a copy unit, for usually they are not in tonal balance and two separate camera exposures will be required to handle them.

Other Precautions

For photographs a No. 2 glossy Velox paper is recommended for normal contrast. Retouching grays should be of the same brand and color cast; otherwise it

Pen-Line and Wash Drawing for Gravure Fig. 8-5 With combination pen-line and wash drawings for gravure monotone, both art media go on the illustration board because both are photographed on continuous-tone film. If the pen-line drawing were to go on high-contrast film, some of the fine lines would be burned out, not reproduced. However, any other 100 percent black lines to be combined with gravure tone should go on an overlay.

may be difficult to make good negatives. A bluish gray and a brownish gray may look fine but require extra engraving time.

With newsprint, avoid fine line reversals such as scratchboard and the reduction of pen-line drawings from sizes larger than size and one-half. The absorbency of the paper makes it liable to fill-ins.

Jet blacks do not reproduce at their full value on newsprint. The poorest art for reproduction is art that is too light, in too high a key.

Gravure makes wide use of allover tints and panels. When the area is large, the boundary is usually outlined in red, so that copy can contain type or a design to surprint. If the tint wanted is noted on a tissue overlay, the engraver will take care of the flash tone. Headlines or prices can be flash-toned by giving necessary instructions.

SPECIAL ADVANTAGE OF GRAVURE

When there is no tone on the press cylinder from the nonimage areas of artwork, the arc lights will burn in enough thickness on the carbon tissue to prevent any etching. As a result, a faint tone does not appear in nonimage areas, as it does with the halftone process unless masking is used.

PROCESS COLOR ON NEWSPRINT

In the advertising sections of Sunday color supplements to newspapers, every other page is usually in process color. The artwork for about half of the material consists of color transparencies. The illustrations tend to be in a large, dramatic size with backgrounds in complementary colors. Backgrounds may be airbrushed or painted, but frequently they are flash tones produced in two or three colors to match a color swatch.

The limitations of process reds and blues apply to rotogravure as they do to the other printing processes. Colors will vary with the paper used, particularly between uncoated and coated paper; the difference is a matter of absorbency as well as of the smoothness of the paper surface. Hand artwork in color should be guided by gravure color charts for the paper to be used. The allover contrast required by the paper is the responsibility of the engraver.

ART MEDIA

Any of the usual art media can be used in gravure, but those using transparent pigments are the simplest to color-separate. Of the two kinds of opaque watercolors, gouaches give the engraver less trouble than tempera, which is composed of two types of pigments. Engravers say that

COPY EXAMPLE 21

Fig. 8-6 Key camera copy.

Fig. 8-7 Reproduction with tints from overlays.

Gravure Flash Tones

Since gravure does not use the halftone method, the equivalent of halftone tints is flashed onto the film by light exposure in the camera. In this example three different tint strengths were used: 30, 50, and 70 percent. Camera copy for the tints is prepared on overlays, with a separate overlay for each strength, registered to the key copy. Each overlay is opaqued for its part of the design, as shown below. The resulting negatives serve as stencils when light is flashed onto the unit film. A tint panel carrying reversed type is prepared with a Photostat negative. If a copy unit carries only one flash tone strength (or reverse), the copy can go on the key copy without an overlay. A single large tint area is outlined in red so that the area can carry design or type. The strength of a tint is indicated on the margin of the mechanical or on a tissue overlay.

Overlays for Flash Tones

Fig. 8-8 Copy for each tone strength is executed in solid black or with red masking film on a separate overlay registered to the key copy. This copy method is also used for offset unless there is a space of at least 1 inch between tones to take the stripper's tape.

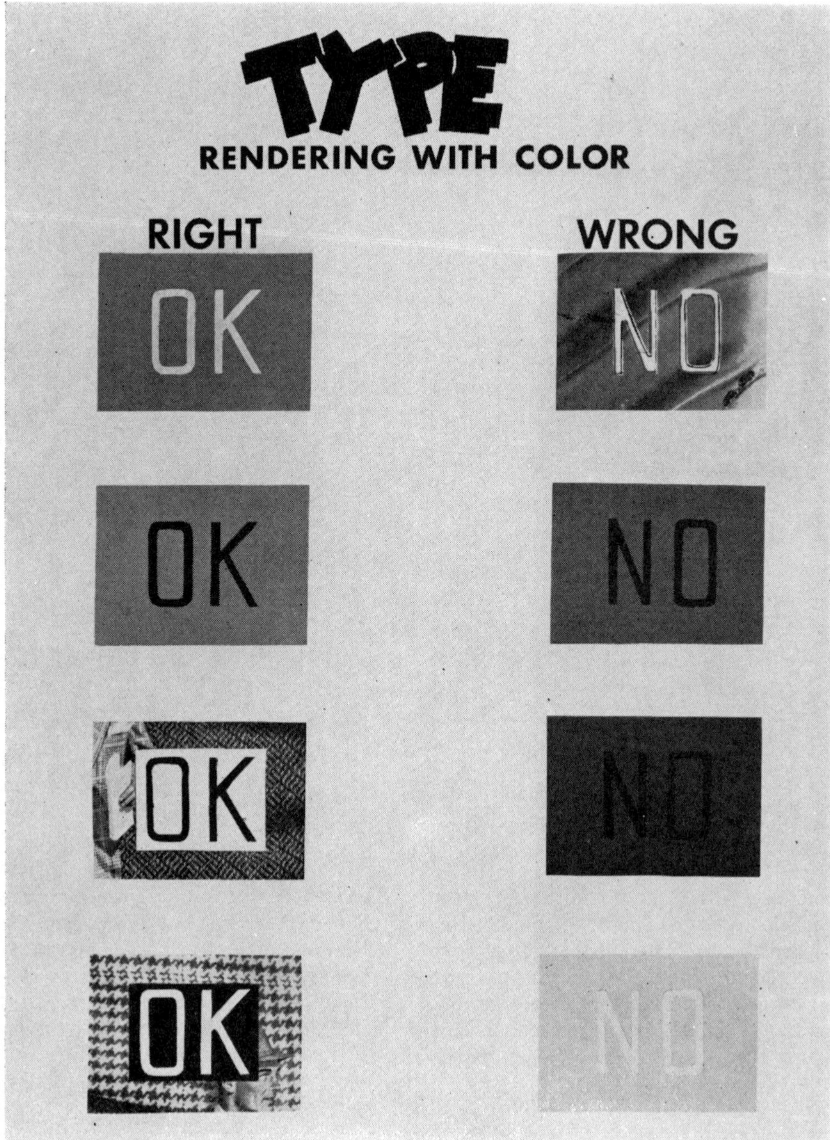

Fig. 8-9 [*Courtesy* Gravure *magazine*]

Right Uses, Top to Bottom

1. Reverse type on all 50 percent or darker primary colors except yellow.
2. Overprint on all light tones and primary colors except dark blue.
3. Use black type on a white mortise in questionable background or color swatches, etc.
4. Reverse type on black panel within multicolor background colors.

Wrong Uses, Top to Bottom

1. Do not reverse small type on a multicolor background (this causes register problems).
2. Do not overprint type on dark blue process color.
3. Do not overprint on any dark process color background. With swatches, overprint on light swatches and reverse on dark swatches.
4. Do not reverse type on any value of process yellow or pastel shades.

IN A ROTOGRAVURE PUBLICATION PLANT

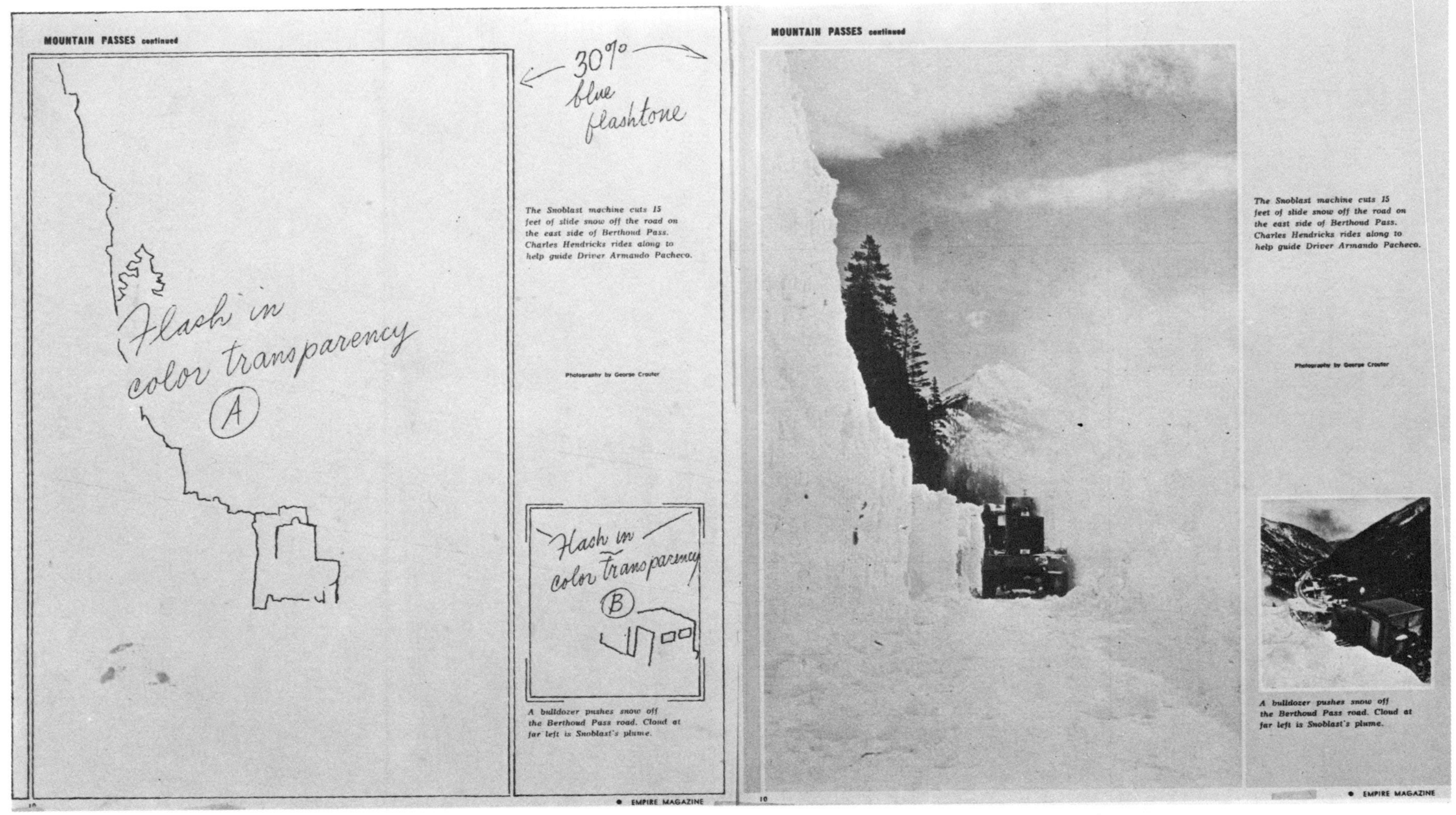

The Mechanical

The Printed Page

Fig. 8-10*A* As with offset, a Photostat is usually placed for size and position, and process artwork is supplied as a separate element. A gravure publication that does its own printing sometimes merely positions an outline of the art.

In gravure, "Flash in" means the equivalent of "Strip in halftone tint." To get the continuous-tone positive films necessary for platemaking (copper cylinder), gravure requires a series of continuous-tone negative contact prints (at least two) to complete the positives: high-contrast film negatives for type and 100 percent black and continuous-tone film negatives for all other elements.

Fig. 8-10*B* Gravure goes through a series of negatives of copy elements (line copy on high-contrast film, tone on continuous-tone film), followed by a series of contact prints on continuous-tone film to get the completed unit positive films for each page. For publications these films are pin-registered on a jig for the imposition, in strips of pages on the carbon tissue plate coating carrier sheet. [*Courtesy* Denver Post] using gouache and tempera together presents difficulties, as does the mixing of Chinese white or lampblack with any of these colors.

Gravure is an excellent medium for reproducing oil paints, but colors such as magenta, deep purple, peacock blue, and some greens can only be approximated with the standardized process inks used by publications. As we have stated, however, this is true of all printing processes.

An artist preparing to enter the commercial field should understand that the brilliance and color purity of transparencies cannot be reproduced by printing or, for that matter, by a quality color photoprint. The visual qualities of color photoprints are much closer to the printed result, and some advertisers prefer to use prints made from transparencies. Their use also makes color adjustment and changes easier. Newsprint, of course, lacks some of the advantages of coated paper for process color reproduction.

PREPARED COPY

All types of gravure color production use photo color studios to convert original artwork to copy for the camera as described in Chapter 7. If the artwork is to be color-separated by electronic scanning machines, the instructions should specify that it is to be for rotogravure. It is advisable to obtain the gravure producer's recommendations in advance.

ARTWORK FOR MAGAZINES

The instructions for monotone and color gravure on newsprint also apply to publications that use coated papers. The minor differences in the artist's work arise from the paper to be used: tonal detail need not be accentuated on coated paper, and more subtle tonal gradations can be used. Minimum type sizes for monotone and color are set forth in each publication's production specifications. Each magazine also supplies separate color charts printed on its paper because colors look different on different papers. Magazine color plates or offset halftone separations to be converted for gravure production should usually be sent to a gravure engraving service and not to the gravure publication itself, but this should be checked.

Bibliography *Gravure Packaging Copy Preparation,* Gravure Technical Association, Inc., 60 East 42d Street, New York, N.Y. 10017, 1967.

CHAPTER NINE
Posters

COMMERCIAL POSTERS ARE printed in standard sizes to fit posting boards or frames placed in transportation facilities or retail outlets. Car cards in various sizes are another form of display advertising. Used in conjunction with posters, they employ the same pictorial material, for which separations are already available.

The twenty-four-sheet posters seen on billboards along highways and in cities are so large that they are printed on ten sheets of paper, which are positioned by billboard posters. The lithographed press plates are produced by the photographic projection of fine halftone negatives; the halftone dot becomes the size of a BB shot. A three-sheet poster requires one and one-half sheets of paper; the one- and two-sheet sizes can fit on a single sheet in normal halftone screen.[1]

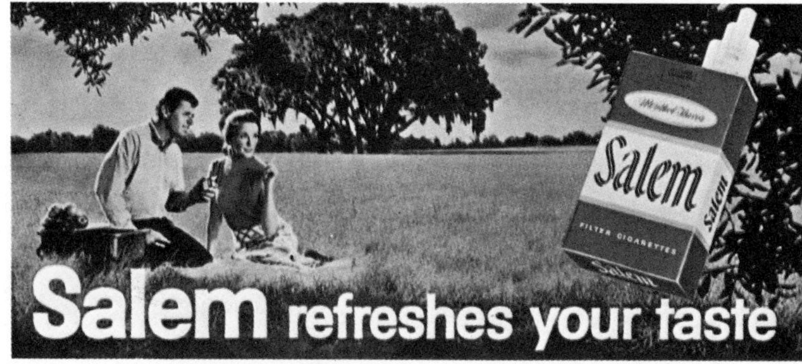

Fig. 9-1 Twenty-four-sheet poster.

POSTER DESIGN

Since posters almost always are a form of collateral material in national advertising campaigns, they should be integrated and coordinated with campaign themes. The pictorial material is usually a key illustration from the magazine advertising, and the package or product is generally presented.

According to the Institute of Outdoor Advertising, experience and research show that an outdoor advertising design should contain no more than three elements: identification, copy, and illustration. The effectiveness of the design will depend on the relationship of these elements to each other. The impact of the design can be increased by varying the size, color, type, background, and spacing of the basic elements.

For posters that are exposed to the weather for at least thirty days, colors should contrast boldly. Fugitive colors do not stand up in sunlight. Certain types of pinks, purples, blues, and greens tend to fade. Such shades should not be used for large areas of color unless the producer is allowed to approximate them with permanent inks. Shades that can be guaranteed for thirty days require very expensive inks.

SKETCH RATIO

The sketch for a twenty-four-sheet poster must always be made in a ratio of 1 to 2¼. A popular size is 16 by 36 inches, but if tone detail is desired, the finished art for camera should be even larger, measuring up to 20 by 45 inches. For the plain lettering and line copy designated as "flat treat-

[1]Illustrations and data on twenty-four-sheet posters are presented courtesy of the Institute of Outdoor Advertising, New York; data on smaller posters, courtesy of Transportation Displays, Inc., New York.

Fig. 9-2 Three units of design is the maximum.

A one-unit design combines in a single unit the three basic elements: identification, copy, illustration. Usually this is possible only when all three are already combined, perhaps on the package or display. If you see that this situation exists, keep the design simple. Do not add another element.

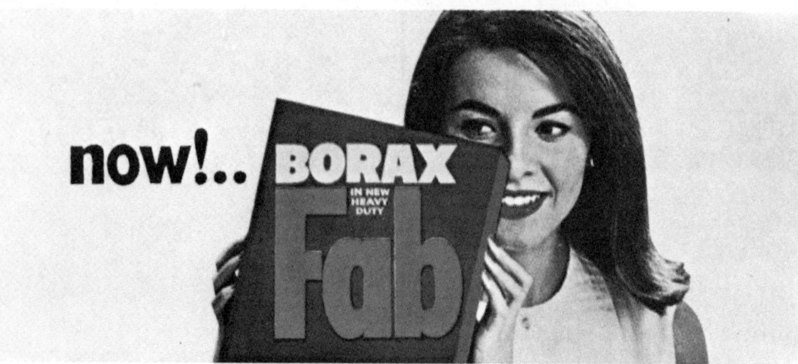

Two units of design are most often practical when two of the basic elements are already united, possibly on the package itself. It is then a simple matter to relate the third element, probably copy, directly to the other two. When you exert creative discipline, you will not allow your design to become complicated.

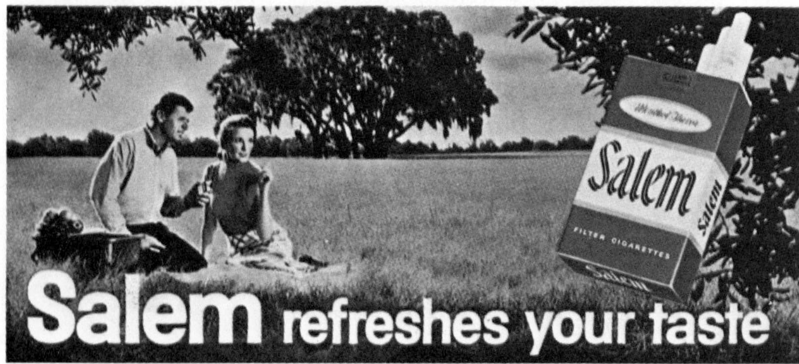

Three units are the maximum number to be used if your design is to be effective. Each unit may well be one of the three basic elements. If they are properly related, the total impact will be much greater than the effect of the elements individually. However, if you complicate the background, it becomes a fourth unit; don't do it.

ment," the finished copy should measure at least 10 by 22½ inches.

SHEET LAYOUT

An approved poster layout in rough form is usually the result of many preliminary sketches. Before any artwork is prepared, however, the sketch is submitted to several poster producers, who make color and composition sketches to show their sheet "layout," which may include slight adjustments to reduce the amount of printing and to avoid bad posting caused by a sheet edge running across a tone illustration. (A low quotation may be based on a risky layout of sheet position.) Alternatively, the approved poster sketch may be sent to a poster artist, who performs the same service and also produces the finished art and poster. The camera copy should be complete: lettering, illustration, background, and all other elements should be positioned. Color photography and some art are supplied separately, their position and size being shown by comprehensive color prints.

The average twenty-four-sheet poster requires forty-five press plates for the ten 44- by 60½-inch sheets (work size, 42 by 58½ inches) to provide a margin for lapping the sheets when they are posted. A three-sheet poster requires ten plates for the one and one-half sheets needed for process work. Every effort is made to reduce plate costs: a sheet may be laid out for cutting into two half sheets to provide parts of the design and thus save a set of plates.

One device of art production is to work on a plastic of some opacity. The camera operator places copy in the transparency holder of the copyboard, exposes it for reflective copy, and then backlights the copy, thus burning out the highlights on the film. This method may save $500 in plate costs.

The minimum quantity required for twenty-four-sheet posters is 1,000 (750, if separations or conversions are available).

MECHANICAL REQUIREMENTS

As shown in the accompanying table, there are three standard sizes of large

	24-sheet	30-sheet	Bleed
Copy area (length)	19′6″	21′7″	21′7″ Live area
Copy area (height)	8′8″	9′7″	9′7″ Live area
Top and bottom blanking	10½″ Top and bottom (21″ total)	5″ Top and bottom (10″ total)	5″ Top and bottom (10″ total)
End blanking	19″ (38″ total)	6½″ (13″ total)	6½″ (13″ total)
Frame width	11″	11″	11″
Total exposed area including bleed: 10′5″ by 22′8″			

Courtesy Institute of Outdoor Advertising.

posters that may be posted on regular billboards. Posters should be printed on 70-pound offset stock suitable for outdoor use. Allow a 1-inch free margin around all four sides of the poster to provide for overlap of the display frame. Uncoated paper is preferred; paper coated on one side is acceptable. Sizes are as follows:

	Overall size	Visible copy area
1-sheet posters	46″ high by 30″ wide	44″ high by 28″wide
2-sheet posters	46″ high by 60″ wide	44″ high by 58″ wide
3-sheet posters	84″ high by 42″ wide	82″ high by 40″ wide

Car cards should be printed on 4-ply stock with a horizontal grain for side and overdoor spaces and 5-ply stock with a vertical grain for end spaces. Allow a ½-inch free margin around all four sides to provide for overlap of the display frame. Sizes are as follows:

	Overall size	Visible copy area
End spaces	33″ high by 21″ wide	32″ high by 20″ wide
End spaces	22″ high by 21″ wide	21″ high by 20″ wide
Overdoor spaces	16″ high by 38″ wide	15″ high by 37″ wide
Side spaces	11″ high by 21, 18, or 42″ wide	10″ high by 20, 27, or 41″ wide

Courtesy Transportation Displays, Inc., New York.

POSTERS AND SHEET LAYOUT

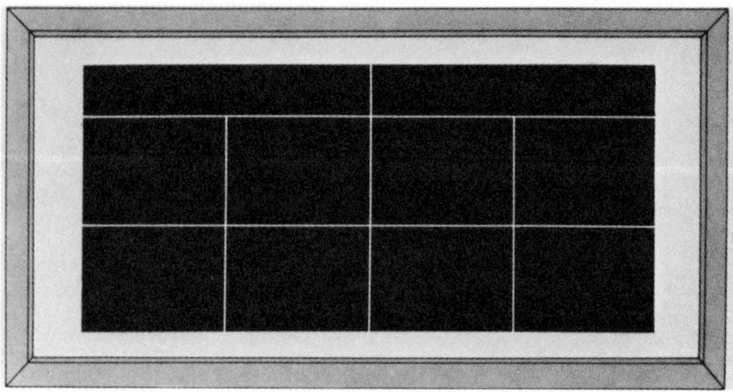

Fig. 9-3 Twenty-four-sheet poster. When printing presses were smaller, a poster panel required twenty-four sheets of paper. Today, with larger presses, fewer sheets are needed, but the original term is still used to describe the size. On the left is a typical paper pattern for a twenty-four-sheet poster. The area between the design and the frame is covered with white blanking paper.

Fig. 9-4 Thirty-sheet poster. The thirty-sheet poster provides approximately 25 percent more space for your design. The width of the blanking paper is considerably smaller. A typical paper pattern is shown, but considerable variation in the pattern is possible, often providing production economies when the design is reproduced.

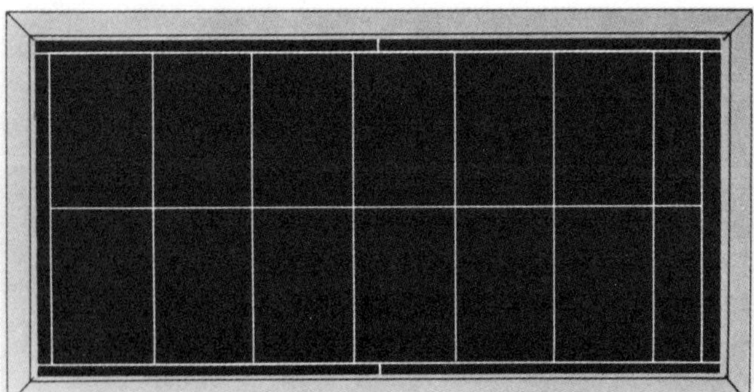

Fig. 9-5 Bleed poster. The bleed poster carries the design out to the frame. This is achieved by printing the blanking paper, producing the bleed effect often used in magazine layouts. The frame crops the illustration rather than a band of white. A typical paper pattern for a bleed design is shown at the left. It offers 40 percent more design space than a twenty-four-sheet poster.

HAND POSTERS

Some poster producers have skilled lithographic artists who can take a rough color sketch and make all the necessary press plates by hand (the original lithographic method). This procedure is used for short runs, particularly for two- and three-sheet theatrical posters when only 400 or 500 posters are wanted. If the technique is suitable for the original design, the cost of finished artwork and photographic press plates is avoided.

Hand methods are also employed for much large lettering, tints, and flat color backgrounds. A projector is frequently used to help the artist outline the work he is to put on the press plates.

SILK SCREEN AND COMMERCIAL COLLOTYPE

When 50 to a few hundred posters with a design in flat color and lettering are required, a silk screen is often used. If the screen stencil is made photographically, some tone work is possible.

Commercial collotype (gelatin printing) is used for short-run tone designs, particularly for two- and three-sheet theatrical posters. A screenless photographic printing process, it is usually handled on a direct litho press.

CHAPTER TEN
Placing the Order

IN SELECTING THE printing producer for a specific job, you are buying the necessary facilities and skills. In smaller cities producers handle the needs of the community. In larger cities they tend to be more selective in soliciting business because of their equipment and the quality of their workmanship, some of them specializing in particular types of production or service. Reliability and organization are important.

KNOWLEDGE OF FACILITIES AND SERVICE

Large users of a variety of printing requirements, such as advertising agencies and national accounts, do business regularly with many different printing organizations. Their lists range from A (top-quality) and B (commercial-quality) process color producers, through specialists in posters, dealer displays, and labels, and producers geared for simple color and single-color printing, to letter shops and contract "production" printers, who handle fast ordinary-quality work.

In addition to a printer's facilities, reliability and quality standards are very important. Before large users put a printing producer on a list for bids, they generally inspect the printer's shop, check its organization, and list the press sizes, process, and other facilities of interest. It may be obvious that the quality of the shop's work is not up to the standard wanted or that the organization consists of one key man. If that man is absent, questions will not be answered or instructions taken by telephone.

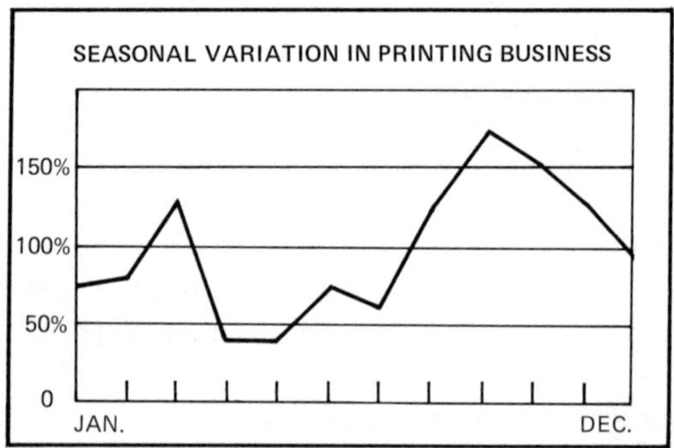

Fig. 10-1 The graph shows the number of orders received monthly in a major printing center and indicates the monthly variation in the area. It is a coincidence that the variation closely checks with the sale of consumer goods.

SEASONAL VARIATION AND PRINTING VOLUME

As in most industries, the supply and demand for printing varies seasonally, ranging from 50 percent below to 50 percent above the annual average. Demand is low from April to July and high in early spring and in autumn. To retain their organizations printers must keep their presses busy. This necessity influences their prices, and in extreme situations a volume job quotation may be very low.

Pricing policies may change. For example, a producer's quotation may be cushioned for such customer's errors as in accurate or incomplete camera copy or a greater number of focuses than were specified. If the cushion is removed from the quotation, extra charges are added because copy has not been supplied as specified.

GETTING BIDS

The purpose of getting bids from several producers on a sizable job is to determine the going market rate on printing and the current situation with the producers selected. A low bid does not always secure the order; usually the order is given to the most suitable producer for the job if the price is in line with the market.

Bids should be obtained only from shops of comparable quality and service. Quality printers usually insist on knowing which shops have been asked to bid; if what they consider to be a lower-grade shop is included, they will refuse to bid. Estimates cost money. It is meaningless to get bids from unknown printers. Their conception of quality work varies widely, and there will be a correspondingly wide variation in quotations, particularly if few specifications have been supplied.

Very large multicolor printing jobs, such as an annual calendar, are frequently placed in a slack season regardless of the date when they are needed. In a slack season a printer with large four-color offset presses will usually offer a very low bid for work that will keep such a press running for a week or two.

Industrial advertisers generally do all their ordering through a purchasing director, who bases the choice on price. In such a case the advertising department generally provides a bid list, which does not include printing producers who are unqualified for the quality and service wanted.

The delivery date frequently is more important to the user than price, and it always has a bearing on the producer's price. When the user eliminates rush work by planning, overtime costs are avoided.

PLACING AN ORDER WITHOUT A QUOTATION

Most small orders are placed without getting bids because of lack of time and the small cost involved. Sufficient work of such a nature should be placed with two or three producers to warrant the special attention given a regular account. This policy also affords a method of checking prices.

Among the specialists in various types of production are contract shops that want a steady volume from a limited number of accounts. Costs are usually determined on a price list basis, under a contractual arrangement that provides the producer with a volume of a particular type of production without the usual sales expense. This arrangement is common with small orders for ordinary-quality black-and-white printing for delivery in a day or two: bulletins, notices to salesmen or distributors, and so on.

COMPLETE INFORMATION FOR ACCURATE ESTIMATE

As camera-ready copy nears completion, job specifications should be prepared, and the sales representatives of selected producers should be shown the layout and camera copy (at least the roughs). The producers' estimators will want to see the color art or at least pencil tracings with notations. Polaroid cameras are sometimes used if the artwork cannot be taken to the printer's shop. Sales representatives usually make out a standard form, "Request for Estimate," which should contain all the data necessary for an accurate estimate. This producer's estimate should be in written form for the customer. A delivery date earlier than conditions require should be avoided because such a date may necessitate overtime and raise the price.

The winning producing organization is usually advised as early as possible so that it can order the paper and schedule the job in its production department. The formal purchase order is accompanied by the job specifications and dummy, together with all camera copy except process copy, which should be sent earlier because it requires more time. A list of what is being sent helps the producer check to make certain that nothing is missing and that specifications do not differ from data on which the quotation and delivery date are based.

Jobs using the same process art in different plate sizes should always be placed with the same producer, the producer who makes the color separations. If copies of the separations are to be supplied to another producer (for posters, displays, and so on), this proviso should be included in the specifications. However, quotations frequently include all work even though some pieces are jobbed out to specialists (canvas banners, wall hangings, and so on).

For a firm quotation, complete specifications are usually necessary, and the form of the copy and the delivery schedule should be as originally specified to the producer's sales representative. Quoted prices are usually based on "copy ready for the camera" and are "subject to inspection of artwork."

A producer schedules work for various departments, and if artwork is not ready as specified, the resulting delay will remove the job from the schedule. Overtime may be required to adhere to the original delivery date. If the budget requires a low price, extra time is a factor. Not only will overtime be avoided, but the job may be scheduled, at least in part, as a filler. The user should have an understanding from each producer of the length of time in which a quotation and delivery date will remain firm.

By trade custom, negatives and plates supplied by a producer remain the property of the producer, and any other arrangement should be in writing. Moreover, 10 percent over or under the quantity ordered constitutes delivery unless specified otherwise in writing.

CHECKLISTS OF PRINTING SPECIFICATIONS

The specification checklists that follow will be helpful as reminders for all the processes, although they apply primarily to the offset process.

PREPARATION OF ART AND TYPE FOR THE CAMERA

1. Know exactly what you want to do and be able to explain your job to the producer clearly.
2. Consult with the producer during the preparation of the copy, and accept the producer's advice.
3. Provide a complete dummy with specifications for the job.
4. Submit all the copy for the job complete before shooting, neatly prepared, clean, and clearly marked with all instructions.
5. Don't request changes while the job is in progress.
6. Provide with the job samples of the paper and the colors to be used.

Preparing Mechanicals

Here are some helpful hints to be kept in mind when preparing mechanicals:

1. Prepare mechanicals for the same size.
2. Be sure that they are accurately squared.
3. Be sure that the type lines up.
4. Be sure that your Photostats or vandykes are accurately pasted down.
5. Key mechanicals with page and code numbers.
6. Identify all marks for corners, trim, folds, and bleeds in red ink.
7. Indicate reverses on an overlay. Circle reverses in red ink or, better still, paste in reverse Photostats.
8. Indicate tint areas with a solid black panel or a red outline, and provide a sample of the precise tint wanted.
9. Indicate the breakdown of color on an overlay as solids, if possible, or outlined in red ink. Be sure to provide samples of colors.
10. Prepare spreads in imposed form if possible.
11. Paste up mechanicals on clean white heavy board.
12. Erase all pencil guidelines, and remove all rubber cement.

Preparing Type and Proofs

The following are pointers for preparing and organizing type:

1. Pull type proofs in the same size.
2. When possible, set type areas in the exact position.
3. Select typefaces with strong serifs and body, especially when you know that they will be used as a reverse area (white on black).
4. Check for clean, even reproduction proofs on white coated stock. Desirable papers are Lusterkote, Kromekote, and Relyon reproduction paper.
5. Examine type for worn and broken letters and missing serifs.

6. Avoid smearing.
7. Supply extra proofs.

Line Copy

Here's a checklist to be used when preparing line copy:

1. Be sure that all line copy is drawn in solid, dull black on white paper.
2. Be sure that outlines are sharp and free from smears.
3. Be sure that all copy is clearly marked for size.
4. Check vertical and horizontal proportions against each other.
5. Prepare as much copy as possible for the same proportionate reduction or enlargement to permit money-saving grouping.
6. Prepare overlays on clear acetate, Vinylite, or white tracing paper, in black ink or dull black color for large areas.
7. When converting from letterpress proofs, be sure that proofs show unsmeared solid-dot reproductions.
8. Be sure that drawings on Rossboard are jet black and clean.
9. Be sure that Craftint copy and Zip-a-Tone tints are clean and smooth.
10. Examine the completed copy for dirt, smudges, extraneous pencil lines, and so on.

Tone Copy

Keep in mind these pointers when planning pictures for halftone reproduction:

1. Mark photos for their correct size and precise proportions.
2. Indicate crop and bleed positions.
3. Outline silhouettes in Chinese white.
4. Prepare pictures for the same proportionate enlargement or reduction.
5. Avoid excessive enlargement or reduction.
6. Mount photos on smooth white board. Avoid ferrotyping, which can cause trouble.
7. Don't write on the backs of prints; don't stamp prints with rubber stamps.
8. Be sure that photos are rich in detail and have good-quality highlights and shadows. Be sure that middle tones are clearly defined.
9. Indicate dropouts when you want them; use Chinese white.
10. Retouch with grays of the same cast throughout a job.
11. Avoid delicate vignettes in pencil or wash drawings. Be sure that the board is white and that there is a definite step between background and art.
12. Maintain scrupulous cleanliness.

Art for Color Reproduction Transparencies

These ideas may be of help in preparing art for color reproduction with transparencies (Kodachromes, Ektachromes):

1. Use a standard viewing light.
2. Maintain the balance of color.
3. Avoid excessive contrast, dark shadows, and burned-out highlights.
4. Prepare for some compromise because the range of color and tone in transparencies is twice that of a printed sheet.
5. Use a color photo laboratory to enlarge small transparencies for color correction or to produce larger prints. Scale or proportion tone for same-focus economies. Color-correct a duplicate instead of using an expensive transparency. Convert a single opaque subject to a transparency if other subjects are transparencies, or vice versa. Prepare an assembly for electronic scanning machine separations.
6. Keep the copy clean. Protect it with a cellophane envelope.

Opaque Process Copy (Paintings, Color Photo Prints, and So On)

1. Keep the copy clean.
2. Scale and position with color photo prints or proportion subjects in one or more groups for a reduction in size.
3. Convert a transparency to a color print if the group for same-focus reproduction is opaque.
4. Use clean colors in the same brand for a group. Don't overpaint, but remove old work.
5. Accept a compromise when particular colors are unobtainable with the four-color process.
6. Use overlays for knockouts or for overprinting type, or prepare overlays on Photostats.
7. Avoid knockouts when printing several colors within an area, for the register is difficult.

CHECKLIST OF OFFSET PRINTING SPECIFICATIONS

General

Customer's name; brand name
Present or last supplier
Address
Credit rating (source)
Sales representative
Date when estimate is wanted
Approximate date on which order is to be placed
Quality required:
  Equal to sample
  Regular commercial

Best
Have we printed or figured this or a similar job before?
Approximate unit price or total price customer wants to pay (arrived at from best sources available at the time estimate was requested)
Subject (kind of job and description)
Quality
Size:
Page size; flat size; sheet size; folded size
Size of backs
Gang size
Size of pad
Trimmed or untrimmed
Can dimensions be altered slightly for economy purposes?
Layout:
Number on; allowances between subjects; printing allowance
Sheet size
Number of pages
Number of leaves if calendar pad
Margins (white; bleed; even color; number of sides)
Cover (self or separate; flush or extended)
Glue laps (size—left or right; free from color; varnish)
Form number or imprint:
Litho; printed or made in the United States; company imprint
Union label,
Copyright notice
Instruction sheets:
Furnished by us?
Specifications
Number of samples (for customer; for salesman's file)
End use:
Customer intends to use subjects as giveaway, point of purchase for resale, in packaging product
Will be packed by hand or by machine; will be applied by machine
Will be in contact with food products; should be resistant to fingermarks and soiling; will be exposed to weather or bright sun; other uses

Artwork

Please furnish pencil tracing, rough sketch, printed sample to show nature of job
When will art be ready? (Size of art or reduction)
Condition of art:
Completely assembled—ready for camera
Complete black-and-white paste-up; full-color art separate but properly assembled
Other (Describe fully number of scales in black and white and in color)
Type of art:
Full-color (transparency; oil painting; watercolor; pastel; color print; other)
Black-and-white (photos retouched; photos not retouched; airbrush; other)
What lettering can be set in type?
Composition and reproduction proofs furnished; number of pages
If by us, what size and face, page size, number of pages?
What special colors must be matched in printing?
On completion, return artwork to:
Nature of art:
Are illustrations still lifes or figures? (Give description of illustrations, including size, nature, number, etc.)
Does the customer's production of the package reproduce in the illustration?
How much of design consists of lettering?

Printing

Method of printing (process); sheet-fed; web; other
Number of printings
Print from deep-etch, albumen, other
Special operations:
Imprint (number of colors; number of imprints; number of lines per imprint)
Number
Press perforation
Press score
Pen rule; sides; ways
Bronze (area)
Emboss (number of subjects)
Is enclosure material printed? (envelopes, containers)
Rerun possibility (assured; possibly; no)
Grind off plates
Wash off glass
Kill standing type

Ink and Varnish

Ink coverage percentage area (submit sample, tracing, description)
Regular, gloss, or metallic inks
Special requirements (permanent or fadeproof; odorless; acid-resistant; nontoxic)
Varnish (printed; spirit; lacquer; other)
Gum (spot; strip; solid)

Positives and Negatives

Plates, positives, or negatives:
On hand; furnished by customer

If furnished
Negatives (glass or film)
Positives (glass or film)
Will negatives or positives fit our step-and-repeat machine?
Type of reproduction:
Process halftone
Special colors
Benday; strip tints
Duotone
Line only; flat colors
Fake
Proofs:
Quantity required
Full color
Partial (Which part?)
Blueprint; ozalid; salt print
Press
None
Proof date necessary

Stock

We to supply
Customer to furnish (If furnished, will moisture content be in balance with our requirements, or will conditioning be necessary?)
Grain of printing sheet if furnished
Weight basis (paper); thickness (board)
Texture and finish (CW1S; CW2S; super; offset MF; bond; other)
Color of stock
Grain of subject on sheet
Specific brand of stock if required

Finishing Operations

Emboss
Gum (spot, strip; solid; which dimension?)
Varnish; lacquer; other
Mount (number of points finished thickness; kind of board liner)
Die cut (irregular; square)
Score (one side; two sides)
Guillotine cut; corner cut
Easel (kind and size; stock)
Drill and punch (size; rounds or slot or Kalamazoo)
Eyelet (size; kind)
String (kind; length)
Fold (number of folds)
Insert
Stitch (saddle; side; number)
Sewing
Pad (number up; edge)
Hinge (cloth or invisible; top or bottom cover)
Enclose (in envelopes, containers, bags, tubes; stiffener; seal; tuck-in flap; clasp; paper ends)
Tipping
Collate (How many signatures?)
Round corners (How many?)
Perforate (pin or slot; Damon one or two ways)
Glue (pasting)
Slip sheet; tissue; wax
Machine or print ruling
Binding (manila top; strawboard back; cloth strip; full duck tight back; single thread; double thread; quarter bind; green edge)
Laminating bind (size of comb; color)
Plastic
Crimp

Packing

Band (paper or rubber)
String tie
Completely wrapped
Chipboard
Bundle
Individual folders; bulk corrugated; wooden cases; skids or pallets
Special copy for stenciling or printing of containers
Size or weight limit
How many in?
Zoning; addressing; typing labels; attaching labels and postage; bundle; handling; stamps (regular; precanceled; furnished with order)

Delivery

Hold (How long?); deferred billing (give details)
When? (partial; complete) Where?
Method of shipment; transportation charges (prepaid or collect); advance copies
Amount of overrun
Drop shipments (How many? Will labels be furnished?)

Invoicing Instructions

Mail to attention of:
Transportation prepaid? Collect?
How many copies?

Index

Adhesives for paste-ups, 55
Advertising:
collateral material, use of, 1, 3, 5, 157
creative planning, control of, 2, 3, 15
integrating and coordinating all parts of, 2, 3
Art department:
changed character of, 2–4
composition prepared by, 6, 24–25
copy fitting, 32–33
specified, 30–31
equipment for, 57, 76–77
materials for, sources of, 118
offsets, extra capabilities of, 4–5
paper as cost factor, 13
plate costs: scale method (photoengraving), 6, 127
time method, 6
services for artwork, 78–79
(*See also* Art production)
Art media, reproduction qualities same for all processes, 4, 120
Art production:
control of, 15
how changed, 2–4
shift to art, 143
development of, 3–4
in creative planning stage, 162–163
in preparation of camera-ready copy, 163–164
process color (*see* Process color copy)
simple color (*see* Simple color copy)
single color, 62
TAPPI survey of change, 4, 15, 143
(*See also* Art department)
Artists, production, 62

Camera copy:
form of, copy elements and units, 51
illumination, 130
kinds of, line and tone, 5–6
mechanical paste-up, 49
rough layout, designer's sketch as, 53
in one-piece method, 51, 82, 85
overlay (*see* Copy overlay)
physical form, 50, 52
line-and-tone, 54
tone mechanicals, 69, 71
transparent overlay, 55
in pieces, 51
single color: preparing line elements, 62–76
autopositive by artist, 115
book pages, paired, 64
brownline prints, 59
combining with tone, 59
contrast with tints, 69
Camera copy, single color, preparing line elements (*Cont.*):
holding line (boundary), color of, 68
areas of tints shown, 68
line surprinted, 68
phototype as art medium, 44
reversing type, 62, 67
scaling and positioning, 51, 57
screened copy: Kodak PMT prints, 72
Velox prints, 162
simple color (*see* Simple color copy)
stock art, 48, 74–75, 136
surprinting on tone, 60
tone to line copy, 70, 73
tone and pattern sheets, 74–75, 136
type reverses, copy for, 67, 87
preparing tone elements: assemblies of components, 152
combining tone with line, 59
cropping and scaling, 57
halftone prints by printer, 69
keying separate elements, 51
knockouts for inserts, 95
line reverse into tone element, 59
materials, services, and tools, 48, 76–79
proportioning, 56, 58
publication production specifications, 60
publication spread, 65
reproduction qualities, 6, 62
reproduction size, percent of original, 57
restrictions removed, paper, 16
retouching, 61, 122
same-focus reduction, economies of, 58
separate tone elements, 59
tonal contrast, extra, 17, 131, 171
tone on color, 110
type proof and lettering on tone, 60
Camera-ready copy:
color assemblies, 147
color mechanicals, 154
copy resulting from intermediate steps from original, 4, 141–144, 147
cropping and scaling elements, 57
mixed art media to single medium, 4, 163
photocomposition, 152
proportioning copy for same-focus reduction, 58
reversed elements, 67
screened prints for line copy, 72
tone mechanicals, 71
Checklists of printing specifications, 184–187
Composition methods:
cold-type, 43–47
for display and text, 45–47

Composition methods (*Cont.*):
metal type: anatomy, 22
classification of faces, 28
contrast on tints, 69
copy fitting, 32
character count, 33
cost of, line or ems, 29
faces of, traditional and contemporary, 29
family and series of, 24
galley repro proofs, 143
hand-set, 23
kinds of proofs, 25
layout for type, 34
leading, 22
machine-set, 23
markup of copy (specification of), 30
monotype, 23
proofreader's marks, 31
reversed type, 67
spacing of lines and letters, 26
stock symbols and designs, 48
surprinting on tone, 60
type gauge, 33
working with type, 27
(*See also* Phototypesetting)
Copy overlay, 102–118
for copy elements, 103
element overlays with large mechanicals, 104
highlight knockouts, 95, 111
pin-register overlays, 116
for plate economy, color, 104
separate line and tone to be combined, 55
when tint areas are too close, 104
(*See also* Simple color copy, overlay copy for)

Flexographic process (*see* Letterpress process, flexography)

Gravure services (*see* Rotogravure)

Keying separate elements, 51

Letterpress process:
artwork: commercial, 119–122
capabilities of category determines suitability of art media, 120
lockup and makeready, 126
paper determines halftone screen, 120
for magazines, 119, 128–129
design and layout for, 129
production specifications, 128
smaller publications, two colors for, 128
standardized inks, color charts, 128
for newspapers, 119, 129–136
coarse-screen halftones, 131
photographs, wash drawings and line drawings in, 131–136
copy in paste-up form, use of, 125

Letterpress process (*Cont.*):
flexography, 133, 137–138
critical measurement, compensating for distortion, 137–138
paste-up copy, 133
precautions for, 137
(*See also* Photoengraving)

Overlays (*see* Copy overlay)

Paper:
as cost factor, 13, 17, 19
kinds of, 16–17, 19
maximum work area of sheet, 21
mill brand selected by printer, 19
offset, economy of, 13, 17, 19–20
printing form or plate, 11
spoilage factor, 19
standard sizes, kinds of, 18
uncoated, tone copy on, 16
Pen, fountain, technical, 76
Photoengravings:
camera copy, reproduction qualities same for all processes, 120
carbon pencil for line art, 133, 135
engraving costs, 125
cost comparison by square inch, 127
extra detail and less reduction on coarse-screen halftones, 122
graphite pencil for tone medium, 133
halftones, types of, 123–124
line engravings, 120–121
paper surface and suitable screens, 120
prepared copy and art production, 129
process color engravings: maximum size, 125
three-color process and line, 161
use of scanning machines, 129
retouching, 61
simple-color engravings, 126
(*See also* Letterpress process)
Photographers, working with, 58
Phototypesetting:
as art medium, 44
composition in art department, 24, 35, 39, 45
cost of, 41
economies, 41
direct-entry systems, 38
flexibility of spacing, 43
International Typographic Composition Association, 22
OCR (optical character recognition), 6, 35, 37
paper tape, perforated, computerized specification unit activated by, 34
perforating keyboards operated by typists, machine operators replaced by, 34, 36
range of phototype equipment, 6
retrieving old composition, 6, 7
terminology of metal type, 22
three generations of photo equipment, 36
type face specimens, 39–43
type fonts, faces of, 41, 42

Placing the order, 182–184
estimate, complete information for, 183
getting bids, reason for, 183
seasonal variation of printing, 182
trade customs, 184
Platemaking:
photomechanical, 7–11
plate coatings, action of light on, 9, 10
printing form, one-piece, 15
Posters, 177–181
design of, 177
hand, 181
sheet layout, 178, 180
silk screen and commercial collotype, 181
standard sizes of, 179
three units, maximum, 179
Printing processes:
action of light on plate coatings, 9, 10
binder's imposition, 21, 64, 66
copy form determines plate cost, 6
makeready: letterpress, 15
offset, 5
multiple images, 13
multiple imposition, 13
negatives, difference between offset and photoengraving, 10
offset process, 9, 11
one-piece plate, advantages of, 15
ordering related jobs, 15
page makeready, two methods for, 49
photomechanical platemaking, 7
printing forms, 11
printing production, change in, 2–4
step-and-repeat machine, 12
work-and-turn imposition, 21
Prints:
blueprints: copy unit proofs, 99
two-color, 101
brownline, 99
contact, 58
dye transfer, 4, 141–143
Kodak Autoscreen Ortho, halftone, 70
photostats, 57, 67, 71
positive Kodak PMT prints, 72
prepress color, 162
projection prints, 58
silver, halftone, 99
Velox, 70, 72, 75
Process color copy:
art production: assembly of two or more elements, 4, 153–155
creative planning stage, 163
preparing camera-ready copy, 163–164
procedures of, 141–158
black copy on overlay, 152
Chinese white, 61
collateral material, 2, 5, 15, 157
color photo studios: list of, 148
major development of, 141
production steps, 141–158
services of, 147
transparencies and color prints, 143–144, 151
use of components to make illustration, 152
Process color copy (*Cont.*):
conversion of process separations for different process, 158
economy process separations, use of photo masking alone, 80–81, 146
enlargement or reduction, 14, 156
Flexichrome process, 160
folding cartons, 159
limitations of reds and blues, 139
masking system, 80–81, 146
mixed art media to single, 143–144
multiple images, 12
overpainting art, avoidance of, 140
paintings, choice of pigments used in, 140
paper, specify kind of, 140
photoprints: dye-transfer color, 4, 143
Type C, 143–144
"prepared" process copy, 4, 14, 143–147
proof, prepress color, 162
reflection and transmission copy not grouped for camera, 146, 148, 150
same-focus reduction, economies of, 6, 58, 142
scanning machines, electronic: used for color separations, 147
used for laser halftones, 149
separations, conventional, 139
shift of production to art department, 141
simple color (*see* Simple color copy)
step-and-repeat machine for multiple images, 12
theory and control of color, 164–167
tonal qualities measured by instrument, 145
type and lines in color, limitations of, 140
viewing light, use of, for transparencies, 145
watercolors keyed to standard process inks, 140
Process mechanical, 143
Process printing plates, 13
large size, 13, 148, 163
multiple sizes, 14, 157
related jobs, 15
Production artists, 62
Proofreader's marks, standard, 31

Rotogravure, camera copy for, 168–176
art media, 172
backgrounds, color, 172
cabriolet (cab) film carrier, 169, 170
engraved cylinder, 10, 169
flash tones, use of, 169, 173
mechanicals: black-and-white, 54
process color, 175
monotone, limitations of, 170
pen-line copy, 171–172
process color on newsprint, 172
proofs, 171
publication production specifications, 168
rotoprints, 168
screened copy, danger of, 168
sent directly to publisher or engraver, 168
type: rendering with color, 174
reversed, on tone, 171
sizes of, 171
Rough layout, 53

Scale, photoengraver's, estimating, 6, 127
Screen printing, 10
Simple color copy:
  boundary (holding) lines, 68, 80
  color register provided, 86
  color swatches, 141
  designing for split-fountain work, 100
  duotone process, 162
  form of copy: for plate cost, 61
    for quality planned, 15
  ink colors, specifying, PMS system, 19
  keylining techniques, 92–95
  masking film, use of, 80, 81
  overlay copy for, 102, 109
    design knockout touching colors, 108
    individual elements, 104
    loose and lap color register, 104
    preseparated color by artist, 104, 112–114

Simple color copy, overlay copy for (*Cont.*):
    shadow detail on flat color, 110
    tone color to black-and-white copy, 112
    type to surprint tone, 70
  prepress color proofs, 101
  register of colors: provision for, in copy, 86–95
    types of, 86–90
  surprinting color, 94
Specifications:
  printing, checklists of, 184–187
  publication production, 60, 168
Split-fountain work, designing for, 100

Technical Association of the Pulp and Paper Industry (TAPPI), 4, 15, 143
Time-estimating methods, 2, 5, 6
Tools and equipment for art studios, 57, 76–77